THE BREAD OF LIFE
by Greg Litmer

2013 One Stone Press.
All rights reserved. No part of this book may be reproduced
in any form without written permission of the publisher.

Published by:
One Stone Press
979 Lovers Lane
Bowling Green, KY 42101
1.800.428.0121

Printed in the United States of America

ISBN 10: 0-985-4938-368
ISBN 13: 978-0-985-4938-68

www.onestone.com

Introduction

We stand together at the threshold of the most important and exciting study into which a person can enter – the study of the life of the Savior of the world. Jesus, the central figure of all history, lies before us. Every true step that we take will be accomplished only by placing our feet directly in His footsteps. Peter wrote in 1 Peter 2:21, "For even hereunto were ye called: because Christ also suffered for us, leaving us an example, that ye should follow his steps." By examining the life of Jesus one learns the true meaning of love, compassion, sympathy, faithfulness, holiness, justice, and learns the way to heaven.

This book is a harmony of the four gospel accounts: Matthew, Mark, Luke, and John. The exact order of all the recorded events in the life of Christ is not known. But many of the events can be placed in chronological order. This book is meant to help all who read it learn what is truly important, Jesus Christ--who He was, what He did, and how we might be like Him.

The Prologue (Luke 1:1-4)

It is apparent as one turns his attention to the first four verses of Luke 1, that the early years of Christianity saw many attempts by various individuals to produce a recorded account of the acts and words of Jesus. Without disparaging these early efforts, Luke saw the need for something more accurate and complete. Such a need would become more obvious as the Lord's church grew and those who had been eyewitnesses died. Luke undertook this task.

There was, in these early writings, a consensus of belief. Certain acts, certain events, and certain teachings concerning Jesus were universally accepted among believers as being absolutely true. What was lacking was infallibility and completeness. There seems to be an indication on Luke's part that these earlier writers did not have his knowledge of the events. Perhaps they had not gone back to the beginning as he had and were not as complete and orderly in their writings as was necessary. Luke went to the eyewitnesses, and followed up in a step by step fashion all things from their source. Additionally, as Colly Caldwell wrote in his *Truth Commentaries, Luke*, 44, "The Holy Spirit of God was not only a willing participant but a cause and a safeguard to accuracy in the writing of this gospel narrative." His purpose was to present to Theophilus a record arranged in an orderly fashion (which is the meaning of "kathexes", or "in order", of v. 3), that he might know. Who was Theophilus? The name is derived from two Greek words and means "Friend of God." Theophilus was probably a Greek and a Christian. That Luke referred to him as "most excellent" may indicate a high office of some sort.

The Gospel of Luke is the most carefully arranged account of the life of Christ, evidently written to satisfy the needs of an educated, cultured individual Theophilus might have been. It is obvious that the gospel, while beneficial for all people of all time, was written for the Gentile mind.

The Pre-existence and Incarnation of Jesus (John 1:1-18)

When we discuss the life of Christ we must go back before the beginning. Now it might be asked, "What beginning?" and the answer is the beginning of creation, the beginning of time. John starts his gospel with the same phrase used by Moses in Genesis 1:1, "In the beginning…"

At the "beginning", the Word already was. The significance of that concerns the essential elements of time: a beginning and an ending. With the Word already existing at the beginning of time, it is an inescapable conclusion that the Word must have been "timeless." The Word had no beginning. The Word existed at the beginning of creation and hence, was not created. The Word is eternal.

Not only is the Word eternal, the Word was "with God." The phrase "with God" means a great deal more than simple co-existence; it conveys the idea of active communication and sharing. By affirming that the Word was "with God," at least three things are shown. First, the Word was co-existent with God in a personal way, as the presence of one person with another. Second, the separate personality of the Word and God was emphasized. Third, the inseparable relationship of Christ with God was also emphasized.

There is another point brought out in verse 1. Not only was the Word eternal and co-existent with God in a personal way; the Word was God. Notice that John did not write that the Word was "a god." He did not write that the Word was "the" God. He wrote that the Word was God with no definitive article. The Word was eternal, co-existent with God, and "was" God. That affirms His absolute deity, but recognizes separate personalities. Also, it affirms that the Word was God in His nature and His being, having all the power and attributes of deity. The Hebrew writer expressed it in this way in Hebrews 1:3, "Who being the brightness of his glory, and the express image of his person…"

What of the use of the title "Word?" I think it is best explained in the following way. According to *Vine's Expository Dictionary of New Testament Words*, the basic meaning of "logos" or word, is "the expression of thought – not the mere name of an object – (a) as embodying a conception or idea." As it relates to Jesus, the title "logos," or Word, would imply the "personal manifestation, not of a part of the Divine nature, but of the whole Deity." Others have mentioned that the title, "Word," emphasizes Jesus' mission to reveal.

Verse 2 of John 1 further establishes that the Word was not only eternal, His relationship with God the Father was, and is, eternal.

The Greek word for "all things" in verse 3 emphasizes all things, one by one, separate and particular. It tells us that Jesus made all things; He was the active agent of creation. The same idea is expressed in Colossians 1:16-17, "For by him were all things created, that are in heaven, and that are in earth, visible and invisible, whether they be thrones, or dominions, or principalities, or powers: all things were created by him, and for him: and he is before all things, and by him all things consist."

In Jesus was the very essence of life, all and complete. Through His life light was given to men. It is the light that illuminates and appeals to reason and to the conscience and that promotes a response. In John 8:12 Jesus said, "I am the light of the world: he that followeth me shall not walk in darkness, but shall have the light of life." But conflict was introduced. The light came into the world and "shineth in the darkness," but the darkness "comprehended it not." This means that it did not perceive or understand. From the very moment that the light entered into the world there was conflict between it and darkness – moral darkness. Wescott says, "The whole phrase is indeed a startling paradox. The light does not banish the darkness: the darkness does not overpower the light. The two co-exist in the world side by side." It could be said that there is also an intimation of tragedy when we consider what would happen because of the failure of the darkness to understand the light.

In verses 6-9 the Apostle John introduces John the Baptist and tells us of his work. He was a messenger divinely sent with a divine message; but he was not the Light. His job was to bear witness to the Light, to announce His coming. Jesus was the Light.

Jesus was in the world, the very world He created. Many believe verse 10 is speaking of the incarnation of Jesus. Homer Hailey gives the correct meaning in his book, *That You May Believe*, 22. He wrote, "He had been in it all the time, ordering, controlling, guiding, 'upholding all things by the word of his power' (Heb. 1:3), as the one in whom 'all things consist' (Col. 1:17). But that world, the rational world of humanity, which should have recognized Him because of a divine kinship, 'knew him not'." Consider also 1 Corinthians 1:21 and Romans 1:21, 25. He came unto His own, which could be referring to the Jews or to both Jew and Gentile for all were created by the Lord, and they rejected Him through the chosen people, the Jews. Again, we note an intimation of tragedy.

Not all rejected Him. Some believed Him, or believed in Him; and to them He gave the power to become the "sons of God." It was by being, "born again" of water and Spirit (John 3:3, 5). It was not by the natural birth, "not of blood"; and it was not by irrational will, "nor of the will of the flesh"; and it was not by rational will, "nor of the will of man." It was spiritual, "of God." It is interesting that those who believed were said to have been given power to "become" sons of God, not that they were sons of God already merely on the basis of their belief. They had to be "born again" by water and Spirit, and that is baptism.

In verse 14 we find the incarnation, a truly incredible idea to contemplate. God was made flesh and dwelt among man. Deity in the flesh, visible and tangible, walking the streets of the world that He had created. When He came, men beheld His glory. In the Old Testament the "glory" of God abode in the Tabernacle. Exodus 40:34-35 describes that beautiful picture. With the coming of the Word, God took up residence among men and mankind was privileged to behold His glory. The uniqueness of the situation is indicated by "the only begotten of the Father." The incarnation was absolutely unique; nothing like it had occurred before and nothing like has occurred since.

Once again the work of John is mentioned. He bore witness to Jesus, declaring Him to be the One whose arrival he was sent to announce. We might ask how Jesus was "preferred" above John? He was preferred by His superiority–a truth to which John often referred. How was Jesus before John? He was before him both in preeminence and in pre-existence.

Jesus is the fullness of Deity. Colossians 1:19 states, "For it pleased the Father that in him should all fullness dwell." In Colossians 2:9, we find, "For in him dwelleth all the fullness of the Godhead bodily." Fullness is defined as "that which is completed, i.e., the complement, the full tale, the entire number or quantity, the plenitude, the perfection" (Lightfoot). Therefore, the perfection, the plenitude, the fullness of Deity is in Jesus, and from Him proceeds grace and truth in its fullness. The grace of God flows to us from Jesus. When we look at Jesus in the gospels, we see God--the personal manifestation of, not a part of Deity, but of the whole of Deity.

The Genealogies (Matt. 1:1-17, Luke 3:23-38)

Why study the genealogies? This is a valid question when we consider the amount of space devoted to the genealogies in Matthew and Luke. The answer is readily apparent. In the infancy of Christianity the genealogies played a role of great importance. We get an idea of their importance from an exchange we find in Matthew 22:41-42. "While the Pharisees were gathered together, Jesus asked them, saying, What think ye of Christ? Whose Son is He? They say unto him, The Son of David."

The Jews of the first century knew that the Messiah was to be of the lineage of David. They were well versed in such passages as 2 Samuel 7:12-16, Psalm 89:3-4, and Psalm 132:11. The genealogies trace Jesus back to David and solidly connect him with the Messianic prophecies. Isn't it interesting that Matthew begins his account of Jesus by establishing this fact? Surely that demonstrates the importance of Jesus' ancestry, especially in a gospel that was evidently written to the Jewish mind. Luke includes his genealogical record of Jesus immediately following the Lord's baptism and just prior to the beginning of His public ministry. The fact that Luke's gospel was written to be read by the Gentiles and includes the genealogy demonstrates it was of universal interest and importance.

Today we have the benefit of the passing of centuries and recognize the ancestry of Jesus as proven. The first century Christians did not have this advantage and needed to be properly prepared to teach that Jesus was the promised Messiah in light of Old Testament prophecy. As we look at the genealogies themselves, let us recognize that they are different and a study of them comes with a certain number of difficulties.

Matthew's genealogy is the shorter of the two. It goes from Abraham forward 42 generations ending with "Joseph, the husband of Mary, of which was born Jesus, who is called Christ." It is divided into three groups of 14 each, the first being from Abraham to David, the second from David to the Babylonian Captivity, and the third from the Captivity to Jesus.

There are difficulties. For instance, certain names are omitted. In verse 8 we find, "Joram begat Uzziah," but what about Ahaziah, Joash, and Amaziah?

In verse 11 we read, "Josias begat Jechonias," but that omits Jehoiakim. However, these are all recognizable names and easily supplied by the Jewish readers.

We must consider what Matthew is seeking to accomplish. Not only is he demonstrating the connection of Jesus to David, he is also supplying an abbreviated history lesson. He traces the origin of the house of David from Abraham to David. He shows its rise to power and its decline from David to the Captivity, and he shows how it has risen again as promised from the Captivity to Jesus. There is a definite historical movement to Matthew's genealogy that demonstrates a twofold purpose. He is connecting the ancestry of Jesus to David and he is tracing the rise, fall, and rise again of the house of David.

Luke's genealogy is different from Matthew's. Instead of running forward from Abraham 42 generations, it runs backward from Jesus to Adam, 76 generations. From Abraham to David the two genealogies are the same, but from David to Joseph they are different except for two names, Zerubbabel and his father, Shealtiel. The major difficulty is that these two different genealogies are presented as the line of Joseph. How do we explain that?

There have been several explanations offered. One is that one genealogy is giving the natural line of descent and the other is giving the legal line of descent. It has been suggested (and this was the ancient explanation of most of the early Fathers), that Joseph was the legal son and heir of Heli, but the real son of Jacob. What seems more plausible is that Joseph was the son-in-law of Heli and that Luke is actually tracing the line of Mary. This certainly would fit in the character of Luke's gospel for he gives more attention to the experiences of Mary than the other gospel writers.

The point of the study is this: the Old Testament prophets had declared that One would come of the line of David who was to be the Savior of the world. He has come and these genealogies prove his ancestry.

The Birth of John and the Birth of Jesus Announced
Mary Visits Elizabeth (Luke 1:5-56)

The marvelous birth of Jesus began to unfold in the days of Herod the Great. Herod the Great was the son of Antipater, founder of the Herodian line. This Herod ruled from 41 to 4 B.C. The emperor of Rome at the time was Octavian, Caesar Augustus. This is extremely important for it places the events surrounding Christ in the days of the fourth world empire, Rome, as prophesied in Daniel 2.

There was a "certain priest" by the name of Zacharias, described as "of the course of Abia." When the number of priests multiplied and became so numerous that they could not all administer at the altar at one time, David divided them into 24 courses or classes. Each of these courses would officiate for a week (1 Chron. 23:1-6, 24:1-31). Abia, or Abijah in Hebrew, was the eighth in order. Zacharias' wife was named Elizabeth, also a descendant of Aaron; showing that on both his father's and mother's side John was a descendant of priests. Zacharias and Elizabeth were described as being exemplary in their conduct; they were righteous individuals. Obviously the purpose of this description was to show why they were chosen for this great honor. Their age, "well stricken in years," was introduced to show the extraordinary nature of the events that were beginning to take place.

According to Jewish writers, lots were drawn by the priests in the morning and the evening of each day. In the morning, four were chosen to care for the golden candlestick, the showbread, and to burn incense. In the evening, only one was chosen to burn incense. This was a tremendous honor. There were so many priests that no priest could have the honor of serving in the Holy Place more than once in his life. The Altar of Incense was located just outside of the double veil that separated the Holy Place from the Most Holy Place, or the Holy of Holies. According to Exodus 30:7-8, incense was offered in the morning and the evening. What the incense was made of is found in Exodus 30:34, while verses 37-38 indicate that this compound was to be used in no other fashion and in no other place. The account indicates this was apparently the evening hour of incense, and the multitude that came to worship remained in the outer courts of the temple and prayed as the incense was being offered.

As he was performing his function of offering incense, an angel appeared to Zacharias, standing on the right side of the altar of incense. Zacharias' troubled and fearful reaction is quite natural when we consider a few things: (1) This was a great moment in his life, offering the incense right before the Holy of Holies; an extremely solemn and emotional moment; (2) The appearance was totally unexpected. It was the breaking of a period of approximately 400 years of silence on the part of God; (3) The Bible is filled with examples of individuals bring troubled when suddenly placed in the presence of the supernatural.

The angel spoke immediately to calm his fear. His prayer had been answered. A son would be given to Zacharias and Elizabeth. Obviously they had prayed for a son. It is well documented that the Hebrew women placed great importance upon child-bearing, particularly a son. For a woman to be barren was considered a reproach from God. This would be an unusual child. His birth would be an occasion of great joy for many. He was to be a Nazarite (Numbers 6:1-8). He would be filled with the Holy Spirit even from his mother's womb. His life would greatly affect many of the children of Israel as he came in the spirit of Elijah, turning the hearts of the people and preparing the way of the Lord. This was in fulfillment of Malachi 3:1, 4:5.

What the angel was saying was contrary to nature, and men are generally slow to believe. So Zacharias requested a sign, proof that it was going to come to pass. The sign he was given was to be struck dumb, unable to speak. He would remain that way until those things promised had come to pass. So spoke Gabriel, the "mighty one" or "hero of God." He is one of two angels that we know by name. Michael is the other one.

All of this took time and the multitude in the outer courts were surprised he tarried so long in the temple. When Zacharias came out, through his signs and gestures, he communicated to them he had seen a vision. After the completion of his course, Zacharias returned to his home in the hill country of Judaea and his wife Elizabeth conceived.

In the sixth month after Elizabeth's conception, the angel Gabriel was once again sent from God with a divine message. This time it was to a town in Galilee called Nazareth. There he appeared to a young virgin named Mary who was espoused to a man named Joseph. Both Mary and Joseph were of the house of David. Gabriel announced to Mary the magnificent event that was going to happen to her. She was highly favored and blessed among women. To her would be born a Son whose named would be called Jesus (Jehovah is salvation). He would be great, called the Son of the Highest, and He would be given the throne of His father, David. He would reign over the house of Jacob forever and of His kingdom there would be no end. This marvelous event would happen through the power of the Holy Spirit. Her child would have no earthly father. This would be a miraculous conception. Certainly this brings to mind the beautiful Messianic prophecy of Isaiah 9:6-7.

Some have suggested that verse 34 indicates that Mary doubted. No, she did not understand. She was overwhelmed. How could this happen? She was espoused to Joseph but not yet married. As espousal among the Hebrews generally lasted ten to twelve months and was a contract to marry. This contract was so binding that any unfaithfulness during the time was considered an act of adultery.

It is interesting that Zacharias, full of doubt, was given a sign as punishment for his lack of belief. Mary, full of faith but still filled with questions, was also given a sign. Her sign was meant to encourage and strengthen her. Her "kinswoman" (sungenis–not necessarily a cousin), Elizabeth, who was well past the age of childbearing and previously barren, was in her sixth month with a son. Truly with God nothing is impossible. With great faith and humility Mary accepted the words of the angel, Gabriel, and quickly made her way into the hill country of Judaea to the home of Zacharias and Elizabeth. She made the journey out of conviction in the truthfulness of the angel's message and to seek counsel and comfort from her older kinswoman.

Upon hearing the salutation of Mary, the babe, John, in Elizabeth's womb displayed a very human emotion. He leaped, or started, in her womb. Elizabeth, filled with the Holy Spirit, again announced the unique position Mary occupied among women. She had been chosen to be the mother of the Son of God. Elizabeth likely knew of Mary's condition by revelation, just as she knew the identity and position of the child she was carrying. Elizabeth herself had been blessed by being chosen to bear the one who was to prepare the way for the Lord; but her humility was displayed by her words, "And whence is this to me, that the mother of my Lord should come to me?" Mary was blessed for believing and would be further blessed when the promised things came to pass.

Mary's statement or poem of praise is known as the Magnificat. That is from the Latin word with which it begins, "magnificat," meaning "does magnify." It is filled with Old Testament references and magnifies the name of God. It praises God for the wondrous things He had done and for the great love, compassion, and mercy He had shown. As the promised arrival of the Messiah was beginning to occur, what better way to begin than in praise to the One who so loved the world as to send His only begotten Son to die for all mankind? After staying with Elizabeth for approximately three months, Mary returned to her home.

The Birth of John (Luke 1:57-80)

The marvelous story continued to unfold as Elizabeth reached full term and delivered her promised son of her old age. When word of the great event reached the ears of her neighbors and kinfolks, they rejoiced with Elizabeth. They viewed the birth of John as God's removal of her reproach.

In Genesis 17:10-12 we find, "This is my covenant, which ye shall keep, between me and you and thy seed after thee; every man child among you shall be circumcised. And ye shall circumcise the flesh of your foreskin; and it shall be a token of the covenant betwixt me and you. And he that is eight days old shall be circumcised among you, every man child in your generations, he that is born in the house, or bought with money of any stranger, which is not of thy seed." In compliance with this command, the child was circumcised on the eighth day. Generally the child was named on the same day and, according to Jewish custom, he was named Zacharias after his father. Immediately Elizabeth intervened and gave him the name John, the name that had been supplied by Gabriel to her husband. It is interesting that among the Jews, tribes and families were kept distinct. To facilitate this, and to avoid confusion in genealogical tables, it appears that generally only names common among a family's ancestors were given. None of John's kinsmen had the name John and that made it just a bit more unusual.

To make certain that John was to be his name, those involved in the circumcision communicated by signs to Zacharias concerning what the child should be called. *Is it possible that this indicates that he was not only dumb, but deaf as well?* He wrote upon a writing tablet, "His name is John," and immediately he was able to speak and hear again.

Concerning verses 65-66:

The word 'fear' often denotes religious reverence. The remarkable circumstances attending the birth of John, and the fact that Zacharias was suddenly restored to speech convinced them that God was there, and filled their minds with awe and veneration. Such were the remarkable circumstances of his birth, that they apprehended he would be distinguished as a prophet, or that great events would result from his life (Albert Barnes, *Barnes' Notes of the New Testament*, 186).

John enjoyed the protection and favor of God as signified by "the hand of the Lord was with him."

Filled with the Holy Spirit, Zacharias begins to prophesy and spoke a two-part prophecy. The first part praised God for bringing to pass those things spoken of by His prophets of old concerning the coming of the Messiah. It deals with Jesus and continues through verses 68 to 75. The second part predicts the future character and ministry of John. It begins in verse 76 and continues through verse 79.

The First Section – God had looked upon his people, knew their needs, and was taking steps to redeem them. Using a horn, a symbol of strength, Zacharias speaks of the One who was even yet in the womb of His mother. He would be of the house of David and would bring the power of salvation to the people.

All that was taking place had been spoken by the prophets of old, and it was now happening. Zacharias referred to the oath made to Abraham which brings to mind Genesis 22:16-18. That passage says, "By myself have I sworn, saith the Lord, for because thou hast done this thing, and hast not withheld thy son, thine only son: that in blessing I will bless thee, and in multiplying I will multiply thy seed as the stars of the heaven, and as the sand which is upon the sea shore; and thy seed shall possess the gate of his enemies; and in thy seed shall all the nations of the earth be blessed; because thou hast obeyed my voice." Surely Abraham's posterity was being blessed.

The Second Section – Beginning with verse 76, the focus shifts to John. He would act as a spokesman for God, preparing the way of the Lord (Malachi 3:1). He would announce that the kingdom of heaven was at hand. He would give them the knowledge of salvation through the remission of sins. In other words, the salvation that John would announce as being imminent was via the remission of sin. Truly, it could be no other way. Man could not work his way to heaven as was generally held to be true by the Pharisees. Sinful man had to repent and be forgiven, and it was for this salvation that John would prepare the way. Only through this salvation, made actual by the coming of Jesus, could man know the true mercy, light, and peace of God.

The young man John would now step into obscurity. He would reside in the wilderness of the hill country of Judaea. He would wax strong in his spirit, acquiring the aspects of character necessary for when he would step into the public conscience and shake them from their lethargy.

Joseph Informed of the Impending Birth of Jesus (Matt. 1:18-25)

After her visit with Elizabeth, Mary returned home, and the fact that she was with child was evident. Can we take the statement, "She was found with child of the Holy Ghost," to mean that was the explanation given to Joseph? It certainly seems reasonable.

What was Mary's situation? In Deuteronomy 22:23-24 we find, "If a damsel that is a virgin be betrothed unto an husband, and a man find her in the city, and lie with her; then ye shall bring them both out unto the gate of that city, and ye shall stone them with stones that they die; the damsel, because she cried not, being in the city; and the man, because he hath humbled his neighbor's wife: so thou shalt put away evil from among you." Mary would have been viewed as being guilty of adultery and Joseph would have been humiliated because his espoused wife had committed such an act. She could have been put to death. However, Joseph was described as a just man, the obvious meaning being that he was a man of tender heart and mercy with true feelings for Mary. So he determined to put her away privately in order not to expose her to further public shame. Deuteronomy 24:1 would be applicable here. "When a man hath taken a wife, and married her, and it come to pass that she find no favor in his eyes, because he hath found some uncleanness (or matter of nakedness) in her: then let him write her a bill of divorcement, and give it in her hand, and send her out of his house." According to Alfred Edersheim in *The Life and Times of Jesus the Messiah*, 108, this was the most private form of legal divorce, handing the letter to her privately in the presence of two witnesses who did not have to be told the reason.

This was quite a situation--a kind and tender-hearted man espoused to a young woman of obvious high character; she was chosen by God to be the mother of His Son, found to be with child. The only explanation she can offer is she conceived by the Holy Spirit, for that is what an angel told her. As you will recall, it had seemed incredible and difficult to understand to Mary. Imagine how it must have sounded to Joseph. But, he was not inclined to humiliate her publicly, so he intended to exercise his right of divorce in a private fashion. Joseph's view would change.

While considering his course of action, Joseph was visited by the angel of the Lord in a dream. He received assurance that corroborated what Mary had apparently told him. The child she was carrying was of the Holy Spirit. He would be called Jesus; that is Savior (being derived from the verb signifying to save). Again we make the point that if Matthew gave the genealogy of Joseph, then Jesus was the "legal" son of Joseph and legally of the line of David. If Luke gives the genealogy of Mary, then He was the biological son of Mary and naturally of the line of David.

All of this was taking place in fulfillment of a prophecy spoken approximately 740 years earlier in Isaiah 7:14. This has proven to be one of the more controversial Messianic prophecies. It has proven to be so because many refuse to accept the idea of a virgin birth and choose to reject a plain statement made by Matthew concerning the fulfillment of the prophecy. The prophecy was uttered during the time of Ahaz, king of Judah. At that time Israel and Syria joined forces to overthrow the southern kingdom over which Ahaz ruled. King Ahaz was frightened and in despair. Jehovah sent Isaiah and his son, Shearjashub, to assure King Ahaz that his enemies would not prevail. To validate the prophecy, Isaiah told Ahaz to ask the Lord for a sign, a miracle, either "in the depth, or in the height above" (Isa. 7:11). Ahaz refused and Isaiah spoke the prophecy to "the house of David" (Isa. 7:13). A virgin would conceive and bear a son.

Much attention has been paid to the Hebrew word translated "virgin" in Isaiah 7:14. Many contend that "virgin" is an incorrect translation; that it should be rendered "young woman." The word itself is "almah." Actually, of the two words rendered "virgin" in the Old Testament, "bethulah" and "almah", almah is the one always used of a virgin. It never means anything else.

I have searched exhaustively for instances in which almah might mean a non-virgin or a married woman. There is no passage where almah is not a virgin. Nowhere in the Bible or elsewhere does almah mean anything but a virgin" (William F. Beck,"*What Does Almah Mean? The Lutheran News*, April 3, 1967).

The word occurs in the following instances and in each obviously designates an unmarried woman and a true virgin – Psa. 68:15, Ex. 2:8, Prov. 30:19, Gen. 24:43, Song of Solomon 1:3, 6:8, and Isaiah 7:14" (Guy N. Woods, *The Living Messages of the Books of the Old Testament*, 261).

Ahaz had refused the proffered sign, and the Prophet was compelled to relinquish the hope of raising him to confidence in Jehovah. But he must have been desirous that the deliverance should not be regarded, when it came, as the work of chance, but ascribed to the mercy of the Supreme Ruler of the theocracy: and that the confidence of the pious in Him should be confirmed. He therefore gives a sign, even against the will of Ahaz, whereby the confidence of every true member of the theocracy, in the prediction already given concerning the deliverance from the confederated kings, must be strengthened. I behold, he declares, the wonderful event of futurity, the birth of a Divine Redeemer of a virgin" (E.W. Hengstenberg, *Christology of the Old Testament*, 152).

Being thus assured, Joseph took Mary to wife and did not consummate the marriage until after the birth of our Lord.

The Birth of the Savior (Matt. 2:1, Luke 2:1-7)

The world was about to be blessed in an immeasurable way: the Savior was to be born. What occurred is not what one would expect when discussing the entrance of the Son of God into the world. The birth of the Savior was not attended by a host of physicians. It did not take place in the luxurious surroundings of a royal palace. It was not trumpeted throughout the world and accompanied with great fanfare. It took place in the most humble of surroundings and was known only to a few.

It came to pass in the days surrounding the birth of Jesus that a decree came forth from the emperor of Rome, Octavian, Caesar Augustus, that a census should be taken of the world under Roman rule. The purpose of such an enrollment would be to assist in the work of taxation and also to determine how many were subject to military service. Octavian ruled in Rome from 31 B.C. to A.D. 14.

This enrollment took place when Cyrenius (Quirinius) was said to be governor of Syria. Luke 2:2 has caused considerable difficulty and has been a favorite verse of the critics because historical records indicate that Cyrenius was governor of Syria from A.D. 6 to 11, and this enrollment would have taken place in approximately 4 B.C. However, *The Pulpit Commentary*, Vol. 16, 36, explains, "It has been now satisfactorily demonstrated that, strangely enough, this Quirinius – who then years later was certainly governor of Syria – at the time of the birth of the Savior held high office in Syria, either as governor or imperial commissioner." Roman custom was for each person to be enrolled in their place of residence. The Jews, however, went to be enrolled in their ancestral homes.

Joseph and Mary, both of the lineage of David, and Mary about to be delivered of a child, made their way to Bethlehem, the city of David, to be enrolled. As I envision this scene of the humble carpenter and his very pregnant wife making the arduous 80 mile journey from Nazareth to Bethlehem for enrollment in the city of their great ancestor, I am reminded of Isaiah 11:1. There we find, "And there shall come forth a rod out of the stem of Jesse, and a Branch shall grow out of his roots." The world did not know that the house of David, referred to as the "stump of Jesse", cut down and brought low as evidenced by the poverty and obscurity of Joseph and Mary, was about to have the Branch spring forth of it and be raised to greater heights than it had ever known during the time of David.

While in the city of David, Jesus was born. No more humble surroundings could be imagined. Our Lord was born in a stable because the enrollment had brought a large number of people to Bethlehem and there was no room for them in the inn. His first bed was a manger.

What was the significance of the birth taking place in Bethlehem? Approximately 750 years earlier these words had been written in Micah 5:2: "But thou, Bethlehem Ephratah, though thou be little among the thousands of Judah, yet out of thee shall He come forth unto Me that is to be Ruler in Israel; whose goings forth have been from of old, from everlasting."

The Shepherds and Angel (Luke 2:8-20)

In the hill country pastures around Bethlehem, shepherds were watching over their sheep by night. As they watched, suddenly an angel of the Lord came upon them and there was a great brightness as the glory of the Lord shone around them, and they were very afraid.

Why appear to shepherds? There is significance to this. First, they were Jews; but why not appear to the scholars in Jerusalem, or the elders of the people? Why not announce the birth to the influential Jewish leaders? Interestingly, at this time shepherds were held in low esteem by the people. According to the Talmud, in the treatise *The Sanhedrin*, shepherds were not allowed to be used in the courts as witnesses. Why appear to men of such low estate?

It was to demonstrate the very nature of Christianity. It is for all men, from the least to the greatest, recognizing no class distinction in terms of the love of God and the availability of salvation. It was, as Mary said in the Magnificat, "He hath put down the mighty from their seats, and exalted them of low degree."

On that day, in the city of David, a Savior was born. He was the Christ, the Anointed One. They were given a sign to confirm their faith and to assist them in identifying the Child. They would find Him lying in a feeding trough for animals wrapped in swaddling clothes.

Suddenly there was a multitude of heavenly beings praising God with the words, "Glory to God in the highest, and on earth peace, good will toward men." Can there be any question of the appropriateness of this praise? God had brought His Son into the world for man's salvation. All that He had promised He was bringing to fulfillment.

The New American Standard's rendering of the last phrase of verse 14 is a much better rendering than the King James Version and indicates that man has a part in his salvation. It says, "And on earth, peace among men with whom he is pleased." Jesus' coming into the world brings peace to those who accept Him; to those who will live in obedience to His commands and be the recipients of God's pleasure.

With haste the shepherds made their way to Bethlehem to see the thing the angel had made known to them. They found Mary and Joseph, and the Child Jesus lying in a manger just as they had been told. Thus these men, on the low end of the social scale, became the first preachers of Jesus. They told abroad what had been told to them, and those who heard it wondered at what they had been told.

Mary thought deeply on all of these events, trying to understand and comprehend their wonderful significance.

Jesus Named and Circumcised (Luke 2:21)

Jesus was born into a devout Jewish family. As Paul tells us in Galatians 4:4, "God sent forth his Son, made of a woman, made under the law." In keeping with the requirements of that law, Jesus was circumcised on the eighth day. It was customary for the child to receive his name at the time of the circumcision, and it was no different for the Lord. He was called Jesus in keeping with the angel's statement to Joseph.

The Presentation in the Temple (Luke 2:22-38)

As we begin to examine the presentation in the temple, we present Leviticus 12. It reads as follows:

> And the Lord spake unto Moses, saying, speak unto the children of Israel, saying, If a woman have conceived seed, and born a man child: then she shall be unclean seven days; according to the days of the separation for her infirmity shall she be unclean. And in the eighth day the flesh of his foreskin shall be circumcised. And she shall then continue in the blood of her purifying three and thirty days; she shall touch no hallowed thing, nor come into the sanctuary, until the days of her purifying be fulfilled. But if

she bear a maid child, then she shall be unclean two weeks, as in her separation: and she shall continue in the blood of her purifying threescore and six days. And when the days of her purifying are fulfilled, for a son, or for a daughter, she shall bring a lamb of the first year for a burnt offering, and a young pigeon, or a turtledove, for a sin offering, unto the door of the tabernacle of the congregation, unto the priest: who shall offer it before the Lord, and make an atonement for her; and she shall be cleansed from the issue of her blood. This is the law for her that hath both a male or female. And if she be not able to bring a lamb, then she shall bring two turtles doves, or two young pigeons; the one for the burnt offering, and the other for a sin offering: and the priest shall make an atonement for her, and she shall be clean.

Exodus 13:2 is also important in this case. It reads, "Sanctify unto me all the firstborn, whatsoever openeth the womb among the children of Israel, both of man and of beast, it is mine."

After the period of purification prescribed by the law (40 days for a male child, 80 days for a female), and in accordance with the dedication of the firstborn to the Lord, Mary fulfilled the rules of ceremonial cleansing and brought the child to the temple for presentation. Being of lowly circumstances, Mary and Joseph did not offer a lamb and a pigeon, but a pair of turtledoves or young pigeons. One was for a burnt offering and the other for a sin offering.

In Jerusalem there lived a man by the name of Simeon. Some have conjectured that he was the son of Hillel, the famous scholar of Jerusalem and president of the Sanhedrin. All that is known for certain of this Simeon is what is revealed in this passage. He is described as a just and devout man, one who clung fervently to the expectation of the coming of the Messiah (beautifully termed "the consolation of Israel"), and the Holy Ghost was upon him in a miraculous way. It had been revealed to Simeon by the Holy Ghost that he would not die until he had seen the Anointed One. In fact, it was the Holy Ghost who led Simeon to the temple at the very time Mary and Joseph brought Jesus there for His dedication. Seeing Jesus, Simeon took Him in his arms, praised God and acknowledged that the promise made to him by the Holy Ghost concerning his death had been fulfilled. He could now die for he had seen the "Lord's Christ." Part of Simeon's statement brings to mind Isaiah 42:1-6:

Behold my servant, whom I uphold; mine elect, in whom my soul delighteth; I have put my spirit upon him: he shall bring forth judgment to the Gentiles. He shall not cry, nor lift up, nor cause his voice to be heard in the street. A bruised reed shall he not break, and the smoking flax shall he not quench: he shall bring forth judgment unto truth. He shall not fail nor be discouraged, till he have set judgment in the earth: and the isles shall wait for his law. Thus saith God the Lord, he that created the heavens, and stretched them out; he that spread forth the earth, and that which cometh out of it; he that giveth breath unto the people upon it, and spirit to them that walk therein: I the Lord have called thee in righteousness, and will hold thine hand, and will keep thee, and give thee for a covenant of the people, for a light of the Gentiles. Men like Isaiah, who lived several centuries before the nativity, with their glorious far-reaching prophecies, such as Isa. 52:10 (another reference to "light of the Gentiles" g.l.), were far in advance of the narrow, selfish Jewish schools of the age of Jesus Christ. It was, perhaps, the hardest lesson the apostles and first teachers of the faith had to master – this full, free admission of the vast Gentile world into the kingdom of their God. Simeon, in his song, however, distinctly repeats the broad, generous sayings of the older prophets (*The Pulpit Commentary*, Vol. 16, 40-4).

We need not wonder at the surprise and astonishment of Mary and Joseph. All of the circumstances surrounding the birth of Jesus had been incredible. They did not understand all that was happening to them and now a stranger had spoken such significant words concerning the future of their Son.

There is disagreement concerning the meaning of Simeon's next statement, "Behold, this child is set for the fall and rising again of many in Israel." The word "again" is not expressed in the Greek, and that has led many to believe that Simeon is referring to the same persons, that they would both rise and fall as a result of Jesus. Foster says it, "refers to the humiliation that repentance brings and the glorification which accompanies forgiveness and salvation" (*Gospel Studies*, Vol. 1, 30). It means that with the coming of Jesus many, by their reaction to Him, would be lost; and many others, because of their reaction to Him, would be saved.

Most assuredly Jesus was a sign "spoken against." This brings to mind Isaiah 53:3: "He was despised and rejected of men; a man of sorrows, and acquainted with grief: and we hid as it were our faces from him; he was despised, and we esteemed him not."

Mary was told "a sword shall pierce through thy own soul also," an indication of future tragedy. Think of the anguish Mary would feel as the public ministry of her Son came to a close. Think of the pain Mary would experience as she stood and watched Him hang on the cross. Yet, through that very act, the true character of so many would be revealed as their hatred for righteousness and holiness culminated in the death of the Lord.

There was yet another person in the temple who would acknowledge the position of the Child. Her name was Anna, described as a prophetess and of the tribe of Asher, a woman of great age. Most hold that she was about 84 years old due to verse 37. Some believe that she had been a widow for 84 years, married previous to that for 7 years (based upon verse 36), and probably would have been 15 to 20 years old when she was married. That would put Anna well over 100 years old.

The tribe of Asher was one of the ten northern tribes that, through exile and intermarriage at the time of the Assyrian captivity, had all but disappeared.

Some individuals, such as Anna, were able to trace their genealogy back to that tribe. Anna remained in the temple, serving God with prayer and fasting. It is apparent that by inspiration Anna knew who Jesus was and she spoke to all who would listen about what she knew.

The Magi (Matt. 2:1-12)

It appears evident that the visit of the magi took place after the presentation of our Lord in the temple. This would be true for several reasons. First, it is certainly reasonable to believe that if Joseph and Mary had already received the valuable gifts before going to the temple, then they would not have offered the two turtledoves. They would have offered a lamb and a dove. Second, with Herod's reaction to the visit of the magi, a trip to Jerusalem would have been very dangerous. Third, when the magi leave, Joseph is told to take the child and his mother to Egypt.

Three things stand out in verse 1. Jesus was born in Bethlehem of Judaea. It was in the days of Herod the king, and wise men came from the east. The birthplace of Jesus was identified as Bethlehem of Judaea to distinguish it from Bethlehem of Zebulun, in the region of Galilee. The significance of this is pointed out in verses 5 and 6. Jesus was born in the days of Herod the king. This helps us to date the birth. Only Herod the Great and Herod Agrippa II held the legal title of "king." Herod the Great reigned from 41 B.C. to 4 B.C., while Herod Agrippa reigned from A.D. 48 to A.D. 100. This obviously eliminates Herod Agrippa II as the Herod under consideration here. Thus we can date the birth of Christ in 4 B.C. The four years' mistake in our present calendar was made in the sixth century by a monk named Dionysius Exiguus.

Wise men, or magi, came to Jerusalem from the east. They were learned men of eastern nations, principally Persia and Arabia. They were devoted to the study of astronomy, religion, and medicine. They were held in high regard as counselors. In verse 2, the magi made the purpose of their journey clear. They had come searching for the newly born king of the Jews. They had seen His star and desired to pay homage to Him. It is apparent at this time there was a prevalent expectation in the east that some remarkable personage was to appear in Judaea. There were Jews living in all parts of the known world and as they spread, they took their expectations of a Messiah with them. Mention of this expectation appears in different secular works of the time:

> An ancient and settled persuasion prevailed throughout the East, that the Fates had decreed some one to proceed from Judaea, who should attain universal empire" (Seutonius, *Vespasian*, 4).

> Many were persuaded that it was contained in the ancient books of their priests, that at that very time in the East should prevail, and that some one should proceed from Judaea and possess the dominion" (Tacitus, *Annals*, 5, 13).

Josephus and Philo, two Jewish historians, also mention this expectation.

Ancient astrologers often considered the appearance of a star or comet as an omen of some remarkable event. These magi were no different. It is important to note that none of the theories that have been set forth to give a natural explanation of the appearance of this star do so. They all fall short. This was a miraculous occurrence.

Herod's reaction to the visit of the magi and their purpose was not surprising. This was a man who had already executed several of his relatives that he viewed as possible threats to his throne. News of these events agitated Herod as yet another possible threat to his throne was born. He knew of the expectation of the Messiah and he knew that the Jews expected a temporal king. So, he gathered together the chief priests and the scribes to inquire where they looked for the Christ to be born. The answer was provided by Micah 5:2, Bethlehem of Judaea. This shows the Jews understood this prophecy to apply to Christ.

The next step Herod took to eliminate the possible threat was to summon the magi to him privately and inquire as to the time of the appearance of the star. He did this to ascertain the age of the Child. Having done so, he sent the magi to Bethlehem to look for the baby, telling them that after they found Him, they were to return to Herod and give him word of the Child's whereabouts that he might worship Him as well.

The reaction of the magi when they saw the star indicates that it had not been visible to them throughout their whole journey. Now, at the conclusion of their trip, the star reappeared to guide them to the exact location of Jesus. When they entered into the place where Jesus and His parents were staying, they fell down and offered homage to Him, along with gifts of gold, frankincense, and myrrh. Frankincense was a fragrant gum of a tree obtained by cutting the bark. Myrrh also comes from trees and was used chiefly in embalming the dead. To foil the murderous plans of Herod, the magi were warned in a dream not to return to him. Consequently, they departed to their own country by another route.

The Flight to Egypt (Matt. 2:13-18)

After the departure of the magi the angel of the Lord appeared to Joseph with the warning to take Jesus and Mary and go to Egypt. There he was to remain until the angel appeared to him again. All of this was necessary because Herod was seeking to destroy the Child.

Why Egypt? First, to fulfill prophecy. Hosea 11:1 says, "When Israel was a child, then I loved him, and called my son out of Egypt." Second, Egypt was only about 60 miles southwest of Bethlehem and there was certainly a precedent for troubled Jews going to Egypt. Third, Herod's jurisdiction ended at the River of Egypt (not the Nile), and Joseph with his family would be safe there.

When Herod saw that the magi did not return as he had expected, he was very angry. He issued orders for all the male children, two years old and under, in Bethlehem and its surrounding regions be executed. He did this to be certain that he had the right child killed. As was so often the case in scripture, evil men, totally unbeknownst to themselves, behaved in such a way as to bring about the fulfillment of prophecy. Such was the case with Herod's wicked intention to kill Jesus. It brought about the fulfillment of Jeremiah 31:15. That passage says, "Thus saith the Lord: a voice was heard in Ramah, lamentation, and bitter weeping: Rachel weeping for her children refused to be comforted for her children, because they were not."

To understand this prophecy it must be viewed contextually, and we must realize that initially Jeremiah wrote of the carrying away into Babylonian Captivity of the nation of Judah:

> Ramah – In Benjamin, east of the great northern road, two hours journey from Jerusalem. Rachel, who all her life had pined for children (Gen. 30:1), and who died with "sorrow" in giving birth to Benjamin, and was buried at Ramah, near Bethlehem, is represented as raising her head from the tomb, and as breaking forth into "weeping" as seeing the whole land depopulated of her sons, the Ephraimities. Ramah was the place where Nebuzaradan collected all the Jews in chains, previous to their removal to Babylon (Jameison, Fausett, Brown, *Commentary on the Whole Bible*, 634).

However, this prophecy was primarily fulfilled when Herod had the male children, two years old and younger, slaughtered in Bethlehem and the surrounding regions.

> Besides the temporary reference to the exiles in Babylon, the Holy Spirit foreshadowed ultimately the Messiah's exile in Egypt, and the desolation caused in the neighborhood of Rachel's tomb by Herod's massacre of the children (ibid, 634).

Return and Settlement in Nazareth (Matt. 2:19-23, Luke 2:39)

Archaeological data indicates that Herod the Great died in March of 4 B.C. and was succeeded by his son, Archelaus. When he died an angel of the Lord appeared once again to Joseph in a dream, this time in Egypt. He told Joseph to take Jesus and His mother back to the land of Israel because the one responsible for endangering His life was dead.

Joseph did as he was told and it appears that he initially intended to return to Judaea, perhaps Bethlehem, but changed his mind when he found out that Archelaus reigned in his father's stead in Judaea. He received an additional warning of this in a dream so he took his family to the region of Galilee and settled in the city of Nazareth. It should be mentioned that at this time Herod Antipas ruled in Galilee. This was also in fulfillment of prophecy, "He shall be called a Nazarene."

Albert Barnes made some very enlightening comments about the statement found in verse 23, "That it might be fulfilled which was spoken by the prophets, he shall be called a Nazarene."

> The words here are not found in any book of the Old Testament; and there has been much difficulty in ascertaining the meaning of this passage. Some have supposed that Matthew meant to refer to Judges 13:5, to Samson as a type of Christ; others that he refers to Isa. 11:1, where the descendant of Jesse is called "a Branch"; in the Hebrew, Netzer. Some have supposed that Matthew refers to some prophecy which was not recorded, but handed down by tradition. But these suppositions are not satisfactory. It is a great deal more probable that Matthew refers not to any particular place, but to the leading characteristics of the prophecies respecting him. The following remarks may make this clear. First, he does not say, "by the prophet", but "by the prophets", meaning no one particularly, but the general character of the prophecies. Second, the leading and most prominent prophecies respecting him were, that he was to be of humble life, to be despised, and rejected. Third, the phrase, "he shall be called", means the same as "he shall be". Fourth, the character of the people of Nazareth was such that they were proverbially despised and condemned. To come from Nazareth, therefore, or to be a Nazarene, was the same as to be despised, and esteemed of low birth…And therefore, that the prophecies were fulfilled, it means that the predictions of the prophets that he should be of humble life, and rejected, were fully accomplished in his being an inhabitant of Nazareth, and despised as such (Albert Barnes, *Barnes' Notes on the New Testament*, 10).

Luke did not speak of the visit of the magi, the flight into Egypt, or the slaughter of the children, but went directly from the presentation in the temple to their settling in Nazareth.

The Childhood of Jesus (Luke 2:40-52)

After the return from Egypt and settlement in Nazareth, verse 40 is all that we know of the first twelve years of our Lord's life. In the older manuscripts the words "in spirit" do not appear. What that verse says is, "And the child grew, and waxed strong, filled with wisdom, and the grace of God was upon him."

Jesus developed as other children develop. He was subject to the law of growth and attainment of knowledge as other children. We do know that Jesus did not sin, so He must have acquired the wisdom necessary to avoid evil and resist temptation. To state any more about His development and childhood would be pure speculation. We are told that "the grace of God was upon him." In normal New Testament usage, grace means "unmerited favor." Here it means favor. Jesus was well pleasing in the sight of God and blessed by Him.

Every year the parents of Jesus went to Jerusalem for the Passover. This was one of three feasts a year in observance of which Jewish males were to present themselves before the Lord. This requirement is found in Exodus 23:14-17.

> Three times thou shalt keep a feast unto me in the year. Thou shalt keep the feast of unleavened bread: thou shalt eat unleavened bread seven days, as I commanded thee, in the time appointed of the month Abib; for in it thou camest out from Egypt; and none shall appear before me empty: and the feast of harvest, the firstfruits of thy labours, which thou hast sown in the field: and the feast of the ingathering, which is in the end of the year, when thou hast gathered in thy labours out of the field. Three times in the year all thy males shall appear before the Lord God.

When Jesus was twelve years old, He accompanied His parents. After they had fulfilled the day, which would have been eight in total, one day for the killing of the Paschal lamb and seven days in observance of the feast of unleavened bread, they began their journey home. As they left, Mary and Joseph believed that Jesus was with them. Actually, He had remained behind in Jerusalem.

We might be tempted to ask how Mary and Joseph could have been so negligent as to leave their twelve-year-old son behind, but there are many possible explanations. First, a Jewish boy in the first century, twelve years of age, was much more advanced and independent than a twelve-year-old boy of our day and time. Second, families and neighbors, making up a large company, would travel to the feasts together. It was very reasonable to assume that Jesus was in the company with His friends and relatives. Third, often the men and women, while in the same company, traveled separately. Perhaps Joseph thought Jesus was with Mary and Mary thought He was with Joseph.

Ultimately they discovered that Jesus was not with them, and after searching among the company, returned to Jerusalem to find Him. After three days (this would probably be three days total; one day in leaving, one returning, one day searching in Jerusalem), they found Him. Jesus was sitting in the temple among the rabbis, listening to them and asking them questions.

According to the Talmud, in the temple enclosure there were three synagogues – one at the gate of the court of the Gentiles, one in the southeast part of the inner court, and one at the entrance of the court of the Israelites. It was in these structures that the doctors, or rabbis, would sit and expound the Law.

Everyone who heard the young boy was amazed at the depth of understanding He displayed concerning the Law and at the intelligence of His answers. Some have supposed that Jesus was confounding the doctors of the law, but there are no facts to support this. It is far more consistent to believe He was asking questions and answering them.

There is a slight reproach in Mary's words, "Son, why hast thou thus dealt with us? Behold, thy father and I have sought thee sorrowing?" The following comments are very good.

> To the gently veiled reproach of Mary, Jesus replies, apparently with wonderment, with another question. It had come upon him so quietly and yet with such irresistible force that the temple of God was his real earthly home, that he marveled at his mother's slowness of comprehension. Why should she have been surprised at his still lingering in the sacred courts? Did she not know who he was, and whence he came? Then he added, 'Know ye not that I must be about my Father's business?' There was an expression of Mary's which evidently distressed the child Jesus. Godet even thinks that he discerns a kind of shudder in his quick reply to Mary's 'my father and I'…'In my Father's house, where my Father's work is being done, there ought I to be busied. Didn't you know this?' But the 12 uneventful years of life at Nazareth, the poor home, the village carpentry, the natural development of the sacred Child, had gradually obscured for Mary and Joseph the memories of the infancy. They had not forgotten them, but time and circumstances had covered them with a veil. Now they were very gently reminded by the Boy's own quiet words of what had happened 12 years before (*The Pulpit Commentary*, Vol. 16, 43).

Mary and Joseph did not understand the meaning of what Jesus had said and now the veil of silence descends again as Jesus returns to Nazareth with His mother and Joseph; there to subject Himself to them as an obedient child. But Mary kept these things in her heart. In every way Jesus continued to grow as He moved toward the beginning of His public ministry.

John Begins His Work (Matt. 3:1-6, Mark 1:1-6, Luke 3:1-6)

Luke, as an historian, dates these events in four ways; by emperor, governor, tetrarch, and high priest. Tiberius was the emperor. In A.D. 11 Tiberius began to reign as joint emperor with Augustus. Augustus died two years later and Tiberius became sole emperor. Luke sets his date from the beginning of Tiberius' joint reign. Pontius Pilate was the governor of Judaea, having been appointed in the twelfth year of Tiberius' sole reign. Herod Antipas was the tetrarch of Galilee, his brother Philip was tetrarch of Ituraea and Trachonitis; and Lysanias was the tetrarch of Abilene. Tetrarch properly means "ruler of a fourth part of the country." Annas and Caiaphas were the high priests. Annas was the rightful high priest, but he had been deposed by the procurator, Gratus, in A.D. 14. Caiaphas was his son-in-law and had been appointed in his place by the Romans.

"In those days" or during this particular time, "the word of the Lord" came to John in the wilderness. He came clothed in the rough and simple garments of the desert (the rough coat of camel's hair, the plain leather girdle, eating wild locusts and honey) to the wilderness of Judaea in the region around Jordan. The wilderness of Judaea was located along the western side of the Dead Sea and a small strip of land to the north of the Dead Sea. His primary message was one of repentance for the kingdom of heaven was at hand. Multitudes responded to John and they came from Jerusalem, Judaea, and the region around the Jordan River, confessing their sins and to be baptized by John.

John preached the "baptism of repentance unto the remission of sins." The primary message of John was repentance in preparation for the coming kingdom of the Messiah. His baptism was "unto the remission of sin." A person sincerely baptized with John's baptism had their sins forgiven in the same way a devout Jew had his sins forgiven on the Day of Atonement. Confronted by the full gospel of our Lord Jesus they would have to respond and be baptized into the death of the Lord.

There are certain differences between the baptism of John and the baptism in the name of Jesus. One, the baptism in the name of Jesus is final. It is the "one baptism" of Ephesians 4. John's baptism was temporary. Two, the baptism in the name of Jesus is "into Christ." John's baptism was preparatory. Three, the baptism in the name of Jesus is into the death of Christ. At the time of John's baptism Jesus had not yet died. Four, one baptized in the baptism of Jesus received "the gift of the Holy Spirit" (Acts 2:38). There was no such result from John's baptism. Fifth, the baptism in the name of Jesus is offered to everyone. John's baptism was to the Jews only.

John's appearance and his message were in fulfillment of prophecy. Isaiah 40:3-5 is mentioned, and Mark refers to Malachi 3:1. John's task was to remove the obstacles, to herald the coming of the Messiah, and to prepare His way.

The Preaching of John the Baptist
(Matt. 3:7-12, Mark 1:7-8, Luke 3:7-18)

It must have been thrilling, and at the same time unsettling, to hear the uncompromising message of John the Baptist delivered in as plain and simple a fashion as the garments he wore. This was a man who was different. This was a man who would not be subservient to the Jewish leaders. This was a man who would not hesitate to rebuke sin. This was a man whose message was meant to placate no one. His words were clear, forthright, and eminently practical. He was "the Voice" of one crying in the wilderness and what he taught demanded change as he prepared the way for the Lord.

Such preaching, as was being done by John, alarmed and disturbed the religious leaders of the Jews and stirred the hearts of the common people. Whatever might have been their motivation, members of all classes of Jewish society came to hear John and to be baptized by him. Matthew specifically mentions the Pharisees and Sadducees coming to John's baptism and being the recipients of a scathing rebuke from him. Luke shows that the entire multitude was included in the rebuke. That rebuke was, "Ye offspring of vipers, who warned you to flee from the wrath to come."

"Offspring of vipers" is a metaphor used by John because of their likeness to vipers; so much like them to have been begotten by them. The viper was an extremely poisonous serpent, two to five feet in length and about an inch in diameter. It symbolized guile and malice, cunning and venom. That is how John characterized the Jewish religious leaders and the multitude that followed them. They came to hear him and to be baptized of him, but John wanted to know why. "Who warned you to flee from the wrath to come?" Did the Jewish leaders come because their knowledge of prophecy told them that the coming of the Messiah would be accompanied by wrath and suffering; generally known as "the woes of Messiah" among Jewish scholars? Did they view John's baptism as some sort of talisman to keep them safe from it? Did the multitude view John's baptism as some sort of mystical guarantee of salvation?

Regardless of their motivation, John made it clear that what he was demanding was change. They could not continue to lead a sinful life and assume they were safe. They could not continue as "offspring of vipers." They had to put their sinful activities from their lives. They had to repent.

As though reading their minds, John responded to a possible retort from his hearers. "Think not to say within yourselves, we have Abraham to our father: for I say unto you, that God is able of these stones to raise up children unto Abraham." In this way John struck at the heart of the vaunted Jewish pride. They truly believed their descent from Abraham was all that was needed to guarantee their citizenship in the kingdom of the Messiah. All Gentiles would be outside of that kingdom. The Talmud tells us of the value Jews placed upon their Abrahamic descent. In it we find such statements as, "The world was made for Israel's sake," and "Abraham sits next to the gates of hell, and doth not permit any wicked Israelite to go down into it," and "A single Israelite is worth more before God than all the people who have been or shall be."

To this way of thinking John said, "No." Their natural descent from Abraham gave them no more merit than descendents of Abraham made from the stones along the banks of the Jordan River would have. Indeed, the axe was already laid at the root of the tree and those found barren would be cut down. Their Abrahamic descent would not be sufficient to ensure citizenship and their old sinful ways would absolutely preclude it. They had to bring forth fruit in their lives that demonstrated repentance.

The mere preaching of principles without practical application to the lives of the hearers accomplishes very little. Application must be made, and John did not hesitate to do that. As the multitudes asked him, "What then must we do?" John gave them simple, practical answers. Be unselfish, be generous. Show your repentance in your lives. If you have two garments and another has none, give him one. If you have food and another has none, feed him. The publicans came to John and asked him what they should do. His response was to collect only what they had the legal right to collect.

Concerning Luke 3:12:

This is the first time this class of men, who on several occasions come before us in the gospel story, is mentioned. The English rendering is most unhappy, for to many of our people it either suggests nothing, or else supplies a wrong chain of reasoning. The Latin 'publicani' were men who collected the Roman taxes or imposts. These imperial taxes, the most painful and ever present reminder to the Jew of his subject and dependent position, were in the first instance leased out to jobbers and speculators of the equestrian order; these were properly publicani. Beneath them and in their employ was a numerous staff who performed for these farmers of imperial revenue the various disagreeable duties connected with the collection of the taxes. Then, as now in the East, bribery, corruption, oppression, and unfair dealing, were too common among all ranks of officials. First, then, the duty itself, the being concerned in the collection of a tribute – for that is what these taxes really were – for Gentile Rome, and, secondly, the various iniquities connected with the gathering of this tribute, made the tax or tribute collectors of all ranks odious among the Jews dwelling in Palestine (*The Pulpit Commentary*, Vol. 16, 67).

Even soldiers came to hear John and asked him what they should do. These were probably Jewish troops serving Herod. John's answer was to be content with their wages, and not try to increase those wages by extorting from others through violence or blackmail. All people, from any rank or position in society, could apply John's preaching personally.

To a people of heightened Messianic expectation it was only natural that upon hearing the thrilling words of John the Baptist, some would begin to speculate as to whether or not He might be the Christ. Aware of their private reasoning, John moved to lay to rest their speculation.

Yes, he did indeed baptize them in water unto repentance, or in the direction of repentance, signifying the washing away of what the individual was repenting of from their life. However, there was One coming Who was inherently superior to John; One whose shoes John was not even worthy to loosen. This was a display of humility and truthfulness on John's part. He used the illustration of the removal of shoes, an act that was performed by the lowest of slaves, to picture the marvelous superiority of the Messiah. John was His forerunner. Surely we all must be of the same mind as John when we compare ourselves with Jesus.

The One who was coming would baptize with "the Holy Spirit and with fire." I am of the conviction that the "baptism with the Holy Spirit" has reference to what took place on the feast day of Pentecost in Acts 2 when the apostles were completely immersed in the Holy Spirit. It occurred again in Acts 10 with Cornelius and his household. The "baptism with fire," contextually, must refer to eternal punishment. It corresponds to the unfruitful trees being cast into the fire and the chaff being burned.

That brings us to John's next illustration. In the days of John the Baptist, wheat and other grains were harvested by hand. After it was picked, the grain was beaten or trodden upon by oxen on a smooth, hard piece of ground called the threshing-floor. Then it was picked up in a winnowing fan and tossed into the air. The wind blew the chaff away and the clean grain fell back to the threshing-floor. The grain was kept, the chaff was burned. So would the One who was coming after John separate the good from the wicked.

Jesus Is Baptized (Matt. 3:13-17, Mark 1:9-11, Luke 3:21-22)

Jesus left Nazareth of Galilee to make the 60 to 70 mile journey to the region around Jordan where John was baptizing. We are specifically told that He went there to be "baptized of John." This was not merely to be baptized, but to be "baptized of John", at his hands, thus linking John's work to His own.

It is interesting how different writers have taken different views of Luke's statement in Luke 3:21, "Now it came to pass, when all the people were baptized..." Some have used that to try to determine at what stage of John's ministry this event took place. R.C. Foster believed this indicated that it was at the end of John's ministry; that the great multitudes had come and gone and the crowds were waning. McGarvey and Pendleton suggested that it meant it was in the midst of John's work, when the crowds were the greatest. Perhaps the simplest explanation is the best. On the particular day that Jesus was baptized, He was the last.

As Jesus came to be baptized, John sought to hinder Him from doing so, saying, "I have need to be baptized of thee." This is interesting and warrants some consideration. In John 1:31-33, John said that he did not know that Jesus was the One who was to come until the Spirit descended upon Him. That leads to the following questions. Why did John try to hinder Jesus from being baptized and why did he say, "I have need to be baptized of thee?" Two answers seem logical. One deals with our understanding of the Baptist's remarks in the Gospel of John. Perhaps the significance is that he did not know Jesus in His full Messianic character until the Spirit descended. But here, at the Lord's arrival, either by involuntary impression or revelation, he recognized the superiority of the One before him. Second, and perhaps more probably, he had previous knowledge of Jesus and His character. Remember, they were related.

In His response, Jesus intimates John was correct. He did not need the baptism of repentance unto the remission of sins, for He was sinless. Nevertheless, to "fulfill all righteousness," and to carry out the righteous decrees of God, He would be baptized. Luke adds that Jesus was praying as well.

> Jesus came not only to fulfill all the requirements of the Law, but also all that wider range of righteousness of which the Law was only a part. 1. Though John's baptism was no part of Mosaic ritual, it was, nevertheless, a precept of God, given by His prophet (Jn. 1:33). Had Jesus neglected or refused to obey this precept he would have lacked a portion of the full armor of righteousness,

and the Pharisees would have hastened to strike Him at this loose joint of His harness (Matt. 21:23-27). 2. It was a divinely appointed method by which the Messiahship of Jesus was to be revealed to the witness John (John 1:33-34), (*The Fourfold Gospel*, 83).

As Jesus came up out of the water the "heavens were opened unto him." It appeared as though there was a tear in the sky, and the Holy Spirit descended upon Jesus in bodily form as a dove. Accompanying this was a voice from heaven, saying, "This is my beloved Son, in whom I am well pleased."

This event deserves further consideration. In the first place, the descent of the Holy Spirit upon Jesus was in fulfillment of prophecy. In Isaiah 11:2 we read, "And the Spirit of the Lord shall rest upon him, the Spirit of wisdom and understanding, the Spirit of counsel and might, the Spirit of knowledge and of the fear of the Lord." Contextually, this is a most interesting prophecy. At the close of Isaiah 10, Isaiah had foretold the humbling of the mighty Assyrians. In contrast to the humbling of the mighty, he tells of the exaltation of the lowly in chapter 11. Out of the family of Jesse, of the House of David, which had fallen into humble circumstances, would come forth a Branch. This Branch is the Messiah. Verse 2 of Isaiah 11 indicates that the Spirit of God would dwell with Him; that He would be abundantly endowed with the Holy Spirit.

> Perhaps the circumstance, that the Messiah is first said to be endowed with the Spirit of God in general terms, and that then particular gifts are mentioned by way of example, indicates that he would not, like all other servants of God, be endowed with any merely particular gifts. Although the word 'rests' is elsewhere spoken of the Spirit of God, when it takes possession of the mind, yet here it seems to be particularly emphatic. The Prophets were powerfully seized by the Spirit, and then again deserted; but His influence with the Messiah shall be uniform and permanent (Hengstenberg, *Christology of the Old Testament*, 188).

When the Holy Spirit descended upon Jesus, and John would later testify that he "saw the Spirit descending from heaven like a dove, and it abode upon him" (Jn. 1:32), our Lord received the promised anointing of the Spirit. Many are of the opinion that the fact the Spirit "abode" upon Jesus signifies the abiding, permanent anointing of Christ.

Second, the message from heaven shows that God recognized Jesus as His only begotten Son and expressed His pleasure in Him.

Third, what of the multitudes? Did they hear the voice and see the dove? If the multitudes saw and understood that would have been a very early announcement of the Messiahship of Jesus, and our Lord often said on later occasions that His time had not yet come. John and Jesus saw, heard, and understood. The multitude may have seen and heard, but they did not understand. Much more would have been made of this if they had.

Temptations (Matt. 4:1-11, Mark 1:12-13, Luke 4:1-13)

The reality of what Jesus went through should be addressed first. These temptations were real. Having taken upon Himself humanity, the reality of temptation and the possibility for failure were things that Jesus had to face. Hebrews 4:15 states, "For we have not an high priest which cannot be touched with the feeling of our infirmities; but was in all points tempted like as we are, yet without sin." Hebrews 2:17-18 tells us, "Wherefore in all things it behooved him to be made like unto his brethren, that he might be a merciful and faithful high priest in things pertaining to God, to make reconciliation for the sins of the people. For in that he himself hath suffered being tempted, he is able to succor them that are tempted."

Those who argue that Jesus was God, and therefore did not feel temptation the way that we do, miss the point entirely. No one knows temptation to the extent that Jesus did. At some point all of us have given in and succumbed to temptation. Jesus reached that point and went beyond, never failing. Do we want to know how to endure temptation? Look to the One who experienced it at its zenith and never sinned.

By combining Matthew's and Luke's accounts, we know that immediately following His baptism, Jesus, full of the Holy Spirit (the result of the Spirit descending upon Him), was led by the Spirit into the wilderness to be tempted by the devil. There He fasted for 40 days and 40 nights. Luke adds, "during the forty days being tempted of the devil" and Mark wrote, "And he was in the wilderness forty days tempted of Satan." Was Jesus tempted throughout the 40 days or did the temptations not come until the fast ended? Matthew certainly makes it appear that the temptations occurred after the fast, while Mark and Luke make it appear continuous. There are two possible explanations. One would be that during the 40 days, temptations of various kinds were presented to our Lord with the three specifically mentioned coming after the fast and being representative of them all. Another explanation could be that the fast itself promoted desires in the Lord and became the basis for further temptation. The first explanation seems most reasonable. After the 40 days and nights of isolation and deprivation, Jesus was hungry. Thus the stage was set for the first recorded temptation.

"If thou art the Son of God, command that these stones become bread." This brings to mind the "lust of the flesh" of which John speaks in 1 John 2:16. Jesus was hungry. Would He use His miraculous powers in a selfish way?

> Weakened and exhausted by long abstinence from food, the temptation to supply his wants by this easy means at once was great. Still, had he consented to the tempter's suggestion, Jesus was aware that he would have broken the conditions of that human existence to which, in His deep love for us fallen beings, He had voluntarily consented and submitted Himself (*Pulpit Commentary*, Vol. 16, 86).

Jesus' response is a lesson for all people for all time. He quoted Deuteronomy 8:3, resorting to God's Word, the source of all answers. In His answer Jesus showed that which is most important is not physical in nature but spiritual. He who lives by bread only does not truly live, but he who places God's Word before his physical needs has attained spiritual maturity.

The second temptation according to Matthew (Luke places it third), was for Jesus to be placed on a high pinnacle of the temple. There the devil said, "If thou art the Son of God, cast thyself down: for it is written, he shall give his angels charge concerning thee; and, on their hands they shall bear thee up, lest haply thou dash thy foot against a stone." This calls to mind John's words, "the pride of life," in 1 John 2:16.

What was the temptation? Satan, by misusing scripture (Psalm 91:11-12), was tempting Jesus to endanger His life for no other purpose than to prove the protection of and close communion with His Father. Again, our Lord responded with scripture. He quoted Deuteronomy 6:16. Who is man to tempt God? What He says, He will do! That is enough!

The third temptation (second in Luke's account), has the devil taking Jesus to an exceeding high mountain and showing Him all the kingdoms of the world and the glory of them. Luke tells us that was done in a "moment of time," illustrating the supernatural nature of what was happening. Satan said to Jesus, "To thee will I give all this authority, and the glory of them: for it hath been delivered unto me; and to whomsoever I will I give it. If thou therefore wilt worship before me, it shall all be thine." This brings to mind John's words of 1 John 2:16, "the lust of the eyes."

> From the standpoint of Christ's humanity, how overwhelming the temptation! It was the world's honors to one who had for thirty years led the life of a village carpenter: it was the world's riches to him who had not where to lay his head (*The Fourfold Gospel*, 97).

Jesus again quoted from the scriptures, this time Deuteronomy 6:13, and demanded that Satan depart, which he did. With this terrible period of trial and testing at an end, the angels came and ministered unto the Lord.

John Identifies Jesus as Christ (John 1:19-34)

After going into the wilderness and being tempted of the devil, Jesus returned to the scene of John's ministry, and to the region around Jordan. There is a natural linking of the Lord's beginning ministry with John's ending ministry. When John saw the Lord, he declared, "Behold the Lamb of God, which taketh away the sin of the world."

There is so much included in that brief testimonial. First, by referring to Jesus as "the Lamb," John immediately introduced to his Jewish hearers the idea of sacrifice. Lambs were commonly used for sin offerings (Lev. 4:32). A lamb was killed for the celebration of the Passover. By using that term, John identified Jesus as the sacrificial hope of the Old Testament-- but not just the hope, the actual sacrifice itself. This sacrifice would not be for the Jews only, but for the whole world.

By referring to Jesus as "the Lamb of *God*", John pointed Him out as the lamb or sacrifice that God provided and as the one true and perfect offering for sin. I am reminded of Abraham's words to Isaac in Genesis 22:8, "My son, God will provide himself a lamb for a burnt offering." In the ultimate sense He most certainly did in Jesus. Consider also Hebrews 10:4-10:

> For it is not possible that the blood of bulls and of goats should take away sins. Wherefore when he cometh into the world, he saith, sacrifice and offering thou wouldest not, but a body has thou prepared me: in burnt offerings and sacrifices for sin thou hast had no pleasure. Then said I, Lo, I come (in the volume of the book it is written of me,) to do thy will, O God. Above when he said, sacrifice and offering and burnt offerings and offering for sin thou wouldest not, neither hadst pleasure therein; which are offered by the law; then said he, Lo, I come to do thy will, O God. He taketh away the first, that he may establish the second. By the which will we are sanctified through the offering of the body of Jesus Christ once for all.

By saying that as the Lamb, Jesus would "take away the sins of the world", John was speaking of the expiatory effect and the vicarious nature of the sacrifice of Christ. It should also be mentioned that Jesus had been depicted as a lamb in prophecy. Isaiah 53:7 says, "He was oppressed, and he was afflicted, yet he opened not his mouth: he is brought as a lamb to the slaughter, and as a sheep before her shearers is dumb, so he openeth not his mouth."

John continued with his testimony, saying that Jesus was the One about whom he had spoken. Though He came after John, Jesus was to be preferred before him, for He was before him. This is true in the absolute sense for Jesus is eternal.

John further rehearsed what had happened at the baptism of the Lord. He knew what his mission was. He was to prepare the way for the One to come, the Messiah. God had given John his mission and had given him the way to identify the Messiah, "Upon whom thou shalt see the Spirit descending, and remaining on him, the same is he which baptizeth with the Holy Ghost."

When Jesus came to be baptized of John, John knew *of* Him. He was his kinsman and John could very well have known the quality and character of Jesus. What he did not know until the Spirit descended was that Jesus was the Messiah. "The knowledge which John had of Jesus was as nothing to the blaze of light which burst upon him when he realized that Jesus was the Son of God" (*Pulpit Commentary*, Vol. 17, 32).

John stated that he saw the Spirit descend and that Jesus was the Son of God.

The First Disciples (John 1:35-51)

The very next day the effect of John's testimony concerning Jesus began to be seen as the first disciples of the Lord began to come to Him. Two of John's disciples, Andrew and John, were standing with the Baptist and heard him testify of Jesus. Again the words are stated, "Behold, the Lamb of God." This John was the author of this gospel for the following reasons. (1) From this time on he writes as an eye-witness; (2) There is no other account in the gospel of his call to discipleship; (3) Several other times in the gospel John withholds his name.

The immediate nature of their response is striking. They heard and they followed. Therefore, there must have been awe and reverence. And, they were naturally hesitant to address Jesus. So they followed Him from behind. It was Jesus who opened the way for them by asking, "What seek ye?" They responded by asking where He lived, and then comes what is really the challenge of Christianity. Jesus said, "Come and see."

It was four in the afternoon according to the Jewish method of keeping time when Jesus gave His invitation to those two men, and they were able to spend the day with Him. But Andrew, before he did anything else, gives us our first example of the passionate evangelism that should characterize all disciples of Jesus. He "first findeth his own brother Simon, and saith unto him, We have found the Messiah."

Andrew brought his brother, Simon Peter, to Jesus; and our Lord saw in Peter what he could be and traced the course of his future with the words, "Thou art Simon, the son of Jona: thou shalt be called Cephas." Cephas means "stone." More specifically, it means a rock detached from the strata or bedrock on which the earth rests.

The next day as Jesus began to make His way to Galilee, He came across Philip. To Philip was offered the simple and powerful invitation "Follow me." Philip was of the same city, Bethsaida, as were Simon and Andrew. The passage tells us, "Philip findeth Nathanael, and saith unto him, We have found him, of whom Moses in the law, and the prophets, did write, Jesus of Nazareth, the son of Joseph." Just as Andrew had gone to share the good news, so too did Philip. Moses wrote of Jesus as the Prophet, David wrote of Him as Lord. Isaiah wrote of Him as the son of a virgin and the suffering servant. Jeremiah beautifully wrote of Him as the Branch. Ezekiel prophetically called Him a shepherd and other prophets in still different ways. Perhaps Philip didn't understand the significance of his statement to Nathanael, but what a profound statement it was.

Who was Nathanael? *The International Standard Bible Encyclopedia* identifies him as "Simon, the son of Cleopas, and one of the Twelve." McGarvey identifies him as Bartholomew with the following reasoning, while admitting that the identification is not perfect or clear:

> One – The name Bartholomew is only a patronymic, and hence its bearer would be likely to have an additional name. Two – John never mentions Bartholomew, and the Synoptists never mention Nathanael, though John mentions him among the apostles at

the beginning and at the close of Christ's ministry. Three – The Synoptists, in their list of apostles, invariably place Philip next to Bartholomew, and show a tendency to place brothers and friends together. Four – All the other disciples mentioned in this chapter become apostles, and none are so highly commended as Nathanael (McGarvey and Pendleton, *The Fourfold Gospel*, 111).

Nathanael's reaction is interesting. He did not immediately burst forth with rejoicing. He was a Galilean (John 21:2), and well aware of the reputation of Nazareth. Galilee in general lacked the culture of Judah, had a crude dialect for speech, and a large population of Gentiles. It was viewed disparagingly; Nazareth even more so. But again, there is the invitation, "Come, and see."

In the Lord's words to Nathanael, "Behold, an Israelite indeed, in whom is no guile!" some see a reference to Jacob. Jacob was a man full of all subtlety and guile in his earlier years, but his experience at Penuel in Genesis 32 changed his nature and his name. He became Israel, the spiritual father of the Israelites. Nathanael's surprise shows that Jesus could not have naturally known who he was, but had seen Nathanael when he was all alone and that miraculous ability caused faith in Nathanael. He regarded the revelation of his character and whereabouts as a great thing, yet Jesus assured him that he was destined to see far greater things.

In Jesus' words of verse 51, there is an obvious reference to the dream of a ladder Jacob had in Genesis 28. Here, because the angels are said to be ascending and descending *upon the Son of man*, the idea seems to be that of Jesus as the mediator between heaven and earth.

The First Miracle (John 2:1-11)

On the third day, either after His return to the region of Jordan or three days after the last day described, we witness the first public miracle of Jesus. The miracle took place at Cana of Galilee. While there have been a number of places in Galilee that have claimed to be the site of the first miracle, it is generally believed that Cana was a small village located about three hours journey northeast of Nazareth. Historically the village was rather insignificant. We do not find it mentioned in the Old Testament and it is not mentioned in the works of Flavius Josephus. It was just one of many small villages located in the region of Galilee. So the first miracle occurred not in the city of Jerusalem where it would have been witnessed by the greatest number of people. It did not even take place upon the highway of the small village of Cana. The first public miracle of the Lord took place in the relative privacy of a wedding feast.

The occasion of the miracle deserves consideration. It happened at a "wedding feast." His presence at this feast demonstrates a number of things: (1) The honor with which Jesus viewed marriage. He did not view celibacy as inherently better than marriage. Indeed, in revealing the will of Jesus, the Holy Spirit made it clear in 1 Timothy 4:1-3 that those who forbid marriage were teaching the "doctrine of devils." (2) The "wedding feast" was an occasion of joy and happiness in which Jesus readily participated. Jesus was not a withdrawn ascetic. He took part in the innocent joys of life and His participation sanctions them as being good and pure. Being a follower of Jesus does not mean a life without joy or constant denial of anything of a physical nature that brings happiness. Being a follower of Christ actually enables us to enjoy to the fullest the pure and innocent things of this life.

It is important to consider what prompted the miracle. The wine was gone. The supply had proven inadequate and those responsible for the feast would have to face the embarrassment of not having sufficient refreshments for their guests. Numerous reasons have been given as to why there was a shortage of wine. Some have speculated that it was due to the arrival of Jesus and His disciples, making a greater number in attendance than had been expected. Others have thought that it might have been due to the protracted nature of Jewish wedding celebrations. Still others have thought that it might have been due to the humble circumstances of those giving the feast. Whatever might have been the reason, this miracle can be viewed as an example of the kindness of Jesus. He relieved suffering, elevated the lowly, and demonstrated concern for all people, even those of the humblest circumstances. Considering the Middle Eastern attitude toward hospitality, running out of wine would have been a tremendous embarrassment. In kindness, Jesus alleviated the problem.

Note the interesting way in which Jesus came to know of the problem and His response to it. Mary, His mother, informed Him, "They have no wine." Much has been written about what Mary meant by that statement. Was her comment an implied suggestion that they leave so as not to embarrass their hosts? Some have suggested that it was. Was her statement a request, an implied appeal for Jesus to do something? The reply of Jesus and the further actions of His mother seem to suggest that was the case. It does not appear that Mary knew *what* Jesus would do, but that she knew He *could* do something. She was aware of the unique nature of her Son. To what extent she understood we can only guess. But earlier in our study we saw the statement of Luke 2:51, indicating that she thought deeply about her Son, about His relationship to His Father, and the work He was to do.

Jesus' reply, "Woman, what have I to do with thee? Mine hour is not yet come" is a statement of respect and mild rebuke. Two things are apparent in His answer: (1) The time of His subjection to Mary was over. His work as the Messiah had begun. (2) The time, the hour to *reveal* His full work, had not yet come. It was not time to reveal His Messianic claims. It was not time to reveal to the general populace His power. Yet, in a quiet way, the request would be met.

Mary's statement to the servants, "Whatsoever he saith unto you, do it," shows that Mary knew Jesus was going to come to the assistance of the wedding couple. She had faith in the ability of her son to take care of the problem. Six stone waterpots with a capacity of two or three firkins apiece, possibly as much as 134 gallons, were filled to the brim with water at the word of Jesus. A sample was taken to the governor of the feast, again at the word of Jesus. That which had been water was now wine, not retaining the physical qualities of water. It did not retain the physical qualities of water. Without a recorded word from Jesus the water was changed and was done immediately. There were no delays, no long incantations, no anxious moments over whether or not it would work. It was done perfectly. The governor of the feast pronounced the wine to be "good," better than the wine originally served.

The text tells us, "This beginning of miracles did Jesus in Cana of Galilee." This was the beginning of many signs that Jesus would perform; signs that would show forth His glory and lead to faith in many who witnessed them.

Change of Residence (John 2:12)

After performing His first miracle in Cana of Galilee, Jesus, Mary, His brethren and His disciples went to Capernaum. This is not to say that He moved there at this time (that would occur later), but perhaps Jesus went there to make arrangements for the future move. Nazareth was isolated. Capernaum was more centralized and accessible. It was located on the northwest shore of the Sea of Galilee, about 2 ½ miles southwest of the point where the River Jordan enters into the sea. There will be more about Capernaum and the significance of Jesus locating there in future studies.

> "Brethren of the Lord" if found in any but a Jewish book would have meant full or half brothers. That evidently is the meaning here also. Catholics argue for the perpetual virginity of Mary saying they were sons of a sister of Mary who was also called Mary. This sister is known to have at least two sons by the same name as two of Jesus' brothers, James and Judas, but these were very common names and are not conclusive proof. Some argue that they were children of Joseph by an earlier marriage. However, if we study the *nine* places in which the "Lord's brothers" are mentioned, we will find that six times they are spoken of as being with Mary, which strongly indicates that she had a least four other sons and some daughters, Jesus being the oldest (R.C. Foster, *Gospel Studies*, Vol. 1, 54).

The First Cleansing of the Temple (John 2:13-22)

The first cleansing of the temple took place at the Passover Feast, the first of four such feasts that Jesus would observe during His public ministry. It was one of the three great annual feasts of the Jews. Vast crowds would flock to the city of Jerusalem for its observance and the temple would be the focal point of activity. To give an idea of the crowds involved, Josephus estimated that in one year 256,500 lambs were slaughtered for Passover in Jerusalem and there were ten men present for every lamb. That means 2,565,000 men were present in Jerusalem for the feast. Even though that is an estimate, it is a tremendous number of people. The streets would have been thronged with multitudes moving toward the temple and further crowded by the merchants selling sheep, oxen, and doves; as well as the tables of the money-changers. Why were the money-changers necessary? Because of a law established in Exodus 30:11-16.

> And the Lord spake unto Moses, saying, When thou takest the sum of the children of Israel after their number, then shall they give every man a ransom for his soul unto the Lord, when thou numberest them; that there be no plague among them, when thou numberest them. This they shall give, every one that passeth among them that are numbered, half a shekel after the shekel of the sanctuary: (a shekel is twenty gerahs:) an half shekel shall be the offering of the Lord. Every one that passeth among them that are numbered, from 20 years old and above, shall give an offering unto the Lord. The rich shall not give more, and the poor shall not give less than half a shekel, when they give an offering unto the Lord, to make an atonement for your souls. And thou shalt take the atonement money of the children of Israel, and shalt appoint it for the service of the tabernacle of the congregation: that it may be a memorial unto the children of Israel before the Lord, to make an atonement for your souls.

Twenty days before the Passover the priests began to collect this half shekel paid yearly by every adult Israelite, rich or poor, as atonement money for his soul and to be applied to the expenses of the Tabernacle, or temple, service. All different kinds of money were in circulation at that time from many different countries and governments and some of it was defiled with heathen symbols and inscriptions. It was not lawful to pay with this kind of money and each was obliged to pay with a little silver coin. Consequently an individual would go to the money-changers to receive this coin in exchange for his own currency and would generally be charged 5% interest on the exchange.

All of this merchandising would have been excusable as necessary if it had been confined to the streets leading to the temple. It had not been so confined. The considerable space of the Court of the Gentiles had been used by the merchants and money-changers, with the approval of the Sadducees, as their marketplace. Note the following vivid description:

> There, in the actual Court of the Gentiles, steaming with heat in the burning April day, and filling the Temple with stench and filth, were penned whole flocks of sheep and oxen, while the drovers and pilgrims stood bartering and bargaining around them. There were the men with their great wicker cages filled with doves, and under the shadow of the arcades, formed by quadruple rows of Corinthian columns, sat the money-changers with their tables covered with piles of various small coins, while, as they reckoned and wrangled in the most dishonest of trades, their greedy eyes twinkled with the lust of gain. And this was the entrance court to the Temple of the Most High! The court which was a witness

that that house should be a House of Prayer for all nations had been degraded into a place, which for foulness, was more like a shambles, and for bustling commerce, more like a densely-crowded bazaar; while the lowing of the oxen, the bleating of the sheep, the Babel of many languages, and huckstering and wrangling, and clinking of money and of balances (perhaps not always just), might be heard in the adjoining courts, disturbing the chant of the Levites and the prayers of the priests! (Frederick Farrar, *The Life of Christ*, 159).

Filled with righteous indignation at this abuse of His Father's house, Jesus fashioned a whip out of several small cords and unleashed His divine wrath upon those who prostituted God's house. He drove out the sheep and the oxen with those who tended them. Then He turned His attention to the tables of the money-changers and turned them over, spilling their coins onto the floor of the Court of the Gentiles. He told those who sold doves to remove them from the temple and with divine authority and justification He said, "Make not my Father's house a house of merchandise." Seeing His righteous indignation, His disciples found their minds drawn back to Psalm 69:9 where David had written, "For the zeal of thine house hath eaten me up; and the reproaches of them that reproached thee are fallen upon me." Three years later this same scene would be repeated at the beginning of Jesus' final week.

It is interesting that the leaders of the Jews did not dare to condemn Jesus for what He had done. Instead, they asked only for some sign that would indicate He had the right or authority to act as He had. Jesus responded with a truly greater sign, "Destroy this temple, and in three days I will raise it up." They thought He meant the destruction of the physical temple that had been in the process of being built for 46 years since Herod had begun its construction. They did not know Jesus spoke of His crucifixion and resurrection, two events that this day certainly helped to set in motion. Later, after the Lord had risen from the dead, His disciples would remember these words and have their faith strengthened.

Conversation with Nicodemus and the Growing Ministry in Judea (John 2:23-3:26)

While in Jerusalem for the Passover Feast, Jesus performed many miracles that were witnessed by a number of people. This caused many to believe in Him, but Jesus, knowing all men, knew the nature of their faith and would not commit or entrust Himself to them. Obviously Jesus knew that their faith was not a solid faith. He knew their thoughts, discerned their character, and knew the actual meaning of, and the reason for, their faith.

There was present among those who witnessed the miracles of Jesus a man by the name of Nicodemus. He was a Pharisee, a ruler of the Jews, and a scholar. Nicodemus was a man who was willing to investigate, and yet he came by night. There are at least two plausible explanations for why Nicodemus chose to come to Jesus by night: (1) As an earnest seeker of truth, he desired the in-depth, private conversation that could not be had in the day because of the crowds. (2) Perhaps there was a degree of timidity in Nicodemus. He wanted to know of Jesus, but not in full view of the public. This timidity idea seems to be borne out at other times when we see Nicodemus in the gospel of John. In John 7:50-51 we find Nicodemus trying to check the injustice and the rash actions of his fellow leaders, but his objection was based upon a general principle and gave no indication of his personal feelings concerning Jesus. Again in 19:38-39, He stepped forward to bury Jesus after someone else, Joseph of Arimathea, had apparently taken the initiative.

It appears that as Nicodemus came to Jesus he had two things on his mind, one of which he would state; the other of which Jesus understood. As a scholar, Nicodemus presented what he believed to be the only logical conclusion to be reached based on the evidence he had seen. In verse 2 he said, "Rabbi, we know that thou art a teacher come from God: for no man can do these miracles that thou doest, except God be with him."

Bear in mind that Nicodemus was a scholar, a learned man. His first remarks to Jesus indicate his philosophic turn of mind. He had weighed the evidence and had reached a logical conclusion, so he was equipped to discuss that subject. But being a scholar also presented some problems. Oftentimes great learning can cause a man to be slow to learn. This appears to have been the case with Nicodemus. Something that a simple Galilean fisherman might quickly grasp by simple intuition or faith, a scholar must reach by the sometimes cumbersome path of evidence and conclusion. So often those with great education have the most difficulty grasping the simple truths of the gospel because they are encumbered by their great learning. However, when a scholar like the apostle Paul comes to believe in Jesus and accept those simple truths, his great mental abilities then serve to increase his faith and the power of his convictions.

Nicodemus' conclusion fell so far short of the truth that Jesus moved directly to what must have truly been on the scholar's mind in the first place. This was his opportunity to speak to one whom he believed to be a teacher sent from God and to hear what was necessary for one to go to heaven.

Sweeping aside the insufficient conclusion that Nicodemus had reached, Jesus went right to the heart of the matter. Verse 3 says, "Verily, verily, I say unto thee, except a man be born again, he cannot see the kingdom of God." With this statement Jesus focused upon individual responsibility and the nature of the kingdom.

Failing to grasp the spiritual significance of what Jesus had said, Nicodemus took a literal course, approaching it purely from the physical standpoint. "How can a man be born when he is old? Can he enter the second time into his mother's womb, and be born?"

Jesus responded with a reaffirmation and a further definition of the new birth in verse 5: "Except a man be born of water and of the Spirit, he cannot enter into the kingdom of God."

It is important to note that in the Greek there is but one preposition, "of", and no article with either "water" or "spirit"; it is "except one be born of water and spirit." The significance is that it refers to one single action, the redemption of one individual soul. The birth of water means baptism, the completing step in the rebirth of an individual. The birth of Spirit seems to suggest the whole spiritual transformation that takes place in an individual as he turns through faith and repentance to solemnly dedicate himself to God in the act of baptism for the remission of sins. The Holy Spirit comes into contact with the spirit of man in the preaching of the Word of God, and man comes from the world into the glorious kingdom of God through the new birth.

Jesus continued his explanation to Nicodemus by pointing out that the physical birth to which Nicodemus had referred and the spiritual birth of which Jesus spoke were two separate and distinct things. The possibility of God bringing a man forth into a new, spiritual kingdom should not have astounded Nicodemus any more than the very forces of nature which are controlled by God but surpass human understanding. Jesus said in verse 8, "The wind bloweth where it listeth, and thou hearest the sound thereof, but canst not tell whence it cometh, and whither it goeth: so is every one that is born of the Spirit."

Nicodemus could only answer with a statement of amazement, "How can these things be?" to which Jesus replied, "Are you the teacher of Israel?" The word for teacher is "chakam," or "wise man," thought by some to indicate that Nicodemus was the third highest member of the Sanhedrin. Jesus' response can be paraphrased in this way, "Art thou a man of such position and yet you do not know this simplest lesson?" Jesus spoke of things of which he had personal knowledge. If Nicodemus could not understand the earthly things, how would he understand the heavenly?

In His continued conversation with Nicodemus, Jesus spoke of the coming salvation of man made possible through the sufferings and exaltation of the Son. His reference to the serpent being lifted up calls to mind Numbers 21, in which Moses constructed a fiery serpent of brass and lifted it up. Those who looked upon it were saved from the bites of the serpents in the camp. Those who did not look upon it perished. In much the same way Jesus would be lifted up and those who came to Him in obedient faith would be saved. Those who did not would perish.

Jesus spoke of the love of God, manifested in the sending of His only begotten Son, not to judge, but to save. He spoke also of the deliverance of those who have faith in Him and are faithful to Him. He also spoke of the condemnation that would fall on those who willfully rejected the truth.

After His conversation with Nicodemus, Jesus left the city of Jerusalem and went into the country of Judaea, tarrying there a time with His disciples. While there Jesus did much teaching and many were baptized. John 4:2 indicates that it was the Lord's disciples who did the baptizing, not Jesus Himself.

Even after his testimony concerning Jesus, John continued his work as long as he had opportunities. Both Jesus and John were in Judaea at this time -- John teaching and baptizing in Aenon near to Salim, and places where there was "much water", sufficient for the immersion that is baptism. People were still coming out to hear John; coming to be baptized by him. While there, a dispute arose between John's disciples and some of the Jews concerning purification, or religious washing. In conjunction with this, John's disciples came to him with a complaint about Jesus.

> They suggest that Christ's setting up a baptism of his own was a piece of presumption, as if John, having first set up this rite of baptizing, must have, as it were, a patent for the invention: "He that was with thee beyond Jordan, behold, the same, baptizeth." They suggest that it was a piece of ingratitude to John. He "to whom thou bearest witness" baptizes; as if Jesus owed all his reputation to the honourable character John gave him…They conclude that it would be a total eclipse of John's baptism: "All men come to him" (Matthew Henry, *Matthew Henry's Commentary in One Volume*, 1521).

In his answer John did several things: (1) He acknowledged the divine authority of what Jesus was doing. (2) He reminded his disciples of his own testimony concerning both himself and Jesus. (3) He spoke of the great satisfaction he had in the advancement of Christ. He was happy about it. (4) He spoke of the need for Jesus and His work to increase, and for his to decrease. (5) He acknowledged the superiority of Jesus, even speaking of His divine origin. (6) He spoke of the teaching of Jesus, acknowledging its divine origin and veracity.

Jesus in Samaria (John 4:1-42)

Jesus had been in Judaea for a time beginning with the cleansing of the temple at Passover. Probably because of the reaction of the crowds, along with the reaction of the Jewish leaders in Jerusalem over His actions in the temple, Jesus had gone out into the country and His ministry began to gather momentum. The crowds were getting larger, bypassing even John, and this was not lost on the Pharisees. It could well be that the animosity that they felt toward Jesus, the animosity that would continue to grow throughout His life and reach its climax in the death of Calvary, was beginning to be expressed already. Jesus determined that it was time to move on and He left Judaea to depart for Galilee.

Jesus was on His way to Galilee, yet the passage says, "He must needs go through Samaria." Why? Why was it necessary for Jesus to go through Samaria? Normally the Jews would have retraced their steps and gone through Jerusalem, taking a more round-about route that would have enabled them to bypass the land of the despised Samaritans. It appears this may be an indication of the danger already facing Jesus in Jerusalem at the hands of the Jewish leaders. So, He chose to go through Samaria, and for at least a few glorious days, the Samaritans would hear Jesus.

The journey was arduous and by the sixth hour, noon according to the Jewish method of accounting time, Jesus and His disciples had reached Sychar, near to the site of Jacob's well. Jesus, fully God and fully man, was weary from His journey and sat on the well to rest. While He was there a Samaritan woman came to draw water. Jesus, alone at this time for His disciples had left to purchase food in the city of Sychar, requested a drink of water from the woman. Her reply introduces a number of things for consideration.

"How is it that thou, being a Jew, askest drink of me, which am a woman of Samaria? For the Jews have no dealing with the Samaritans?" Two things make this unusual. First, Jesus was a Jew and she was a Samaritan. The woman herself had said, "For the Jews have no dealing with the Samaritans." Second, she was a woman. Jewish social customs of the time precluded speaking to a woman on the street.

Who were the Samaritans? They were a hybrid race of people that had arisen out of the intermarriage of the remnant of the ten tribes of Israel left in Israel with the colonies of heathen nations brought in after Samaria fell in 722-721 B.C. The Assyrians took the best of Israel into captivity and deported the intellectual and political elite of the nation. Only the feebler elements of the nation were left in Israel, and as they intermarried with the heathen brought in by Assyria, they eventually lost their Jewish identity. We can see bitter hostility between the Jews and the Samaritans as early as the reconstruction of Jerusalem during the time of Ezra and Nehemiah. It would continue even to the time of the destruction of Jerusalem in A.D. 70.

In His reply Jesus immediately turned the discussion to the subject of God. "If thou knewest the gift of God, and who it is that saith to thee, give me to drink; thou wouldest have asked of him, and he would have given thee living water." You may remember that in the discussion with Nicodemus Jesus had introduced the subject of the new birth. Here He speaks of the "gift of God." He continued on with a beautiful and stimulating comparison of salvation with "living water." Just as Nicodemus had taken Jesus' words in a purely physical sense, so too does this Samaritan woman.

"Sir, thou hast nothing to draw with, and the well here is deep: from whence then hast thou that living water?"

Jesus continued in the spiritual. Those who drank the water of Jacob's well would thirst again. But those who drank of the living water would never thirst. They would have a well of water springing up into everlasting life.

Staying in the physical the woman requested this "living water" so that she would never be thirsty again or have to come to the well to draw water. Now the Lord moved to stir her conscience and to bring into sharp focus individual responsibility.

"Go, call thy husband, and come hither."

With this simple request Jesus shows this woman's need for what He had. She had had five husbands and was with a man now who was not her husband. So when she replied, "I have no husband" to that extent she was telling the truth. But with reference to her checkered past, Jesus had revealed Himself a little more fully. How could He have known these things if He were not a prophet of God? Notice that she had arrived at the same conclusion with which Nicodemus had started his conversation. Nicodemus had said, "Rabbi, we know that thou art a teacher come from God..." This woman said, "Sir, I perceive that thou art a prophet."

There are two ways to look at this woman's next question. It is possible percieving the One she was speaking with to be a prophet and realizing her need of truth and salvation, she was seeking an answer to an old controversy. Being a member of an outcast race, Jerusalem was not readily open to her for worship. Her forefathers had worshipped at Mt. Gerizim. Which was the proper place for worship, Jerusalem or Mt. Gerizim? It is also possible that being confronted with her sinful past, she was trying to change the subject.

Whatever might have been her motivation, in Jesus' answer the appeal for Mt. Gerizim was flatly denied. The claims of the Samaritans were invalid. They had abandoned all but five books of the Old Testament. Whenever a person abandons God's Word he or she then worships what they know not. The Old Testament was the Word of God, salvation was of the Jews, and the Samaritan claims were absolutely false; but if she was appealing for an approach to God for forgiveness and a higher manner of life, that was not denied. Jesus taught her that it was not a matter of location, but of spirit and truth in finding God. The heart must be involved in worship; it cannot be mere thoughtless ritual. The heart must be combined with the truth, God's truth, or the worship is worthless. Indeed, a new revelation was about to be granted from heaven that would fulfill the Old Testament and introduce something new. All of this was contained in Jesus' answer and makes it one of the most profound and revolutionary statements He made.

In their conversation Jesus had risen above the need of physical refreshment from Jacob's well and offered "living water." He revealed miraculous insight into her unworthy past and condemned it. He had even, in a veiled way, claimed superiority to the Old Testament itself and the authority to reveal a new way from God. The conversation turned to the Messiah.

"I know that Messiah cometh, which is called Christ, when he is come, he will tell us all things."

There, sitting at a well in the outcast land of Samaria, talking to a woman of questionable reputation, totally alone with her and away from all crowds, Jesus revealed Himself as He truly was and is: "I that speak unto thee am he." He was, and He is, the Messiah.

Just as the climax of the conversation had been reached, the disciples came back with the provisions they had purchased. They were surprised to find Jesus talking to this woman, yet their reverence and respect for Him prohibited them from uttering a word against it. The woman, who had come to Jacob's well to draw water, left her water pot and ran into the city. She had come seeking physical water; but she left consumed with a thirst for "living water." Her enthusiastic announcement to the men of the city caused them to abandon all and come see for themselves.

In the meantime Jesus taught His disciples that the truly important things of life are not the physical needs we feel and experience. The truly important thing is doing the work of God while the harvest is ripe.

For two days Jesus stayed in the midst of the Samaritans, teaching them and having their faith in Him as the Messiah grow and be confirmed.

"Now we believe, not because of thy saying; for we have heard him ourselves, and know that this is indeed the Christ, the Savior of the world."

John Arrested (Luke 3:19-20)

The arrest of John the Baptist is placed here for three reasons: (1) We know that John was present in Judaea at the close of the early Judean ministry (John 3:23-26). (2) The next time we read of John, he is sending messengers to Jesus from prison (Luke 7). (3) Matthew and Mark both indicate John being "cast into prison" was one of the reasons for Jesus' departure to Galilee.

Who was this Herod?

> Herod Antipas was the son of Herod the Great and Malthace, a Samaritan woman. Half Idumaean, half Samaritan, he had therefore not a drop of Jewish blood in his veins, and 'Galilee of the Gentiles' seemed a fit dominion for such a prince. He ruled as 'tetrarch' of Galilee and Peraea from 4 B.C. to 39 A.D. The gospel picture we have of him is far from prepossessing. He is superstitious, foxlike in his cunning and wholly immoral. John the Baptist was brought into his life through an open rebuke of his gross immorality and the defiance of the laws of Moses (*The International Standard Bible Encyclopedia*, Vol.III, 1381).

John boldly rebuked Herod because he had taken his brother Philip's wife, Herodias, to be his own wife. Leviticus 18:16 comes to mind: "Thou shalt not uncover the nakedness of thy brother's wife: it is thy brother's nakedness." Through his actions, Herod was in open rebellion to God's law. Who was Herodias?

> Herodias was daughter of Aristobulus, son of Herod the Great, by Mariamne, daughter of Hyrcanus. Herod Antipas was the son of Herod the Great by Maltache. Herod Antipas was thus the step-brother of Aristobulus, father of Herodias (ibid, 1383).

Because of the rebuke, Herod cast John into prison. Matthew 14:5 informs us that he would have put John to death, but he feared the multitude who held John to be a prophet. So adding to his list of sins was the unlawful and unwarranted imprisonment of John the Baptist.

Galilean Ministry Begins (Matt. 4:12-17, Mark 1:14-15, Luke 4:14-15, John 4:43-54)

After learning of John's arrest Jesus left Judaea for Galilee. As already seen, He chose to travel through Samaria. In Galilee, Jesus made the city of

Capernaum His base of operations. It may appear difficult to rectify this with the statement made in John 4:44 which says, "For Jesus himself testified, that a prophet hath no honor in his own country." Jesus had been raised in Galilee, thus making Galilee and not Judaea His "own country." However, it is no problem if that statement was made with reference to Nazareth. Jesus made Capernaum His primary city, not Nazareth, His home town. We know in Matthew 13:57 and Mark 6:4, Jesus would use the same expression in reference to what was Nazareth. There is no reason to think that it is different here. He left Judaea, went through Samaria into Galilee, Nazareth to be specific, and He left there to go to Capernaum.

Matthew points out the significance of Jesus making Galilee the recipient of the bulk of His ministry. It was in fulfillment of prophecy.

> Nevertheless the dimness shall not be such as was in her vexation, when at the first he lightly afflicted the land of Zebulun and the land of Naphtali, and afterward did more grievously afflict her by the way of the sea, beyond Jordan, in Galilee of the nations. The people that walked in darkness have seen a great light: they that dwell in the land of the shadow of death, upon them hath the light shined (Isaiah 9:1-2).

Galilee of the nations, or Galilee of the Gentiles, was the region primarily held by the tribes of Zebulun and Naphtali. This area constituted the border with a number of heathen nations. Not only were there many Gentiles living in the vicinity of Galilee, many lived in the region itself. It would appear that the less than favorable view most Jews held of Galilee, as evidenced by Nathanael's statement in John 1 and the questions of the Jews in John 7, was primarily a result of the mingling of its inhabitants with the Gentiles. But there was glory and honor to be had for this region. A "light" would shine among them. This occurred when Jesus fixed His residence in Capernaum.

> Christ passed the greatest part of the time of his public ministry in Galilee; there lay Capernaum. His ordinary place of abode; in Galilee were most of his disciples; there he performed many miracles; there the preaching of the gospel met with much success...Altogether similar is the passage in the first verse of the fifth chapter of Micah...As there, the birth of the Messiah shall confer honor upon the hitherto obscure Bethlehem, so here shall Galilee, hitherto held in contempt, upon which the Jews cast reproach that no prophet arose there, be raised to honor and rendered illustrious by the manifestation of the Messiah (E.W. Hengstenberg, *Christology of the Old Testament*, 174).

Thus Jesus, filled with the Holy Spirit who had come upon Him at His baptism, went to Galilee in fulfillment of prophecy. It was time for Him to manifest Himself more fully. Capernaum was made the base of His operations and the people of Galilee were ready to receive Him. They too had been in Jerusalem for the feast of the Passover and many of them had witnessed the miracles He performed in Judaea. As Jesus went through Galilee teaching in the synagogues, He called upon the Jews to repent and believe His gospel, for the kingdom of heaven was at hand. As He labored, His fame spread throughout the region.

There are four things about the miracle in John 4:46-54 that make it extremely notable: (1) It opens this major portion of the Galilean ministry. (2) It was the second miracle performed in the small village of Cana. (3) It was a cure performed at a distance from the one healed. (4) It was performed for a nobleman, a distinguished officer of the king. There seems to be little doubt that this particular individual would have been a member of the government of Herod Antipas.

The situation is one that touches the heart of every parent. Disease and death enter into the home of every man, whether he is a common working man or a nobleman. We can all identify with the anguish in his home over the critical illness of his son. Perhaps this man, Jesus, about whom he had heard, who had performed so many miracles in Jerusalem, could heal his son. What father would not have determined to do all that he could to save his son from death?

The nobleman left Capernaum to go to Jesus personally. It would have been a long and difficult journey from Capernaum to Cana. Cana was 2849 feet above sea level, while Capernaum was on the northwest shore of the Sea of Galilee at 682 feet below sea level. The distance between the two cities was approximately 20 miles, and it would have been 20 uphill miles through rugged mountain roads. He would have been motivated by urgency that only the father of a sick child can understand. When he arrived he asked Jesus to come down with him and heal his son who was at the very point of death.

The reply of Jesus is most interesting: "Except ye see signs and wonders, ye will not believe." The plural form of the verb was used, and that is important as we seek to understand the meaning of Jesus. The reply, at first glance, seems almost out of character. It seems to indicate a certain degree of impatience on Jesus' part with the urgent appeal of this distraught man for his son. But the plural form of the verb indicates Jesus was not rebuking this man, but more likely a multitude that had gathered. That is not difficult to envision either. Multitudes followed Jesus constantly, and now with the arrival of this nobleman and his urgent request, their excitement and curiosity would have grown as they anxiously awaited the reaction of Jesus. There appears to be no weakness of faith on the part of the nobleman but a good deal of weakness on the part of the multitude. The people who had received Jesus in Galilee did so because they had witnessed the works Jesus had done in Jerusalem and anticipated more of them in Galilee.

Jesus' statement did not deter this distraught father. "Sir, come down ere my child die." The desperation in the man's request can be seen. What followed was a mighty test of this man's faith.

"Go thy way; thy son liveth." This man had come with the conviction that if he could reach Jesus in time and persuade Him to come to his home, his child could be saved. Now Jesus demanded further faith on his part. He was being asked to believe that it was not necessary for Jesus to accompany him to his home and that Jesus could heal his son from a distance.

"And the man believed the word Jesus had spoken unto him, and went his way." As he made his way back to Capernaum he was met by his servants with the news that his son lived. He had gotten better at the exact hour Jesus said he would. The man's faith was strengthened and his whole house believed.

First Rejection at Nazareth (Luke 4:16-30)

It is very difficult to place all of the events of the Galilean ministry in their exact chronological order. Generally speaking, they are not recorded that way and not much emphasis is given to the importance of their order in the scriptures. We will examine them in what appears to be a logical progression. The order presented is by no means definitive.

Before we begin to examine the first rejection of the Lord at Nazareth, it should be noted both Matthew and Mark record a visit to Nazareth that appears to have taken place at a later time in the Galilean ministry. Some hold that all three accounts are talking about the same visit. There are many similarities in the accounts, but also many differences. The differences seem to indicate Matthew and Mark were referring to a different visit than Luke. In Luke we have an extended description of the synagogue service, the text of Jesus' reading and the first favorable effect of His words. Then we see a rising tide of anger and scorn, the reply of Jesus, and the ensuing disturbance in which they attempted to kill Him. We do not find any of this in Matthew and Mark. Luke also makes it clear Jesus worked no miracle on this first visit to Nazareth, while Matthew and Mark both declare He healed a few sick people.

At the time of Jesus, Nazareth was a relatively obscure village. As was His custom, Jesus went into the synagogue wherever He was on the Sabbath day. Standing to read, He was delivered the book of the prophet Isaiah. The passage He chose was Isaiah 61:1-2.

Some may wonder why Jesus went back to this small town. He could have labored exclusively in the large centers of commerce and population. Why go to such a small and insignificant place, even if it was His hometown? The answer to this question lies in the text He chose to read. The gospel is not just for the rich, the best educated, or those of the most desirable reputation. It is for all. So, in this little village of Nazareth, in its one synagogue where it had been Jesus' custom during His youth to attend, He revealed Himself to those among whom He had lived. Of all the prophetic passages Jesus could have chosen concerning Himself, He chose one that presented the Messiah as a minister to the sick and afflicted, as a teacher of the neglected, as a savior and comforter of the oppressed. With all the eyes of the people in the synagogue fastened upon Him, Jesus said, "This day is this scripture fulfilled in your ears." Jesus was saying, "He that is speaking to you is that Promised One."

All present heard Jesus and spoke well of Him, marveling at the gracious words falling from His mouth. It is obvious they did not initially comprehend the import of what Jesus said, but slowly doubt and scorn began to be voiced.

"Is not this Joseph's son?" In other words, "We know this fellow. What makes Him so different? Who does He think He is?"

Jesus knew their thoughts. To this growing current of anger and unrest, Jesus said, "Ye will surely say unto me this proverb, physician, heal thyself: whatsoever we have heard done in Capernaum, do also here in thy country." In other words, "If you claim to be the Messiah, do Messianic things. Show us the mighty works we have heard that you did in Capernaum."

Jesus addressed their unbelief in a most forceful manner: "No prophet is accepted in his own country." Two Old Testament examples were used by Jesus. Elijah was sent of God to a Gentile home for shelter, sent to the widow of Sarepta, because she had the faith to share even the last morsel of meal and oil with God's prophet. Elisha, with many Jewish lepers living and dying within his reach, helped Naaman, the Syrian, because Naaman had the faith to come, ask, and to ultimately obey. The implication is that of the Messiah, rejected by His own people, but received and honored by the Gentiles. The blessings of God would be poured out on the Gentiles because the Jews rejected and scorned His Chosen One.

This was the implied in Jesus' statement and seen in the reaction of the people. They were filled with wrath. The normally quiet synagogue became a place of turmoil as they reacted like a mob. They removed Jesus from the synagogue and herded Him through the narrow streets of the little village, intent upon taking Him to the brow of the hill on which their village was built and casting Him to His death. But somehow, the Lord passed through their midst and departed.

Calling of the Four Fishermen
(Matt. 4:18-22, Mark 1:16-21, Luke 5:1-11)

This was not the first time Peter and Andrew, James and John had seen or been associated with Jesus. John gave us the account of their association with Jesus, as well as their first meeting with Him, in his account of the early Judean ministry. John 1 described the meeting, and chapters 2-4 mentioned the "disciples" of the Lord who had accompanied Him. There is no reason to believe these "disciples" were any other than Peter and Andrew, James and John, Philip and Nathanael, and probably others. The indication is that after returning to Galilee with Jesus they had scattered to their homes and resumed their occupations. It doesn't appear any of them had been with Jesus when He experienced His first rejection at Nazareth.

Both Matthew and Mark represent Jesus walking along the shore to where Peter and Andrew were casting their net into the sea; and further on, to where James and John were in their boat mending nets. Jesus called them to leave all, with the words, "Come ye after me, and I will make you to become fishers of men." They obeyed Him immediately and without hesitation. That would be difficult to understand were it not for the fact John had described their earlier association.

Luke, however, shows there was much more to this tremendous event. He describes the multitudes being so vast they were pressing upon Jesus as He preached to them the Word of God. He tells of the fishing expedition that followed and bringing the miraculous catch of fish. Some look at the different settings given in Matthew's and Mark's accounts, compare it with Luke's, and see some difficulty there. But there is no difficulty. Luke shows that the disciples had spent the whole night unsuccessfully fishing. The scene described in Matthew and Mark occurred early in the morning. They had returned and were mending their nets. They answered the call of Jesus and abandoned their work for Him. The crowds gathered and grew larger and larger as Jesus preached unto them. Luke shows Jesus requested the use of Simon's boat because of the immense crowd of people. In the boat, out a little from the land, all would be able to see and hear Him. After finishing His sermon, Jesus commanded the disciples to go out farther and lower their nets for a draught. All of this appears to be most reasonable in terms of order of occurrence.

"Launch out into the deep, and let down your nets for a draught" (Luke 5:4). This was the command the Lord gave to these fishermen after He had finished speaking. Peter registered the surprise and the implicit faith of the men with his reply, "Master, we toiled all night, and took nothing: but at thy word I will let down the nets."

These men made their living by fishing. All night long they had thoroughly tested the fishing and had come up empty. They knew the best places and the best time for a catch. Yet at the word of Jesus, they were willing to try again.

Luke tells us the catch was so great the nets were breaking. Their partners in another boat had to help them and both boats were filled with fish to the point of almost sinking. A large catch of fish was not really the point. These men were being asked to leave their businesses and homes, and come follow Jesus. Their faith had to be tested and strengthened. The command to cast their nets into the deep, contrary to what their experience as fishermen told them would be beneficial, served that purpose.

"Depart from me, for I am a sinful man, O Lord" was Peter's humble confession. It was a natural reaction of a noble and good man who finds himself in the presence of God in a way he had not before realized. It calls to mind Isaiah's confession when he had a vision of God seated in majesty and holiness upon his throne, "Woe is me! For I am undone; because I am a man of unclean lips"(Isa. 6:5). This did not mean Isaiah had been particularly vulgar or blasphemous in speech. It meant his conscience was keen and sensitive. In the presence of God, all men, no matter how fine or noble they may be, must cry out, "I am a sinful man!"

Even though Peter said, "Depart from me" separation from Jesus was the farthest thing from his mind. His cry meant the exact opposite. It is the extreme expression of humility as he declares himself unworthy of remaining another minute in the presence of the Lord. Peter's statement actually contains a fervent appeal that, in spite of his human frailty and sinfulness, Jesus would permit him to remain in His company.

Jesus responded by saying, "Fear not; from henceforth thou shalt catch men." Thus the miracle confirmed their faith and enabled Jesus to confirm their call by this emphatic repetition of His promise to make them "fishers of men." The word used means to "take men alive." Here begins a close association with Jesus, the likes of which no other men, but the rest of the apostles would ever have as they were trained and prepared to take the gospel to the rest of the world.

Ministry in Capernaum
(Matt. 8:14-17, Mark 1:21-34, Luke 4:31-41)

Having called four of His apostles along the shore of the Sea of Galilee, Jesus entered into the city of Capernaum. On the Sabbath day He went into the synagogue and began to teach the people. The reaction of those who heard Jesus speak in the synagogue is similar to the reaction of the temple officers sent by the Pharisees and chief priests to take Jesus in John 7. When questioned why they had not fulfilled their mission and brought Jesus back to them, these officers replied, "Never man spake like this man." The astonishment with which the people of Capernaum heard Jesus was very similar. He taught them as one "having authority, and not as the scribes." Jesus spoke with authority of His own right and power, instead of quoting the authority of the Old Testament or perhaps of some famous rabbi of the day.

> There were several things which caused his teaching to differ from that of the scribes. There was no lack of self-assertion in their teaching; but their words did not carry weight. Their teaching was based chiefly on tradition; it dwelt much on the "mint and anise and cumin" of religion, but neglected "judgment and mercy and faith." Christ's teaching, on the contrary, was eminently spiritual. And then he practiced what he taught. Not so the scribes (*Pulpit Commentary* Vo. 16, 5).

Jesus spoke with the authority of the Father, and to demonstrate that authority, a miracle followed. There was in the synagogue that day a man possessed by an unclean spirit, or literally, "in an unclean spirit." That means the man was in the power of a demon. The origin and exact nature of demons is not conclusively known, but there is no doubt that during the time of Jesus they took possession of men and inflicted bodily and mental torture upon them. It appears the demons were fallen angels, cast out of heaven and in service to the devil. Jude 6 helps to substantiate this view.

This demon recognized Jesus and the nature of the conflict between God and Satan, between good and evil. This is evidenced by what he said, "What have we to do with thee, Jesus thou Nazarene? Art thou come to destroy us? I know thee who thou art, the Holy One of God." Jesus silenced the demon, rebuked him and cast him out of the man. The vindictiveness of the demon is demonstrated by his throwing the man into convulsions and casting him down in the midst of the synagogue. Luke informs us that after the demon departed, the man suffered no lasting physical effects.

Once again the people were amazed. They had not heard, nor seen, anything like this before. Jesus' words rang with authority and He exercised power even over the demons. As they left the synagogue, the rumors and reports concerning Jesus began to spread all over the region of Galilee.

From the synagogue Jesus went to the house of Simon Peter in Capernaum. Upon entering Peter's house, Jesus was informed that Peter's mother-in-law was sick with a great fever, and they besought Jesus on her behalf. Luke tells us that Jesus "stood over her, and rebuked the fever", while Mark informs us that "he took her by the hand, and raised her up." With such a simple action on the part of Jesus, she was able to rise from her sick bed and immediately begin administering to them as Oriental hospitality demanded.

This occurred on the Sabbath day and the Jewish interpretation of Sabbath laws appears to have given Jesus a brief period of rest. The multitudes waited until sunset. As soon as the sun went down the crowds began to come, bringing their sick with them to be healed. The city was gathered at the door of Simon Peter's home, and in their midst were those suffering from all manner of disease and many that were possessed of demons. Jesus laid His hands on every one of the sick and healed them. Those suffering from demon possession had the demons cast out. What a beautiful and awe-inspiring picture this presents of the close of this day in Capernaum during the early period of Jesus' Galilean ministry.

First General Tour of Galilee
(Matt. 4:23-25, Mark 1:35-39, Luke 4:42-44)

"And in the morning, a great while before day, he rose up and went out, and departed into a desert place, and there prayed" (Mark 1:35).

In the gospels we find Jesus would often remove Himself from the crowds and the attention, then go to His Father in prayer. This was such a case. Jesus "departed into a desert place." "Desert place" does not always mean a barren region, void of vegetation. It is often used as a place of solitude, uninhabited, where privacy was available.

Jesus taught us the value and importance of prayer. The ministry of Jesus affected people like nothing else before, but it also affected Him. Jesus was a man as well as God, and as He began to give Himself so unrelentingly and unselfishly to the service of the sick and dying, to men and women lost in sin, He felt the pressure and the tension. Regularly Jesus availed Himself of the comfort, strength, help and inspiration that communication with His Father would provide. Here, early in the morning following such a great day in the city of Capernaum, Jesus sought that help. Since Jesus is the example in whose footsteps we are to walk (1 Peter 2:21), our lives should also be characterized by regular prayer.

As Jesus devoted Himself to prayer on that morning, Simon Peter was leading a multitude of people on a search for Him. It is not hard to imagine the scene and what Peter was thinking at the time. The previous day had been a wonderful day as Jesus performed miracles in Capernaum. Now the excitement of the city would have reached a high pitch, word of the works of Jesus would have spread even farther, and the city of Capernaum would have been filling with people anxious to see and hear Him. But there was no Jesus. Peter, an impetuous sort of person and still very early in his discipleship, took it upon himself to remedy the situation. Finding Jesus he said, "All are seeking thee." The multitude sought to persuade Jesus to remain in Capernaum, but Capernaum was not the only city to which Jesus had been sent. He would go to other towns and other cities of Galilee, teaching them the good tidings of the kingdom of God.

So Jesus went throughout Galilee teaching in the synagogues, preaching the gospel of the kingdom, and healing the sick and demon possessed. News of the work of Jesus spread north into Syria, the region just north of Palestine under Roman rule. Great multitudes came from many different places to follow Jesus. They came from Galilee, Jerusalem, Judaea; even Decapolis.

> Decapolis – The Decapolis was a region southeast of the Sea of Galilee, comprising ten Greek cities, nine east of the Jordan and one (Beth-sham) west. These cities were founded by followers of Alexander the Great, and were reestablished by Pompey (63 B.C.) who hoped to use them to establish Roman rule in Palestine. Pliny, the first writer to mention the Decapolis, lists the original ten cities as Beth-sham (Scythopolis), Pella, Dion, Kanatha, Raphana, Hippos, Gadara, Philadelphia (Rabbath-ammon), Damascus, and Gerasa (Jarash) (*Baker's Bible Atlas*, 192).

Cleansing of a Leper
(Matt. 8:2-4, Mark 1:40-45, Luke 5:12-16)

Jesus left Capernaum and His campaign carried Him through the cities of Galilee. Many were healed and the gospel of the kingdom of God was proclaimed. The healing of this leper is recorded as a striking example of the healing ministry of Jesus. What is leprosy?

> A slowly progressing and intractable disease characterized by subcutaneous nodules, scabs, or cuticular crusts and white shining spots appearing to be deeper than the skin. Other signs are (1) that of the hairs of the affected part turn white and (2) that later there is a growth of 'quick raw flesh.' This disease in an especial manner rendered its victims unclean; even contact with a leper defiled whoever touched him, so while the cure of other diseases is called healing, that of leprosy is called cleansing" (*The International Bible Encyclopedia*, Vol. III, 1867)

This miracle took place in an unnamed city of Galilee and demonstrates the great faith of this man. As he approached Jesus, it was necessary to enter into the city which was contrary to the letter of the law of the Law of Moses. Leviticus 13:45-46 says, "And the leper in whom the plague is, his clothes shall be rent, and his head bare, and he shall put a covering upon his upper lip, and shall cry, unclean, unclean. All the days wherein the plague shall be in him he shall be defiled; he is unclean: he shall dwell alone; without the camp shall his habitation be." His faith caused this man to drop to his knees before Jesus, even falling on his face and offering homage to the Lord, saying, "Lord, if thou wilt, thou canst make me clean."

It is thrilling to learn of the motivation of the Lord's action that Mark reveals in verse 41: "And being moved with compassion, he stretched forth his hand, and touched him, and saith unto him, I will; be thou made clean."

But what about Jesus? Did He break the Law by this obviously intentional touching of a leper?

> We should note the spirit and purpose of this law. Touch was prohibited because it defiled the person touching, and aided not the person touched. In Jesus' case the reasons for this law were absent, the conditions being reversed. Touching defiled not the toucher, and healed the touched (*The Fourfold Gospel*, 179).

> Some hold that Jesus had the right to touch the leper because he was a priest after the order of Melchizedek. But he transcends the Old Testament since he was the maker of both the Old Testament and the New Testament. He shows his sympathy for the man and his absolute power over the disease by touching the leper. He was in no danger of taking or spreading the disease. He is the 'Great Physician' who can heal all the ills of man. The law of love, Jesus held, superceded the ceremonial law (R.C. Foster, *Gospel Studies*, Vol. 2, 13).

At the word of Jesus, the man was cleansed of his leprosy. Two commands were then given to him: "See thou tell no man," and "Go, and show thyself to the priest, and offer the gift that Moses commanded, for a testimony unto them." I will deal with the second command first.

He was told to go to the priest. There are three reasons why he was thus commanded: (1) It was part of the Law of Moses (Leviticus 14:1-32). (2) It was for his cleansing. The priests were the health officials of the nation, and before the leper could be received back into society, he had to go to them for inspection. (3) It was for the priests themselves. They and other national leaders of the Jews did not believe in Jesus. So, a man thus healed by the Lord of this terrible disease made them confront the evidence.

The first command was, "See thou tell no man." The man did not obey this command and it is obvious why. He had been cured of leprosy and was so overjoyed that it appears he could not contain himself; he began to spread abroad the word of his cleansing. The reaction was so great that Jesus had difficulty in the cities because of the multitudes coming to hear Him and to be healed. Ultimately, Jesus resorted to uninhabited places and the crowds would come to Him. Again, Luke also shows us Jesus withdrew Himself to pray.

Why command the man to tell no man? Several reasons come to mind. (1) The Messianic expectations of the people. They expected a political messiah who would throw off their Roman yoke in a military fashion. (2) To allow time to complete His work, thus avoiding the final confrontation with the Jewish leaders. (3) To demonstrate what kind of Messiah He was.

The Healing of a Paralytic
(Matt. 9:1-8, Mark 2:1-12, Luke 5:17-26)

After an absence of some time, Jesus returned to Capernaum, referred to as "his city" in Matthew 9:1. He was sitting in what is called "the house," likely the home of Peter. The dwelling was crammed to capacity, filling the doorway. Outside the streets were crowded with people clustered around the house. Part of the audience listening to Jesus is described by Luke as "Pharisees and doctors of the law sitting by, who were come out of every village of Galilee and Judaea and Jerusalem." Even the religious leaders of the nation had their representatives present, some coming all the way from Jerusalem. The rapid rise in the popularity of Jesus was a source of concern to the leaders of the Jews.

Into this crowded situation came four individuals, bearing one sick of the palsy on a bed. The crowd was so great that they could not get through to bring this individual to Jesus. But they thought of a way. They would go to the rooftop of the house and lower the man down into the presence of Jesus. In Palestine it was not a difficult or far-fetched idea. Most of the homes in Palestine were built with flat roofs and many had outside staircases that led to the roof. The roof itself would be composed of tiles that could easily be removed and then replaced without damage to the house. Luke makes it clear this particular house did indeed have a tile roof. So with determination borne of faith, they carried out their plan and lowered the man sick of the palsy into the presence of Jesus. It is hard to imagine a more dramatic way of bringing this man to the Lord. How would Jesus respond? What would He do, and what was palsy?

> The disease is one characterized by extreme loss of the power of motion dependent on some affection either of the motor centers of the brain or of the spinal cord. It is always serious, usually intractable, and generally sudden in onset (*The International Bible Encyclopedia*, Vol. IV, 2236).

The narrative indicates Jesus was impressed by their faith and He was moved. No matter what those in the house might have been expecting, It is difficult to imagine that they expected Jesus to say what He did.

"Son, thy sins are forgiven thee." It is important to note that the forgiveness of this man's sins and the healing of his affliction were not synonymous, nor were they simultaneous. Jesus first went to the highest need, and it was not physical healing; it was forgiveness of his sins and a right relationship with God. That was first and foremost; the healing would come later.

The first statement, in addition to showing us the proper priorities, also illustrates a marvelous character trait of Jesus. He was the Son of God. He knew such a statement in the presence of the "Pharisees and doctors of the law" would elicit a severe denunciation. He knew it would certainly be repeated in Judaea and Jerusalem, yet He did not fear controversy or its consequences. Jesus' actions speak directly to those today who say that we should not say, do, or teach anything that might offend someone or generate controversy.

What was the controversy? Only God can forgive sins, and the Jewish leaders were absolutely correct. For Jesus to make such a statement was blasphemy as far as they were concerned. One of the definitions of blasphemy is to "arrogate or claim any attribute, power, or authority which belongs exclusively to God." To their way of thinking such a statement as "Thy sins are forgiven thee" made Jesus guilty of blasphemy. This was a very serious charge. Leviticus 24:16 said, "And he that blasphemeth the name of the Lord, he shall surely be put to death, and all the congregation shall certainly stone him: as well the stranger, as he that is born in the land, when he blasphemeth the name of the Lord, shall be put to death." If Jesus had been a mere man, or even an extraordinary man, their accusation would have been just and correct. But He was not; He was the Son of God. Jesus' statement was a dramatic and direct claim to deity. It implied absolute perfection on the part of the one who claims the ability to forgive sin. It implies supreme authority. Jesus claimed this authority and then proved it by a miracle.

The first evidence of Jesus' claim was to read their hearts and declare out loud what they were thinking. He then laid down the proposition that He would prove "…that the Son of man hath power on earth to forgive sins" by a miracle. "Which is easier to say to the sick of the palsy, thy sins be forgiven thee, or to say, arise, and take up thy bed and walk?"

Obviously it would be easier to pronounce forgiveness of the man's sins for they would have no visible means of testing the truth of His claims to such authority. But if He commanded the man to rise up, healed of the dreadful disease that had rendered him helpless, they would be able to test the reality of His authority. Thus Jesus proved the less difficult by the more difficult, and the reason His argument was valid was because it was only by the authority of God that He could do either.

"But that ye may know that the Son of man hath power on earth to forgive sins, Arise, take up thy bed, and go unto thine house." The palsied man was healed immediately and the reaction of the people who saw it was, "We never saw it on this fashion." Luke adds, "We have seen strange things today." Both reactions were absolutely correct and natural. Jesus' declaration offered something aside from the Old Testament provisions for the forgiveness of sins – there was no temple, priests, or sacrifice. The only reason the Pharisees and doctors of the law did not object to His astounding declaration as being contrary to those ordinances in the law was because all of that paled in comparison to the larger, implied claim of Jesus to be deity – to have authority in Himself and upon earth to forgive sins.

The Call of Matthew
(Matt. 9:9-13, Mark 2:13-17, Luke 5:27-32)

After healing the paralytic and entering into the controversy with the Pharisees and doctors of the law, another event took place that caused additional controversy. Jesus left the house of Peter and was walking by the seaside. Once again multitudes followed Him and He taught them as He went. As He walked, He passed the collection booth of a publican, Matthew (Levi, the son of Alphaeus). The publicans had a very profitable occupation, but it was one held in low esteem. They were considered by the populace to be outcasts and traitors because they assisted Rome in the collection of taxes. Their wealth, the natural temptations of their work, and the way they were viewed by the people often led them into less than honorable lifestyles. You will notice in the gospels that "publicans and sinners" are often linked together. Yet Jesus called this man to follow Him, and he did.

Matthew made a great feast in his home. Certainly Jesus would have been the guest of honor. Present at this feast were many of Matthew's colleagues, as well as Jesus and His disciples, of which there were many. This prompted murmuring on the part of the Pharisees and scribes: "How is it that he eateth and drinketh with publicans and sinners?"

The love of Jesus took Him into some of the most unlikely places in search of those who needed Him. His love took Him into the highways and byways. The scribes and Pharisees could keep their self-righteous distance from the publicans and refuse to go into their homes for fear of defiling themselves and they could condemn and belittle Jesus for His association with them, but our Lord went immediately to the heart of the matter. In response to their murmuring Jesus said, "They that are whole have no need of the physicians, but they that are sick. But go ye and learn what this meaneth, I desire mercy, and not sacrifice: for I came not to call the righteous, but sinners."

There is so much to be found in Jesus' statement. He was the physician in His answer, the publicans were the ones who were sick, and the Pharisees and scribes were the ones who were whole. However, "whole" and "righteous", as applied to the Pharisees and scribes, was their own estimation of themselves. They thought they were well, but were desperately sick and did not even know it. The publicans were sick, yes, sin-sick; but to help and to cure them was the very reason Jesus had come. The charge that Jesus associated with sinners was to His glory, not to His shame. Out of this association came Matthew, faithful apostle and author of the gospel that bears his name. The Pharisees and scribes could not understand the significance of Hosea 6:6. The ordinances of the Law meant very little if they were not underscored by love and compassion, the very attributes of character so sorely lacking in their lives.

Controversy about Fasting
(Matt. 9:14-17, Mark 2:18-22, Luke 5:33-39)

After seeing Jesus and His disciples partaking of a feast in the home of Matthew, a publican, it appears the Pharisees sought to enlist the disciples of John in their campaign against Jesus. John was a man noted for his austere lifestyle, a lifestyle that would have been emulated by his disciples, at least to a degree. It stood in sharp contrast to that of Jesus and His disciples. They partook of the innocent pleasures of life, and did in fact eat with publicans and sinners taking the truth about the kingdom of God to them. This was something the disciples of John had difficulty understanding. Previously we noted a certain degree of jealousy among John's disciples toward Jesus (John 3:26). The Pharisees recognized that feeling and sought to use it to their advantage against the Lord.

The Pharisees had designated Monday and Thursday as days of fasting, and it is reasonable to believe that John's disciples observed those days as they sought to imitate the lifestyle of their teacher. Jesus and His disciples did not observe these traditions of men, and the Pharisees and disciples of John wanted to know why.

Jesus used four illustrations, called parables by Luke, to explain. The first was a wedding, a time of great joy and feasting. At a time such as that, fasting was inappropriate. Notice a possible indication of tragedy to come in the words, "But the days will come, when the bridegroom shall be taken away from them, and then will they fast in that day." Second, Jesus used the illustration of a person attempting to sew a piece of cloth that was not shrunk on an old garment. When the new patch did shrink, it would rend the old material, thus ruining it. It was inappropriate to put the new with the old. Luke added that the "new" piece was torn from a new garment, thereby ruining not only the old garment, but the new one as well. Third, Jesus spoke of putting new wine in old wine-skins. Old wine-skins had already expanded as far as they were going to go. When new wine was put into them it would ferment and increase in volume via the gases. Already stretched to their limit, the old skins would burst. Fourth, found in Luke 5:39, also used wine. The old wine was good, the new wine inferior. To drink the old wine and immediately follow it with new wine was disappointing. It was inappropriate to do so.

The point of all four parables was to show things that do not harmonize should not be put together. Fasting was not a part of the Lord's current ministry. There would be a time for it, but it was not commanded by Jesus.

At the Pool of Bethesda (John 5:1-47)

The Galilean ministry was evidently interrupted by a visit to Jerusalem for one of the great feasts of the Jews. It seems reasonable to believe this was the Passover, the second of four Passovers John mentions in connection with the ministry of Jesus.

One year earlier Jesus had cleansed the temple and aroused the anger of the Jewish leaders in Jerusalem. We have been witnessing the growing controversy in Galilee and now can understand the bitterness and hatred toward Jesus that was gaining momentum in Jerusalem.

The miracle took place at the Pool of Bethesda, a spring-fed pool of water that had for a long time been thought by many to have been in the southeast area of the temple; now many believe it to have been in the northeast area. Before proceeding it should be noted that the best and earliest manuscripts of the Gospel of John do not include verse 4, which is believed to have been a scribal insertion in an attempt to explain the belief of the people. The fact that the water was "troubled" is attributable to the siphon spring that fed the pool.

A great multitude of sick and crippled people were lying in the five porches surrounding the Pool of Bethesda. Why did Jesus choose this particular individual from among all the sick and lame? There are a few indications given in the account. (1) This man appears to have been a most helpless case and his healing would be a powerful illustration of the power of Jesus. (2) The man's state was made all the more pitiful by the fact that he was alone and constantly pushed aside by others as he attempted to make his way to the water. (3) This man had been in his condition for 38 years and the account states Jesus knew he had been this way for some time. Thus, the compassion and sympathy of Jesus certainly enters into the picture.

In the cases seen thus far, the sick and the lame came to Jesus seeking help. In this case, Jesus approached this man who did not know Him and had made no effort to seek His help. Jesus came into the world to lead men to faith in Him that would bring eternal salvation. That was the point of the miracles He performed. The love of Jesus moved Him to pity the man both in his physical ailments and in his spiritual suffering. Jesus used His miracles to bring faith as well as health. The miracles gave opportunity to stir and confirm faith. An important point to make is this — the miracles of Jesus and His apostles were faith producing, not faith dependent!

The first thing Jesus did for this lame man was to stir anew in his heart the great desire to be healed and the belief that he could be, "Wilt thou be made whole?...Rise, take up thy bed, and walk...immediately the man was made whole." It happened immediately and completely. There were no failures, no charges that the man's faith was not strong enough. The cure depended upon the one doing the healing, not on the one being healed. This man did not know who Jesus was. Later, when the man was being persecuted by the Jewish leaders for carrying his bed on the Sabbath day, Jesus revealed Himself to him more completely. He had made his body whole; He then sought to give him the more needed spiritual health as well. "Behold, thou art made whole: sin no more, lest a worse thing come unto thee." The man went out and told the Jews that it had been Jesus who had made him whole.

This second visit of Jesus to Jerusalem created a great furor. The manner in which this miracle was performed aroused heated discussion. Why did Jesus heal this man on the Sabbath day, knowing it would bring such bitter criticism against Him? He made deliberate choices in the matter concerning the man and the time. He approached the man. He told him to take up his bed and walk, even though He knew the sight of a person carrying such a burden through the Sabbath day crowds would create controversy. Notice the difference in the methods Jesus used. In Galilee, where such intense excitement accompanied His ministry to the point it threatened to get out of hand, Jesus told a leper He had healed to tell no one. But in Jerusalem, a city so filled with hostility toward Him that even those who believed on Him did so privately for fear of the Jewish leaders, He boldly threw down the gauntlet by sending this man right through the midst of the people on the Sabbath day carrying his bed.

On His first visit Jesus had cleansed the temple of the worldly merchandising and proclaimed, "Behold, a greater than the temple is here." Now He denounced the false leadership of the Pharisees, who by their traditions had nullified the Word of God. He deliberately sent this man walking through the crowds carrying his bed on the Sabbath day. By so doing He was declaring to the nation and its leaders, "Behold, the Son of man is Lord even of the Sabbath" (Matt. 12:8).

When they knew that it had been Jesus, the attitude of the Jewish leaders turned ugly. "And therefore did the Jews persecute Jesus, and sought to slay him, because he had done these things on the Sabbath day."

The stage was set for the first recorded public discourse of Jesus of any length. It arose in defense against the charge that He was a Sabbath breaker (a crime punishable by death – Leviticus 23:29-30, Numbers 15:32-36), but it quickly moved to the larger claim that He was the Son of God.

The fundamental proposition of Jesus' defense is found in v. 17, "My Father worketh hitherto, and I work." He didn't defend His actions by attacking the traditions of the Jews concerning the Sabbath – traditions they had allowed to supersede the scriptures. Jesus went right to the heart of the matter. He based His actions upon His unity and equality with God. The things He did were those things that God does. He was declaring His own authority over the Sabbath, as absolute as God Himself. The Jewish leaders were able to see instantly that the declarations of Jesus were implicit and explicit claims to deity. Jesus did clarify a mistake the Jews made in their reaction to His statement. He made it clear that He was subject to God; but at the same time He was His very Son and acting in conjunction with Him. Jesus showed in His argument that those who did not honor Him were not honoring His Father who had sent Him. He also showed that their reaction to Him, the Son of God, would determine what their fate would be in judgment.

Jesus spoke of witnesses that attested to who He was. The first witness Jesus offered was Himself; but it was not a witness given independently of God. It was a witness given with God. This is borne out by another statement Jesus made in John 8:18, "I am one that bear witness of myself, and the Father that sent me beareth witness of me."

The second witness was John the Baptist. Jesus pointed out that the testimony of John was known to all. The Pharisees could not deny this for they had sent a delegation to John and had heard his testimony concerning Jesus.

His third witness was even greater than John. It was the miracles Jesus performed. This was evidence of the direct work of God through Him. Even Nicodemus understood this to be true when he said to Jesus, "Rabbi, we know that thou art a teacher come from God, for no man can do these miracles that thou doest, except God be with him" (John 3:2). They could not deny Jesus worked miracles.

In the miracles was the fourth witness to be found, God Himself. His testimony was found in the ability of Jesus to perform these mighty works.

The fifth witness was the scriptures. "Search the scriptures; for in them ye think ye have eternal life: and they are they which testify of me." The testimony of the Old Testament was clear and powerful. In fact, His coming was the story of the Old Testament, but they would not believe.

Now the battle lines were drawn. The Sabbath controversy would continue to rage. The Jews would "seek the more to kill him" until that day approximately two years later when Jesus would die on the cross.

Controversy (Matt. 12:1-8, Mark 2:23-28, Luke 6:1-5)

Sadly, the Sabbath controversy did not remain in Jerusalem. It followed Jesus as He returned to Galilee. Matthew gives the fullest account of the next event with Mark adding the statement, "The Sabbath was made for man, and not man for the Sabbath."

It was the Sabbath day, and Jesus and His disciples, in the midst of His exciting and busy ministry, were walking on roads that led them through ripened fields of grains. Perhaps their work and the fevered pace of it had not allowed time for a leisurely meal, so as they moved through, the disciples reached out and plucked the heads of the wheat which was now ripe.

> When thou comest into thy neighbor's vineyard, then thou mayest eat grapes thy fill at thine own pleasure; but thou shalt not put any in thy vessel. When thou comest into the standing corn of thy neighbor, then thou mayest pluck the ears with thine hand; but thou shalt not move a sickle unto thy neighbor's standing corn (Deuteronomy 23:24-25).

This was understood to mean that the hungry were permitted to take any grain they might reach from the highway to satisfy their hunger, but they were not permitted to enter the field itself. Stealing was not the charge being leveled by the Pharisees. They were charging the Lord's disciples with breaking the Sabbath. They were charging them with reaping, threshing, and winnowing as they plucked the grain, rubbing it out in their hands, and blowing the chaff away.

The defense of Jesus was based upon five points. (1) The case of David when he ate the showbread to appease his hunger. (2) The conduct of the priests in carrying out temple sacrifices on the Sabbath. (3) The principle set forth by

Hosea that God desires mercy above sacrifice. (4) The fundamental purpose of God in ordaining the Sabbath for man and not creating man for the Sabbath. (5) The crowning declaration that the Son of man was Lord of the Sabbath. We will look at these points one by one.

The first argument refers to an event in the life of David. It is found in 1 Samuel 21:1-6. Notice in Jesus' defense there was no attempt to discuss the propriety of what David did when he sought food for himself and his hungry men while in flight from Saul. The only food available was the showbread, which the Law of Moses strictly forbade anyone to eat other than the priests (Leviticus 24:5-9). The Jews accepted what David did. Since they did not criticize David for eating the showbread under those trying circumstances, why did they criticize the disciples?

The second argument shows there were certain inevitable conflicts of duty arising from the Law which God had left man to decide according to his own conscience. The Law forbade any work on the Sabbath, but the Law also commanded certain sacrifices to be offered in the temple. When these sacrifices came on the Sabbath, the priests gave precedence to the law for sacrifice in the temple rather than the law of no work on the Sabbath. The argument is simple. Why criticize His disciples when they did not criticize the priests for thus apparently breaking the Law?

Jesus concludes this argument with a majestic declaration, "In this place is one greater than the temple." Early in His ministry Jesus showed His authority over the temple before the whole nation by cleansing it so forcefully of the merchandisers. If the priests of the temple were without guilt in their work of offering sacrifices on the Sabbath, how much more the disciples of the eternal High Priest, whose ministry superseded and ended all such sacrifices?

Jesus' third argument was derived from a statement found in Hosea 6:6 which says, "For I desired mercy, and not sacrifice; and the knowledge of God more than burnt offerings." This is a Hebraism which more precisely means, "I desire not only sacrifice, but also mercy." This argument incorporates the fourth as well, "The Sabbath was made for man and not man for the Sabbath." The Lord's point was that His disciples were without guilt in this matter and the Pharisees would have recognized that if they had understood Hosea's words. Mercy was behind it all. Mercy had led to the saving of the lives of David and his men even though they broke the regulation regarding the eating of the showbread. Mercy permeated the sacrifices offered in the temple. Mercy was the underlying theme of the ministry of Jesus which overshadowed the temple.

Jesus' final argument was a clear declaration of His personal authority, "The Son of man is Lord even of the Sabbath day."

> Even as Jesus proclaimed himself greater than the temple, so he declares himself Lord of the Sabbath. This is a clear declaration of his deity. The temple and the Sabbath were the two central figures of the Old Testament law. Jesus transcends the Old Testament Law. He does not here abrogate the law, but claims authority over it and relates it to the great principles of mercy and love. He

later set it aside when he died on the cross and gave at Pentecost God's final plan of salvation (R.C. Foster, *Gospel Studies*, Vol. 2, 34).

Son of Man – This is the favorite self-designation of Jesus. It is found over 30 times in Matthew, 15 times in Mark, 25 times in Luke, and 12 times in John. It has often been viewed as a designation that sets forth the human element of Jesus' person. However, there is much more to this title.

The phrase is often found in the Old Testament, such as in Psalm 8:4, where it appears in the midst of a psalm that sets forth the lowliness and loftiness of mankind. It also appears in Psalm 80:17, which has a decidedly Messianic flavor. Ezekiel used the phrase of himself over 90 times. It is also found in the book of Daniel in Daniel 8:17. In this verse, Daniel is addressed by that designation. It is also used in one of Daniel's apocalyptic visions in Daniel 7. Very similar to Daniel's usage of the phrase in his apocalyptic vision, is the Lord's usage of it in Matthew 24:30, 25:31, and 26:64.

> The usage of this self-designation by Jesus is especially frequent and striking in passages referring to his future coming to judgment, in which there is necessarily a certain resemblance to the apocalyptic scene in Daniel. In such utterances the Messianic conscious of Jesus is most emphatically expressed; and the passage in Daniel is also obviously Messianic. In another considerable series of passages in which this phrase is used by Jesus, the references are to his sufferings and death; but the assumption which explains these also most easily is that they are Messianic too; Jesus is speaking of the fortunes to which he must submit on account of his vocation…In short, every passage where the phrase occurs is best understood from this point of view, whereas, from any other point of view, not a few appear awkward and out of place (*The International Standard Bible Encyclopedia*, Vol. 5, 2829).

To simplify, it appears that Jesus used this designation of Himself because it is Messianic, because it concealed and revealed to His hearers, and because of the connection it gave Him with all men.

The Man with the Withered Hand
(Matt. 12:9-14, Mark 3:1-6, Luke 6:6-11)

The combined accounts of Matthew, Mark, and Luke give a clear picture of what happened on this particular Sabbath day. Each one of the accounts provides information peculiar to it. Mark gives us Jesus' question to the Pharisees in verse 4, "Is it lawful to do good on the Sabbath days, or to do evil? To save a life, or to kill?" He also mentions the Lord's reactions to the lack of an answer to His question by the Pharisees in verse 5, "And when he had looked round about on them with anger, being grieved for the hardness of their hearts." Luke informs us Jesus knew their hearts and what motivated their questions to Him.

On this Sabbath day Jesus entered into a synagogue. Also present was a man with a withered hand. Whether the deformed man was there by custom or by design is not known. The scribes and Pharisees were certainly watching the proceedings very closely. Their question, "Is it lawful to heal on the Sabbath day?" was an obvious attempt to ensnare Jesus. What would He do?

Jesus commanded the man with the withered hand to stand forth and stretch out his hand, focusing all attention on the critical issue. The Lord could have healed this man later in the day or in private, but He did not. Jesus healed him on the Sabbath day in the synagogue where all could see. Thus His answer to the Pharisees was as direct and impressive as possible. Jesus helped the man and exposed the hypocrisy of the Pharisees at the same time. His illustration of the sheep in the pit showed the Pharisees had more mercy concerning a dumb animal in distress on the Sabbath day than they did for a fellow human being in need.

The question of Jesus in Mark 3:4, "Is it lawful to do good on the Sabbath days, or to do evil? To save life, or to kill?" warrants close consideration. The Pharisees did not answer Him and Jesus knew their silence was caused by the hardness of their hearts. Some have interpreted the Lord's question as meaning to save the man's life by healing him or to kill him by refusing to heal him just because it was the Sabbath. Contextually it means "to save a life" (as Jesus was doing by helping this man) or "to kill" (as the Pharisees were planning to do to Jesus). Thus Jesus laid bare their hypocrisy to them. The Pharisees objected to Jesus healing this man on the Sabbath day; but they were spending the day plotting to kill Him. They were growing more bitter and more desperate in their desire to be rid of Jesus. He was continually defeating them in argument, proving their teaching and customs false, uncovering their hypocrisy, and wresting the leadership of the populace away from them. It is interesting that after this event the Pharisees left the synagogue and went out to take counsel with the Herodians concerning the death of Jesus according to Mark. The Herodians were a powerful political party in Galilee devoted to the interests of the Herod family. As such, they were enemies of the Pharisees, but shared a common hatred of Jesus and were ready to join forces to destroy Him.

Jesus and the Multitudes (Matt. 12:15-21)

Aware of the plot of the Pharisees, Jesus left the synagogue and great multitudes followed Him. Jesus taught them and healed the sick. The last two verses of this passage, quoted from Isaiah 42, are a beautiful picture of the mercy of Jesus to the sinful, the sick, the suffering, and the downtrodden. A "bruised reed" suggests the man oppressed by sin or misfortune would not be destroyed by Jesus if he seeks forgiveness and help. "Smoking flax" is the wick of a lamp which is about to flicker for lack of oil or because of an imperfection of the wick. The light is feeble and the smoke annoying, but Jesus will not snuff it out. He will replenish it and fan it to flame again. Jesus was a man of mercy, standing in sharp contrast to the bitter spirit and hatred of the Pharisees.

Selection of the Twelve Apostles
(Mark 3:13-19, Luke 6:12-16)

As noted before, Jesus often availed Himself of the opportunity to commune with His Father in prayer. The night before He chose His twelve apostles was one such time. It was on a mountain somewhere near Capernaum that this momentous event took place. Of His disciples, Jesus chose twelve to be especially appointed as apostles. The word "apostle" means "one who is sent." It is a fitting title for these twelve men. They were sent forth in a special way to preach the gospel. They were to be peculiar ambassadors of Jesus.

The names of these men were Peter, James (son of Zebedee), John, Andrew, Philip, Bartholomew (possibly Nathanael), Matthew, Thomas, James (son of Alphaeus), Thaddaeus (called Judas son of James by Luke), Simon the Cananean (called Zealot by Luke) and Judas Iscariot. Matthias would be added later to replace Judas Iscariot, and Paul was specially called to be an apostle. Altogether there would be fourteen apostles, but only twelve originally.

There is significance to Simon being called Peter and, the brothers, James and John, being called Boanerges. Peter means "rock", although not an immoveable object. It speaks of the character he would develop. Boanerges means "sons of thunder." Luke 9:51-56 illustrates this character trait of those two men.

> In selecting twelve at first, it is probably that he was somewhat guided by the number of the tribes of Israel. Twelve was, with them, a well-known number, and it was natural that he should select one for every tribe. Their office was clearly made known. They were to heal the sick, raise the dead, preach the gospel, etc. They were to be with him, receive his instructions, learn the nature of his religion, be witnesses of his resurrection, and bear his gospel then around the globe. The number twelve was the best for these purposes that could be selected. It was sufficiently large to answer the purpose of testimony; and it was so small as not to be disorderly, or easily divided into parties or factions. They were not learned men, and could not be supposed to spread their religion by art or talents. They were not men of wealth, and could not bribe men to follow them. They were not men of rank and office, and could not compel men to believe. They were just such men as are always found the best witnesses in courts of justice – plain men, of good sense, of fair character, of great honesty, and with favorable opportunities of ascertaining the facts to which they bore witness. Such men everybody believes, and especially when they are willing to lay down their lives to prove their sincerity.
>
> It was important that he should choose them early in his ministry, that they might be fully acquainted with him; might treasure up

his instructions, and observe his manner of life and his person, that by having been long acquainted with him they might be able to testify to his identity, and be competent witnesses of his resurrection. No witnesses were ever so well qualified to give testimony as they; and none ever gave so much evidence of their sincerity as they did (Albert Barnes, *Barnes' Notes on the New Testament in One Volume*, 47).

The Sermon on the Mount (Matt. 5:1-8:1, Luke 6:17-49)

Matthew and Luke are describing the same occasion and sermon. In Matthew 5:1 we find Jesus going up the mountain, probably due to the press of the multitude. We know He spent the night in prayer to His Father and then chose the twelve apostles. Luke informs us that Jesus came down the next day from the mountain to a level place with His apostles, and a great multitude of people from Judaea and Jerusalem, Tyre and Sidon, were there. Included were the sick and others troubled by unclean spirits. They had come to be healed. At this time Jesus delivered the great Sermon on the Mount. It will be approached topically, focusing primarily on Matthew's account, beginning with the Beatitudes.

The Beatitudes (Matt. 5:3-12, Luke 6:20-26)

The first of the Beatitudes is "Blessed are the poor in spirit; for theirs is the kingdom of heaven." Luke says, "Blessed be ye poor: for yours is the kingdom of God." The word "poor" is not describing what a man has but what a man is, and there is an important difference.

In the New Testament two words are used to express degrees of poverty. One word means total destitution (ptochos), absolute poverty. The other word (penichros) means having only the bare necessities, needy. The word Jesus used was the first. He was saying, "Blessed are the spiritually destitute, those who are utterly helpless; for they are the ones who will gain access into the kingdom of heaven."

The point Jesus was making is this--man must come to feel his total dependence upon God rather than upon himself. He must come to the place where he realizes his helplessness. He must be willing to say, as Jeremiah wrote in Jeremiah 10:23, "O Lord, I know that the way of man is not in himself; it is not in man that walketh to direct his steps." Those who are not willing to bow in humble submission to the will of God will never enjoy the blessings of citizenship in the kingdom of heaven. Entrance is gained by an attitude of humility and recognition of our own insufficiency. That attitude leads to obedience.

"Blessed are they that mourn: for they shall be comforted." This is not a verse of consolation for those who have lost loved ones. Nor is it a proof-text for the "mourner's bench." It is a reference to those who mourn because of sin. It is a reference to those who are mourning over the lost condition of their souls. This describes an individual with a broken heart, broken because of the realization of his sin. To such a one, comfort is promised.

This brings to mind Isaiah's prophecy of Isaiah 61:1-3, "The Spirit of the Lord God is upon me; because the Lord hath anointed me to preach good tidings unto the meek; he hath sent me to bind up the broken hearted, to proclaim liberty to the captives, and the opening of the prison to them that are bound: to proclaim the acceptable year of the Lord, and the day of vengeance of our God; to comfort all that mourn; to appoint unto them that mourn in Zion, to give unto them beauty for ashes, the oil of joy for mourning, the garment of praise for the spirit of heaviness; that they might be called trees of righteousness, the planting of the Lord, that he might be glorified." Jesus fulfilled that prophecy by making salvation available through His death and resurrection. The second Beatitude is an announcement of that coming fulfillment.

In contrast to those who mourn over their soul's condition is the statement of Luke 6:25, "Woe unto you that are full! For ye shall hunger. Woe unto you that laugh now! For ye shall mourn and weep." They are the ones with no realization of their soul's condition. They are the ones with no feeling of godly sorrow brought about by their sins. They may be delighting in the things of the world now, oblivious to their true spiritual condition, but eventually they will mourn and weep. For them there will be no comfort.

"Blessed are the meek; for they shall inherit the earth." The Greek word for "meek" (praus) describes a condition of the mind and heart.

> In its use in Scripture, in which it has a fuller, deeper significance than in non-scriptural Greek writings, it consists not in a person's outward behavior only; nor yet in his relations to his fellow-men; as little in his mere natural disposition. Rather it is an inwrought grace of the soul; and the exercises of it are first and chiefly towards God. It is that temper of spirit in which we accept His dealings with us as good, and therefore without disputing or resisting (*Vine's Expository Dictionary of New Testament Words*, 55).

Meekness is an inward virtue. Those who possess it do not show resentment when they are wronged. It is an evenness of spirit, level temperament. It is the opposite of bitterness and violence. Jesus said that those who had such a disposition would inherit the earth. Here again, people have misunderstood what Jesus meant. The "inheritance of the earth" is a proverbial expression used to suggest great and bountiful blessings. The Jews used the expression to denote any great blessing. Originally it meant the land of Canaan but soon came to refer to the totality of God's blessings. It has absolutely nothing to do with the future inheritance of this old physical earth. This earth will ultimately be destroyed (2 Peter 3:10). When Jesus said, "Blessed are the meek, for they shall inherit the earth" He was saying that those who are meek would be in His kingdom and would receive God's blessings here and now as well as in the future heavenly land of promise.

"Blessed are they which do hunger and thirst after righteousness: for they shall be filled." To paraphrase, "Blessed are those who vehemently desire to be right before God, for they will obtain it."

All men are sinners (Rom. 3:23). Man must depend upon God for forgiveness in order to be righteous. This is made possible through obedience to the gospel of Christ (Heb. 5:9). Hungering and thirsting after righteousness shows a man must want to come, he must desire it and need it as strongly as he does nourishment for his body. When he does, Jesus says that he will be filled.

"Blessed are the merciful, for they shall obtain mercy." Our Lord attached a great, and often over-looked, significance to mercy. Many times Jesus would refer to Hosea 6:6, "For I desire mercy, and not sacrifice; and the knowledge of God more than burnt offerings."

Many of the Jewish leaders during the time of Christ were without mercy. The Roman world in which Jesus lived was extremely unmerciful, particularly to slaves and children. Slaves were treated no better than property and were put to death at any whim of their owner. Unwanted children were discarded in the streets. Against this kind of backdrop, Jesus taught mercy. One of the best explanations of this mercy is, "To be merciful is to have the same attitude to men as God has, to think of men as God thinks of men, to feel for men as God feels for men, to act towards men as God acts toward men." (I do not remember the author of this statement, but it is practical and I thank him for it.) This is the opposite of self-centeredness and selfishness.

Jesus said that the merciful would obtain mercy. If we want God to be merciful to us, we must be merciful to others. James wrote in James 2:13, "For he shall have judgment without mercy, that hath showed no mercy; and mercy rejoiceth against judgment."

"Blessed are the pure in heart: for they shall see God." To be "pure in heart" is to have a singleness of mind, an honesty that has no hidden motives, no selfish interests; to be true and open in all things. The "heart" means "the inner man, the faculty and seat of intelligence." Jesus was saying, "Blessed are those whose understanding is clear; whose spiritual vision is singular, and whose motives are honest, for they shall see God."

All we know about the will of God and our Lord Jesus Christ is through the revealed Word. Those who know and love the truth follow it with a singleness of mind and with no ulterior motive; they are "pure in heart." To "see God" means to have a relationship with Him, both here on earth and ultimately in heaven.

"Blessed are the peacemakers: for they shall be called the children of God." Jesus was not talking about an arbiter in disputes between people. He was not talking about one who settles disagreements among men. He was talking about peacemakers who preach the gospel of peace and show the world the way back to God.

When a man sins he separates himself from God. There is a need for a restoration. That is the function of the peacemaker. He preaches the gospel of peace and thereby helps to reconcile the sinner to God. In Ephesians 2:16-17 Paul wrote, "And that he might reconcile both unto God in one body by the cross, having slain the enmity thereby. And came and preached peace to you which were afar off, and to them that were nigh." Those who spread the peace Jesus brought and preached are peacemakers, makers of peace between God and man.

Romans 10:14-15 states, "How then shall they call on him in whom they have not believed? And how shall they believe in him of whom they have not heard? And how shall they hear without a preacher? And how shall they preach, except they be sent? As it is written, How beautiful are the feet of them that preach the gospel of peace, and bring glad tidings of good things!" All who proclaim the gospel of peace, all who make known to others the possibility of reconciliation to God and the restoration of peace, are the peacemakers. This is everyone who teaches someone the gospel of Christ. These shall be called "the children of God."

"Blessed are they which are persecuted for righteousness' sake: for theirs is the kingdom of heaven. Blessed are ye, when men shall revile you, and persecute you, and shall say all manner of evil against you falsely, for my sake. Rejoice, and be exceeding glad: for great is your reward in heaven: for so persecuted they the prophets which were before you." To be a follower of Jesus would not be easy. He spoke of "counting the cost" (Luke 14:28). There would be persecution of all forms, and yet for the ones who stood firm no matter what, there would be strength to endure now and eternity in heaven.

Light of the World (Matt. 5:13-16)

In these verses Jesus addressed the need for God's people to be useful in His service and their responsibility to exercise influence for good. There are at least four important characteristics of salt that should be mentioned. (1) Salt suggested purity. To the Romans salt was the purest of all substances. Thus the follower of the Lord was to be an example in purity. (2) Salt preserves, it keeps things from corrupting. In the ancient world it was the most common preservative. A follower of the Lord must preserve himself from corruption, and have a preserving effect upon those he comes into contact with. (3) Salt seasons. Being a follower of Christ is to life what salt is to food. Life without Christ has no flavor. Being a believer makes it palatable. It is the responsibility of the Christian to exercise that influence. (4) Salt promotes thirst. A follower of Christ must live in such a way as to stimulate a thirst in others for Jesus. When salt loses its properties and ceases to perform its functions, it is useless and should be cast out. A Christian who has ceased to perform his function has become useless as well.

Light dispels darkness. That is the same function that a follower of Christ performs as he reflects the light of Christ in the darkness of the world. Light that is hidden is useless. So too is a follower of Jesus who hides that fact. A Christian's responsibility is to be useful in service to God – to exercise influence for good.

The Relationship of Jesus' Teaching to the Traditional Interpretation of Old Testament Teaching (Matt. 5:17-48)

Jesus lived His entire life while the Mosaic Law was in effect. He taught many things that were not specifically set forth in that Law as He was preparing for the "law of faith" (Rom. 3:27), the "perfect law of liberty" (James 1:25). He often exposed the fallacy of some of the traditional interpretations of the Law. This led to charges He advocated breaking the Law of Moses or doing away with it. This was obviously not true. Jesus taught that the Jews were to respect and obey the Law of Moses, but they were to understand it correctly.

Jesus did not come to destroy the Law but to fulfill it, to bring it to fruition and completion. Until He had completed His task, not even the smallest letter of the Hebrew alphabet, the jot, or even the smallest part of a letter, the tittle, would pass from it. Indeed, obedience to that Law was essential for the Jews to be saved at that time. Failure to obey it, or to teach others not to obey it, would result in condemnation. But it had to be properly understood. Obedience had to come from the proper motive or it was useless. A follower of the Lord had to exceed the shallow righteousness of the scribes and Pharisees.

Jesus referred to the sixth commandment, "Thou shalt not kill" (Exodus 20:13). He expanded it and showed the initial stages of unjust anger leading to such an act are wrong. Unjust anger places a person in danger of an earthly court, which is the meaning of "judgment" in both verses 21 and 22. If it progresses to name calling, "Raca" – meaning stupid or empty-headed, he stood in danger of the council. This would have been the Sanhedrin, the highest Jewish court. If it continued to progress to the point of calling someone a fool, "moros" – a scoundrel, morally worthless -- he stood in danger of hell. The difference is the Law of Moses taught that the act of murder was wrong. Jesus showed the inward feelings that lead to it are just as wicked.

The Lord taught that in wrongs committed among brethren, the wrongdoer has the God-given responsibility to face the one he has wronged and rectify the situation. So serious is the responsibility that even if the wrongdoer was in the midst of making an offering to God, he was to stop and make the situation right.

Jesus continued to teach His lessons in ways His audience could understand. He used the metaphor of the civil court as He continued to talk about sins against others. The "adversary" is the one who has been sinned against. Jesus illustrated the seriousness of it by showing the failure to reconcile quickly placed one in danger of divine judgment without mercy.

Jesus introduced the subject of adultery, and more completely, the subject of lust. He was not talking about the passing thought of sexual desire through the mind. Jesus was talking about gazing upon someone, letting the mind linger and build lust toward another individual. That is as wrong as the act itself. It is not the act itself, but equally sinful. To illustrate the seriousness of this sin Jesus referred to an eye and to a hand, making the point it would be better to lose such a valuable part of one's body than to permit it to contribute to the loss of our soul.

As we consider verses 31 and 32, the following is very helpful:

This Pharasaic tradition which the Lord cites is based on a distortion of Deuteronomy 24:1-4. The meaning of these verses had been hotly disputed among the rabbinical schools. Shammai, insisting on a criminal and legal cause for the divorce, emphasized the words "some unseemly thing", and limited it to adultery. Hillel stressed the word "find no favor in his eyes", and allowed divorce for anything displeasing to the husband. Rabbi Akiba went even further, permitting divorce if a man found a more appealing woman.

From other information available to us in the New Testament, it is evident that the Pharisees shared the very loose views of Hillel if not worse ones (Matt. 19:3, 7), and were less concerned about the reason for the divorce and its unholy consequences on the victim than for the following of proper forms. Their obsession with legal niceties to the complete disregard of moral principle is again revealed. The Pharisees viewed divorce as a right, and saw the words of Moses as a command (Matt. 19:7) rather than a permissive allowance. By so doing they had wholly misapprehended the law and its purpose.

God's attitude toward divorce had been made abundantly clear in the Old Testament whose canon had virtually closed with the ringing words, "I hate putting away, saith Jehovah, the God of Israel" (Mal. 2:16). Consistent with that divine sentiment the words of Deut. 24:1-4 were intended to put a check on already rampant divorce, not to introduce and encourage it. Jesus describes the teaching of the law on divorce as a concession to Israel's "hardness of heart" (Matt. 19:8); not surely a "hardness" of stubborn rebellion, which would have been intolerable (Heb. 3:7-11), but one borne of spiritual backwardness (Mk. 6:52) (Paul Earnhart, *Christianity Magazine*, April 1985).

Jesus' teaching concerning divorce is that fornication on the part of one of the marriage partners is the only valid reason. The one "put away" for fornication cannot marry another.

As we consider verses 33-37 it should be noted the exact wording of the traditional teaching Jesus mentioned is not found in the Old Testament. More than likely Jesus was giving a summary of the Law's teaching concerning oaths from such passages as Leviticus 19:12, a teaching that sought to regulate an already prevalent practice. The problem was in the application of the regulation of the Law. Apparently the scribes and Pharisees saw the teaching of the Law concerning oaths as permission not to be truthful when one was not under an oath.

The evil Jesus addressed in verse 34 was not the taking of oaths, but lying and deception. In just a few short words, He swept away the vain oaths of the Pharisees and their deceitful subtleties. He did it by making the observation that there was nothing by which they might swear, be it heaven or earth, Jerusalem, or even their own heads, which was not ultimately tied to God and His power. The point was that every single word a follower of the Lord utters, whether under oath or not, is before God and must be the truth. A simple yes or no puts a man under no less obligation to tell the truth than does an oath.

The general rule Jesus taught in verses 38-48 was that we are not to be ruled in our lives by vengeance. "An eye for an eye, and a tooth for a tooth" expresses the idea that the penalty should match the offense (Deuteronomy 19:18-21). Under the Old Law this was to be carried out as a legal act, not a matter of personal retaliation. Jesus was teaching that our personal lives must be guided by love, restraint, and forgiveness, not by vengeance, retaliation and hatred. He illustrated this principle in verses 39-42, showing His followers should be the oppressed, not the oppressors.

In verse 43, Jesus addressed the human tradition teaching "love thy neighbor and hate thy enemies." This teaching was probably arrived at due to the tenor of some of the imprecatory psalms, such as Psalm 109, but it was not a valid interpretation of the Old Law. Consider Proverbs 25:21, and the book of Jonah. By saying "love your enemies," Jesus was once again focusing attention upon God. The love that embraces its enemies does not find its origin on earth. Men don't normally act that way. Paul put it very succinctly in Romans 5:7 when he wrote, "For scarcely for a righteous man will one die…" But God is not like that. He has consistently loved His enemies and this divine love has nothing to do with some attractive quality found in man. The book of Ecclesiastes 7:20, makes it clear what mankind has succeeded in doing making itself morally repugnant. Yet, God loves us. God loves the unlovable (Rom. 5:8). Followers of Christ must strive to have that kind of love.

Pride – Illustrated in Almsgiving, Prayer, Fasting (Matt. 6:1-18)

Jesus addressed the problem of pride, self-seeking, self-first attitude that is not compatible with true devotion and service to God. We might wonder what attraction there would be for the self-seeking, prideful man in almsgiving, prayer, and fasting. These things grow out of humility before God and a concern for others. Why would a prideful man even bother being involved in these things? Therein lies the heart of what Jesus was addressing. Even acts of religious piety and service can be turned into wickedness for the doer of them, when they are motivated by pride.

Almsgiving refers to giving to the poor, something very familiar to the Jews of the first century and dealt with extensively in the Law of Moses. Jesus makes it clear that giving to the poor, like all other expressions of devotion to God, can be turned into wickedness if it is done with an evil motive. If it is not done with a God-centered heart of love, it is soiled and corrupt.

In our almsgiving, we must be content God knows what we have done. We must not announce our deeds to others. In verse 3, Jesus taught us not to announce it to ourselves. Obviously we are going to know what we do, so what was the Lord's point? Jesus was talking about the motive behind our giving. Do we give to the needs of others out of our love for God and the needy? Do we do it unselfishly with no thought about possible credit that might come our way? Or do we give in secret, hoping what we have done becomes know to our glory?

The Lord's prayer is found in verses 9-15 of Matthew 6. A similar sample prayer will be examined when Luke 11:1-13 is studied. For now our focus is upon the problem the Lord was addressing – pride.

Prayer is a marvelous privilege given to Christians. It is the opportunity to speak directly with our Father in heaven. By its very nature it requires we open our hearts in simplicity and humility before God. When we use prayer in a prideful way, seeking our own glory, we have perverted a wonderful blessing. We must not pray to be heard of others. This is not a condemnation of public prayer. The sin is not in being seen and heard, it is in praying to be seen and heard. The hypocrite prays, not because he loves God, but because he loves himself.

The "closet" Jesus spoke of in verse 6 is purely figurative. It is the closet of our hearts. There is no room, no nook into which we can enter, that can keep us from our pride. Even private moments of prayer can become occasions of sin if we allow pride to get in the way. Have you ever had someone tell you about the many hours they spend in private prayer to God? Have you ever had someone expound upon his or her "prayer life?" When they do such, it is no longer private.

Verse 7 speaks of "vain repetitions." Jesus was speaking of the Gentiles. They wanted to be heard by God, but were so woefully ignorant of the true nature of God. Pagan prayers corresponded to the nature of pagan deities. Pagan deities were not like God. They were often indifferent, mean, and unpredictable in the minds of the people. The Gentiles lived in fear of their gods and sought to placate them or to gain their favor through a system of endless, ritualistic prayer, repeated over and over. "Vain repetitions" referred to the idea of the Gentiles that the effectiveness of prayer was found in the words themselves and not in the heart of the one doing the praying. Repetition for repetition's sake does not involve the heart, and the heart must be involved in our conversations with God.

Fasting was an established part of Old Testament worship. There was only one ordained public fast, the Day of Atonement, but at times of special crisis both the nation and individuals fasted. It had a spiritual significance. It was not intended to be therapeutic or ascetic. It was a way of humbling the spirit before God in times of distress and was almost always linked with prayer. By the time of Jesus, pride had entered even into this. The Pharisees had turned private fasting into a hard and fast, twice-weekly ritual, and they wanted everyone to know.

Jesus did not institute any days of fasting for His church, public or private. There is no indication He ordained fasting as a matter of regular devotion.

He did indicate that fasting was appropriate at times of mourning (Mark 2:18-22), and that it would be a natural companion of prayer (1 Cor. 7:5). It was not commanded as a law for Christians.

Singleness of Mind (Matt. 6:19-24)

To be a true follower of Jesus, He must be the center and focal point of all aspects of our lives. Jesus used the illustration of material possessions to make His point. If we succeed in laying up for ourselves the eternal treasures of heaven, it will be because we have put our whole heart into the matter, and only because we have put our whole heart into the matter; anything less dooms man to failure.

> He compares the function of the eye for the body with the influence of one's life-controlling perspective on the heart. The eye acts as the source of light for the body. A "single" (sound, healthy) eye fills the body with light. An "evil" (unsound, defective) eye leaves the body in darkness. The application comes in his concluding observation. (v. 23b): "If therefore the light that is in thee be darkness, how great is the darkness!" As the eye is the window by which the whole body is either lighted or darkened depending on its condition, so the "eyes of the heart" (Eph. 1:18) determine whether the spirit of man is flooded with illumination or plunged into a Godless gloom. It is tragic enough to be physically blind, but when the spirit is denied true sight, how much deeper is that darkness of the soul! A single heart brings clarity and wholeness. A divided heart brings confusion and disarray (Paul Earnhart, *Christianity Magazine*, Nov. 1986, 27).

"Mammon" is the Aramaic word for "riches." Jesus was showing again that a true follower of His cannot vacillate or seek to divide his loyalties. With God, it is all or nothing.

Do Not Worry (Matt. 6:25-34)

Jesus warned His true followers not to engage in worry and anxiety over material things.

> A person should not worry and be anxious about the accumulation of earthy treasures because (1) The spiritual life is more important than the physical; the physical body more important than the clothes with which we adorn it. (2) God cares for the birds of the air. He will care for us if we trust Him and do our part. We are more precious in God's sight than the birds. V. 26. (3) Anxiety and worry are useless: we cannot thus increase our stature. (4) Anxiety over raiment is wrong: since God makes the

lilies and even the grass so much more beautiful than man can adorn himself, we should trust God to clothe us if we are <u>full of faith</u>. (5) Anxiety for earthly treasures is the chief concern of the worldly; the Christian should be different. V. 32. (6) God knows our needs so we should not be anxious, but seek first the doing of His will; He in turn will care for us. V. 33. (7) Every day brings sufficient burdens and problems for our strength; give yourselves to the doing of these things instead of worrying over the future. V. 34 (R.C. Foster, *Gospel Studies*, Vol. 2, 50,51).

Hypocritical Judgment (Matt. 7:1-6)

Here again Jesus lays down a general principle in the form of universal prohibition. This principle is, of course, to be limited by other scriptural laws concerning judgment. It does not prohibit: (1) Judgment by the civil courts, which is apostolically approved (2 Pet. 2:13-15; Heb. 13:17, Tit. 3:1). (2) Judgment of the church on those who walk disorderly; for this also was ordered by Christ and His apostles (Matt. 18:16,17; Tit. 3:10; 2 Thess. 3:6,14; 2 John 10; 1 Tim. 1:20, 6:5). (3) Private judgment as to wrong-doers. This also is ordered by Christ and His apostles (Matt. 7:15,16; Rom. 16:17; 1 John 4:1; 1 Cor. 5:11). The commandment is leveled at rash, censorious and uncharitable judgments, and that fault-finding spirit or disposition which condemns upon surmise without examination of the charges, forgetful that we also shall stand in the judgment and shall need mercy (Rom. 14:10; James 2:13) (McGarvey and Pendleton, *The Fourfold Gospel*, 260).

While verse 6 is somewhat difficult to understand, the connection seems to be that holy and precious things are not to be given to animals. Therefore a Christian must exercise wise judgment. He must be able to judge the dogs and swine, figuratively speaking.

Ask, and It Shall Be Given You (Matt. 7:7-11)

It is imperative that this passage be kept in its context. It is not a guarantee that everything we ask of God, every possible human desire, will be granted. Indeed, when we think soberly about it, such a situation is not one that intelligent men and women would want.

The thought of being able to ask God for anything with the absolute assurance of receiving it would be a frightening one. Alex Motyer expresses it well: "If it were the case that whatever we ask, God was pledged to give, then I for one would never pray again, because I would not have sufficient confidence in my own wisdom to ask God for anything…" There are few of us who have not lived long enough to thank our heavenly Father for prayers that went unanswered (Paul Earnhart, *Christianity Magazine*, July 1987, 27).

Jesus had set forth some lofty standards in the sermon thus far. Lest any despair of ever enjoying the blessings of the kingdom because of those standards, Jesus makes it clear they are available to all who come seeking them. That is an important point. The "everyone" Jesus mentions in verse 8 must be contextually understood to be the spiritually-minded, humble man of the Beatitudes who truly is seeking and searching. To such a one the blessings of the kingdom are promised. God will grant their prayers. By way of illustration the Lord referred to an earthly father who willingly gives to his son the good things he needs. If an imperfect, earthly father will do this, how much more will the perfect Father in heaven, Who knows our every need before we do, grant those things unto us?

The Golden Rule (Matt. 7:12)

At the core of the Old Testament teaching concerning relationships is Leviticus 19:18, "Thou shalt not avenge, nor bear any grudge against the children of thy people, but thou shalt love thy neighbor as thyself: I am the Lord." What Jesus presented at this point of His sermon was not a new ethical teaching.

Followers of Jesus must treat others as they want to be treated themselves. It is really simple and clear. In every circumstance, we must ask ourselves how we would like to be treated in the same situation. To do this, God must be the center and focal point of my life. Matthew 22:36-40 summarizes the Golden Rule, "Master, which is the great commandment in the law? Jesus said unto him, thou shalt love the Lord thy God with all thy heart, and with all thy soul, and with all thy mind. This is the first and great commandment. And the second is like unto it, thou shalt love thy neighbor as thyself. On these two commandments hang all the law and the prophets."

The Strait Gate (Matt. 7:13-14)

The Strait Gate was an illustration familiar to all in Jesus' audience. Two city gates, approached by two roads, represent destruction and life. One is narrow and the other is broad. The narrow road is the way of life. It is God's way and it is narrow. There is only one way to be saved, one road of life. The broad road is the way of destruction. It is the devil's way. There are many, many ways of being lost. It is easy to drift along the broad way. The narrow way requires effort. Few will find and walk the narrow way; the vast majority will tread the broad way. It has always been so and it will always be so.

Dangers in the Narrow Way (Matt. 7:15-23)

As one seeks the kingdom of God, he must be aware that there are many lies and deceptions in the world seeking to lead him in the broad way. There are dangers even from those who appear to be walking in the narrow way. Such would be the "false prophets" or "false teachers." Both the Old and New Testaments are filled with warnings about false teachers. They will always exist.

False teachers are to be judged objectively. Are they teaching the truth? Are they living the truth? How do we make such judgments? By their fruits. The very word out of their mouths will be corrupt--false. Since the mouth speaks "out of the abundance of the heart" (Matt. 12:34), eventually their evil will reveal itself in their character as well. The apparent good things that they do must also be judged objectively. Are they obeying the Lord, or are they going outside of the realm of God's Word into the realm of things God has not authorized? That is how God judges them.

Two Builders (Matt. 7:24-27)

This is a simple illustration. Two men were building houses. One built his upon a firm foundation, which is the gospel of Jesus. When the rains and winds came upon his house, representative of the experiences and trials of life, his house stood. It stood because it was built upon the solid foundation of his obedience to the teachings of Jesus. The other man built his house upon the unstable foundation of sand, which represents the opinions and doctrines of man. When the experiences and difficulties of life came upon it, it could not stand. When it fell, representing judgment day, great was the fall.

In Conclusion (Matt. 7:28-8:1)

As Jesus concluded His teaching, those who heard Him were amazed at His words. Jesus taught them as one having authority in His own right. He revealed aspects of the Law that they had not understood before. He sought to open their understanding to the principles behind God's Law. His teaching was very different from that of the scribes and Pharisees.

One other point needs to be made. We were told in Matthew 4:23 that Jesus went all about Galilee "preaching the gospel of the kingdom." As we come to the conclusion of the Sermon on the Mount, we find "the people were astonished at his doctrine." There is no "gospel-doctrine" distinction. That is an invention of man.

The Centurion's Servant (Matt. 8:5-13, Luke 7:1-10)

We are now moving into the middle period of the Galilean Ministry with the Sermon on the Mount having acted as the dividing point between the early and middle. No one is absolutely certain about the chronology of the events.

Rome was the world power of the time. Its territory was vast, encompassing entire countries that had been defeated and being held as Roman provinces. All of the naturally born Roman citizens combined could not have made an army large enough to properly occupy each of the conquered countries. Because of this, Rome would draft or enlist men from the occupied countries to serve in the army in that land. They were not able to do this in Israel because the Jews refused to serve. So in Palestine the occupation army was comprised primarily of recruits from Samaria and Greece. However, Rome was always careful to keep these non-Roman battalions officered by true Romans.

The Roman army was a study in efficient leadership. During the time of Christ, there were 25 legions in the Roman army. Ordinarily each legion consisted of 6,000 men. Those men were divided into ten cohorts. Each cohort contained three maniples, and each maniple contained two centuries. In each province the governor was the commander-in-chief of all troops within his jurisdiction. An officer from the senatorial rank of Roman society was entrusted with the command of each legion, and under him were six tribunes. Over the centuries, each containing 100 men more or less, were the centurions. Under the centurions were the principales, or non-commissioned officers. This organization worked extremely well.

Historically, armies of occupation in conquered countries have been vulnerable to greed, oppression, and riotous living. It was true before Rome, during the time of Roman domination, and it is true now. But the Roman centurions presented on the pages of the New Testament are favorably pictured. They appear to have a high degree of valor, good judgment, and honesty. In Acts 10, Cornelius is probably the best known and shown to be a man of remarkable character. The centurion in charge of the crucifixion of Jesus made that memorable statement, "Truly this was the Son of God." The centurion in charge of Paul during his journey to Rome showed himself to be a man of strong character when he kept the soldiers under him from killing the prisoners, Paul included, after their ship ran aground. Now our attention focuses upon the centurion at Capernaum. This man was apparently in charge of the garrison at Capernaum, a very important commercial center, and he had been for some time. He had occupied his position long enough to show the people of the city his true character. He had won the respect of the religious leaders of the city. He had even constructed a synagogue for the Jews.

In his first appeal for help, the centurion sent the elders of the Jews to Jesus asking for Jesus to come and save his servant. Luke tells us that this servant was "dear" to the centurion, and Matthew informs us that he was suffering from palsy, grievously tormented. Indeed, this servant was at the point of death. The Jews' assessment of this centurion and his request was, "He is worthy that thou shouldest do this for him."

There is a difference in the two narratives of this event and may present some difficulty until consideration is given to how this man felt about his servant and the emotional distress he was enduring. By combining the two accounts concerning the centurion first thought it best to send the elders of the Jews to Jesus with his request. Next he sent some of his friends. Out of respect for Jesus, he had his friends ask the Lord to heal his servant from a distance; merely speak the word and his servant would be healed. In this way Jesus would not even have to come into his home. Finally, the centurion went to Jesus personally.

What he said was such a marvelous example of faith. When Jesus heard it he said, "I have not found so great faith, no, not in Israel." The centurion, a Roman officer, first declared his own unworthiness to come to Jesus, much less to have Jesus actually come and enter into his home. He also recognized that such a thing was totally unnecessary, for Jesus only had to say the word and his servant would be healed. Notice that the centurion understood the whole thing to be a matter of authority, and authority was a field in which he had some experience. He said, "For I also am a man set under authority, having under me soldiers, and I say unto one, go, and he goeth; and to another, come, and he cometh; and to my servant, do this, and he doeth it."

This man's statement was truly amazing. To paraphrase his words, he was saying, "I understand that this whole matter is one of authority. I know about authority in my own life. I have a certain degree of authority and people under my authority respond to it. But you have authority over all things. You can do whatever you think is right and proper. You don't have to come to my home. All that is necessary for you is to but speak the word and it will be done." Even Jesus marveled at this man's faith and understanding. What an example of faith and what depth of understanding!

Matthew recorded the application Jesus made for the people present at this Gentile's magnificent faith. Jesus said, "And I say unto you, that many shall come from the east and west, and shall sit down with Abraham, and Isaac, and Jacob, in the kingdom of heaven. But the children of the kingdom shall be cast out into outer darkness, there shall be weeping and gnashing of teeth." The whole world was included in that statement, and it was a prophesy of the part the Gentiles would have in the final redemption to come.

Jesus' final words of love, compassion, and kindness to this centurion, "Go thy way; and as thou has believed, so be it done unto thee" are thrilling. That very hour the centurion's dear servant was healed.

The Widow's Son (Luke 7:11-17)

Nain was a city located on the northern slope of a mountain often called Little Hermon. It was situated about 25 miles southwest of the city of Capernaum. Luke makes it clear that this event was soon after Jesus had healed the centurion's servant in the city of Capernaum. Being 25 miles away, Nain would have been a day's journey.

As Jesus drew near to the gate of the city, two groups of people met. One group consisted of Jesus' disciples and a host of other people who were following Him; while the other group was going in the opposite direction. They were coming out of the city and comprised a funeral procession. Being borne on a bier in the funeral procession was the only son of a widow. There are few things as sad as the funeral of an individual who has been survived by a parent. This one was particularly sad since the woman had no husband to help share the burden of grief.

Luke tells us that upon seeing her, Jesus "had compassion on her" and told her to "weep not." It is oftentimes easy to overlook the element of compassion in so many of the Lord's miracles, yet Jesus was a most compassionate man. His was a compassion brought about by a realization of the human suffering and anguish people feel. Jesus understood. He could feel anguish and sorrow for He was fully man even as He was fully God.

Having said, "Weep not" Jesus went to the funeral bier, touched it, and said, "Young man, I say unto thee, arise." His command was simple and the method without ostentation; yet the very simplicity of it makes this miracle incredible to contemplate. Jesus could raise the dead as easily as one might raise someone who is asleep.

Notice the last part of verse 15, "And he delivered him to his mother." Again, the tenderness and the compassion of Jesus is seen. After performing this mighty wonder, Jesus delivered her restored son to the widow. It calls to mind Elisha and the tenderness with which he presented the Shunammite woman with her restored son (2 Kings 4:36).

What was the reaction of the crowd? First a stunned silence, Luke describes it as a fear upon all; then the cries of "A great prophet is arisen among us; and, God hath visited his people." Throughout Judaea and the whole region round spread about word of what happened in Nain.

John's Doubt and Jesus' Comments about Him (Matt. 11:2-19, Luke 7:18-35)

After witnessing the miracles of Jesus, John's disciples informed him of what they had seen. By examining both accounts we can see that John sent two of his disciples to Jesus from his prison cell. It is generally believed that by the time of this event, John had already been in prison for at least six months. There are even those who hold to the idea that John had been in prison for a year when he sent these messengers to Jesus. Exactly how long he had been incarcerated is not known, but it is certain he had been in prison for a considerable period of time. Josephus says that John was imprisoned in the castle of Machaerus, or Makor. This was a strong and extremely gloomy castle located on the border of the desert to the north of the Dead Sea, on the frontiers of Arabia. It was a place of wild and eerie surroundings, said by Jewish legends to be haunted by "goats and satyrs." This was the site of Herod's winter palace.

"Art thou he that should come, or do we look for another?" Was this a question for the benefit of the one who had first recognized and pointed out the Lamb of God? Was this for the benefit of the one who had seen heaven open and the Spirit descending upon the head of Jesus like a dove? Many have suggested that this message was intended to merely satisfy the doubts of the followers of John. Others contend that his question really meant, "Art thou truly the Jesus to whom I bore my testimony?" Still others say it implies no real doubt on John's part, but was meant only as a push, as an attempt to get Jesus to change His approach and to strongly manifest Himself as the Messiah of the nation. Others yet find in John's question a gentle rebuke of Jesus for allowing him to languish in prison when a simple statement of Jesus would have been sufficient to miraculously tear down the walls that held him. All of these suggestions, while worthy of consideration, seem to be meant to save the reputation of John, as if to say there was no possibility that John could have felt any doubt. Such of a view of John is not necessary.

John had been in prison for some time. This would have been a very trying situation for a man of the wilderness, accustomed to a free and open life. Being confined with no work, with no release for his considerable energies, very probably affected the spirit that had been so strong. Perhaps John found himself sinking into melancholy like his prototype, Elijah. It may very well have been so. John was a man of strength, bold and courageous; but let us not forget that he was a man, subject to weaknesses and inconsistencies. No man lives at his highest level at all times, and the Bible is very clear that even great men of God sometimes fail, and sometimes they fail in what had appeared to be their strongest attribute. For example, Elijah failed in courage, Moses in meekness, and Peter in steadfastness. Perhaps John was a case in point. He had waited for a long time, locked in prison. Why should we be surprised if he had become impatient and despairing? Surely John had heard reports of the actions, works, and teachings of Jesus. They were holy, and yet in some respects, unlike his own. It is no wonder John was perplexed.

The Bible consistently presents men as they really were. It does not paint idealized pictures. It shows the imperfections as well as the good. In the Scripture, it is encouraging to see real men, truly great men of God, men who fought the good fight and won the race, yet they failed from time to time. They occasionally wavered, sometimes even doubted; yet triumphed. In his troubled state, John sent directly to Jesus.

With kindness and gentleness Jesus responded to the two disciples of John. "Go and show John again those things which ye do hear and see." What was it that they had seen and heard? The blind received their sight, the lame walked, the lepers were cleansed, the deaf made to hear, the dead were raised, and the poor were having the gospel preached to them. This was substantially a quote from Isaiah 35:5-6. Included in Jesus' response was a word of encouragement to John. "Blessed is he, whosoever shall find no occasion of stumbling in me." In other words, "John, don't find me a stumblingblock to your faith. Remain strong and believe."

In Matthew 11:7 and in Luke 7:24-25, there is a warning for all who would preach God's Word today. What had the people seen when they went to see John; a reed shaken with the wind? A reed did not have sufficient strength to withstand the elements. It yielded to every wind that blew. Many modern preachers are like that. They bend in every direction of the compass to avoid any kind of controversy or conflict. Had the people seen a luxuriously clad preacher when they went to see John? What a searing condemnation of the materialism of so many today! But this was not what the people had seen when they went to see John. They had gone to hear a prophet, and that is what John was. He was not just any prophet; he was the promised prophet of Malachi 3:1. Of all of those born of women at that time, there was not one greater than John the Baptist.

An important point must be made here. At this time the kingdom of the Lord was not yet in existence; the church had not been established. Yet, as great as John was, a little one in that kingdom would be greater. John was never in the church and the relationship of one in the church is closer to Jesus than John had been. The point being made is that it is a marvelous blessing and privilege to be a member of the body of Christ.

The Jews of Jesus' day wanted action against Rome. The constant effort of the zealots was to seize the movement of Jesus and turn it to their violent ends. With the coming of John, the end of the Law and the prophets was at hand; the Messiah was nigh. Let the Pharisees argue that the Messiah could not come until Elijah, for John was that promised Elijah of Malachi 4:5. If they would accept it, they could be saved.

Verses 16-19 of Matthew's account and verses 31-35 of Luke's account constitute an interesting use of sarcasm by Jesus. They are a comparison of the unbelieving generation to contrary children in the marketplace who refuse to play with the other children. One group holds up to their lips imaginary pipes as though they were playing wedding songs, but the contrary group of children refused to play along and dance. So, the other changed and played at mourning and weeping, acting as if at a funeral, but the contrary group wouldn't join in that as well. No matter what they did, the other group would not accept it. It was the same with that contrary, unbelieving generation. John came neither eating nor drinking, in the solemn austere manner of the children playing at the funeral, and the Jews would not accept that. Jesus came eating and drinking and they wouldn't accept that. They accused Jesus of being a "man gluttonous, and a winebibber, a friend of publicans and sinners." However, the results of John's ministry demonstrated the wisdom of the course he had followed, and the results of Jesus' ministry were proving the wisdom of His course. The unbelieving Jews would be satisfied with no one.

Condemnation of Unbelief and the Great Invitation (Matt. 11:20-30)

These verses help us understand the full force of what Jesus had said concerning the contrary, unbelieving generation. His "headquarters" during the Galilean ministry was Capernaum, and Jesus mentioned it with two of its suburbs, Chorazin and Bethsaida. They had witnessed so many works at the hands of Jesus, works that evil cities as Tyre, Sidon, and Sodom, cities notorious for their idolatrous wickedness, would have repented had they seen. The unbelievers Jesus mentioned saw and refused the evidence. They refused to repent. They would be held responsible for their deliberate refusal to believe, and their torment would be worse because they would know what they had. They would know that they had the opportunity and had rejected it.

Not all rejected the Lord; not all proved themselves to be unworthy. Not all of the Jews sought the pleasures of this world rather than the blessedness of heaven.

Who else but God could invite the whole world? What we see in verses 28-30 is the love of God shown in the divine love of His Son. These words are directed to all the hearts of mankind lost in sin and despair. What is offered is peace, complete and total contentment, and rest, both here and in the world to come.

Simon the Pharisee (Luke 7:36-50)

Before we examine the events in Simon's home, a false idea needs to be addressed. It is widely believed that this woman was Mary of Magdala, mentioned in 8:2, as having had seven demons cast out of her. The Bible does not identify the two as being the same. Actually, it appears to give the opposite impression. There is nothing in the account indicating this well-known sinful woman of Luke 7 had ever been a demoniac. Also, the earliest church writers do not identify the two as being the same. The earliest assertion that they were the same was made by Gregory the Great (590 – 604 A.D.).

As already noted, the relationship between Jesus and the leading religious parties of His time was rapidly deteriorating. There had been heated exchanges and charges leveled, but the Pharisees had not publicly declared Jesus to be an enemy of the people and a blasphemer. They were watching Him closely, but the indication is some were undecided in their opinion of Jesus. Evidently Simon the Pharisee was one of the still undecided.

An interesting facet of Middle Eastern life, and one that is very well illustrated in this account, is the emphasis placed upon hospitality. At feasts, the houses were open and uninvited guests were free to enter the open courtyard of the home and look in on the guest chambers. At this time an uninvited guest entered, one whose way of life was well known to Simon and several others guests. She had heard Jesus was eating at Simon's house and her desire to see Him spurred her. It was bold to enter, uninvited, into the home of a rigid individual as Simon, but the knowledge that Jesus was there and the urgent need to see Him gave her the courage to go. Perhaps what she had heard of Jesus indicated He would not turn her away. Jesus was different from the religious leaders of which she was accustomed. He called the weary, the down-trodden and the sinful to come to Him. He did not turn them away. So she came, bearing an alabaster box of ointment with which to anoint the feet of Jesus. As her tears fell on His feet, she used her hair to wipe them away.

Alabaster is a material slightly softer than marble that could be used to form vessels and bottles. It was the common material used in containers that held ointments and expensive cosmetics like those worn by wealthy Roman women.

The sight of this woman – her shame, penitence, tears -- did not evoke feelings of compassion and sympathy in Simon. His were feelings of disgust and disapproval. There was no sympathy in his heart. It was not enough for Simon that Jesus had allowed this woman to kiss and anoint His feet without speaking even one word of encouragement to her as of yet. Simon thought to himself that if Jesus had really been a prophet, He would have known what manner of woman this was, and knowing, He would have been repulsed by her and would have sent her on her way with contempt and indignation.

While Simon did not say all of this, Jesus knew his thoughts. He proceeded to teach Simon, as well as all of the others, a wonderful lesson. "Simon, I have somewhat to say to thee."

The parable Jesus spoke was taken from the everyday life of the Jews. Lending and borrowing was an ever-present feature in the economy of the Jews. The Old Testament, particularly the book of Deuteronomy and later in the book of Proverbs, contains many warnings against greed and covetousness and the sin of usury. In this particular case the two debtors were just common people and the amounts of money in question were relatively small. One was about $8.00 and the other about $80.00. Both were unable to pay and both received a generous release from their debt by their creditor. Obviously the larger sum represented the great catalogue of sins that the penitent woman acknowledged she had committed; the smaller sum represented the few transgressions that even a self-righteous Pharisee would admit. Both were sinners before God and both were equally unable to pay.

When Jesus asked Simon, "Which of them will love him most?" there was a touch of indifference to the whole matter in his answer. "I suppose (or I presume) that he, to whom he forgave the most." To which Jesus replied, "Thou hast rightly judged." Thus the stage was set for something similar to what Nathan said to David in 2 Samuel 12:7, "Thou art the man..."

When Jesus had entered Simon's house, He had not even been treated with the normal courtesy that would have been extended to a special guest. There had been no water given to wipe His dusty feet, but this woman washed them with her tears and wiped them with her hair. There had been no kiss of greeting from Simon, but this woman had not ceased to kiss Jesus' feet. There had been no soothing oil applied to the Lord's head by Simon, but this woman had taken expensive ointment and anointed His feet. She who needed so much gave so much; and he who thought he needed little gave little in return.

With the power Jesus had while on earth, He forgave this woman her sins. With the simple statement, "Thy faith hath saved thee; go in peace," our Lord sent this woman back into the world; but not back to her previous way of life. Now, she had something priceless. She was forgiven and possessed the promised peace of Jesus, the peace that passes all understanding.

Second General Tour of Galilee (Luke 8:1-3)

Jesus and His apostles went throughout the region of Galilee teaching the good tidings of the kingdom of God. They were accompanied by a small band of women. Included in the group of women were Mary Magdalene (out of whom Jesus had cast seven demons), Susanna, and Joanna, the wife of Chuza who was Herod's steward. A steward would have been one in charge of the royal household.

The last clause of verse 3 indicates certain things about these women and what they did. When the Lord and His apostles were not being fed in the homes of friends and supporters, they had to have some means to buy food. It appears this group of women may have performed that function, ministering unto them out of their own substance.

Pharisees Charge Jesus in League with Devil (Blasphemy against the Holy Ghost) A Sign Demanded (Matt. 12:22-45, Mark 3:19-30, Luke 11:14-36)

The focus is on Matthew's account. An individual who was possessed of a demon was brought to Jesus. The account certainly indicates that the blindness and dumbness of the man was a direct result of the possession. Just as Jesus had done in the case of the dumb man possessed by a demon in Matthew 9, He cleansed this individual, casting the demon out enabling him to both see and speak.

The reaction of the people who witnessed this cleansing was one of amazement, leading some to the conclusion that this was the promised son of David, the Messiah. But the Pharisees were not of the disposition to accept this conclusion. They were gradually forming their own opinion of Jesus, and that He could be the Son of David was not part of it. Still, it was obvious to all present this individual had been freed from the demon that had possessed him and was now able to both see and speak. Some sort of explanation was necessary. A wondrous thing had been done and it could not be denied.

The explanation of the Pharisees was that Jesus did cast out demons, but He did so by the power of the prince of demons, Beelzebub. Their explanation was more than a simple assertion that Jesus did what He did by the power of Beelzebub. It was a declaration that He could have done it by no other means. God was dismissed from the picture altogether. In the time of Christ, Beelzebub was the name used for the chief of the demons, and was identified with Satan himself. Jesus showed that such an action on Satan's part, which would effectively be casting out himself, was ridiculous and self-destructive.

The Pharisees should have hesitated before making such an accusation because their own disciples claimed to be able to cast out demons. Acts 19:13 gives evidence that there were some Jews who tried to practice exorcism, and Josephus in his work *Antiquities*, also mentions Jewish exorcists.

Jesus neither confirmed nor denied that the disciples of the Pharisees cast out demons. He mentioned it by way of argument. The obvious implication is they would have to reply that their disciples cast out demons by God's help and if that be so, then they would be convicted of dishonesty and insincerity. How could they attribute divine assistance to their disciples and deny it to Jesus? All had witnessed what Jesus had done. To be consistent, the Pharisees would have to admit divine assistance to Jesus and that in Jesus the kingdom of God had arrived.

The "strong man" is Satan and the demons his "goods." Jesus had to be more powerful than Satan or He could not be casting out Satan's demons. As far as Jesus was concerned, neutrality concerning Him was impossible. They had to choose. A person was either for Jesus or against Him. **The foolish charges and illogical reasoning had to stop.**

Blasphemy against the Holy Spirit (Matt. 12:31-32)

The parallel passage from Mark states, "Verily I say unto you, all sins shall be forgiven unto the sons of men, and blasphemies wherewith soever they shall blaspheme: but he that shall blaspheme against the Holy Ghost hath never forgiveness, but is in danger of eternal damnation: because they said, he hath an unclean spirit" (Mark 3:28-30). Luke adds in Luke 12:10, "And whosoever shall speak a word against the Son of man, it shall be forgiven him: but unto him that blasphemeth against the Holy Ghost it shall not be forgiven."

The three most popular interpretations concerning the blasphemy against the Holy Spirit are: (1) The blasphemy against the Holy Spirit was committed by these Pharisees when they said Jesus was in league with the devil and was casting out demons by the power of the devil. Those who hold this view usually maintain it is not a sin which is committed today, but was this particular charge made against Jesus during His ministry. (2) It is the sin of rejecting the invitation of Jesus to become His follower. It is committed by everyone who refuses to believe and obey when they hear the gospel. (3) It is the sin of continuous malicious attacks upon Christ and the Holy Spirit. It is not a single word or insult, but a continuous assault by word or deed. A combination of the second and third views appear to be most correct.

In Luke 4:17-19 we find Jesus in the synagogue of the city of Nazareth. The passage says, "And there was delivered unto him the book of the prophet Isaiah. And when he had opened the book, he found the place where it was written, the Spirit of the Lord is upon me, because he hath anointed me to preach the gospel to the poor; he hath sent me to heal the broken-hearted, to preach deliverance to the captives, and recovering of sight to the blind, to set at liberty them that are bruised, to preach the acceptable year of the Lord."

This passage, and the statement Jesus made in Matthew 12:28, "But if I cast out demons by the Spirit of God, then the kingdom of God is come unto you", indicate to us an important function of the Holy Spirit as far as the Lord was concerned. Jesus performed the miracles through the Holy Spirit. The gospel accounts are clear that Jesus was anointed of the Spirit and that the Spirit was a vital agent in His work. This needs to be kept in mind as we seek to understand the nature of blasphemy against the Holy Spirit from the accounts themselves.

Jesus had worked a notable miracle in the presence of witnesses. The subject of the miracle was both blind and dumb, afflictions that were evidently brought about by the fact he was a demoniac, possessed by a demon. But Jesus cleansed him, "insomuch that the blind and dumb both spake and saw." The crowd of witnesses was convinced. They cried out "Is this not the son of David?" Is not this miracle worker the Messiah? Didn't the prophecies portray Him as a worker of miracles? Who could dispute that the Spirit of God was with Jesus? Who could dispute that He was the Anointed One, the Messiah, the Christ of God?"

The Pharisees disputed it. Against the clearest of evidence, because of their pride and envy, they refused to accept what they had seen. Truly there are none so blind as those who refuse to see. To defend their opinion of the Lord and to retain some credibility in the eyes of the people, they invented the ludicrous charge that Jesus was casting out demons through the prince of the devils. Thus, they blasphemed the work of the Holy Spirit by attributing it to a diabolical agency, the very prince of demons. What had they done? They had rejected the clearest of evidence, the work of the Spirit through Jesus, and blasphemed God.

It is my conviction that the blasphemy against the Holy Spirit is the final rejection of the evidence produced by the Spirit through Jesus – the miracles He worked. Obviously such an individual will reject Jesus as well. There is no forgiveness for such a sin while the sinner remains involved in it. But Jesus did say, "And whosoever speaketh a work against the Son of man, it shall be forgiven him." What would that be? It is the resistance to the testimony of Jesus without the demonstration of the miracles. But to speak against the Holy Spirit, to blaspheme against the Holy Spirit, is to resist that testimony when it is confirmed by the miracles.

Jesus spoke of the significance of His miracles in John 10:25, 37-38. Verse 25 states, "Jesus answered them, I told you, and ye believed not: the works that I do in my Father's name, they bear witness of me." Verses 37-38 tell us, "If I do not the works of my Father, believe me not. But if I do, though ye believe not me, believe the works: that ye may know and believe, that the Father is in me, and I in him."

The sin denounced as blasphemy against the Holy Spirit is the rejection of the evidence of the Messiahship of Jesus through the work of the Holy Spirit – the miracles He performed. Can it be committed today? Yes it can! The same evidence they had in the first century, we have today. It is presented to us for the same reason: "And many other signs truly did Jesus in the presence of his disciples, which are not written in this book: but these are written, that ye might believe that Jesus is the Christ, the Son of God; and that believing ye might have life through his name" (John 20:30-31).

The ludicrous charge of the Pharisees had shown the condition of their hearts. A man who was truly good would not speak such wicked things. They, by their speech, had shown the abundance of their hearts, and it was wickedness. To the Pharisees and to all, Jesus gave a warning. Every word that we speak we will be held accountable for. Idle words spoken thoughtlessly, without giving true consideration to their meaning or their effect, can condemn us.

A Sign Demanded (Matt. 12:38-45, Luke 11:24-36)

Despite all of the miracles the Pharisees and scribes had witnessed, they still had not seen a sign that would convince them of who Jesus was. Perhaps they were looking for some sort of sign from heaven, like Elijah calling down fire on Mt. Carmel. But no sign would be given just to appease these individuals who had shut their eyes and closed their ears. The sign they could look to would be that of the prophet Jonah. For three days and three nights Jonah was in the belly of the great fish, so too would Jesus be three days and three nights in the belly of the earth. As Jonah came forth from the fish, so too would Jesus come forth from the earth. The Lord's resurrection was the sign.

The Ninevites had heard the preaching of Jonah and believed. These Jews had heard and seen Jesus, but had not believed. Thus, the Ninevites will stand in condemnation of these Jews in the judgment. The Queen of Sheba would also rise in judgment on that generation, for she came to see for herself concerning Solomon, and she saw and believed. They were seeing and hearing one much greater than Solomon and believing not.

The illustration of the man with the unclean spirit departing him was indicative of the condition of the unbelieving Jews. The man had been relieved of the unclean spirit, but put nothing in its place. Consequently the unclean spirit returned with seven like him. In the same way that generation of unbelieving Jews was getting worse and worse. In their attempts to conquer sin they were maintaining a vacuum, so to speak, by refusing to accept Jesus. They needed to fill their hearts with the truth, and not leave it empty to be filled with wickedness and evil thoughts.

Luke 11:33-36 is very interesting in the context of this teaching:

> Jesus uses a very apt illustration; a lamp was used for light, and no one would put it in a secret place, or "in a cellar", or "under a bushel"; when lighted, it was placed on a stand that it might give light to those who were in the room. The Greek word for "secret place" or "cellar" means any concealed place, like a vault, crypt, or covered way, or place like a cellar, a mere hole where persons would not enter.

> As the lamp is made for light and its useful purposes, so the eye was made for vision, needing therefore to be in perfect condition so as to fulfill its functions. In like manner the moral light of God comes into this world through Christ to be accepted by men honestly and with unprejudiced mind. For as a blurred eye dooms the whole body to darkness, so does a prejudiced, worldly heart shut off the light of God and doom the miserable man to the darkness of delusion and death. The "eye is single" when it is undimmed and has its natural and proper powers for straight and clear seeing; when the eye is evil, that is, it lacks its power of clear and correct sight, the body is full of darkness.

> If the only source of light be darkness, great indeed is the darkness. The eyes give expression and radiance to the face and person; when the eye is dark the whole person is gloomy and sad. The eye has been called "the window of the soul"; hence through the

eye the different moods of the soul are expressed. Disputing and questioning the work and authority of Jesus as these Pharisees and others were doing, and demanding unreasonable signs, and disbelieving the signs which he had already given them, was like having an eye that is dark; the whole spiritual man is soon filled with evil, with deep spiritual darkness (Boles, *Luke*, 238,239).

Mother and Brethren
(Matt. 12:46-50, Mark 3:31-35, Luke 8:19-21)

The physical family of Jesus, including Mary and His brothers, were outside looking for Him while the Lord was still speaking. When informed of this, the Lord took the opportunity to teach yet another spiritual lesson. It would be incorrect to view the Lord's response to be in any way dismissive or disrespectful toward His family. Jesus was referring to His mission. It was to gather all into His spiritual family and that family would include all who would listen and obey the Will of the Father.

The Parable of the Sower
(Matt. 13:1-23, Mark 4:1-20, Luke 8:4-15)

The parable of the Sower is one of the best known and most beloved of the Lord's parables. A parable is:

> A somewhat lengthy utterance or narrative drawn from nature or human circumstances, the object of which is to set forth a spiritual lesson (*Vine's Expository Dictionary of New Testament Words*, Vol. 3, 158).

This is an example of the Lord using things and circumstances of everyday life familiar to His listeners to teach a vital spiritual lesson. While best known as the Parable of the Sower, its emphasis is upon the soil into which the seed falls and not upon the one doing the sowing. It is taken for granted that the sower does his job and that the seed is good. What results depends upon the type of soil that receives the seed.

Matthew began his account by writing that this parable was presented as Jesus "was sitting by the sea." This would have been the Sea of Galilee near the city of Capernaum. A crowd gathered and Jesus got into a boat, removed a small distance from the shore, and taught the multitude. It is a story about a man planting seed. It was something of which the Lord's audience would have been aware. As the sower cast his seed, some of it would fall on ground conducive to growth and some would not. It seems apparent that the sower is anyone who teaches the gospel to others and, as Luke wrote in Luke 8:11, "The seed is the word of God." Four different types of soils were identified by the Lord and they are the focus of the parable.

During the presentation of this parable, Jesus was asked by His followers and apostles why He spoke to the people in parables. Parables were not meant to hide; they were meant to teach and increase understanding by drawing vivid pictures that the common man could understand. It was not a matter of the Lord preventing anyone from understanding, but as Isaiah had prophesied in Isaiah 6:9-10, many refused to see, hear, and understand the truth. However, for those who did listen and understand, they were seeing and understanding things that the prophets themselves had desired to know.

Jesus spoke of the wayside soil. In between the various plots of cultivated land were pathways. They were hard from constant use and any seed that fell on this type of soil had little or no chance of growing. Many people are the same. They hear the message, but it has little or no chance of having an effect upon them because they have hardened their hearts. The second type of soil the Lord spoke of was rocky and of little depth. When the seed fell on such shallow ground, it would spring up quickly, but when the rain ceased and the heat of the sun beat upon it, it would wither and die. So it is with the faith of some. The Word is received with joy and they appear strong for a time, but when the difficult times of life arise, their faith is so shallow they fall away. The third type of soil the Lord spoke of was thorny. Jesus identified these thorns with "the worry of the world and the deceitfulness of riches." Jesus was speaking of concern for earthly things. Even innocent physical things can become "thorns" when they choke the Lord out of first place in our hearts. The fourth type of soil Jesus spoke of was the good soil. Matthew tells us this represents the "man who hears the word and understands it." Mark indicates that it is the individual who hears the Word and receives it, while Luke writes of the one who hears and keeps the Word. The good soil produces fruit and that is the responsibility of all faithful children of God.

Take Care What You Listen To (Mark 4:21-25, Luke 8:16-18)

Through the use of parables, Jesus was not concealing His teaching. He was here to reveal the truth; but to receive it would require a receptive heart. Those with a receptive heart will find their understanding enlightened; but for those who will not receive the truth, whose hearts are hardened, they will not understand.

The Parable of the Tares
(Matt. 13:24-30, 36-43, Mark 4:26-29)

Some believe that Mark 4:26-29 is a separate parable from the well known Parable of the Tares. They should be considered as one. When Jesus said, "The kingdom is likened unto…," He was setting forth the principles of its establishment and full development. In the parable itself, Jesus used circumstances that would be familiar to His hearers. What does the word "tares" refer to?

A general word used to denote any kind of vetch, but in Matt. 13:25, referring probably to the bearded darnel (Lolim temulentum). In the blade these tares resemble wheat, but if the biblical counsel be followed and both are allowed to grow together till harvest (Matt. 13:30) the weed is clearly distinguished, and usually to women and children falls the tedious task of separation. The tares are often used as chicken food. Sowing tares in a field for the purpose of revenge was a crime under Roman legislation (*New Bible Dictionary*, 1238).

Jesus' explanation of the parable is simple. The sower of the good seed was Jesus Himself. The field in which the seed was sown was the world, and the good seed was the children of the world. The tares were the children of the wicked one, and the wicked one was representative of the devil. Both were allowed to grow together until the harvest, which represented the end of the world. At that time the angels would be the reapers; both the good and the bad would be gathered. The bad would be cast into a furnace of fire, where there would be weeping and gnashing of teeth. The good, or righteous, would go home to the Father.

It is interesting that this parable sets forth the gradual growth of the kingdom and shows both good and bad exists simultaneously on earth. While there might be the natural desire to get rid of the bad and the wicked immediately, they shall grow right along with the good. However, we can be assured that at the proper time full separation will be made by the proper agents. In Jesus' explanation of the parable, greater attention and more detail are given to the work of the reapers than to the other aspects of the parable. Jesus drew special attention to the fact the tares will one day be separated and the wheat will appear in full splendor.

The Mustard Seed and Leaven (Matt. 13:31-35, Mark 4:30-34)

The point of the parable of the mustard seed was to show the gradual growth of the kingdom. From such a small beginning as was taking place in the land of Canaan at that time, the kingdom would grow tremendously. The mustard seed was the smallest seed ordinarily sown in Palestine at that time. It is not the smallest seed of all, but Jesus was using something familiar.

The significance of the parable concerning the leaven was to show the gradual growth of the kingdom from within. In Luke 17:21 Jesus said, "Neither shall they say, Lo here! Or, lo there! For, behold, the kingdom of God is within you." Leaven has permeating qualities that take place within the dough. So too does the kingdom of God grow within a man and affect him from within.

The point of Matthew 13:34 seems to be twofold. One is that the parables presented in this chapter are representative of many Jesus spoke at this time. Secondly, it means that on this occasion and in this particular sermon Jesus spoke only in parables.

The reference to Psalm 78:2 appears to have a threefold meaning. First, no teacher compares in history to Jesus in the use of parables. What about the second clause of that quotation?

> Truths never before revealed have now been revealed by Christ's parables, especially by those two which have just been related. For in these it has been affirmed that outsiders, i.e., those belonging to other nations than the Jewish nation, shall seek protection of the kingdom of heaven, and also that the whole world, including, therefore, these Gentile nations, shall become permeated with its principles. It may well be though that the clause refers to the announcement of these great truths. (3) But this interpretation, however, if taken alone, is not enough. For the evangelist is not speaking of Christ revealing truths to men generally. On the contrary, he says that Christ does not reveal them to multitudes (v. 10) a contrast which the emphatic language of v. 34 would probably suggest, even though it is not expressly mentioned. It is, therefore, likely that it was this latter fact to which the evangelist specially wished to refer by his quotation of the second clause. Hence, to make his meaning clearer, he has modified its language. As he quotes it, not merely "enigmatical saying", but "things hidden" (and that from the foundation of the world) are uttered by Christ; but these are now no longer "hidden" to those to whom he speaks them. This complete meaning of the clause – revelation to his disciples of truths before hidden – corresponds to the idea in v. 11 (*Pulpit Commentary*, Vol. 15, 10).

Hidden Treasure, Pearl of Great Price, the Net, the Householder (Matt. 13:44-53)

It is important not to dwell upon too many of the details of these short parables. The point of the parable of the hidden treasure is to show the immense value of the kingdom of heaven. The man sells all to secure it. It is the hidden treasure which must be sought and found at all costs.

The principle is the same in the parable of the pearl of great price. Perhaps Jesus meant to point out the difference in the method in which it was pursued. The one man happened upon the treasure not knowing that it was there. The individual in this parable found it only after a long and persistent search. Both recognized it when they found it, and both gave all they had to secure it.

The parable of the net makes the same point concerning the judgment day as did the Parable of the Tares. There are good and bad in the world, just as there are good and bad fish in the sea. When the net is cast and the fish hauled in, the good and bad are forever separated. The same will occur on the Day of Judgment when the good and the bad will be forever separated.

There are some who believe the net refers more specifically to the church, while the parable of the tares dealt with the entire world. They believe that within the church there are those who appear to be good, but are wicked. At the judgment they will be separated.

The parable of the household is an interesting short parable. Jesus had explained His parables to his disciples. He had given them the method of understanding. Then He compared them to a householder. A homeowner retains the valuable old things and adds the necessary new things. Thus the scribe should treasure the best of the old and be ready to do all that is new, true and valuable. With that, Jesus ended His private instruction to His disciples following this sermon of parables.

Total Commitment (Matt. 8:18-22, Luke 9:57-62)

The constant press of crowds during the Galilean ministry caused the Lord to request that His disciples take Him in a boat to the eastern shore of the Sea of Galilee. As Jesus was making His way to enter the boat, a "certain scribe" volunteered to follow Jesus, as a pupil would follow a particular teacher or rabbi. The Lord's response indicates the type of commitment He required, a commitment this scribe did not quite understand. Life as a disciple of Jesus demanded steadfast, total commitment. It would not be easy, as demonstrated by the Lord's statement, "The foxes have holes, and the birds of the air have nests; but the Son of Man has nowhere to lay his head."

The scribe had not understood what he was asking. Other disciples gave reasons for not committing wholly to the service of the Lord. One expressed his willingness to follow, but first he had to bury his father; still another expressed the desire to follow, but only after returning home to say goodbye to his family. There is nothing wrong with burying a parent; indeed, to do so would be a responsibility. There is nothing wrong with saying goodbye to a family member before leaving home. The point the Lord taught was that of absolute obedience and commitment. Being a faithful disciple is more important than anything else.

Stilling the Tempest
(Matt. 8:23-27, Mark 4:35-41, Luke 8:22-25)

Now our attention is on one of the most stupendous miracles recorded in the New Testament. It is a miracle that reveals another aspect of the power of Jesus and a miracle that should inspire awe in our hearts as it did in the hearts of those who first witnessed it, moving them to ask, "What manner of man is this, that even the winds and the sea obey?"

It had been a busy day in the life of Jesus. As "even" descended upon Him, Jesus and His disciples entered into a ship and began to make their way across the Sea of Galilee, traveling from the northwest corner to a point about midway on the eastern side. We know this because of where the boat landed, the country of the Gadarenes. Under normal conditions this would be a journey of about two hours with a favorable light wind pushing the boat.

There is a statement made by Mark that is often overlooked in discussion of this event, yet gives us insight into the nature of the ministry of Jesus. In describing their departure, Mark wrote, "and they took him even as he was in the ship." What was meant by "even as he was?" Could it mean without food or time to procure food? Is it possible that it means without rest and exhausted from the day's labors? It seems to be an indication of the humanity of Jesus and it reminds us that He feels, as shown when Jesus sat down by Jacob's well in John 4. In verse 6 we read, "Now Jacob's well was there. Jesus therefore, being wearied with his journey, sat thus on the well." The "thus" of John 4:6 is very much like the "even as he was" of Mark 4:36; exhausted, worn-out by the tremendous strain and effort of His ministry.

The small flotilla disembarked. Mark informs us "There were also with him other small ships." Since we do not read of these other ships reaching the country of the Gadarenes with Jesus, the indication is that they were soon scattered and left or were perhaps frightened by the signs of the gathering storm and turned back. As the journey proceeded, Jesus retired to the stern of the boat, laid His head upon a pillow, and slept. Once again the humanity of Jesus is underscored as He took advantage of this brief opportunity to rest from His labors.

Two different words are used by the gospel writers to describe the storm that arose. Mark and Luke use the word "lailaps." This word is commented upon by Thayer as "never a single gust of wind, but a storm breaking from black thunderclouds in furious gusts, with floods of rain, and throwing everything topsy-turvy." Matthew describes it as "seismos", a word that can mean an earthquake, but is also a common word for a tempest in that a storm of such volume causes a shaking or a commotion. Both words put an emphasis upon the severity of the storm. Evidently this was something that was not at all unusual on the Sea of Galilee.

> The heated tropical air of the region, which is so low that the surface of the Sea of Galilee lies 600 feet beneath the level of the Mediterranean, is suddenly filled by the cold and heavy winds sweeping down the snowy ranges of Lebanon and Hermon, and rushing with unwonted fury through the ravines of the Peraean hills, which converge to the head of the Lake, and act like gigantic funnels (Thomson, *Land and Book*).

The storm, which arose so quickly, raged about the small boat. Mark says, "The waves beat into the ship, so that it was now full." Matthew tells us, "The ship was covered with the waves." Luke informs us, "And they were filled with water, and were in jeopardy." So violent was the storm that the apostles of Jesus, many of them experienced fishermen who knew these storms well, feared for their lives. Let us not fail to notice that in the midst of such a violent storm, Jesus continued to sleep. How exhausted He must have been! How all-consuming were His labors!

The action of the disciples to rouse Jesus was obviously a last resort. They felt death was close. When we consider all three accounts together it is clear they did not wake Jesus in a calm fashion, but fearing for their lives, one cried out one thing and another something else. It is easy to envision the scene with the waves beating upon the boat, the wind howling and the rain pouring down. One cries out, "Lord, save us, we perish." Another cries, "Master, carest thou not that we perish?" Still another pleads, "Master, master, we perish." Surely they had faith enough to know that if Jesus was awake, He could save them. They did not have faith enough to understand that with Him in their midst, they were safe.

The first thing Jesus did when He awoke was to rebuke His disciples. "Why are ye fearful, O ye of little faith?" Then standing up in the boat, Jesus spoke directly to the wind and the sea, "Peace, be still." Both the wind and the sea obeyed Him. Where once had been a raging, life-threatening storm, there was now calm; no crashing waves, no howling wind, no torrential downpour, just calm.

> Some have asked whether we may not suppose that the fact which underlies the narrative was in reality not a miraculous exercise of power over those elements which are most beyond the reach of man, but that Christ's calm communicated itself by immediate and subtle influence to His terrified companions, and that the hurricane, from natural causes, sank as rapidly as it had arisen? I reply, that if this were the only miracle in the life of Christ; if the Gospels were indeed the loose, exaggerated, inaccurate, and incredulous narratives which such an interpretation would suppose; if there were something antecedently incredible in the supernatural; if there were in the spiritual world no transcendent facts which lie far beyond the comprehension of those who would bid us see nothing in the universe but the action of material laws; if there were no providences of God during these nineteen centuries to attest the work and divinity of Christ – then indeed there would be no difficulty in such an interpretation. But if we believe that God rules; if we believe that Christ rose; if we have reason to hold, among the deepest convictions of our beings, the certainty that God has not delegated His sovereignty or His providence to the final, unintelligent, pitiless, inevitable working of material forces; if we see on every page of the Evangelists the quiet simplicity of truthful and faithful witnesses; if we see in every year of succeeding history, and in every experience of individual life, a confirmation of the testimony which they delivered – then we shall neither clutch at rationalistic interpretations, nor be much troubled if others adopt them. He who believes, he who knows, the efficacy of prayer, in what other men may regard as the inevitable certainties of blindly directed accidents of life – he who has felt how the voice of a Savior, heard across the long generations, can calm wilder storms than ever buffeted into fury the bosom of the inland lake – he who sees in the person of his Redeemer a fact more stupendous and more

majestic than all those observed sequences which men endow with an imaginary omnipotence, and worship under the name of Law – to him, at least, there will be neither difficulty nor hesitation in supposing that Christ, on board that half-wrecked fishing boat, did utter His mandate, and that the wind and the sea obeyed; that His word was indeed more potent among the cosmic forces than miles of agitated water, or leagues of rushing air (Frederick Farrar, *The Life of Christ*, 259,260).

Immediately after the miracle, the disciples were afraid. Moments before they had been afraid for their lives in the midst of the storm; they were afraid now of being in the awesome presence of the supernatural. The presence of Jesus was even more awesome to them in the stillness that His words had wrought. What a privilege we now have to be able to answer the question the disciples asked one another at that time, "What manner of man is this? For He commandeth even the winds and the water, and they obey Him."

The Gadarene Demoniacs
(Matt. 8:28-34, Mark 5:1-20, Luke 8:26-39)

After that most eventful journey at sea, Jesus arrived in the land of the Gadarenes. You may notice in the readings that Matthew says this transpired in the country of the Gadarenes, while Mark and Luke say it was the country of the Gerasenes. The explanation of the difference is very simple. It appears Mark and Luke were referring to the local village nearest to the place where Jesus landed called Khersa, while Matthew was referring to the important city of Gadara which was located approximately 16 miles to the southeast of where Jesus landed. It is quite natural for the name of the larger city to be given to an entire region, as well as the name of the local village or smaller city. For example, when living in Ohio I wrote my address as Cincinnati because it was the name of the larger city; but the local community in which I lived was Deer Park. Each was acceptable.

Just as the storm presented a striking situation, so too does our Lord's encounter with the demoniacs. Matthew gives us the information that there were two individuals involved, but it is obvious from Mark and Luke that only one of them was dominant and thus became the primary character of the account.

These men dwelt in the mountainous region, in tombs that had been hewn out of the rock and doubtlessly abandoned. This was the only home or shelter such an individual could find. Living among the rest of the people would have been impossible because of their conduct. They were wild and violent. Mark describes the dominant individual in this way: "No man could bind him, no, not with chains: because that he had been often bound with fetters and chains, and the chains had been plucked asunder by him, and the fetters broken in pieces, neither could any man tame him. And always, night and day, he was in the mountains, and in the tombs, crying, and cutting himself with stones."

Matthew added "no man could pass by that way" and Luke states us they "had worn no clothes." So these violent, naked, wild individuals were what confronted Jesus when He landed on the eastern shore of the Sea of Galilee.

When Jesus arrived the demoniac did not react as he normally would have. He did not viciously attack. Instead, he came running and fell down before Jesus in a position of worship, crying with a loud voice, "What have I to do with thee, Jesus, thou Son of the Most High God? I beseech thee, torment me not." Just a short time ago the men who were with Jesus in the boat had asked, "What manner of man is this, that even the winds and the sea obey him?" Here, from the mouth of demons, is the answer. This was Jesus, the Son of God. The reaction of the demoniac brings to mind a statement made by James in James 2:19, "Thou believest there is one God; thou doest well, the devils also believe, and tremble." The response of the demoniac was prompted by the demand of Jesus, "Come out of the man, thou unclean spirit."

Jesus directly addressed the unclean spirit, "What is thy name?" The answer is very interesting. The demon replied, "My name is Legion, for we are many." Legion is a Latin word obviously associated with Rome. It was a term used for a division of the Roman army that numbered 6,000 men. The demon was not saying there were actually 6,000 demons in this individual, but that they were a large number. The demons show not only keen intelligence, but supernatural knowledge. The manner in which the identity of Jesus and His divine person were instantly recognized is united with their terror of impending doom.

The demons did not want to be cast into the "abyss" as Luke tells us, or to be cast from the country, means the same thing, as Mark tells us. They requested they be sent into a great herd of swine that numbered about 2,000 feeding nearby. One suggested explanation was that it was an attempt to discredit Jesus and to turn the people of the region against Him when the swine ran into the sea and destroyed themselves. This may have been the thinking of the demons, but a greater lesson was being taught by Jesus. He knew what would happen. He knew that the 2,000 swine would be lost and He knew the people would react as they did and ask Him to leave. But it is certainly possible that Jesus was seeking to shock the people of the region. He could have been attempting to teach them a lesson concerning the relative value of a soul as opposed to the animals and the material lost for their owners. We know Jesus ultimately returned to this region. Is it not possible that this marvelous miracle, coupled with the loss of the swine, was for the purpose of awakening these people? Later, when Jesus did return, the people were much more prepared to listen to Him.

The demons were cast out of the men, they entered into the swine, and the herd of 2,000 ran violently down a steep place into the sea and perished. Those who cared for the swine ran into the nearby city and countryside and told what had happened. The people who heard the exciting news came flocking to see. They saw the demon-possessed individual, who they knew to have been wild, naked, violent and dangerous, sitting calmly. He was fully clothed and at the feet of Jesus. He was in his right mind, in full possession of his faculties, and in control.

When they saw him, they were afraid. They could not understand what had happened. They evidently did not know of Jesus. In addition, they had suffered a great material loss through the destruction of the herd. They feared this man of such great power might use it again with more destructive purposes. Consequently, they asked Jesus to leave. He left, but He would return to do much good among them.

What about the dominant figure in the account? He wanted to go with Jesus. So much could be said of this man now -- of his gratitude, his desire to be away from the place of such terrible events in his life, perhaps his fear of hostility from the people – any number of things might have entered into his request to accompany Jesus. For him there was another purpose, "Go home to thy friends, and tell them how great things the Lord hath done for thee, and hath had compassion on thee."

Jairus' Daughter and the Woman Touching the Lord's Garment (Matt. 9:18-26, Mark 5:21-43, Luke 8:40-56)

While all three synoptic gospels record these events, Mark supplies the most detail. So, his account will be the focus.

Jesus left the region of Gadara on the eastern coast of the Sea of Galilee and returned to Capernaum, or its vicinity. Awaiting His arrival was a large group of people and two of these individuals were about to have their lives touched and changed forever by Jesus.

The first one was a man of some position, a ruler of the synagogue. If in fact this was taking place in Capernaum, then this man could very well have been one of the elders of the Jews who had come to Jesus earlier on behalf of the centurion. What had been his attitude toward Jesus before? Had he been a believer, only quietly for fear of the reaction of the people? Had he been one of those who questioned Jesus and tried to ensnare Him? Whatever he may have been before, he was now feeling the press of tragedy in his life. His little girl, his only daughter, twelve years of age, was dying. Whatever his attitude may have been before, now he came to Jesus.

Luke declares, "And he fell down at Jesus' feet, and besought him that he would come into his house: for he had one only daughter, about twelve years of age, and she lay a dying." Matthew tells of the position this man took as he came to Jesus, "He fell at his feet and worshipped him." This constitutes a public confession of his faith for he did it in front of all. Isn't it sad that so many times it takes a tragedy before people declare their faith? Nevertheless he did make his request and Jesus accepted, accompanying him to his home. As was so often the case, this was all being witnessed by a large number of people. We are told, "And much people followed him, and thronged him."

Within the crowd there was one who had not been attracted by curiosity. There was one who did not come seeking to witness what would be done for the ruler of the synagogue. There was a woman who had suffered from a disease for twelve years – an issue of blood.

This was apparently very common and difficult to deal with. The Jewish Talmud gives no fewer than eleven cures from such a problem. Some of them are tonics and astringents, but some of them are nothing more than superstitions. For instance, the one suffering could carry the ashes of an ostrich egg in a linen rag in summer and a cotton rag in winter; or she could carry a barley corn that had been found in the dung of a white she-ass. No doubt this poor woman had tried everything. The account certainly indicates she had done everything she could. Not only was her health being affected, but this condition rendered her continually unclean and denied her the worship of God, along with the fellowship of her friends.

> And if a woman have an issue of her blood many days out of the time of her separation, or if it run beyond the time of her separation; all the days of the issue of her uncleanness shall be as the days of her separation: she shall be unclean. Every bed whereon she lieth all the days of her issue shall be unto her as the bed of her separation: and whatsoever she sitteth upon shall be unclean, as the uncleanness of her separation. And whosoever toucheth those things shall be unclean, and shall wash his clothes, and bathe himself in water, and be unclean until the even (Leviticus 15:25-27).

Through all those years the woman had gone from doctor to doctor. She had spent all she had in an attempt to be cured, and the end result was her condition worsened. Having heard of Jesus, she would not let this opportunity pass. She made her way through the press of the crowd, desiring to but touch the hem of His garment, believing touching His clothes would accomplish what all of the physicians had been unable to do. So she did. She touched the hem, or the border, of Jesus' garment from behind. The issue of her blood was immediately dried up and she felt within herself that the plague she had suffered so many years afflicted her no longer. When this occurred, Jesus knew that "virtue" or power, had flowed out of Him and He turned to face the crowd, asking who had touched His clothes.

The exasperation of the apostles can be sensed by the question they asked. Luke specifically identifies Peter in connection with their response. They said, "Master, the multitude throng thee and press thee, and sayest thou, who touched me?" In other words, "Look at all these people, and You want to know who touched You?" Jesus already knew the answer to His question and He had an important lesson to teach. When the woman timidly came forward confessing it was she, there was no rebuke issued, only mercy and kindness. The entire multitude was taught a valuable lesson concerning faith. Jesus said, "Daughter, thy faith hath made thee whole: go in peace, and be whole of thy plague."

Now, our attention turns back to Jairus. Surely in his state of anxiety this interruption by the woman must have been a time to try his patience and to increase his concern. Now comes the words that he most feared, "Thy daughter is dead, why troublest thou the Master any longer?" The response of Jesus to these words is awe-inspiring, "Be not afraid, only believe."

As they came to the home of Jairus, only Peter, James, and John were permitted to enter into the house with Jesus. The other apostles remained outside with the rest of the multitude. As was customary at the time, the home was filled with professional mourners and wailers. These individuals were paid to come and mourn at a death. It is interesting that Jesus dealt with them in such an abrupt manner. "Why make ye this ado, and weep? The damsel is not dead, but sleepeth." The laughter with which these professional mourners greeted Jesus' statement should be viewed in two ways. One was that Jesus was denying what they knew to be fact. The child was dead. Second, His intrusion into the matter jeopardized their livelihood. They were paid to mourn at a death. Perhaps the possibility of losing their wages caused them to react in such a hostile way. Whatever might have been their motivation, they were ejected from the house by Jesus.

Taking only the father, the mother, Peter, James, and John, Jesus went into the area where the dead little girl was laying. Mark and Luke provide exact information as to what took place. Taking her hand, Jesus addressed her. Mark gives us the Aramaic words our Lord spoke, "Talitha cumi: which is, being interpreted, Damsel, (I say unto thee), arise." She arose immediately. Two more commands were given by Jesus. She was to be given food and they were not to go out and reveal what had happened. Surely the miracle would be known because many knew the little girl was dead and now she was alive. There was to be no organized effort to spread the news. No publicity was to accompany the miracles. We might ask why Jesus would make such a request. He had done so before.

Galilee was the hotbed of the Zealots. These individuals were consistently trying to turn Jesus' ministry to their own militaristic aims. They wanted to declare Him king and have Him lead the people in revolt against Rome by popular acclaim. Jesus continually sought to calm the excitement of the people over His miracles to prevent His ministry from coming to an end before the proper time and to continue the spiritual emphasis. Jesus faced a day-to-day battle with the Zealots and all other worldly-minded hearers as His ministry moved toward its inevitable and predestined conclusion.

Last Visit to Nazareth (Matt. 13:54-58, Mark 6:1-6)

There is a distinct difference in time between the visit recorded in Luke which comes early in the Galilean ministry and this visit which comes late in the ministry. It was natural that Jesus should make a second effort to win His own town. There is no attempt to destroy His life on this second visit – only callous unbelief. Note the difference in Mark. Matthew says, 'Is not this the son of the carpenter?' Mark says, 'Is this not the carpenter, the son of Mary?' Mark has omitted any account of the virgin birth and guards his readers from misunderstanding by saying, 'the son of Mary'. Matthew says, 'He did not many mighty works...' Mark also adds that He was not able to do many mighty works because of their unbelief but that He did heal a few sick people. He (Mark) adds that He marveled at their unbelief (R.C. Foster, *Gospel Studies*, Vol. 2, 90).

Matthew explains Mark's statement in verse 5, "And He could there do no mighty work," and when he wrote in verse 58, "And He did not many mighty works there because of their unbelief." The Lord's power was not limited by the belief or unbelief of His hearers. The point is that it would have been useless to the purpose of Jesus' mission to have worked many miracles there. These people were so prejudiced toward Him and their minds so completely made up that they would not be honest judges of evidence and they would not be convinced. Jesus knew this. We are even told that "he marveled at their unbelief."

It is important to note the "brethren" of Jesus. Vine says the word "adelphos" in Matthew 13 means "children of the same mother." It also means near kinsman. There are those who say that these individuals were cousins of Jesus, not children of the same mother. That would at least be arguable if there were not a word in Greek that Matthew could have used to more specifically denote cousins. There is such a word, "sungenis." If Matthew had meant cousins, he could have said so.

Jesus' Third Tour of Galilee, Twelve Sent on Evangelistic Mission (Matt. 9:35-11:1, Mark 6:7-13, Luke 9:1-6)

Matthew 9:35-38 sets the stage for what follows and serves as a marvelous example of the compassion of Jesus. Jesus worked tirelessly, going from city to city, village to village-- healing the sick, teaching in the synagogues, preaching the gospel, and still the multitudes were in desperate need. He could not get to them all. More people needed to hear the good news and feel the touch of God's love and compassion.

As Matthew put it, the multitudes were "distressed" (or fainted) and they were "scattered." The word for "distressed" or "fainted" means, "skinned, flayed, rent, mangled, vexed, annoyed, fatigued, suffering violence" while the word "scattered" means "harassed, importuned, bewildered." This is such a vivid picture of the condition of the multitudes. They were just like sheep without a shepherd, driven in terror, torn by wild beasts, perplexed and frightened. There was a tremendous need for people to be taught, to be touched and comforted. The field was great and the harvest so bountiful that Jesus did not have the time to reach all. Yet the condition of the multitude stirred the love and compassion of the Lord. If He could not go personally, then He would send the twelve that they might go into the midst of the people. He would send the twelve to teach them and prepare the way for Jesus Himself. That is why the admonition "to pray" was given. Pray for laborers to go for the need was very great. It still is.

In response to the situation with the multitude that Jesus observed, He gathered His apostles to Him, twelve in number, and conferred upon them the power to work miracles so they would be able to confirm the truthfulness of what they would tell the people. An important point to make is that the apostles had been freely given this message of the coming kingdom and the power to perform the miracles. Consequently, they were to freely give.

They were commanded to limit their evangelistic efforts to the Jews. It is important to realize we have no record of Jesus ever excluding Gentiles from the multitudes when He taught. Certainly Gentiles came seeking miraculous aid from Jesus and were received on numerous occasions. In the same way the apostles were not to exclude any Gentiles if they gathered with the multitudes. However, the gospel was to go to the Jews first, to those most prepared for its reception as recipients of the Old Testament revelation.

The apostles were not to go out at this time and present Jesus as the Christ. As a matter of fact, the apostles themselves did not truly understand the nature and character of the work of Jesus as the Messiah at this time. They were commissioned to preach that the "kingdom of heaven was at hand"; it was very near and about to be established.

The apostles were sent to the Jews. This nation of people had been trained by the Old Law to care for their spiritual leaders. Probably as a test of their faith, as well as a test of the generosity of the Jews to whom they were sent, the apostles were instructed to take no special supplies or equipment on their mission. They were to take no extra money, food, clothing, shoes, or even extra staffs. This means that they were to take nothing for this mission. The reason why is stated by Jesus, "For the workman is worthy of his meat." When they entered into a community, they were instructed to make a survey of that area. They were to establish a center in the home of some devout person, making that their "base of operations," and branch out into the community from there. Finding such a home, they were to stay there for the duration of their time in that community. When they came to this home, they were to offer a salutation. If their reception was cordial, they should stay; if not, they were to leave. If an entire village or community rejected them, then they were to go their way, warning them that their blood was upon their own head, "shaking the dust off of their feet." Those who should have known better through the preparation given in God's Word had rejected it and would pay the penalty.

Jesus sent His apostles forth with no false ideas of what would happen. He did not give them the impression they would meet with a string of unbroken success in each community they ventured. We would be hard-pressed to find a clearer warning of arrest, persecution, trials, imprisonment, and even death. Jesus made it clear that even the closest ties of blood relationship would not protect them. Jesus warned these men of the most severe persecution which would take place. However, this early warning served to make their hearts more steadfast. Yes, they would meet opposition even on this mission, but that would serve to harden them for the severe trials ahead. In those times of trials, their exact words would be given to them through the Holy Spirit.

There seems to be two explanations for the last part of Matthew 10:23. One is this coming of the Son of Man would be in judgment on the nation – the destruction of Jerusalem. The second means the coming in His kingdom on the day of Pentecost in Acts 2. They were to preach that the kingdom of heaven was at hand. Their work of preparing Israel for the kingdom would not be complete before it was actually instituted. This is the more plausable of the two.

The warning of the terrible persecution that would eventually come upon them was followed by a reminder from Jesus that this was the very sort of thing He Himself would undergo. They had to realize that a disciple cannot expect to be above his teacher. Yes, suffering would come. Yes, they would be persecuted; but they would be prepared and know how to bear it because Jesus, their teacher, had given them the example. This calls to mind Peter's statement in 1 Peter 2:21-25:

> For even hereunto were ye called: because Christ also suffered for us, leaving us an example, that ye should follow his steps: who did no sin, neither was guile found in his mouth: who, when he was reviled, reviled not again; when he suffered, he threatened not; but committed himself to him that judgeth righteously: who his own self bare our sins in his own body on the tree, that we, being dead to sins, should live unto righteousness, by whose stripes ye were healed. For ye were as sheep going astray; but are now returned unto the Shepherd and Bishop of your souls.

The nature of the message could not be done in secret, it could not be whispered in ears – it demanded that it be shouted from the housetops. When this was done, anger and hatred would be directed at them, just as it had been at Jesus. But all was not despair regardless of what happened to them on earth. They had the hope of heaven. The power of men was nothing they needed to fear. By serving God with reverence and respect they would have comfort. The promise to them would be in heaven if they faithfully confessed Christ before men.

The cross was an image familiar to the Jews. Hundreds of their countrymen had been crucified by the Romans in Palestine. They knew what a cross meant. At this point in their development they did not understand all the ramifications of what Jesus was saying, but His words must have returned to them and acted as encouragement in their lives of service. Indeed, how those words can help and encourage us. Yes, from time to time it is difficult. Yes, from time to time we suffer various forms of persecution. Yes, there may even come a time when we will be asked to die. Yet we can take heart and move forward with a resolute determination. Jesus said, "He that findeth his life shall lose it: and he that loseth his life for my sake shall find it."

In a sense, the kindness done unto one of the Lord's disciples was done to Him. It reminds me of Matthew 25:35-45--to receive someone "in the name of" means out of consideration for the person or cause. To receive the apostles was to receive Jesus. Those who did so would receive the proper and fitting reward of a righteous man.

With this, the apostles were sent out. Jesus departed to preach and teach in the cities of Galilee.

The Death of John the Baptist
(Matt. 14:1-12, Mark 6:14-29, Luke 9:7-9)

The death of John the Baptist either brought the mission of the apostles to a close or followed their mission very closely. As Jesus continued His ministry and the apostles went out two by two to the various villages, cities, and towns of Palestine, it was inevitable that word of Jesus and His works would reach the ears of Herod, tetrarch of Galilee. News of His miracles and the crowds that followed Him caused a number of opinions to be expressed. Some thought Jesus was Elijah come again. Still others said He was a prophet. But Herod, driven by a guilty conscience, began to think Jesus was none other than John the Baptist, the holy man of God whose murder he had ordered, back from the grave.

Herod Antipas and Herodias had been considered earlier. To gain further insight into the character of Herod, we need to look at Tiberius, his capital city. It was located only a few miles south of Capernaum. When Herod built Tiberius, he was enamored by the beautiful scenery and the climate of the region around the Sea of Galilee. He chose the site of his city personally. The difficulty was that the site he chose was a graveyard. Jewish custom prohibited the disturbance of those graves, but Herod dug them up and built his city. Once it was built, he could not get people to live there because of what he had done. So Herod emptied the jails and the prisons of the land to get sufficient population for his new city. Roman writers tell us that Tiberias, after such a beginning, was the vilest in all the Roman Empire.

Here is a further description of Herod and an explanation of how Herodias came into his life.

> It was the policy of the numerous princelings who owed their very existence to Roman intervention, to pay frequent visits of ceremony to the Emperor of Rome. During one of these visits, Antipas had been, while at Rome, the guest of his brother Herod Philip, not the tetrarch of that name, but a son of Herod the Great and Mariamne, who, having been disinherited by his father, was living at Rome as a private person. Here he became entangled by the snares of Herodias, his brother Philip's wife: and he repaid the hospitality he had received by carrying her off. Everything combined to make the act as detestable as it was ungrateful and treacherous. The Herods carried intermarriage to an extent which only prevailed in the worst and the most dissolute of the Oriental and post-Macedonian dynasties. Herodias, being the daughter

of Aristobulus, was not only the sister-in-law, but also the niece of Antipas; she had already borne to her husband a daughter, who was now grown up. Antipas had himself long been married to the daughter of Aretas, Emir of Arabia, and neither he nor Herodias were young enough to plead even the poor excuse of youthful passion. The sole temptation on his side was an impotent sensuality; on hers an extravagant ambition. She preferred a marriage doubly adulterous and doubly incestuous to a life spent with the only Herod who could not boast even the fraction of a vice-regal throne. Antipas promised on his return from Rome to make her his wife, and she exacted from him a pledge that he would divorce his innocent consort, the daughter of the Arabian prince (Frederick Farrar, *The Life of Christ*, 295,296).

Herodias proved to be the evil genius behind much of what the spineless Herod did. John rightfully condemned the adulterous and incestuous relationship of Herod and Herodias. Nothing is known about how this condemnation originally occurred, whether face to face or if John expounded upon the subject to the multitude of people who came to hear him. However it occurred, Herodias was incensed and John was arrested and imprisoned by Herod to appease her.

Even imprisonment was not enough for Herodias. Mark 6:19 tells us she "would have killed him, but she could not." Matthew informs us that Herodias must have persuaded Herod, but he decided not to kill John because he feared the reaction of the people who held John to be a prophet. Interestingly, while Herod had John imprisoned, he must have summoned him. Mark tells us, "For Herod feared John, knowing that he was a just man and a holy, and observed him; and when he heard him, he did many things, and heard him gladly."

Among other features in the character of Herod was a certain superstitious curiosity which led him to hanker after and tamper with the truths of the religion which his daily life so flagrantly violated. He summoned John to his presence. Like a new Elijah before another Ahab – clothed in his desert raiment, the hairy cloak and the leathern girdle – the stern and noble eremite stood fearless before the incestuous king. His words – simple words of truth and justice – the calm reasonings about righteousness, temperance, and the judgment to come – fell like flakes of fire on that hard and icy conscience. Herod, alarmed perhaps by the fulfillment of the old curse of the Mosaic law in the childlessness of his union, listened with some dim and feeble hope of future amendment. He even did many things gladly because of John. But there was one thing which he would not do, and that was, give up the guilty love which mastered him, or dismiss the haughty imperious woman who ruled his life (Farrar, *The Life of Christ*, 297).

Herodias waited for a convenient time to have her desire for the death of John fulfilled. Why is it that the one who is most guilty often reacts the most violently before the Word of God? So often, the only way some sooth their battered conscience is by attacking the one who has pricked it with the truth.

Herodias received her opportunity when Herod celebrated his birthday. The Herods were noted for their magnificent banquets and celebrations. They aspired to greatness and imitated the luxurious feasts of the Roman emperors themselves to the extent of their ability. This would have been such a feast with all the notables of his region present. In such gatherings during the days of the Roman Empire, it was quite common for prostitutes to present exhibitions of indecent dancing for the titillation of the gathered men. It was not common for a woman of position or respectability to so debase herself. But Herodias used her own daughter, Salome, to gain her desired end. Having danced in such a way to please Herod and his gathered guests, the drunken king told the debased girl in the presence of his guests, "Ask of me whatsoever thou wilt, and I will give it thee. Whatsoever thou shalt ask of me, I will give it thee, unto the half of my kingdom."

Immediately Salome went to confer with her mother. Here at last was the chance Herodias had been waiting for. Having made the pledge in the presence of his guests, Herod's pride would not allow him to renege. He would feel obligated to pay. Anything she wanted she could have up to half of Herod's possessions. Wealth and land were at her bidding, but Herodias wanted only one thing -- the head of John the Baptist. So that is what Salome was instructed to ask for, and the manner in which she asked certainly seems to indicate that she shared the temperament and personality of her mother. The New American Standard renders her request in this manner, "I want you to give me right away the head of John the Baptist on a platter." She made her request, "straightway with haste."

Herod had been duped. If he had been a truly honorable man he would have rejected her request as one that was totally outside of the spirit and even the letter of his offer. He could have replied that if that was her request, then his oath was more honored by being broken than it would have been by being kept, but Herod was not an honorable man. Because of his guests, he did not see how he could refuse. The executioner was sent and the forerunner of Jesus, the Messiah, was beheaded. At last John, the man who breathed the spirit of the wilderness and man accustomed to the ground for a bed and the heavens as his cover, was no longer a prisoner in the dark recesses of Herod's summer palace. The disciples of John came and took the headless body and laid it in a tomb.

What became of Herod, Herodias, and Salome, three people whose names live in infamy?

> When the Emperor Caligula began to heap favors on Herod Agrippa I, Herodias, sick with envy and discontent, urged Antipas to sail with her to Rome and procure a share of the distinction which had thus been given to her brother. Above all, she was anxious that her husband should obtain the title of king, instead

of continuing content with the humbler one of tetrarch. In vain did the timid and ease-loving Antipas point out to her the danger to which he might be exposed by such a request. She made his life so bitter to him by her importunity that, against his better judgment, he was forced to yield. No love reigned between the numerous uncles and nephews and half-brothers in the tangled family of Herod, and either out of policy or jealousy Agrippa not only discountenanced the schemes of his sister and uncle, he actually sent his freedman Fortunatus to Rome to accuse Antipas of treasonable designs. The tetrarch failed to clear himself of the charge, and in A.D. 39 was banished to Gaul, not far from the Spanish frontier. Herodias, either from choice or despair, accompanied his exile, and here they both died in obscurity and dishonor. Salome, the dancer, disappears from history (Farrar, *The Life of Christ*, 303,304).

Jesus Retires With His Apostles and the Feeding of the Five Thousand (Matt. 14:13-21, Mark 6:30-44, Luke 9:10-17, John 6:1-14)

The climax of the Galilean ministry is approaching. Up to this time the tide of popular opinion was definitely in the Lord's favor. After the feeding of the five thousand and Jesus' sermon the following day in Capernaum, the tide begins to swing. This is the only miracle recorded by all four gospel writers.

Word of John's death must have filled the cities and villages of Galilee. The apostles of Jesus had returned from their mission filled with news of what they had done and what they had taught, yet obviously saddened over the death of John. This was a time when serious teaching needed to be done. It was a time when the apostles would have many questions that needed to be answered. The death of John needed to be placed in its proper perspective for them. Yet solitude and privacy were hard to achieve with the constant press of people around Jesus. They did not have time to eat a leisurely meal.

Jesus and the apostles entered into a boat and launched out into the Sea of Galilee, following a course along the northern coast. This placed a degree of separation between them and the multitudes, yet still allowed the people to know where they were going and to follow. "Come ye apart into a desert place and rest awhile," was the gracious invitation that Jesus extended to the apostles.

Usually when we think of a "desert place," we think of a barren, waterless, sand-filled area. The New Testament usage of the word does not necessarily mean that. In the New Testament it means "uninhabited or empty." Thus Jesus was taking His apostles to an uninhabited place along the northern shore of the Sea of Galilee.

It would be wonderful to know what Jesus said to His apostles while they were in the boat traveling to the site of the miracle. It would be wonderful to know what the apostles said about their mission, how Jesus responded to their enthusiasm, how He encouraged and comforted them concerning the death of John. However, God has not deemed it necessary for us to know.

The crowd was quick to hear of Jesus' departure and quick to see the direction He was going. Their response was to follow Him, running along the shore. That is quite a fascinating picture if we pause to consider it. There would be a crowd strung out along the lake, every person hurrying as best he could. Some would be running and others walking as quickly as possible. We can easily envision the younger and stronger ones in the lead, with the older ones and the handicapped or ill bringing up the rear. As they went past various villages and towns, others joined until a multitude numbering about 5,000 men (not taking into account the women and children) had assembled. Many of them arrived at the Lord's destination before He and the apostles got there.

Upon coming to shore, Jesus "welcomed them" and He went into their midst, teaching them many things and telling them of the kingdom of God. He also healed those who were sick and cured those who were ailing. But more people kept coming. So Jesus went up on a mountain as He so often did, the mountainside forming a natural amphitheater, where the greater number of people would be able to both see and hear.

We are told what motivated Jesus. The Lord was so pressed by people that He did not have the time to eat a normal meal. He was so much in demand that He had to launch out in a boat to get some time in private with His apostles. Yet when He saw the multitude, "He had compassion on them, because they were as sheep not having a shepherd." That is an expression we have seen before and it illustrates the care, protection, and provision Jesus wanted so much to give the people.

The day progressed as Jesus taught and healed. Before they knew it, the day was far spent and evening was upon them. Here was a vast multitude of people in an uninhabited place away from their homes with little, or no, food. To the apostles it seemed that there was only one thing to do – send the crowd away. Let them go into the villages in the countryside where they could find lodging and provisions while there was time.

To Jesus there was no problem. He said unto Philip, "Whence are we to buy bread, that these may eat?" This question was for Philip's benefit, not the Lord's. John tells us that Jesus knew exactly what He was going to do. For Philip, however, the situation presented quite a problem. His answer was, "Two hundred shillings' worth of bread is not sufficient for them, that every one may take a little." What a tremendous lesson Philip was about to learn!

Jesus ordered the apostles to go into the multitude and see what food was available. How long would it take a group of twelve men to go through a multitude numbering well above 5,000? From group to group they went, asking, "Does anyone have any food?" Consider what this did. It awoke in the multitude a sense of urgency. Those who had been patiently listening to Jesus now have their attention focused on the fact that there is no food, darkness is rapidly approaching, and they are in an uninhabited place. Out of the great multitude only Andrew was able to find food. It belonged to a lad and consisted of five barley loaves and two small fish. What were these five loaves and two fishes among so many?

"Bring them hither to me." In Jesus' hands those five barley loaves and two small fish were more than enough. Jesus had His apostles once again go among the crowd, instructing them to sit down in an orderly fashion – groups of about fifty each. In this way what Jesus was about to do could be more easily witnessed by the multitude and the serving of each person could be more efficient. This being done, Jesus looked up to heaven, blessed the bread and fish, gave thanks, and began to break them for distribution.

There is some discussion as to how the miracle happened. Some believe that each time a person broke off a piece of bread for himself the loaf was instantaneously restored. Thus each one of the people witnessed the miracle as it was repeated each time. Others believe Jesus was the center of attention during this miracle. The crowd had been arranged to facilitate their seeing and hearing the Lord. Thus, there must have been a continuous supply of food in the hands of Jesus as He broke it and gave it to His apostles for distribution. There is no definitive proof either way. The point to be emphasized is over 5,000 people were fed until they were satisfied with nothing more than five barley loaves and two small fish. When all had eaten, there was enough left over to fill twelve baskets.

The crowd was moved by what it had seen, heard, and now tasted. Some began to proclaim that surely One who could do such a thing was "the prophet that cometh into the world." That "prophet" was the one spoken of by Moses in Deuteronomy 18:18, "I will raise them up a prophet from among their brethren, like unto thee, and will put my words in his mouth; and he shall speak unto them all that I shall command him." The Jews correctly understood this to be a Messianic prophecy. They began to say that this man, Jesus, was the Promised One.

In a crowd of this size, particularly in the region of Galilee, we would expect to find a number of Zealots. The effect of the miracle on the fanatical Zealots created a desire to seize Jesus, by force if necessary, and make Him a king – their kind of king. The people could not, or would not, see the spiritual significance of the Lord's ministry. His was a kingdom "not of this world," but a worldly kingdom was what they wanted. Soon their worldly desires would turn them against Jesus.

Jesus Refuses Crown and Walks on Water (Matt. 14:22-36, Mark 6:45-56, John 6:15-21)

Jesus took steps to forestall the plan of the Zealots to make Him a king. He constrained, or compelled His apostles to depart by boat from the desert place at which the feeding of over 5,000 had taken place. Their departure would make the dismissal of the multitude easier since they would see His disciples leaving. This they did, entering into a boat, going "unto the other side to Bethsaida" as Mark wrote, or "going over the sea unto Capernaum" as John informs us. Luke had written that the feeding of the 5,000 took place near a city named Bethsaida (Luke 9:10). That would have been Bethsaida Julias, a village that had recently been enlarged and beautified by Philip, tetrarch of Ituraea. It was located on the northeast corner of the Sea of Galilee. The apostles were to travel across the northern end of the lake to Bethsaida on the northwest side, a suburb of Capernaum.

With such a large number of people and the excitement of what had taken place, it is easy to understand that dismissing them would have taken some time. As sunset fell, the crowd had been sent away, the apostles had departed by boat, and Jesus went up into a mountain to pray alone.

> So in the gathering dusk He gradually and gently succeeded in persuading the multitude to leave Him, and when all but the most enthusiastic had streamed away to their homes or caravans, He suddenly left the rest, and fled from them to the hill-top alone to pray. He was conscious that a solemn and awful crisis of His day on earth was to come, and by communing with His Heavenly Father, He would nerve His soul for the stern work of the morrow, and the bitter conflict of many coming weeks. Once before He had spent in the mountain solitudes a night of lonely prayer, but then it was before the choice of His beloved apostles, and the glad tidings of His earliest and happiest ministry. Far different were the feelings with which the Great High Priest now climbed the rocky stairs of that great mountain altar which in His temple of the night seemed to lift Him nearer to the stars of God. The murder of His beloved Forerunner brought home to His soul more nearly the thought of death; nor was He deceived by this brief blaze of false-founded popularity, which on the next day He meant to quench. The storm which now began to sweep over the barren hills; the winds that rushed howling down the ravines; the lake before Him buffeted into tempestuous foam; the little boat which – as the moonlight struggled through the rifted clouds – He saw tossing beneath Him on the laboring waves, were all too sure an emblem of the altered aspects of His earthly life. But there on the desolate hilltop, in that night of storm, He could gain strength and peace and happiness unspeakable; for there He was alone with God. And so over that figure, bowed in lonely prayer upon the hills, and over those toilers upon the troubled lake, the darkness fell and the great winds blew (Frederick Farrar, *The Life of Christ*, 310).

It appears Jesus spent nearly eight hours in solitude and prayer, having gone upon the mountain at sunset and not coming to the apostles until the fourth watch of the night. Each night was divided in four watches of three hours each. They were 6-9, 9-12, 12-3, 3-6. Jesus came to them between 3 and 6 a.m.

While the Lord was on the mountain praying, the apostles were in the boat attempting to make the crossing to Capernaum, a distance by water of only about 6 ½ miles. But there were contrary winds and waves preventing them from using sails, and they were forced to row. John informs us that they had traveled only about 25 or 30 furlongs. A furlong is 1/8 of a mile, so they had traveled about 3 ¾ miles. As the apostles struggled mightily in the storm against the wind and waves, Mark 6:48 indicates Jesus watched their progress.

Seeing His apostles in great distress, laboring with such difficulty against the storm, Jesus came to them in the fourth watch of the night. Evidently Jesus pursued a course parallel to the boat as He came to them. Mark wrote, "He cometh unto them, walking on the sea, and he would have passed by them." Why walk on a parallel course?

> (1)To keep from frightening them too much. (2) To give them a clearer view as He walked past so they might recognize Him. (3) To show His absolute independence of the boat. They could not entertain the idea that they had rescued Him. The boat is helpless in the storm and unable to make progress in the face of the wind, but Jesus comes over the dashing waves in spite of the storm (R.C. Foster, *Gospel Studies*, Vol. 2, 114).

The apostles were frightened when they saw Jesus, not knowing what it was and originally thought that He was a ghost; but He responded "Be of good cheer; it is I, be not afraid." Peter said, "Lord, if it be thou, bid me come unto thee upon the waters." Jesus said, "Come."

> It was characteristic of Peter to speak first and think afterward. It was an exciting moment; his joy and relief at hearing the voice and apparently seeing the person he most loved was struggling with a strong undercurrent of doubt as to the possibility of what he saw; his reckless disregard of the possible consequences to himself was also characteristic. Peter was a born leader of men, impulsive, but courageous. Amid the storm at night, he was quick to challenge the words of Jesus and seek further proof of the reality of His presence (*Gospel Studies*, Vol. 2, 114).

Peter stepped out of the boat and began to walk across the water to Jesus. But as he walked and felt the intensity of the wind, coupled with the fact that all of his life experiences told him that what he was doing was impossible, fear and doubt began to get the better of him. His faith wavered and he began to sink. It was Jesus' power that enabled Peter to walk on the water, but his faith was an essential ingredient of this act and the lesson to be taught. When he closed his heart, he began to sink. "Lord, save me" Peter cried, and Jesus immediately did so with a gentle rebuke, "O thou of little faith, wherefore didst thou doubt?"

Both Peter and Jesus entered into the boat. When they did, "the wind ceased." John wrote, "And straightway the boat was at the land whither they were going." The meaning of John's statement is somewhat difficult to ascertain. It may mean that the sudden calm enabled them to quickly reach the destination toward which they had been struggling for hours. Or it may mean the miracle of walking on the water was followed by a miraculous immediate arrival at their destination, a distance of about three miles from where they met Jesus.

When Jesus and Peter entered into the boat, they all worshipped the Lord, saying, "Of a truth thou art the Son of God." Remember that not long ago, when Jesus had calmed the tempest on the sea, they had asked, "What manner of man is this, that even the winds and the sea obey him?" They were progressing in their conviction. But Mark tells us, "and they were sore amazed in themselves; for they understood not concerning the loaves, but their heart was hardened."

Why was "their heart hardened?" Probably due to the Lord's refusal to be king. They were viewing events from a worldly standpoint. The miracle of feeding the 5,000 lost its power in their minds. Why would He not use His power as ruler of the Jewish nation? Why not use His ability to overthrow the shackles of Roman domination? Two attitudes are shown. Matthew shows there was recognition on their part of His divine character; Mark shows they also had doubt and were confused concerning His purpose and plan. The boat would land along the northwestern shore of the Sea of Galilee, and once again Jesus would be surrounded by people.

The Opinion Begins to Change in Galilee (John 6:22-71)

On the previous day Jesus had sent the multitude away, including His apostles, and had gone into the mountain to pray in solitude. Not all had obeyed; some remained. These were probably the most determined of the Zealots, bent upon making Jesus an earthly king. They remained behind, fully expecting Jesus to come down from the mountain in the morning. The morning came and Jesus did not appear. The night before He had walked on the surface of the Sea of Galilee and joined His apostles in the midst of the sea. They did not know that. All they knew was that there had been one boat and His apostles had entered it, embarked, and Jesus had not been with them.

Evidently during the night additional boats from Tiberius, perhaps seeking refuge from the same storm the disciples had encountered, had landed near the site of the feeding of the 5,000. These individuals who remained behind entered those boats and set sail for Capernaum, seeking Jesus. When they found the Lord, their question was, "When did you come here?"

Instead of answering the question, Jesus focused on their motives. It is important we understand His response. The miracles Jesus performed were proofs He was the Messiah. To seek Him because they had seen the miracles and were convinced by them of who He was would have been completely proper. But to follow Him because they had their physical needs supplied was earthly and purely selfish. This group of people wanted to make Jesus an earthly king. These Zealots had "seen" the miracles of Jesus, but not in the sense they were intended. They sought Jesus' miraculous power to further their own aims, not God's. What they wanted was a Messiah with the power of Jesus, one who could completely annihilate the Roman occupation army with a word. Growing out of the feeding of over 5,000 people came a marvelous discourse emphasizing the spiritual nature of the ministry of Jesus.

Verse 27 is elliptical, meaning it is of "not only – but also" construction. John 12:44 and 1 Cor. 1:17 are other examples of this grammatical construction. What the Lord was saying is, "Labor not only for the meat which perishes, but also for the meat which endureth unto everlasting life…" Thus Jesus turned the discussion to the spiritual. An important point to be made is this, the meat which endureth forever cannot be earned by our work, but it also cannot be received without our work. We are to labor for it. In response to their question, "What shall we do that we might work the works of God?" Jesus said, "This is the work that God would have you to do, believe on him whom he hath sent." That is the primary work God desires all men to do – to believe in Jesus with all that we are and all that we have. He wants people to completely commit to Him.

If we bear in mind that the people taking the lead in this discussion were Zealots seeking Jesus from purely earthly ambitions, their questions and comments in verses 31-34 are easier to understand. They had seen the miracle of the previous day, it had convinced them to view Jesus as the Messiah and to seek to make Him a king. But the discussion was taking a turn they did not want it to take. Moses had been the leader of the people and he had supplied them with physical food. In their view of the Messiah, He would supply the temporal needs of the people as well.

Jesus' response was tremendous. Moses did not give the food in the wilderness, God did. God was now giving them the true bread from heaven; that bread was the One that He sent, and in Him was life to be found. When they requested this bread, Jesus stated, "I am the Bread of Life." This is similar to the discussion with the Samaritan woman at Jacob's well in John 4 and the "Living Water." It is the provision of the spiritual sustenance that we need and never perishes. The people had seen the miracles Jesus performed and had not given themselves and their hearts to Him. This was a warning to them. Those whom the Father gives to Jesus, He will in no wise cast out, and those who have been given to Him, verse 40, are those who believe on Him. These, as long as they continue in belief, have everlasting life, and will rise with Christ in the last day.

Now the Jews murmured among themselves. "This is Jesus. We know His father and we know His mother. How can He say that He came down from heaven?" The people did not understand His spiritual message, so Jesus continued His explanation. No one would come to Him except he was drawn of the Father. The way this "drawing" would take place is in John 12:32, where Jesus said, "And I, if I be lifted up from the earth, will draw all men unto me." Once Jesus was crucified, and the gospel of the cross began to be proclaimed, they would come. That would be the drawing power – the good news of salvation through the cross of Christ.

Jesus again repeated His glorious message. Believing on Him, with all belief involves, would bring everlasting life. He was the "bread of life", the provider of all spiritual sustenance that a person would ever need. They had mentioned manna. Their fathers had eaten manna in the wilderness and were dead. But Jesus, who came down from heaven, was the "living bread" and to partake of Him was to live forever. This would be made possible by the giving of His life.

Again the Jews murmured, wondering how this man would give His flesh to eat.

There is some dispute as to whether Jesus was making reference to the Lord's Supper in His statement concerning eating His flesh and drinking His blood. R.C. Foster is one who believed that was the evident meaning of His statements. Matthew Henry was closer to the truth in his following remarks.

> What is meant by eating this flesh and drinking this blood? It is certain that it means neither more nor less than believing in Christ. Believing in Christ includes these four things, which eating and drinking do (1) It implies an appetite to Christ. This spiritual eating and drinking begins with hungering and thirsting. (2) An application of Christ to ourselves. Meat looked upon will not nourish us, but meat fed upon. We must so accept Christ as to appropriate him to ourselves. (3) A delight in Christ and his salvation. The doctrine of Christ crucified must be meat and drink to us. (4) A derivation of nourishment from him and dependence upon him for the support and comfort of our spiritual life, and the strength, growth, and vigor of the new man. It is to live upon him as we do upon our meat (Matthew Henry, *Matthew Henry's Commentary in One Volume*, 1540).

Verse 55 is particularly interesting. For flesh to be eaten, it must be broken. For blood to be drunk, it must be poured out. Thus, Jesus is speaking of Himself as a sacrifice to be given.

> The thought of drinking blood was startling to the Jew, for he was forbidden to taste even the blood of animals, and the reason assigned was very pertinent - because the blood was the life of animals (Gen. 9:4, Lev. 17:10-14). By insisting, therefore, on the drinking of his blood, Jesus has insisted that his very life be absorbed and assimilated. To be disciples of other teachers, it is only necessary that we accept and follow their doctrine. But to be a disciple of Christ is to do more than this. His divinity permits us to have a spiritual communion and fellowship with Him, an abiding in His presence, an indwelling of His Spirit and a veritable assimilation of life from Him. Were it otherwise He could not be food for the spirit – bread of life. He had started to show to the Jews that He was to the spirit what bread was to the body. It was difficult to bring home to their carnal minds so spiritual a thought, and therefore Jesus clothed it in carnal metaphors and made it as plain as possible (McGarvey and Pendleton, *The Fourfold Gospel*, 389).

This great discourse took place in the synagogue of Capernaum. Now, many of His disciples began murmuring among themselves. "This is a hard saying; who can hear it?" Jesus' response was, "If this disturbs you with your earthly point of view, what will my ascension do?" He plainly told them that He spoke of the spiritual realm and life within it. The flesh and fleshly things were not what was most important. He spoke to them of spiritual things and therein was life to be found.

Not all of Jesus' disciples had followed Him for the right reasons and from the right motives. Jesus knew this to be true from the very beginning. Now the die was cast, the Galilean Ministry was effectively ended, and the tide of popular opinion – even among some of His disciples -- was beginning to turn. Many of His followers would walk no more with Him.

We can truly feel the pain in Jesus' words as He turned to the apostles and asked, "Will ye also go away?" Peter's answer is a tremendous confession, "Lord, to whom shall we go? Thou hast the words of eternal life. And we believe and are sure that thou art that Christ, the Son of the living God."

Jesus closed by speaking of His betrayer, illustrating the truth that no man can be a real follower of Jesus unless he has truly believed and assimilated His life with his own.

Attack of the Jerusalem Pharisees – Traditions (Matt. 15:1-20, Mark 7:1-23, John 7:1)

In John 6:4 we are told that the Passover was at hand. The obvious indication of John 7:1 is that Jesus did not attend this Passover in Jerusalem but rather remained in Galilee. The reason is given. Fear and hatred of Jesus had grown to such a level among the leaders of the Jews in Jerusalem that they were seeking to kill Him.

As reports of the Lord's ministry and the excitement He was generating in Galilee reached the ears of the Jewish authorities in Jerusalem, they sent some of their number to Him. Those they sent were selected Pharisees and scribes, scholars, whose evident mission was to entrap Jesus and discredit His ministry and Jesus Himself. They seized upon the fact that they had seen some of the disciples of Jesus eat without washing their hands. This was contrary to the traditions of the elders. This brings to mind two questions: (1) Why did the disciples eat without washing their hands? (2) What were the "traditions of the elders?"

The first question is easily answered. This was not a question of cleanliness. In the minds of the Pharisees it was a question of religious ceremony. The Lord and His disciples were often so encompassed by crowds that they did not have the time to eat, much less wash their hands before every meal. Since it was a man-made tradition and not decreed by God, Jesus did not teach His disciples to keep it.

The second question requires a thorough explanation.

Belief in the tradition of the elders was the fundamental peculiarity of the Pharisaic system. They held that these traditions, or oral expositions of and additions to the law, were revealed to Moses along with the law, and were communicated by him orally to the elders of the people, by whose successors they had been handed down through each successive generation. They regarded these traditions as equal in authority with the written word. Various uncleannesses are specified in the Mosaic law. Traditions extended the idea of uncleanness so as to hold the man probably unclean who had been in the marketplace, where he might have touched an unclean person, and to hold certain cups, pots and brazen vessels as ceremonially unclean when neither the law of Moses nor the law of hygiene declared them to be so. Since the law of Moses ordered the unclean to dip himself in a bath for his cleansing, the tradition of the elders required a like dipping in these cases of uncleanness which they had invented. When we remember that bathing was a daily practice among the Pharisees, we are less surprised at this observance. As to the theory that the tradition of the elders was derived from Moses, Jesus here flatly contradicts it. There is no trustworthy evidence to show that it is of higher antiquity than the time of the return from the Babylonian captivity (McGarvey and Pendleton, *The Fourfold Gospel*, 394).

Jesus laid bare the hypocrisy of the Pharisees with His response. He did not deny that His disciples violated the tradition of the elders but justified their actions by laying bare the whole traditional system.

Jesus quoted Isaiah 29:13 and applied it to the Pharisees. They were hypocrites. They criticized the Lord and His disciples for disobeying the tradition of the elders, while they were disobeying the law of God through their devotion to their traditions. Yes, they took great pains concerning ceremonial defilement of themselves and even their kitchen utensils. Yes, vocally they honored God, but inside they were corrupt and dishonored Him. They were ready to leave the law of God and obey their traditions, not recognizing that in doing so, they were serving God the way they wanted to serve Him and not in the way He wanted to be served. By clinging to their traditions they were rendering their worship vain – useless and empty. Jesus illustrated this truth in the following way.

The law demanded respect and support for one's parents (Ex. 20:12, Deut. 5:16). But, by their tradition, the Pharisees had circumvented this law. According to their tradition, an individual could declare a possession "corban" or "given to God." Thus a Jew could declare part of his estate, by which his parents would be profited, a gift to God, and be freed from his obligation to his parents. Thus their tradition made void the law. Actually, their whole attitude toward God was out of balance. They were more than willing to sacrifice the spiritual content for their ceremonial traditions.

Jesus utilized this opportunity to instruct the multitude. He laid down the principle that real defilement is moral, not ceremonial; and that which enters the mouth is not what defiles a man, but that which cometh forth out of the mouth from the heart.

The disciples were upset because Jesus' whole speech had offended the Pharisees. He had shown their hypocrisy. He had shown that their traditions, which they held in such reverence, caused them to sin. He demonstrated their traditional, ceremonial cleanliness was worthless compared to the moral cleanliness the law of God demanded and which they chose to ignore. But these were the Pharisees, strict adherents to the law and respected teachers of it. His disciples were concerned by Jesus' response to them.

In essence, the Lord told His disciples not to worry about the Pharisees. God was responsible for the Law as given by Moses. He had planted it. God had not planted the traditions of the elders. Therefore, those traditions were doomed to be uprooted. When Jesus said, "Let them alone", He was not saying let them alone by allowing their false teaching to go unanswered or allowing their hypocrisy to continue unexposed. He was telling His followers to "let them alone" in bowing down to their false teaching and worrying whether or not Jesus' teaching pleased or displeased them. When the blind lead the blind, both are responsible. The Pharisees were leaders who refused to accept the truth of Jesus in spite of all the evidence. They were blind leaders, and blind followers possess the same faults and will suffer the same fate.

The words of Jesus were so perplexing that Peter referred to them as a "parable", meaning in this instance an obscure saying. He asked for an explanation. It was understandable that the multitude, so long swayed by the teaching of the Pharisees, would be slow to grasp the significance of what Jesus was saying. But His disciples who had been with Him and had felt free enough to eat with unwashed hands, should have been quicker to understand. At this point, they were not. So Jesus explained.

> Thus Jesus sets forth the simple doctrine that a man's moral and spiritual state is not dependent upon the symbolic cleanness of his physical diet, much less is it dependent on ceremonial observances in regard to things eaten, or the dishes from which they are eaten. Of course, Jesus did not mean at this time to abrogate the Mosaic law of legal uncleannesses. These uncleannesses worked no spiritual defilement, but were merely typical of such; for the food in no way touched or affected the mind or soul, the fountains of spiritual life, but only the corporeal organs, which have no moral susceptibility. The Pharisees had erred in confusing legal and spiritual defilement, and had added error to error by multiplying the causes of defilement in their tradition. By thus showing that legal defilement was merely symbolic, Jesus classed it with all the other symbolism which was to be done away with when the gospel reality was fully ushered in (Col. 2:16-17)). In saying, therefore, that Jesus made all meats clean, Mark does not mean that Jesus then and there repealed the law. The declaration of such repeal came later (Acts 10:14,15). He means that he there

drew those distinctions and laid down those principles which supplanted the Mosaic law when the kingdom of God was ushered in on the day of Pentecost (McGarvey and Pendleton, *The Fourfold Gospel*, 398).

Retirement to Phoenicia – (Matt. 15:21-28, Mark 7:24-30)

Jesus left the land of Galilee and entered in the "parts of Tyre and Sidon" in the land of Phoenicia. His reasons for leaving are evident. After the feeding of the 5,000 there had been an increase in the desire by certain elements of the Jews to take Jesus, by force if necessary, and make Him a king. His discourse in Capernaum about the "bread of life" had caused a negative reaction. Jesus had also offended the Pharisees by exposing their hypocrisy concerning their traditions. A definite change had taken place. The ministry was becoming more dangerous, there was much teaching to be done with the apostles, and they were about to begin the final stretch that would lead to Calvary. There was a need for rest and seclusion. So Jesus went to a home in that region and desired His location remain unknown, but His fame had spread even into this predominantly Gentile country and He could not remain hidden.

Tyre and Sidon were two famous cities of Phoenicia, a narrow strip of country bordering the Mediterranean just north of Palestine. The people were a sea-faring and colonizing race. Phoenicia was 28 miles long with an average width of approximately one mile. Sidon was 22 miles north of Tyre.

A woman who knew of Jesus and had heard He was in the area, came to Him with an urgent request. "Have mercy on me, O Lord thou son of David: my daughter is grievously vexed with a demon." Several things need to be noticed about this woman and her request. (1) Matthew says she was a "woman of Canaan" and Mark calls her a "Greek, Syrophoenician by race." Is there a difference there? No. She was a Syrian born in Phoenicia, descended from the Canaanites. (2) What is the significance of this Gentile woman calling Jesus "son of David?"

> Living among a mixed population of Jews and Gentiles, she had heard this title applied to Jesus; she knew something of the hopes of the Hebrew nation, that they were expecting a Messiah, a son of the great King David, who should preach to the poor and heal the sick, as she heard that Jesus had done. We know that the reputation of Jesus had spread into these parts, and that persons from this country had come to him to be healed (Mk. 3:8, Lk. 6:17). There is no reason to suppose that the woman was a proselyte; but evidently she was of a humble and religious spirit, open to conviction, and of an enlightened understanding (*Pulpit Commentary*, Vol. 15, 99).

At first Jesus did not respond to her. Matthew tells us, "But he answered her not a word." That seems out of character for Jesus, so we ask "why?" Why did not Jesus answer her immediately? Several explanations have been suggested. (1) Jesus' ministry was to the Jews. This is supported by our Lord's statement in verse 24 of Matthew 15. (2) Jesus was measuring her perseverance and faith.

Whatever the Lord's reasons, this woman was persistent, so much so that His disciples said, "Send her away; for she crieth after us." Her persistence was drawing the type of attention to Jesus that He had sought to avoid. But His answer to the apostles indicates they were asking Jesus to grant her request. However, upon closer examination it appears their request was selfishly motivated. "Send her away, grant her request," in hopes she would leave them alone. Jesus' response to the apostles shows that it was part of the divine plan of His ministry would be to the Jews, the "lost sheep of the house of Israel." It is obvious from the gospel accounts that variations to this divine plan were few and granted to those Gentiles who displayed exceptional faith.

If we follow closely the gospel narratives, it appears that Jesus left the house He was in and the woman followed after Him. She was pleading with Jesus and threw herself at His feet in the dusty road, saying, "Lord, help me."

Jesus' answer to her in Matthew 15:26 and Mark 7:27 was not quite as severe as it might first appear:

> By the use of the word 'first' Jesus suggested that there would come a time of mercy for the Gentiles. He uses the diminutive for the word dog, thus indicating a tame pet, and suggesting rather the dependence and subordinate position than the uncleanness of the dog. By so doing He gave the woman an argumentative handle which she was not slow to grasp (McGarvey and Pendleton, *The Fourfold Gospel*, 401).

Concerning her response in verse 27 of Matthew 15 and verse 28 of Mark 7, note:

> Jesus had suggested that domestic order by which dogs are required to wait until the meal is over before they receive their portion; but with a wit made keen by her necessity, she replies by alluding to the well-known fact that dogs under the table are permitted to eat the crumbs even while the meal is in progress; intimating thereby her hope to receive aid before all the needs of Israel had first been satisfied (ibid, 401).

Her great faith caused her to receive the help she requested. That very hour, from a distance, the demon was cast out of her daughter. In Mark 7:30 reads, "And found the child thrown upon the bed", indicating that the casting out of the demon had been accompanied by convulsions. Consider the faith of this woman. Even when Jesus was silent, she had persisted. She listened carefully to what He said and regarded His assistance to her to be a mere crumb from the table of His abundant powers. She obviously obeyed Jesus and went her way when He sent her, believing that what He promised had occurred.

Third Retirement and Ministry in Decapolis (Matt. 15:29-38, Mark 7:31-8:9)

Mark's account shows us the circuitous route that Jesus took bringing Him into the region of Decapolis. Going from Tyre through Sidon would have taken Jesus through the northern most part of Palestine and then into the east and southeastern regions along the Sea of Galilee. We know that Jesus had gone into Phoenicia seeking rest and seclusion, but had encountered multitudes there. Perhaps His roundabout journey through Decapolis was undertaken for the same reasons, and yet He had encountered multitudes there as well.

Previously, when Jesus had cleansed the Gadarene demoniacs, the people of this region had driven Jesus out after the loss of the swine. Now it is different. Maybe the dominant figure of the demoniacs had fulfilled the commission given him by Jesus, "Go home to thy friends, and tell them how great things the Lord hath done for thee, and hath had compassion on thee." Perhaps word of Jesus' wondrous ministry in Galilee had spread to the region. Whatever the reason, His reception was better this time.

Matthew makes it clear that a great deal of healing took place at this time by Jesus. "The lame, blind, dumb, maimed, and many others" were brought to Jesus and He healed them. The reaction of the multitude was one of wonderment. The Greek verb used by Mark in verse 37 means, "They were struck out of their senses." Mark gives us the details of one specific case of healing. It was a deaf-mute. He was taken aside by Jesus, away from the multitude. We might ask why? It appears to have two possible explanations. (1) The man could not hear Jesus nor could He speak to the Lord. Privacy of a greater degree was needed in order to communicate with the man. (2) It may have been to keep the excitement, which was already growing in Decapolis, to a reasonable level.

Possibly Jesus pantomimed to this person what He was going to do. Whether Jesus put His fingers into the man's ears or into His own, whether He touched the man's tongue or His own doesn't really matter. He was indicating to the man what He was going to do and by looking up to heaven, Jesus demonstrated to the man that it was through God that he would be healed. Jesus sighed, or groaned – indicating pity – and said "Ephphatha" meaning "be opened," and the man could both hear and speak.

There were those who had seen this occur, and Jesus urged them not to speak of it; but excitement got the better of them and they published it widely. Once again, the reason for not wanting it announced seems to have been the desire to keep the excitement to a minimum. They did not obey Him. It has been written, "Like most people they would rather praise Jesus than obey Him."

A great multitude was following Jesus and they stayed with the Lord for three days. During that time, their food supply was exhausted. This does not mean that they had been without food for three days; it means that what they had was gone. Once more we see the compassion of Jesus. He did not want to send them away to their homes with nothing to eat lest they grow faint on the way.

The interesting thing about this, and something that has caused considerable questions, is the question of the disciples. "Whence should we have so many loaves in a desert place as to fill so great a multitude?" Were not these the same men who had asked essentially the same question before the feeding of the 5,000? Had they not learned? Many feel that it is illogical they could have asked such a question again, but is it so illogical as to render the account questionable?

Among themselves the disciples had seven loaves and a few small fish. After sending His disciples into the multitude to have them sit down, Jesus gave thanks for the loaves and fish, broke them, gave them to the disciples, and the disciples gave them to the multitude. The multitude, numbering about 4,000 (not counting women and children) ate their fill, and of the remaining pieces there were enough to fill seven baskets. Those baskets were large hampers, not the small baskets in the feeding of the more than 5,000. Once their needs were met, Jesus sent them away.

Brief Visit to Magadan and Demand for a Sign from Heaven (Matt. 15:39-16:4, Mark 8:10-12)

After leaving Decapolis, Jesus arrived in Magadan (some manuscripts have Magadala). Mark tells us that He "came into the parts of Dalmanutha." Is there a discrepancy here? The answer is no. Magadala was a city on the southern part of the plain of Gennesaret on the northwest shore of the Sea of Galilee. Dalmanutha was most probably a village in the suburbs of Magadala. Matthew identifies the area by the name of the largest city, while Mark identifies the specific site of the encounter.

We are told that the Pharisees "came forth", while Matthew informs us they were joined by the Sadducees. Jesus was near the northwest shore of the Sea of Galilee. The Sadducees were concentrated in Jerusalem. This would suggest that this was a delegation sent from Jerusalem to monitor the movement of Jesus – a movement gaining followers at an alarming rate. It is interesting the Pharisees and Sadducees, bitter enemies and at opposite ends of the spectrum religiously, would join forces because of their mutual hatred of Jesus. They came to "try" or to "tempt" the Lord. While we are told to "try the spirits to see whether they are of God" (1 John 4:1), this was not such a test. They were trying to ensnare Jesus, to trap Him. They were seeking to discredit the Lord in the eyes of the people.

This combined group of enemies demanded a "sign from heaven." There had been ample miracles performed by Jesus, all of them demonstrating He was the Son of God; but they were not satisfied with those. You may recall certain Pharisees had attributed the Lord's miracles to the "power of Beelzebub." They were asking for some visible sign from heaven, such as only God could give. "Let us see something like what happened with Elijah and the fire that came down on Mt. Carmel, maybe a voice from heaven. Show us something like that and we will believe."

There is a statement made in Mark 8:12 concerning Jesus as He began to respond to their request. Mark tells us, "And he sighed deeply in his spirit." Perhaps we are seeing here an indication of the sadness of Jesus over the refusal of the religious leaders to accept the abundant evidence that was all around them; the blind could see, the lame could walk, the deaf could hear and the dumb could speak. Why would they not see? Perhaps there was frustration in the sigh. How often must they be taught? How much must they be shown?

Jesus used a simple illustration in His answer. They could look at certain signs in nature, read those signs, and understand. For instance, a generally accepted rule is a red sky in the evening means fair weather the next day and a red sky in the morning with lowering clouds means foul weather. They could read those kinds of signs. Why could they not read the signs of the times? They could look at Jesus' miracles; they could see that could only be accomplished by the power of God. They knew the prophecies concerning the Messiah. They could not see those prophecies were now being fulfilled.

Jesus placed the responsibility directly upon them. Jesus was saying, "Why should so perverse a generation seek a sign when it has already seen and rejected more signs than any other generation before it?" There would be no additional signs given to satisfy the demands of men who were rejecting the evidence of all the previous signs they had seen. There would be but one more sign. It would be a sign from heaven, and it was not being given just to satisfy the whims of the Pharisees and the Sadducees. It would be the "sign of the prophet Jonah." It would be the Lord's resurrection -- a true sign from heaven only accomplished by God.

The Fourth Withdrawal to Eastern Side of the Lake and a Warning to Disciples (Matt. 16:5-12, Mark 8:13-26)

Following this exchange between Jesus and the Pharisees and Sadducees, the Lord and His disciples once again entered a boat and departed for the other side of the sea. On this occasion they were going to the eastern shore, probably toward Bethsaida Julias, on the northeast shore of the Sea of Galilee.

It is obvious that Jesus did not always miraculously supply food for Himself and His disciples; the feeding of over 5,000 and over 4,000 were two notable and exceptional situations. They usually took what supplies would be needed with them. In this instance the disciples had forgotten, and when they prepared to eat, they had only one loaf of bread among them. Jesus used oversight to teach His disciples a very important lesson.

"Take heed and beware of the leaven of the Pharisees and Sadducees." Frequently, leaven was used in the New Testament to suggest a permeating influence, whether good or bad. In this case, it was obviously bad. Mark also mentions the "leaven of Herod." Herod's court was so corrupt that it could contaminate by its worldliness and hypocrisy just as the religious leaven of the Pharisees and Sadducees.

This was a pivotal time in the ministry of Jesus and in the preparation of the apostles. They had seen Jesus' ministry reach a peak of popularity and then start to decline after the feeding of the 5,000. Jesus had been challenged and taunted by His enemies, yet refused to respond to that taunting by performing a "sign from heaven," even though the apostles knew He could. The apostles had been upset about the way Jesus had offended the Pharisees (Matt. 15:12). They needed to be warned about allowing themselves to be influenced in a negative way by the things that were happening.

At first the apostles thought Jesus was rebuking them for failing to bring bread. Having been with Jesus so long, having witnessed the miraculous feedings, they still did not understand that He was speaking of spiritual things. Forget the bread; they needed to be more concerned about the leaven of the Pharisees' teaching. That is where the real danger was lurking.

After He entered into Bethsaida Julias, a blind man was brought to Jesus to be healed. The Lord took him away from the multitude and healed him.

> The man's eyes were probably sore and Jesus made use of saliva to soften and soothe them. But it was our Lord's custom to give variety to the manifestations of his power, sometimes using one apparent auxiliary means, and sometimes another; and also healing instantly or progressively, as He chose, that the people might see the healing was altogether a matter of His will (McGarvey and Pendleton, *The Fourfold Gospel*, 409).

The healed man was sent to his home and not into the village where the excitement over his healing would have grown.

Peter's Confession
(Matt. 16:13-20, Mark 8:27-30, Luke 9:18-21)

The city of Caesarea Philippi was located at one of the three sources of the Jordan River, approximately twenty five miles north of the Sea of Galilee and two and a half miles east of the city of Dan. It was the capital of the territory of Philip. Philip was a son of Herod the Great, and at the death of his father he inherited the region. It included Panias, Gaulanitis, Trachonitis, and Auranitis. This particular Herod was unlike the rest of the Herodian family. He was dignified, moderate, and just. Herod Philip died in A.D. 34.

Luke includes the fact Jesus was apart from His disciples praying before this conversation. In view of the momentous things that were about to be said at this time, it is wholly consistent for Jesus to have been engrossed in prayer.

Rejoining His disciples, Jesus asked the first of two questions, "Who do men say that I the Son of Man am?" Or, what is the popular opinion about Me?

Jesus wanted to know what the multitudes were saying about Him, not the opinion of the leaders.

The popular opinion at that time did not regard Jesus as the Messiah. This could possibly be traced to the fact Jesus had condemned their current view of the Messiah as a political leader and had refused to be crowned as an earthly king. But some thought He could be John the Baptist. Remember, Herod had thought Jesus might be John back from the dead (Matt. 14:2). Some thought Jesus was Elijah, since Elijah's return had been prophesied by Malachi. Others thought He was Jeremiah. Still others were more vague, thinking that Jesus was "one of the prophets."

Then Jesus asked His second question, "Whom say ye that I am?" This was asked of those who had spent the greatest amount of time with Jesus. They had heard Him teach, and witnessed the miraculous works at His hands. They had been the recipients of special, private instruction from the Lord. They had time to form a more correct opinion.

Peter responded, "Thou art the Christ, the Son of the Living God." There are two things that stand out in Peter's answer. (1) Jesus was the Christ – the Anointed One. (2) Jesus was the Son of God, therefore divine. Peter did not yet fully understand the nature of the work of the Christ nor did he fully understand the sense in which Jesus was the Son of God and thus divine. But his statement is a clear expression of his faith in those two propositions, as imperfect as his understanding might have been. Jesus was the Christ and He was the Son of God.

In the Lord's answer to Peter, He called him Simon Barjona. This was an Aramaic phrase showing that Jesus was speaking in Aramaic, which was the popular dialect used by the Jews after the captivity. "Bar" means "son" and "Jonah" is "Jonah or John." When Jesus said, "Flesh and blood hath not revealed it unto thee, but my Father which is in heaven," He made a statement about which there has been a considerable amount of discussion.

Two interpretations are held: (1) 'Flesh and blood' represents men whose false opinions have just been cited and from whom Peter did not receive his conviction. 'My Father' affirms the deity of Christ and His unity with God. God had revealed the great truth to Peter through the deeds and words of Christ – who is God; Peter had not come to it by unaided human reason. (2) By 'My Father – hath revealed' Jesus means not by oral communication even from Himself, but of that inward reception by silent communication from the Father which is the source of true knowledge of spiritual things.

> Evidently interpretation (1) is to be preferred for Jesus has labored by word and deed to bring them to this conviction and He repeatedly declared His revelation sufficient for faith and condemned the Pharisees for not accepting this truth...There is a sense in which all revelation and comprehension of truth is from God, but to say this was from God apart from the instruction of Jesus is to set aside the importance of the incarnation as sufficient of

itself to bring faith without special immediate aid (R.C. Foster, *Gospel Studies*, Vol. 2, 151,152).

In the statement of the Lord, Jesus is the builder of the church. Petra is the rock; petros is Peter.

> Petra denotes a mass of rock, as distinct from petros, a detached stone or boulder, or a stone that might be thrown or easily moved...in Matt. 16:18, metaphorically, of Christ and the testimony concerning Him; here the distinction between petra, concerning the Lord Himself, and petros, the Apostle, is clear (W.E. Vine, *An Expository Dictionary of New Testament Words*, 302).

The "rock" to which Jesus referred was Peter's confession, "Thou art the Christ, the Son of the Living God." The church is built upon Jesus, not Peter (1 Cor. 3:11).

There has been discussion concerning Jesus' statement, "The gates of Hell shall not prevail against it." Two views seem plausible. (1) The gates of Hades shall not be able to prevail against the church in the sense that the grave shall not be able to hold Jesus when He would be crucified. Hades shall not prevail against it – meaning its establishment by Jesus on Pentecost. (2) Gates are a symbol of power. The strength of a city was measured by the strength of its gates. The greatest foe of Christianity is not death, but the devil. Two great kingdoms are at war in this passage; Satan's kingdom shall never prevail over the Lord's.

Peter was given the "keys of the kingdom." Keys represent the power to open and close. Peter had the "keys" wherein he preached the first gospel sermon, complete with the terms of admission into the kingdom, on the day of Pentecost. It can be said that he "opened" the kingdom to the Jews that day. Peter also preached the first sermon to the Gentiles at Caesarea, to Cornelius and his household, thereby opening the kingdom to the Gentiles as well.

The statement by Jesus concerning "binding and loosing" was made to the other apostles in Matthew 18:18. It refers to their teaching people to observe all things whatsoever the Lord commanded them. They would be binding upon people things already bound by the Lord. They would be loosing those things already loosed by the Lord.

It is important to note the words "kingdom" and "church" are used interchangeably in this passage. If they were not so used, there would be no satisfactory interpretation of the passage possible.

It is apparent from the gospels that the apostles did not understand the significance of Jesus being the Christ, the Anointed One. They were still looking at it as an earthly, political arrangement. If they had proclaimed to the people that Jesus was the Christ, with their own lack of understanding about it, such a proclamation would have been immediately misunderstood by the multitude and would have created difficulty. So, Jesus charged them that they should tell no one He was the Christ.

First Distinct Prediction of Death
(Matt. 16:21-28, Mark 8:31-9:1, Luke 9:22-27)

It needs to be noted in verse 21 of Matthew 16, there is a distinct change in the teaching of the Lord to His apostles. They were only about nine months from the cross. "From that time forth" indicates that change. The apostles had now come to the realization Jesus was the Messiah, but their understanding of what that meant had to grow and mature. They needed to be taught what kind of Messiah Jesus was. Time was beginning to press upon them. The cross loomed in the near future, less than a year away, and they needed to be forewarned and prepared lest they be overwhelmed by the coming events. Every day the plots to kill Jesus were getting bolder and stronger. He needed to inform them that to die was the reason He came.

Several times before this Jesus had intimated that He was going to die, but He had not spoken of it in such detail before. Now it was time. By the use of the word "must" in verse 21 of Matthew 16, Jesus was showing His disciples there was a divine plan unfolding, that it was God's Will all these things come to pass. He must go to Jerusalem, He must suffer many things at the hands of the elders (a general term for the members of the Sanhedrin), the chief priests (the high priest, his family and all eligible to the office), and the scribes (the great scholars of the Pharisees). He must be killed and raised again the third day.

It is appropriate to make some comments concerning the "third day." Many try to get exact about the time element. Some demand 72 hours, thus attempting to place the death of Jesus on a Thursday. Some want to get bogged down in wrangling about such matters. However, the exact time Jesus was in the tomb is not necessary to determine. There is no effort in the gospels to state the number of hours. The time is presented in a general way, "on the third day" or "after three days." These are equivalent expressions as used in the gospels.

It seems strange that Peter, with all his love and devotion to Jesus, would dare to rebuke Him. But Peter is full of joy and love, and had just made a wonderful confession. Hearing the tragic prediction of Jesus, a prediction that would appear to be in utter contradiction to his understanding of the Messiah, Peter could not restrain himself. So he took Jesus aside and said, "Be it far from thee, Lord: this shall not be unto thee."

Peter had unwittingly offered the same temptation to Jesus that Satan had offered in the wilderness. Dissuade Jesus from the cross; offer conquest and victory of the world by earthly means other than death. This is why Jesus calls Peter Satan. He was doing what Satan did and playing Satan's role.

"Get thee behind me" is Jesus' way of telling Peter to get in the role of follower, where he belonged, instead of trying to dictate to Jesus and become a stumbling-block. It was a divine plan that was to be carried out; it could not be viewed from a worldly standpoint as Peter was doing.

To the rest of the disciples and to the multitude, Jesus taught a valuable lesson. To be a disciple one must learn to say "no" to many of the strongest cravings and desires of an earthly nature and perform our daily duty at any cost, even the most painful death. To be a disciple, one must be willing to follow Jesus wherever He goes.

The Lord explained that the person who seeks to save his own life in the selfish and worldly sense shall lose it in the most important sense, the spiritual. But the one who loses his life for Jesus' sake, meaning to deny himself and serve the Lord, shall find his life in the highest and eternal sense. Peter and the apostles, with the multitude, were thinking about a worldly Messiah in a worldly kingdom with its profits, physical benefits, and rewards. But Jesus showed that the riches and wealth of the whole world does not compare with the rewards of the kingdom.

Both Mark and Luke mention Jesus' statement, "For whosoever shall be ashamed of me and of my words, of him shall the Son of man be ashamed when he cometh in his own glory…" Peter had been ashamed of the way that Jesus had portrayed Himself with the humiliation of a shameful death. His warning was clear. If they were ashamed of Jesus in the manner in which He was to die, to fulfill the will of the Father, He would be ashamed of them in the day He judges the world.

Verse 28 of Matthew 16 demonstrates that these things were going to happen, including the establishment of the church or kingdom, in a relatively short period of time. It would occur before all of those standing there at that time had tasted death.

The Transfiguration (Matt. 17:1-8, Mark 9:2-8, Luke 9:28-36)

The event we are about to examine is one of the few placed in its chronological order in the gospels. It followed Peter's great confession at Caesarea Philippi. Matthew and Mark say, "after six days", while Luke says, "about eight days after." There is no contradiction there. Matthew and Mark are obviously counting the intervening days only, while Luke includes the day of the confession and the day of the transfiguration – with six days in between. Additionally, Luke makes it clear that he does not intend to be exact by saying, "about eight days after."

Those chosen by the Lord to accompany Him and witness this event were Peter, James, and John. These three seem to have comprised the inner circle of the apostles. They were with Him at the raising of Jairus' daughter, and were with Him, apart from the other apostles, in Gethsemane on the night of the Lord's betrayal. Luke is the writer who informs us that they went up into the mountain to pray – a constant activity in the life of Jesus.

Matthew and Mark write that Jesus was "transfigured before them," with Luke adding additional information. Luke tells us that when it occurred, Jesus was praying. He also tells us that Moses and Elijah were talking with Jesus about His departure which was to be accomplished at Jerusalem. Luke adds that His disciples (Peter, James and John), were heavy with sleep when the scene began, and that Peter began to speak as Moses and Elijah were leaving.

The transfiguration was something wonderful to behold. The Greek verb used by Matthew and Mark is translated as "transfigured" and means "changed in form." It probably means that Jesus was changed back into a portion of His heavenly glory. Apparently His features remained the same, but there was a tremendous change in His face, garments, and entire person. There was an intense light, an overpowering light, coming from Jesus. Look at how each writer describes it:

> Matthew – "And his face shone like the sun, and his garments became white as light."
> Mark – "And his garments became glistening, intensely white, as no fuller on earth could bleach them."
> Luke – "The appearance of his countenance was altered, and his raiment became dazzling white."

It seems as though the writers were hindered by the language available to them as they attempted to describe the grandeur of what they had seen.

Appearing with Jesus were Moses and Elijah, both the Law and the Prophets being represented by these two great Old Testament figures. Luke tells us they appeared "in glory" and spoke with Jesus. That raises questions. What does "in glory" mean? Does it mean they came from Hades (Paradise), or does it refer to the form in which they were seen? How did the apostles recognize them as Moses and Elijah? Had the description of what these two men looked like been meticulously passed down from generation to generation so that they immediately knew who they were? Did Jesus identify them as Moses and Elijah as He spoke with them? In what kind of form were they? There is a great deal about this event that we just do not know.

As mentioned earlier, Luke is the one who tells us of the conversation between Moses, Elijah, and Jesus. They were talking about His departure that was to be accomplished at Jerusalem. They were talking about His crucifixion. There are a couple of interesting points to be made from Luke's words. The word for departure means "exodus" (the way out). Thus, by His death, Jesus was "going out" of the earth into heaven. At the same time, His death was to be "accomplished" in Jerusalem. "Accomplished" means "to fulfill." By His death, all of the types and prophecies of the Old Testament would be fulfilled, accomplished.

Several different things need to be observed about Peter's proposal. First of all, both Mark and Luke make it clear that Peter really did not know what to say. The three apostles were afraid, amazed, and rejoiced at witnessing this incredible scene. It is easy to understand the different emotions they were experiencing. So Peter spoke up and proposed they make three tabernacles; one for Moses, one for Elijah, and one for Jesus.

A tabernacle was a tent, most often made from cloth, but sometimes constructed from the branches of a tree. It was a temporary dwelling place. This indicates one possible way of viewing Peter's proposal. In his rejoicing at the scene and in his wonderment, it is possible he may have been attempting to prolong it. Luke tells us Peter spoke when "the men were departing." Maybe Peter felt that by providing shelter they would remain. On the other hand, we know from the book of Exodus that a tabernacle had also been built for the honor of God, as a dwelling place of the divine presence. Perhaps Peter's suggestion is best viewed as a way to honor those involved in the transfiguration: Moses, Elijah, and Jesus.

While Peter was speaking, a bright cloud overshadowed them; more specifically, it was diffused and spread over them. The cloud was a symbol of divine presence. Luke tells us that they "feared as they entered the cloud." It is not necessary to search for some deeper meaning to that. They were in the midst of a supernatural occurrence. It calls to mind the pillar of cloud by day and that of fire by night guided Israel through the wilderness.

From out of the cloud comes the voice of God, "This is My beloved Son, with whom I am well pleased, listen to Him." Peter's proposal had placed Moses and Elijah on the same level with Jesus. God's statement set Jesus above all and when they arose they saw only Jesus. That is interesting. Moses and Elijah appeared, only to disappear. Jesus abides. The Law and the Prophets were temporary. The gospel of Jesus is final and eternal. Hebrews 1:1-2 is applicable here, "God, who at sundry times and in divers manner spake in time past unto the fathers by the prophets, hath in these last days spoken unto us by His Son, whom He hath appointed heir of all things, by whom also He made the worlds."

The Discussion of the Vision
(Matt. 17:9-13, Mark 9:9-13, Luke 9:36)

Jesus had strictly forbidden Peter, James, and John from telling anyone what they had seen until Jesus had risen from the dead. Why? The answer would be the same as it was in the previous incidents when Jesus had instructed the individuals involved to tell no man. The miracles would be misunderstood and generate an excitement that would not be founded upon knowledge. Additionally, Peter, James, and John did not yet understand the full significance of what they had seen and heard. After the Lord's death had destroyed the false hopes and His resurrection had made clear His true glory, then they would be better equipped to understand and tell others of what had happened on that mountain. Mark informs us that "they did not understand what the rising from the dead meant."

The apostles continued questioning Jesus about the appearance of Elijah. In their excitement they made a connection between this event and the prophecy of Malachi 4:5, which said, "Behold, I will send you Elijah the prophet before the coming of the great and dreadful day of the Lord."

The scribes were correct in saying the Old Testament predicted Elijah would come and restore all things. Jesus instructed His apostles in this. But the scribes, who were so insistent in offering this prophecy as a ground for rejecting Jesus as the Christ, needed to study the prophecies about the sufferings of the Messiah and see their whole concept of the Christ was incorrect. The prophecy concerning Elijah had already been fulfilled. Elijah had already come; the scribes had failed to recognize him and had rejected his counsel. John the

Baptist, rejected and slain, was the fulfillment of the prophecies concerning the return of Elijah.

While the understanding and faith of the apostles were undoubtedly helped by the explanation of Jesus, there was again the proposition of His death. Here was another prediction. The transfiguration was granted to help them recover from the shock of the first clear prediction. So elated over what they had just witnessed and concerned they would forget what lay ahead, their departure from the mountain was assessed.

The Demoniac Boy
(Matt. 17:14-21, Mark 9:14-29, Luke 9:37-42)

Jesus, Peter, James, and John had departed from the rest of the apostles when they went up the mountain where the Transfiguration took place. Here is evidence of the scribes taking advantage of Jesus' absence to pounce on the rest of the apostles. A man had appealed to them for help in casting a demon from his son and they had failed in their efforts to do so. This gave the scribes opportunity to declare the failure before the public and thus discredit them, and Jesus, by implication.

The multitude that had gathered was amazed and joyful at the return of Jesus at the moment when the defeat and humiliation of the other apostles at the hands of the scribes seemed complete. Jesus calmly walked up to His harassed apostles and scribes, demanding to know what they had been questioning them about.

While there is no comment from the scribes recorded, the father of the boy stepped forward and described the pitiful condition of his son. The King James version says the boy was a "lunatic," a most unfortunate translation. Most say that he was an epileptic, while Mark says that he had a "dumb spirit." The gospels do not affirm all diseases are caused by demons. This is one case, however, where it was. The boy would have fits, throwing himself into fire or water; he would foam at the mouth and grind his teeth. He would wail and scream. This pitiful condition had been upon him since he was a child.

Jesus' response is very interesting. Mark tells us that He answered "them." The Lord's response seems to have involved all who were present. "O unbelieving generation! How long shall I be with you? How long shall I bear with you?" This questioning was to the baffled apostles, to the relentless and vicious scribes, to the father of the boy, and to the multitude. We can feel the frustration of Jesus in His words. When would they learn, when would they understand? Jesus then requested that the boy be brought to Him. When he was brought into the sight of the Lord, the demon further demonstrated its maliciousness by tormenting the child further in a violent fashion. Mark says, "The spirit tare him grievously; and he fell on the ground, and wallowed foaming."

Jesus asked the father a few more questions, and then the father expressed a despairing doubt when he said, "If thou canst do anything, have compassion on us, and help us." Jesus' response is striking and it is emphasized by Mark, "If thou canst believe..." Of course Jesus could help. The only possible lack was not in Jesus, but in the man's faith. Jesus said, "All things are possible to him that believeth." In verse 24 of Mark's account we find, "Straightway the father of the child cried out, and said, I believe; help thou mine unbelief."

> His confession and appeal furnish a model for all prayers. He frankly confessed the common experience of humanity struggling for righteousness and faith and yet sinking in a measure into wickedness and doubt. "Lord I am struggling to believe with all my might, but if I do not believe as much as I should, forgive me and help me to a stronger faith." He claims to possess faith, but does not rest his case on his own merit: he pleads for the mercy of Jesus. He unconsciously reveals a genuine trust in Jesus by this last appeal. The person who does not feel the need of a larger faith, does not possess much faith (R.C. Foster, *Gospel Studies*, Vol. 2, 170).

At his appeal, Jesus rebuked the unclean spirit, and after once more tearing the boy, the demon departed, leaving the boy as though dead. His appearance was so lifeless that most of the crowd thought he was dead. But Jesus took the boy by the hand and raised him up, and all the people were astonished at the majesty of God. Why were they astonished? By putting the event together we can see that astonishing. There had been the failure of the disciples, the attack of the scribes, the pleading of the father, the pitiful plight of the boy, and the wonderful majesty of Jesus in the casting out of this vicious demon.

Later, in private, His disciples asked Him, "Why couldn't we cast out the demon?" Jesus' answer was the lack of faith on the part of the disciples was the direct cause of their failure. Had they possessed more faith they would have been able to accomplish it, but they had not. Jesus also mentioned, "This kind can come out by nothing, save by prayer." This probably refers to the particularly vicious character of this demon, a viciousness emphasized throughout the entire account.

Third Prediction of Death
(Matt. 17:22-23, Mark 9:30-32, Luke 9:43-45)

After these events Jesus and His apostles made their journey from the mountain, upon which the Transfiguration had taken place, "through Galilee." It must have been a leisurely journey, for Matthew says, "While they abode in Galilee" and Mark writes of their "passing through Galilee."

With all that had taken place, it was not possible for Jesus and His apostles to have the privacy necessary for their further instruction. So they took the journey and sought to keep their movements as quiet as possible. There is an interesting statement made by Luke. He wrote, "But while all were marveling at all the things which he did, he said unto his disciples, Let these words sink into your ears…" It is as though Jesus was saying, "Listen to what they are saying now, listen to the praise. It will soon change." All the words of praise were but empty sounds, for He would ultimately be delivered up to die.

The apostles did not understand what Jesus was saying. They did not understand what He meant by "being delivered up" and they could not conceive of how He could let His enemies kill Him. How could the Messiah allow such to happen? They were not ready to accept the obvious meaning of His words, but recognized they could mean nothing else. Much the same thing happens today when people declare a passage of scripture obscure because they are unwilling to accept its plain teaching.

Both Mark and Luke tell us they were afraid to ask Jesus what He was saying. Perhaps they were recalling Peter's protest against a similar statement, receiving a strong rebuke from Jesus. Or maybe they thought if they questioned Him further they would learn more that they did not want to know.

The truth was not concealed from them by God in some miraculous way. The truth was concealed from them because of their clouded understanding and their misconceptions of the Messiah. They could not understand how the Messiah, at least in their view of Him, could allow His death at the hands of His enemies. Even though they did not understand, Jesus' repeated predictions of His death obviously filled them with grief and sorrow.

The Temple Tax (Matt. 17:24-27)

What exactly was this required half-shekel? Was it a temple tax or was it a tax due to the Romans?

> When thou takest the sum of the children of Israel after their number, then shall they give every man a ransom for his soul unto the Lord, when thou numberest them; that there be no plague among them, when thou numberest them. This they shall give, every one that passeth among them that are numbered, half a shekel after the shekel of the sanctuary: (a shekel is twenty gerahs) an half shekel be the offering of the Lord. Every one that passeth among that are numbered, from twenty years old and above, shall give an offering unto the Lord. The rich shall not give more, and the poor shall not give less than half a shekel, when they give an offering unto the Lord, to make an atonement for your souls. And thou shalt take the atonement money of the children of Israel, and shalt appoint it for the service of the tabernacle of the congregation; that it may be a memorial unto the children of Israel before the Lord, to make an atonement for your souls (Exodus 30:12-16).

A dispute existed between the Pharisees and the Sadducees concerning whether or not the payment of this tribute was compulsory or voluntary. Maybe the collectors thought Jesus considered this voluntary, at which point

He would have angered those who thought it to be compulsory. Perhaps they thought Jesus might have considered Himself above it.

Whatever might have been their motive, Peter's answer to the question was, "Yes." When in private, Jesus addressed this issue with Peter before Peter could address it with Him. Jesus' argument was this: if the sons of kings are free from the payment of tribute, then would not He, as the Son of God, be free from paying God's tribute? But, so they would not be totally misunderstood and people think Jesus was teaching it was not necessary to pay this tribute, Peter was instructed to go to the sea. This would have been the Sea of Galilee. There he was to cast a hook into the sea and open the mouth of the first fish he caught; there he would find a shekel. This he could give to the tax collectors as payment for both Jesus and himself.

Discussion of Who Shall Be the Greatest (Matt. 18:1-5, Mark 9:33-37, Luke 9:46-48)

This discussion took place in the city of Capernaum immediately following the temple tax incident. Both Matthew (in the temple tax account) and Mark mention "the house," which must have been the house of Peter. Perhaps we can determine what caused this discussion

Consider what had taken place. There had been the confirmation that Jesus was the Messiah and the promise that Peter would be given the "keys of the kingdom." This could have stirred anew in the hearts of the apostles the dream of future greatness and generated jealousy among them. Jesus had spoken of their need to be willing to die for Him and had predicted the glories of the kingdom to come. That could have produced similar feelings. This discussion had continued among the apostles during the journey from Mt. Hermon to Capernaum. The fact that the tax-collectors had asked Peter to speak for Jesus and that he had presumed to do so may have caused the feelings to flare at the time. Matthew tells us that the disciples came to Jesus with the question. Mark states Jesus asked them about what they had been disputing. Both statements are evidently abbreviated summaries. The disciples came to Jesus asking the question, "Who then is greatest…?" Their question seemed innocent, but Jesus knew their hearts and He answered with a question, "What were ye reasoning on the way?" They were apparently conscience-stricken and "held their peace." On the same journey during which Jesus had again predicted His death, the apostles had been quarreling about who would be the greatest among them.

To answer, Jesus called the twelve close to Him and set forth a basic principle of the kingdom. In the giving of this principle Jesus used a concrete illustration. He took a little child in His arms, set him in the place of the highest honor at His side, and pronounced such a little one as the greatest. He also pronounced a blessing on any who would receive such a little child in His name.

What was the principle? To be first, efface yourself and become last. To be the greatest, become a servant of all. Instead of rebuking their self-first attitudes and their jealousy, Jesus dramatically turned their world upside down and allowed them to figure out just how foolish and wrong their reasoning had been. Not only do humility and service "lead to greatness -- but they are greatness itself." The one who is first in his own thinking will be last in God's estimation and the last in self-seeking (if he is last because he puts Christ first) will be greatest.

When Jesus said, "Except ye repent, or turn..." he meant away from sinful ambitions and toward the true greatness that comes from service and is characterized by the beautiful qualities of the young, unspoiled child. The qualities of humility, trust, the willingness to be taught, the desire to please, to serve--these qualities are pure and unstained in the child and must be in us.

To "receive one such little child in my name" is not necessarily talking about little children physically, but of those who are spiritually as little children, those who possess the characteristics of a child. In affirming the person who receives such a one receives Him, Jesus is again exalting the qualities of humility and service.

The Unknown Worker of Miracles
(Mark 9:38-41, Luke 9:49-50)

It is not known who this fellow was, but he had evidently become a disciple of Jesus at some time. It could have been when the apostles were not with the Lord, for they did not know this man.

If we look at John's statement we can see how the apostles were beginning to think. When we couple this statement with the discussion of who would be the greatest, we can see a problem developing. Because they had the power to work miracles, the apostles had begun to feel that they alone had the right to do so; anyone who did not work in their group had no right to the name and power of Jesus. They had forgotten that Jesus was the Lord and Master and could commission whomever He desired.

The Lord's reply indicates they were not to interfere with such a person. His working of true miracles, in the name of Jesus, showed the fitness of the man for the work. It was seemingly against the man that he did not follow Jesus' immediate company, but there may have been something in the man or in the purpose of Jesus for him that caused this situation. The man was evidently working for the Lord. He could not use the name of Jesus to do miracles and then turn right around and revile Him. Those two extremes do not fit together.

The context shows this man was casting out demons. He could not have been casting them out, an act of hostility toward Satan, and be an agent of Satan at the same time. "A house divided against itself cannot stand."

The Question of Stumblingblocks
(Matt. 18:6-14, Mark 9:42-50)

After what appears to have been an interruption in the discussion of who would be the greatest, the Lord turned to caring for little ones in the faith.

Again the child is the illustration, but Jesus was talking about spiritual matters related to the kingdom.

The Lord emphasized the seriousness of the discussion by mentioning the millstone. Rather than causing a Christian to stumble, it would be better to die. "Occasions of stumbling" refer to the temptations thrown in the way of others that cause them to fall. These need to be expected in this world of sin, but the man who tempts others must answer to God for doing so. This led Jesus to discuss the things within a man that lead him to sin and the comparative value in life. The loss of a hand or an eye is like nothing when compared to eternal life. Gehenna with its fires await those who are earthly.

What exactly is meant by "everyone shall be salted with fire" is difficult to determine. Salt is generally used for preservation and fire is generally used of punishment. So it could mean preserved from destruction (salted) by the suffering (fire) which sin entails and which leads a man to repent. On the other hand it could mean that if a man refuses to heed and be salted by fire here, then he will in eternity be salted (preserved) in the midst of fire (hell) that his punishment may be eternal.

Salt is good and it preserves, but if our lives are devoid of the qualities that make them palatable and worthwhile, then we are nothing but worthless. We have salt in ourselves by adopting and maintaining the attitude of a follower of Christ, by avoiding the things that cause others to stumble and fall, and by maintaining a loving, forgiving spirit toward one another.

The case of the little ones betrayed and saved suggests the touching illustration of the shepherd who seeks, saves, and rejoices over a seemingly insignificant sheep that has been lost. So is God with His erring children.

The statement in verse 10 of Matthew concerning "their angels," when coupled with Acts 12:15, may indicate that each Christian has an angel.

Mistreatment and Forgiveness (Matt. 18:15-35)

In the earlier part of this discourse Jesus showed the seriousness of causing someone to sin and utilized children to make His point. Now He turns the discussion to what an individual should do when sinned against. There is a decided shift in the discussion from the seriousness of sin, and the need to avoid it, to the need for forgiveness. In emphasizing the need for forgiveness Jesus does not in any way minimize the seriousness of sin.

If someone sins against another it is the responsibility of the one who has borne the brunt of that sin to go to the offending brother or sister, tell him or her how they have been sinned against, and seek reconciliation. Interestingly, in Matthew 5:23-24 we find, "Therefore if thou bring thy gift to the altar, and there remember that thy brother hath ought against thee; leave there thy gift before the altar, and go thy way; first be reconciled to thy brother, and then come and offer thy gift."

The question may arise, "Who is to go first?" That misses the point. Jesus taught that the offended is to seek the offender and the offender is to seek the offended. One way or another, the sin is to be resolved. Action is required from both sides.

Initially the offended is to go alone. His purpose is to save the brother from the sin. Therefore, he seeks the best time, place, and approach to save him. If he refuses to hear, reconciliation is still to be sought; but now, two or three witnesses are to be brought. They are there to hear the conversation and seek to aid in the reconciliation. If the witnesses can render a verdict concerning this matter, both the one trespassed against and the one who did the trespassing have the responsibility to hear and be responsive.

If the offender still refuses to hear, then the case is to be brought before the whole congregation. Should he still refuse to correct the wrong, he is to be regarded as a publican and a heathen. That does not mean that the defiant sinner is to be mistreated, but all fellowship, outside of that which is necessary for living, is to be withdrawn from that individual. He would be treated just as the Jews treated a Gentile.

The "binding and loosing" of v. 18 is best explained in the following manner:

> The binding and loosing here mentioned is limited by the context or the subject of which Jesus now treats. Binding represents exclusion from membership. Loosing, the restoration to fellowship in cases of repentance. The church's actions in thus binding or loosing will be recognized in heaven if performed according to apostolic precept or precedent. Hence it is a most august and fearful prerogative (McGarvey and Pendleton, *The Fourfold Gospel*, 436).

Verses 19-20 tell of the incredible power of prayer. As further evidence of the Lord's desire that His followers be united, He promised to be present with them in a special way when they are gathered together in agreement in His name. The numbers are not what is important (two or three), but the cooperation together in the doing of Jesus' Will. The gathering must be "in the name of" the Lord, or by His authority. The cooperation must be in that which is authorized.

The words of Jesus, with His obvious emphasis upon forbearance and forgiveness, moved Peter to ask the Lord to place some sort of limit to help them understand their duty in this area. When Peter asked if he should forgive a brother until seven times he was actually being very liberal, for Jewish Talmudic tradition held that three times was proper. Jesus' answer shows there is no numerical limitation; that was the point of seventy times seven. Jesus was not saying forgive your brother 490 times, but rather to be ready always to forgive. Forgiveness, charity, forbearance; these attributes should know no limits. If a person repents of his sin, he is to be forgiven. Such an answer naturally lends itself to a discussion of the nature of God's forgiveness and leads to the parable that followed.

The situation presented in the parable is that of a certain king who would from time to time take account of his servants. One such accounting revealed a servant who owed him 10,000 talents. It is very difficult to determine the exact amount. The talent may have been made of silver or gold. So, the exact amount could not be calculated. Some have suggested $10,000,000, others $12,000,000, and still others $16,000,000. The man was hopelessly in debt. When he could not pay, the king commanded he be sold, along with his wife and children, and all he had, and payment be made. Even such a sale would not have completely repaid the debt. This kind of sale was legal under the Law of Moses (Lev. 25:39-47, 2 Kings 4:1).

The man showed a willingness to pay, and even though he never would be able to completely alleviate the debt, the king was moved by compassion on the man and promptly released him and forgave him the debt.

The same man went out and found a fellow servant who owed him 100 pence, something like $16, $17, or $20; and demanded payment. When he could not pay, the man had him cast into debtor's prison until payment could be made. He ignored his pleas for mercy and patience, as well as the man's willingness to pay when able.

The cruelty of this servant did not go unnoticed by his fellow servants who informed the king of what he had done. Angered by the man's lack of mercy and unforgiving spirit, the king turned him over to the tormentors until his debt was paid. In the east, torture was used to make debtors confess to possession of goods and property suspected of being hidden. This follow had escaped being sold as a slave only to receive a death sentence by torture for his lack of forgiveness and mercy.

The key words are found in verse 35, "So likewise shall my heavenly Father" and "if ye from your hearts." God will also deliver to the tormentors those who are without mercy and unwilling to forgive, and our forgiveness must be real. It must come from the heart. The magnitude of the debt God has forgiven us makes our debts to each other insignificant. It helps if we remember that.

Unbelieving Brethren (John 7:2-9)

You may recall that John 6 gave the account of the feeding of the 5,000 and the sermon on the bread of life Jesus delivered the next day. Verse 4 of John 6 told these things occurred when the time of the Passover was nigh. John 7:1 summarizes the work of Jesus until we are at verse 2. It is now time for the Feast of Tabernacles. It is six months later. During those six months Jesus had been in Tyre and Sidon, Decapolis and Caesarea Philippi, and occasionally in various parts of Galilee. At this point we see Jesus shift the focus of His ministry. He essentially leaves Galilee and devotes His attention to Judea and Jerusalem.

Let us examine briefly the Feast of Tabernacles.

> And the Lord spake unto Moses, saying, Speak unto the children of Israel, saying, the fifteenth day of this seventh month shall be the feast of tabernacles for seven days unto the Lord. On the first day shall be an holy convocation: ye shall do no servile work

therein. Seven days ye shall offer an offering made by fire unto the Lord: on the eighth day shall be an holy convocation unto you; and ye shall offer an offering made by fire unto the Lord: it is a solemn assembly; and ye shall do no servile work therein (Lev. 23:33-36).

Also in the fifteenth day of the seventh month, when ye have gathered in the fruit of the land, ye shall keep a feast unto the Lord seven days: on the first day shall be a sabbath, and on the eighth day shall be a sabbath. And ye shall take you on the first day the boughs of goodly trees, branches of palm trees, and the boughs of thick trees, and willows of the brook; and ye shall rejoice before the Lord your God seven days. And ye shall keep it a feast unto the Lord seven days in the first year. It shall be a statute for ever in your generations: ye shall celebrate it in the seventh month. Ye shall dwell in booths seven days, all that are Israelites born shall dwell in booths: that your generation may know that I made the children of Israel to dwell in booths, when I brought them out of the land of Egypt: I am the Lord your God (Lev. 23:39-43).

The Feast of Tabernacles came six months before and six months after Passover. It was a most joyous feast, commemorating the time when Israel lived in tents in the wilderness and celebrating the harvest. It was a time of thanksgiving for blessings received. With all the people dwelling in booths, it had a festive atmosphere.

Jesus' brothers wanted Him to go to the feast. Who were "His brethren" from verse 3? They were not His disciples, for they are distinguished from His brethren. The brethren are the sons of Joseph and Mary, half-brothers of Jesus. We learn their names in Matthew 13:55 -- James, Joseph, Simon, and Judas. The disciples mentioned in verse 3 would have been disciples made during earlier visits to Judea and Jerusalem who had been waiting for Jesus to return to the city and openly proclaim Himself as the Messiah. Additional disciples from all regions of Palestine would be in Jerusalem for the feast and expecting Him.

It is interesting that His brothers would charge Him with acting in secret and we might ask why. Certainly the majority of the Lord's work to this point had taken place in the provinces and not in Jerusalem, as would be expected. Also, since the feeding of the 5,000, Jesus had purposely sought seclusion with His apostles, and He had refused to be crowned a king when the crowd wanted to proclaim Him as one.

The lack of belief in Him on the part of His brothers is also interesting. Jesus had indicated as much when He said that a prophet is not without honor save "among his own kin and in his own house." They said in verse 4, "If thou do these things, show thyself to the world." Does this mean they doubted the veracity of His miracles? Does it mean they could not believe their brother was the Messiah because He did not come into Jerusalem, the capital city, and demonstrate His power and might? After Jesus' death, burial, resurrection, and ascension, James would become one of the great leaders in the first-century church.

There were still six months to the Passover, still six months before the terrible agony of the cross. Thus His answer, "My time is not yet come." Complete manifestation at this time could have upset the timetable and hastened what was to occur. As for the brothers, they could show themselves at Jerusalem any time; but not Jesus. Their situation was entirely different. They were not hated by the world; Jesus was. He had laid bare the sins of the world and the world responded with hatred, with the fiercest opposition Satan could muster.

Jesus went to the feast but not according to their timetable. He did not go with the large caravans of people making the journey to Jerusalem. He went later, privately. As the brothers left, Jesus remained in Galilee.

Private Journey through Samaria (Luke 9:51-56, John 7:10)

There is some question whether these passages describe the same journey to Jerusalem. It appears reasonable to say that they do because the late start to the Feast of Tabernacles fits this quick journey through Samaria.

After His brothers had left for Jerusalem, after the regular caravans of pilgrims departed, Jesus secretly began His journey to Jerusalem with His apostles. He would not take the regular route of the pilgrims along the east side of the Jordan River. Jesus took the more direct route through Samaria.

> Taken in its strictest sense, the expression "taken up" (Lk. 9:51) refers to our Lord's ascension, but it is here used to embrace His entire passion. Though our Lord's death was still six months distant, his going to Jerusalem is described as attended with a special effort, ("He steadfastly set His face to go to Jerusalem") because from that time forth Jerusalem was to occupy the position of headquarters, as Capernaum had done, and His withdrawals and returns would be with regard to it. The presence of the twelve alone is sufficient to account for the messengers. He did not wish to overtax the fickle hospitality of the Samaritans by coming unannounced (McGarvey and Pendleton, *The Fourfold Gospel*, 441, 442).

Jesus was coming as a Jew on His way to Jerusalem, not on an evangelistic trip to the Samaritans. As such, He was received as a traveling Jew on His way to Jerusalem to celebrate one of the feasts. Since the Jews and the Samaritans viewed each other with animosity, Jesus was not well received. The two "Sons of Thunder" (Mark 3:17), James and John, seeing the poor reception that Jesus received, requested that He call down fire from heaven to consume those who were rejecting Him. That was not what Jesus was here for, nor was such an action consistent with His character. Jesus rebuked them and moved on to another village.

Jesus at the Feast of Tabernacles (John 7:11-52)

It had been 18 months since Jesus' last visit to Jerusalem at which time He healed the lame man at the Pool of Bethesda. That was at the second Passover of our Lord's ministry. He spent the third Passover in Galilee around the time of the feeding of the 5,000. His prolonged absence made many in Judea anxious for Him to return.

The term "Jews" is used to differentiate between the unbelieving leaders of the Jews and their followers, who were the Lord's bitter enemies, and the common people who heard Jesus gladly.

The crowds were alive with anticipation of Jesus' arrival and debated among themselves about Him. Some thought Him to be a good man and came to His defense; others thought Jesus was a deceiver. These discussions were conducted quietly, however, for fear of the Jewish leaders who opposed Him.

The feast lasted eight days. Sometime between the third and fifth days, Jesus arrived and went into the temple to teach -- into the very stronghold of His enemies. Those who opposed Him were amazed at His knowledge. The great schools of religion were found in Jerusalem, but Jesus had attended none of these. Scholars of the day were expected to have passed through one of these schools, thus preparing to teach. How could this uneducated man possess such knowledge? Jesus' answer shows that He received His wisdom and doctrine from above and not from man. If they had the disposition to willingly receive and obey His teaching, they would have known the truth. Jesus did not come bearing His own message and doctrine seeking glory for Himself. He came bearing the Father's message and seeking His glory.

Verse 19 goes back to the original controversy in Jerusalem and brings up the desire to kill Him. In John 5, Jesus had healed a lame man in Jerusalem on a Sabbath day. John 5:16-18 said, "And therefore did the Jews persecute Jesus, and sought to slay Him, because He had done these things on the Sabbath day. But Jesus answered them, My Father worketh hitherto, and I work. Therefore the Jews sought the more to kill Him, because He not only had broken the Sabbath, but said also that God was His Father, making Himself equal with God."

By bringing the plot to kill Him to the forefront, Jesus was accomplishing several things. (1) He was preparing His disciples for His death. (2) He was giving His enemies time to change their terrible purpose. (3) He was letting them know that He knew of their plots against Him. (4) He was showing their hypocrisy. They charged Jesus with breaking the Law and used that as an excuse to seek His death while their plots to kill Him were contrary to the very intent of the Law.

Evidently some of the common people were not aware of these plots against Jesus and saw His charges as preposterous, so much so that they attributed His comments to demon possession. But Jesus did not let their foolish comments deter Him from His teaching.

The Law did say that no work was to be done on the Sabbath day. The Law also said that a male child was to be circumcised on the eighth day. If the eighth day happened to fall on a Sabbath, the child was still circumcised. It was a case of a specific command making an exception to a general law. If they looked at the act of healing on the Sabbath as a mere work, then it probably could be considered a breach of the Sabbath law. But if they would look at the nature of the act and all the Law had to say about compassion and mercy, then they would judge the healing righteously and see it was amply justified.

There were some present in the crowd who were aware of the plots to kill Jesus. As they listened to Him teach so openly and expose the hypocrisy of the leaders, they began to wonder why He was being permitted to teach. Was it possible the leaders knew Him to be the Christ? But then again, they knew where Jesus was from, or at least they thought they did. He was from Nazareth of Galilee.

They thought they knew all about Jesus, but they did not know. They did not know of His divine origin. After all, they did not know God, and not knowing God, they did not know from whence Jesus came. Those listening knew exactly what Jesus meant. They knew He was declaring them to be ignorant of God and they reacted with a vengeance, seeking to lay hold on Him. However, it was not according to God's timetable that Jesus should die yet.

There were many of the common people who did believe in Jesus and pointed to His miracles as proof of His being the Christ. When this came to the attention of the leaders of the Jews, they felt that it was time to take action. They sent the soldiers of the temple guard to arrest Him. Note the following comments concerning verses 33, 34:

> Knowing their attempt to arrest Him, Jesus tells them that it is not quite time for them to accomplish their purpose. They would soon destroy Jesus; after which they would seek Him in vain. Their violence would result in His return to His Father. In the dark days which were about to come the Jews would long for a Messiah, for the Christ whom they had failed to recognize in Jesus. They, too, would desire the heavenly rest and security of the better world, but their lack of faith would debar them from entering it (McGarvey and Pendleton, *The Fourfold Gospel*, 447, 448).

Since they did not understand, many of the Jewish leaders made light of Jesus' words. Would He go to the Jews dispersed throughout the Roman world and teach them? Would He go into hiding? Where could He go so they could not find Him? Where could He go that they could not come?

The last day of the feast arrived and Jesus pronounced Himself the "Living Water."

> If we may trust the later Jewish accounts, it was the custom during the first seven days for the priests and the people in joyful procession to go to the pool of Siloam with a golden pitcher and bring water thence to pour out before the altar, in commemoration of the water which Moses brought from the rock and which typified the Christ. If this is so, it is likely that the words of

Jesus have some reference to this libation, and are designed to draw a contrast between the earthly water which ceases and the spiritual water which abides, similar to the contrast which He presented to the Samaritan woman at Jacob's well (McGarvey and Pendleton,*The Fourfold Gospel*, 448).

While the specific statement of verse 38 is not found in the Old Testament, when considered in the sense of the spiritual blessings of the Messianic age, the idea is most certainly found. There are many passages that speak of the dry and barren ground abounding with water and becoming fertile (Isa. 35:6-7, 53:2, Prov. 18:4).

Acts 1 and 2 describe the pouring out of the Holy Spirit on the apostles and the promise of the Holy Spirit to all believers.

Many of the people, hearing our Lord's words, were convinced He was the Prophet, like unto Moses (Deut. 18:15). Others were convinced He was the Christ. But there was division, for others objected to these conclusions with questions about His lineage and the place of His birth. Their objections were the result of their ignorance concerning these matters. Some were angered enough to seek Jesus but did not.

Remember the Jewish leaders had sent officers of the temple guard to arrest Jesus. When they returned without Him they were asked why they had failed in their mission. Their answer, "Never man spake like this man." The response of the Pharisees was, how could Jesus be the Christ if none of the Pharisees or rulers of the people had believed on Him. Only the ignorant masses were able to be deceived.

Nicodemus, while not declaring himself a believer in Jesus, still called for an honest hearing and investigation of Jesus. He was met with the snide remark, "Art thou also of Galilee? Search, and look: for out of Galilee ariseth no prophet." They all went to their own homes to think about their next step and to observe the Sabbath.

The Woman Taken In Adultery (John 8:1-11)

This particular passage has been the object of considerable debate concerning its genuineness and its authenticity. Genuineness relates to whether it is a work of John or of someone else. Authenticity relates to whether it is a true account or not. Even those who question its genuineness seem to accept its authenticity; they believe it to be a true story of an incident in the life of Jesus. But several do not accept it as genuine because many of the ancient manuscripts omit it and others put it at the end of the gospel. Some ancient writers, such as Chrysostom and Cyril, do not mention it in their commentaries, therefore it must not have been part of John's original work. However, the evidence in favor of its genuineness and its authenticity far outweighs the evidence against it.

After the dispute with Nicodemus, the members of the Sanhedrin dispersed and went to their homes. Jesus went to the Mount of Olives. This is a mile-long ridge of limestone hills that parallels the eastern elevation of Jerusalem. It is separated from Jerusalem by the Kidron Valley with an elevation of 2,680 feet. Gethsemane, was a garden east of the temple area, across the Kidron Valley, at the base of the Mount of Olives.

Early the next morning Jesus went into the temple, sat down, and began to teach the people. The scribes and Pharisees believed they had found a way to entrap Him. They brought a woman, caught in the very act of adultery, and presented her before the Lord. The Law of Moses was very specific concerning the punishment for the offense. Leviticus 20:10 states, "And the man that committeth adultery with another man's wife, even he that committeth adultery with his neighbor's wife, the adulterer and the adulteress shall surely be put to death." Deuteronomy 22:22 tells us, "If a man be found lying with a woman married to an husband, then they shall both of them die, both the man that lay with the woman, and the woman: so shall thou put away evil from Israel."

Their question to Jesus was, "What do You say?" This was done to give the scribes and Pharisees a means by which to accuse Jesus. If He did not demand death, as the Law required, they would accuse Him before the people of setting aside and disobeying the Law of Moses. If He did demand death, they would accuse Him before Pilate as a traitor to Rome, who had issued a decree that no Jewish court could pass the death sentence without the consent of the Roman governor. Jesus did not answer them with a single word. Instead, He stooped down and began to write on the ground with His finger.

The fact this woman had been caught in the very act of adultery, and yet she was the only one brought before Jesus, shows the hypocrisy of her accusers. The Pharisees wanted Jesus to enforce the Law on this woman but not out of concern for the Law. They wanted to ensnare the Lord. They certainly had not brought the guilty man to be judged who was equally guilty in the eyes of the Law.

Jesus' lack of an immediate response caused the scribes and Pharisees to press Him for an answer. The Lord's silence was deliberate. As they grew more vehement in their demand, their embarrassment would be greater when Jesus exposed their hypocrisy. The silence of the Lord made the crowd focus on the problem and caused the Pharisees to be emboldened. When Jesus finally spoke, His words carried tremendous convicting power.

"He that is without sin among you, let him first cast a stone at her." Then Jesus bent back down and wrote once more upon the ground.

What power was contained in the words of Jesus! Deuteronomy 17:7 taught that the witnesses were to cast the first stone. Jesus did not deny or set aside the Law; He brought out a principle they had overlooked. The one who carried out the Law must be free of the same crime, lest by stoning they condemn themselves as being worthy of the same fate. Jesus did not mean that a person must be perfect before he undertakes the task of punishing for a crime. If that were the case, law and order would cease to exist. But He meant to thrust into their hardened hearts, as well as the hearts of the crowd gathered around, a realization of their own sinfulness. Surely Jesus' words impressed upon them all the fact that freedom from outward sin does not necessarily mean inward purity and sinlessness.

With tremendous force the words of Jesus cut the hardened consciences of the scribes and Pharisees. The older leaders recognized the force of His statements first, and they departed, properly chastised. Eventually all followed suit, from the oldest to the youngest, until there was Jesus and the woman. He said to her, "Woman, where are those thine accusers? Hath no man condemned thee? She said, "No man, Lord. And Jesus said unto her, Neither do I condemn thee: go, and sin no more."

Jesus did not dismiss this woman's sin in any way. He did not pronounce forgiveness as He did the woman in Simon's house. Jesus told her to go and give proof of repentance by changing her life.

The Light of the World (John 8:12-59)

After dealing with the accusers of the woman taken in adultery, Jesus was still in the temple where He made a profound statement. He often used physical objects familiar to His listeners to teach spiritual lessons. Perhaps He had in mind the seven-branched candlestick in the Holy Place as He declared, "I am the light of the world: he that followeth me shall not walk in darkness, but shall have the light of life."

> When Jesus came into the world, He found Himself in a world of darkness – darkness into which it had been plunged by sin. Isaiah's prediction was fully realized, for he had said, "Behold, darkness shall cover the earth, and gross darkness the peoples" (Isa. 60:2). There was a desperate need for light that would illuminate the lives of men, a light by which man could clearly determine what was right and what was sin. Now the long-awaited light was beginning to dawn. John had said of Him in the Prologue of his Gospel, "In him was life; and the life was the light of men. And the light shineth in the darkness; and the darkness apprehended it not" (1:4 & 5). That divine light which was claimed for Jesus, and claimed by Him, would be the light which would kindle a brilliant glow in every man's soul (v. 9). It was a light that "the darkness apprehended not", that is, understood or comprehended it not (Alford, also Dods); or, overcame it not (Westcott). Both interpretations are true, but which idea John intended is not clear. The darkness of the world did not comprehend the light in Jesus, nor did the darkness "put it out", overcome it. History testifies that it has shone through the centuries, and experiences testifies that it shines even now.
>
> All that Jehovah had been to His people in the wilderness as he led them by the cloud by day and the pillar of fire by night, so Jesus would be to those who would follow Him. As the word had been to the psalmist (a lamp unto his feet and a light unto his path (Ps. 119:105), and when opened had given to him light

and understanding (v. 130), so Jesus would be to all who should look to Him. And He would be even more, for in following Him one would have the "light of life" – eternal life.

When preparing to open the eyes of the man born blind, Jesus said, "When I am in the world, I am the light of the world" (9:5). In this statement the definite article is omitted; while in the world He is light to it. Later He said, "Yet a little while is the light among you. Walk while ye have the light, that darkness overtake you not: and he that walketh in darkness knoweth not whither he goeth. While ye have the light, believe on the light, that ye may become sons of light" (12:35-36a). He would have men become sons of light, luminaries reflecting His own light in their lives, walking in the light, that they might have the life He came to provide.

Jesus concluded His claim as light when He said, "I am come a light into the world, that whosoever believeth on me may not abide in the darkness" (12:46). The world was in darkness; but if His claim be true, man would be at that time, and is today, without excuse for abiding in darkness. Jesus claimed to be the embodiment of all spiritual and moral light, light brought into the world from without, brought from above, that men might have the light of life (Homer Hailey, *That You Might Believe*, 73, 74).

In response to the Lord's declaration, the Pharisees, perhaps remembering a statement made by Jesus some eighteen months earlier, "If I bear witness of myself, my witness is not true" (John 5:31), denied the validity of His testimony. "You are bearing witness of yourself, therefore your witness is not true."

Jesus' response was profound. No man is competent to testify of his own nature because he does not know it fully, nor its end. But Jesus, with full knowledge of His eternal existence, was qualified. Only Deity can testify of Deity.

The Pharisees viewed Jesus only from the fleshly standpoint, and that was tainted by their own wickedness and ambition and desire to condemn. Jesus came to save, not to condemn. Yet any judgment He would render would be true, for it would be rendered in conjunction with His Father. Deuteronomy 19:15 called for the testimony of two witnesses to establish the guilt of an individual. Any testimony of Jesus concerning Himself would meet the criterion, for it would also be the testimony of His Father.

Unable, or unwilling, to separate the fleshly from the spiritual, the Pharisees asked, "Where is thy father?" In other words, bring this other witness here that we might hear him. How difficult it must have been for Jesus to be teaching these life-giving spiritual lessons and having the leaders of His people refuse to understand! If they had allowed themselves to perceive the true identity of Jesus they would have understood the true identity of His Father.

This exchange took place in the treasury, the place where the chests for offerings were placed. It was located in the Court of the Women, the most public place in the temple, very near to the place where the Sanhedrin met. Even though the Lord's word's were arousing the fury of the leaders, and where arresting Him would have been easy, no man took Him. It was not yet the right time.

Verse 21 is very similar to Jesus' statement in John 7:33-34. Those who refused to believe on Jesus, even though they would seek the Messiah, would die in their sins. The Lord would ascend to heaven; those who die in their sins will not go there.

> Since Jesus has predicted an eternal separation from them by reason of their dying in their sins, they answer with bitter malice, "Will he kill himself?" The Jews held that those who committed self-murder went into the depths of Hades lower than any faithful Jew could go. Thus they seek to reverse the meaning of Jesus; if they are to be in different places in eternity, then Jesus must be about to send Himself by suicide into the depths of eternal punishment. This vicious and hypocritical answer also attempts to answer His revelation of their plots to kill Him (R.C. Foster, *Gospel Studies*, Vol. 3, 12).

Once again, Jesus made the point that they refused to believe in Him because they were earthly and He was not. It was not a question of it being impossible for them to believe, it was a question of their refusing to believe. Because of their refusal to believe Jesus was the Promised One, they would die in their sins.

We can sense the frustration of the Pharisees as they demanded, "Well, who are you then?" They wanted Jesus to state His divinity, and in a manner that they could justify His stoning. The Lord's response was, "I have already told you."

Verse 26 is very interesting. Up to this point Jesus had been revealing Himself and the Father; now He would reveal His enemies as well, and those things He spoke would be of the Father. Still, the Pharisees refused to understand that Jesus was speaking to them of God.

Next, Jesus referred to His crucifixion and how His identity would become plain to them in His death and the time after. It is obvious that some in the crowd were trying to understand and believe, while others maliciously refused to do so. Surrounded by His enemies and those seeking His life, Jesus gave calm assurance of His belief that He was not alone. The Father was with Him and He would prevail, for He was always doing those things that were pleasing to the Father. There were those present who heard Jesus and believed.

It is only through obedience to the truth that one can be made free from sin and death. This declaration of Jesus, along with others He made, was taken by the Pharisees in a physical sense. They refused to believe that they had any need of being made free. They were Abraham's seed, under bondage to no man – even though the entire nation was under Roman subjection, at the time.

Once again Jesus showed them that He was not referring to physical bondage, but spiritual bondage. They were under bondage to sin, slaves of it.

To paraphrase the Lord, He said, "I know that outwardly and carnally you are Abraham's seed, but not inwardly and spiritually. You are the enemies of God's Son, seeking to kill Him. You are acting as though another is your father."

The intensity of this exchange between Jesus and the Pharisees is obvious. They replied, "But Abraham is our father," and Jesus responded with, "If you were Abraham's children you would act as Abraham did. But you seek to kill me for telling you the truth which I have from God. Abraham would not have done so." They were acting as though their spiritual father was someone entirely different.

As we look at verse 41, the Pharisees recognized that Jesus was not speaking of physical parentage, but spiritual. He had shown they were not acting as Abraham, so they went back even further. They were spiritually begotten of God – and not from some idolatrous fornication.

Jesus' response was powerful, "If you were of God you would love Me, for I am of God and came from Him." They did not understand the word of Jesus because their minds were filled with the thoughts of the devil. Jesus continued on to declare that they were showing who their real father was by their hatred of the truth and their desire to commit murder. Who were they following? Certainly not Abraham! They were showing themselves to be children of the devil. Satan had brought sin into this world. Satan introduced lies and murder, and those were the things in which the Pharisees were involved. They hated Jesus because He told them the truth.

Notice the statement of Jesus in verse 46, "Which of you convinceth me of sin? And if I say the truth, why do ye not believe me?" The point is, if they cannot convict Jesus of sin, then what He said is true. Why didn't they believe Him? Jesus is affirming His sinlessness and they could not point out a character flaw. Jesus had no consciousness of sin. If He was not the Son of God, how could He have made such a statement? If He was another prophet, even the preeminent prophet of all time, there would have been some sin, some missing of the mark, at some point in His life. If He was not the Son of God and yet made that statement, then He was either helplessly deluded or not a good man.

The point is, if God had been their true spiritual father, then they would have received the words of Jesus and believed. But, they were of the devil, their spiritual father, and believed not.

In light of the devastating logic of Jesus, the Jews responded with a lame charge, "Say we not well that thou art a Samaritan, and hast a devil?" Calling Jesus a Samaritan was meant to be malicious and bitter. One commentator wrote that is was the same as saying, "Thou art born of spiritual fornication; thou art of an outcast race; thou art an alien from the worship of God." And, declaring Jesus of possessing a demon, was an old charge. The Pharisees had implied it when they accused Him of casting out demons by the power of Beelzebub (Matt. 12).

To paraphrase the Lord's response to these charges, "You may dishonor Me, but I did not come seeking my own glory. I came seeking the glory of God. Howbeit, the one who accepts and receives My words will never taste of eternal condemnation."

The Jews took Jesus' words as confirmation of their accusations. Their argument was this: God's Word spoken to Abraham and to the prophets did not prevent them from dying; Jesus was saying that if a man were to keep His words, he would never see death. Was He claiming to be greater than Abraham, now dead, and the prophets, also now dead? Just exactly who was Jesus making Himself out to be?

> Jesus answers with a clear-cut statement of His Deity: "My Father that honoreth Me; of whom ye say, that he is your God." He then reiterates the reason they do not understand and believe His claim: because they do not know God. The reference to Abraham meets their question as to whether He was greater than Abraham and affirms again His Deity. God had promised Abraham that all the nations of the earth shall be blessed in him; in light of this prophecy Abraham had seen the day of its fulfillment in Jesus. By faith Abraham looked forward to the fulfillment of the glorious promise made to him and so far as it was possible for him to do so, he saw the time of Christ's coming into the world to save mankind (R.C. Foster, *Gospel Studies*, Vol. 3, 16).

The Jews persisted in a literal interpretation of Jesus' words. Allowing for error, they said, "You are not even 50 years old, are you telling us you have seen Abraham?"

"Before Abraham was, I am!" Using the very name of God revealed to Moses (Ex. 3:13, 14), Jesus identified Himself with God and implied eternal existence; not just existence before Abraham, but eternal existence. Now, they perceived their opportunity to deliver Him as a blasphemer – making Himself God. So, they took up stones to stone Him, but somehow Jesus hid Himself and passed through the crowd.

A Man Born Blind (John 9:1-41)

It is difficult to determine if this particular event is a continuation of the account of Jesus in Jerusalem for the Feast of the Tabernacles, or if it took place two months later at the Feast of Dedication. John 10:22 has led many to believe it was the latter time.

The exact place in the city of Jerusalem where this event took place is not known. Since we are told in verse 8 that this man "sat and begged", it is possible that it occurred near the main entrance to the temple.

As Jesus passed by, He saw a man who had been born blind. The disciples' question indicates a common belief among the Jewish people of that time. It was generally believed that all suffering was retributive, the result of sin. Some have suggested the disciples' question indicates a possible belief in the transmigration of souls; that perhaps this man had sinned in some previous existing state. However, there is nothing to indicate that they knew this man had been blind from birth. They thought he was blind as the result of some sin in his life, or perhaps his parents had sinned before he was born and his blindness was punishment to them (Luke 13:1-5 is an example of this belief).

Jesus' answer is not to be understood that the man or his parents were not sinners. It means their sins were not the cause of his blindness. Rather, it was part of the providential plan of God and through Him the mighty power of God was going to be revealed. The fairness of God may be questioned, but consider what happened with this man in verses 35-38.

The Lord's public ministry was not going to last indefinitely. There was a period of activity ("while it is day") that would be terminated by His death ("the night cometh"). These works needed to be done while He was in the world. Although Jesus is ever the "light of the world," the "light" needed to shine brightly while He was here to illuminate the darkness which permeated the world.

Jesus' method of cure was unusual in this case. He spat upon the ground, made clay with the spittle, and anointed the man's eyes. Then He gave him instructions to go and wash in the pool of Siloam. Why? (1) It served as an aid to the man's faith. He could feel that something was being done for him. (2) It helped draw attention to the miracle by raising the expectation of any who saw it. (3) It served to bring Jesus into conflict with the Sabbath traditions of the Jews, both by applying the clay and telling the man to go and wash it off. The man obeyed the Lord, washed, and was cured.

> Siloam, (sent; specially a sending of water through an aqueduct). A pool at Jerusalem; probably identical with Shiloah, the waters of which go softly (Isa. 8:6), and the pool of Shelah, which was by the king's garden (Neh. 3:15). Josephus says that it was situated at the extremity of the valley of cheesemongers, near a bend of the old wall beneath Ophlas, i.e. Ophel. The name is preserved in the Birket Silwan, which occupies the general site of the ancient pool. It is a rectangular reservoir, 58 feet long, 18 broad, and 19 deep, built of masonry, the western side of which has considerably broken down (*Davis Dictionary of the Bible*, 763).

A man born blind who suddenly received his sight would have a slightly altered appearance. That, coupled with the impossibility of the cure, probably led to the confusion of his neighbors. "Isn't this the fellow who was blind and sat and begged?" they asked. "It looks like him," some replied. Others said, "It is him!" The man himself said, "I am he!" This led to the obvious question, "How? How did you receive your sight?"

The man's response was direct, containing the facts with no embellishment. "A man that is called Jesus made clay, and anointed mine eyes, and said unto me, Go to the pool of Siloam, and wash: and I went and washed, and I received sight." This led his neighbors to consider how the Pharisees would react. After all, the cure had been wrought on the Sabbath day, and Jesus had made the clay. The Pharisees also asked the man how he had received his sight. He told them, "He put clay upon mine eyes, and I washed, and do see."

The reaction demonstrates not all Pharisees viewed Jesus in the same way. Some stressed the Jewish tradition in the face of the evidence and declared Jesus to be a sinner because He had done this on the Sabbath day. Others recognized the significance of the miracle and declared that a sinner could not do these things. Thus, there was division concerning Jesus among the Pharisees.

They turned again to the man and said, "What sayest thou of him, that he hath opened thine eyes?" The healed man's response was, "He is a prophet." This was a logical deduction and showed the man's faith was progressing as he listened to the arguments of the Pharisees and considered the ramifications of what had happened.

The discussion was not going the way the Pharisees wanted. So, they chose to deny the cure. They denied the man had been born blind and had miraculously received his sight. They even called for his parents and asked them, "Is this your son, who ye say was born blind? How then doth he now see?" The parents answered affirmatively the first two questions, "We know that this is our son, and that he was born blind." However, they demonstrated a lack of courage concerning the third question. The Pharisees had already let it be known, however informally, that confession of Jesus would result in removal from the synagogue, the focal point of Jewish life. Fearing that, the parents said, "We don't know how he got his sight, but he is of age, ask him. He will speak for himself."

Verse 24 and the statement of the Pharisees are being considered. "Then again called they the man that was blind, and said unto him, Give God the praise: we know that this man is a sinner." Two different views of this statement are possible. (1) They were urging the man to be as pious as they were. They had judged this Jesus to be a sinner and this man should go along with them. (2) They were seeking to get a confession that he and Jesus had concocted this story together. It is said that the phrase, "Give glory to God" was an adjuration for a criminal to admit what he had done.

No matter how the statement of the Pharisees is understood, this healed man would have none of it. He reinforced the facts. He didn't know Jesus well enough to say if He was a sinner or not, but he did know he had been blind, and now he could see, and there was nothing fraudulent about it.

Unable to answer the honesty of the healed man, the Pharisees again ask for the details about the miracle. His response is inspiring to all those who have faced skeptics. He asked them two questions which laid bare their hypocrisy. First, "I have told you already, and ye did not hear: wherefore would ye hear it again?" and "Will ye also be His disciples?" This man's faith in Jesus, whom he had not known at all prior to this event, was quickly growing under the questioning by the Pharisees.

This upset the Pharisees. "We are Moses' disciples," thus seeking to make it appear that Jesus was in some way opposed to Moses. "We know that God spake unto Moses: as for this fellow, we know not from whence He is." This is a powerful argument. If they could make it appear that Jesus was forsaking Moses and the healed man was that doing the same thing by following Him, they would label the Lord as an apostate.

What courage this formerly blind beggar demonstrated as he exposed the ungodly motives of the Pharisees. "Why herein is a marvelous thing, that ye know not from whence he is, and yet he hath opened mine eyes." This remark was dripping with sarcasm. These were the Pharisees, the scholars of the law, and they could not draw the right conclusion from the evidence before them.

"Now we know that God heareth not sinners: but if any man be a worshipper of God, and doeth His will, him He heareth. Since the world began was it not heard that any man opened the eyes of one that was born blind. If this man were not of God, he could do nothing." In the history of the world, who else had done the things that Jesus did? There was only one logical conclusion that could be reached. Jesus had to be from God. It is interesting that this simple man, healed by Jesus from a lifetime of blindness, reached the same conclusion that Nicodemus had reached in John 3:2, "Rabbi, we know that thou art a teacher come from God: for no man can do these miracles that thou doest, except God be with him."

First the Pharisees had denied the man had been blind. Then they found themselves being outsmarted by this simple and honest man. So they attempted to use his blindness as proof of the fact he was a sinner. As a sinner, how could he possibly teach them? With that, they cast him out, meaning that he would not be welcome in the synagogue or the temple. Jesus, hearing of the persecution of the man, sought him. He had been cast out of that which pertained to Moses, but Jesus was leading him into fellowship with the Son of God. "Dost thou believe on the Son of God?"

"Who is he, Lord, that I might believe on him?" The idea of knowing the Son of God, the long-awaited Messiah, was beyond his wildest dreams.

Here, to an outcast from the synagogue, Jesus identified Himself as the Son of God. The man believed and worshipped Jesus. Only God deserves worship, and this is an example of Jesus acknowledging that He is God even as He is man.

The discussion between Jesus and the healed man has all the earmarks of having been private. Next Jesus turned His attention to the crowds and made a comparison between the physical blindness of the man who had been healed with the spiritual blindness of the Pharisees. Some of the Pharisees made the application and said, "Are we blind also?"

Augustine said that if they had realized their blindness then they would have sought the Light and He would have taken away their sin; but as now they boast of their vision, their sin remains because they reject the Light.

The Good Shepherd (John 10:1-21)

In verse 6 of this passage we find the word "parable." This word is "paroimia", which literally means "beside the way." Thus, we are talking about a speech not of the common or direct form, i.e. a similitude or allegory. A parable is a simple story told to illustrate a moral truth using things familiar to the hearers. An allegory uses symbolic figures and actions to set forth truths or generalizations. It is important not to stretch the symbolism of an allegory beyond what it was intended to convey.

This flows from the previous event in which the Pharisees had cast out the man born blind. Many Old Testament prophecies speak of the false shepherd that would arise and lead God's flock astray. Other prophecies spoke of the true Shepherd of God, the Messiah. The Pharisees were part of the fulfillment of the first type of prophecy, while Jesus was the fulfillment of the second. To His Jewish listeners the details of this allegory were familiar:

> The sheepfolds of the East are roofless enclosures, made of loose stone, or surrounded by thorn bushes. They have but one door. Jesus, the true shepherd, came in the proper and appointed way, thus indicating His office as Shepherd. A thief steals by cunning in one's absence; a robber takes by violence from one's person. The Pharisees are represented as both. They stole the sheep in the Messiah's absence, and they slew the Messiah when He came. They did not come in the ways ordained of God.
>
> Several small flocks were sometimes kept in one fold. The door was fastened from the inside with sticks or bars by the porter, who remained with the sheep during the night, and opened for the shepherds in the morning.
>
> In the East, sheep are not driven, but led, and each sheep has and knows its name. Disciples are also led. There is no rough road or thorny path which the feet of Jesus had not first trod. The Pharisees had put forth the beggar to be rid of him; the true shepherd puts forth to feed.
>
> The mingled flocks are separated by the calling voices of the shepherds. They know the voice of their shepherd and will not follow a stranger. The control of the Pharisees was not like this (McGarvey and Pendleton, *The Fourfold Gospel*, 468,469).

The people did not understand the words of Jesus. The concept of loving care and nurturing was foreign to the way the Pharisees conducted themselves, causing a lack of understanding in the people. They approached things from a completely different standpoint.

Because of their lack of understanding, Jesus gave the people a twofold explanation. First, Jesus presented Himself as the Door, the entranceway into peace and security, protection and nurturing. Those who came before could be referring to the false teachers among the Jews who had led them astray, including the Pharisees. They could be the false messiahs who arose periodically.

Second, Jesus presented Himself as the Good Shepherd, in contrast to the hireling. Obviously the hireling's main concern would not be the welfare of the sheep, but his own personal gain. The Good Shepherd would lay down his life for his sheep. Such was Jesus. Also, the "other sheep I have which are not of this fold" mentioned in verse 16 are the Gentiles. They would also be drawn to the Lord, having the opportunity to hear the gospel and obey. Ultimately the separation between Jew and Gentile would be dissolved and there would be one fold.

What is the significance of the Lord's claim to be the Good Shepherd?

One of Jesus' claims so often overlooked as a claim to the messianic expectation is the reference to Himself as the "good shepherd"... Jesus here uses an allegory of a shepherd and his flock; this was familiar to all His hearers. But His claim to be the good shepherd is more than an allegory used to teach an immediate lesson. The claim identified Him with the Old Testament prophecies which pointed to a shepherd-king who was to come...

In these claims Jesus was identifying Himself with the messianic promises of old. A few of these are here introduced to show the relation between what Jesus said of Himself and what the prophets had said of the shepherd who would come. Isaiah, the great prophet of hope, comforted the people who would be captives in Babylon with the assurance that good tidings of God's presence in their midst would be proclaimed to them. The Lord Jehovah would be in their midst as a mighty one, ruling and rewarding His saints; and 'He will feed His flock like a shepherd, He will gather the lambs in His arm, and carry them in His bosom, and will gently lead those that have their young.' (Isa. 40:11) This was to be the assurance and comfort of the exiles; Jehovah would be their shepherd.

Ezekiel, the prophet to the people of the captivity in Babylon, sees the fulfillment of Isaiah's prophecy in Jehovah as the shepherd of the people in this foreign land. In glowing words Ezekiel portrays Jehovah as searching out His people in and beyond the captivity and bringing them back, Himself being their shepherd and judge. But this picture blends into the messianic hope as Jehovah looks beyond the time of His own shepherding of the sheep to that time when He would care for them through David, His shepherd. 'For thus saith the Lord Jehovah: Behold, I myself, even I will search for my sheep, and will seek them out...I myself will be the shepherd of my sheep, and I will cause them to lie down...Behold, I judge between sheep and sheep, the rams and the he-goats...And I will set up one shepherd over them, and he shall feed them, even my servant David; he shall feed them, and he shall be their shepherd. And I, Jehovah, will be their God, and my servant David prince among them... And ye my sheep, the sheep of my pasture, are men, and I am your God, saith the Lord

Jehovah.' (Ezek. 34:11-31) In this prophecy Jehovah is portrayed as shepherd over His people as He brings them back from the Babylonian Captivity, caring for and judging them. But from this He looks to that time when through David, the 'prince-shepherd', He would shepherd them as their God. Jesus claimed to be the good shepherd. He claimed that it was the Father in Him doing His works. Therefore it was God in Christ, judging and gathering, feeding and shepherding His sheep…

The prophet Zechariah presented a vivid contrast between the false shepherds and the good shepherd. Because of the lies of the false shepherds, the prophet said of the people, 'Therefore they go their way like sheep, they are afflicted, because there is no shepherd. Mine anger is kindled against the shepherds (the false shepherds), and I will punish the he-goats (the leaders); for Jehovah of hosts hath visited his flock, the house of Judah, and will make them as his goodly horse in battle' (Zech. 10:2,3). He hears 'a voice of the wailing of the shepherds! For their glory is destroyed' (Zech. 11:3). As a further contrast, Jehovah presents the false and the true as he cuts off three false shepherds, 'for my soul was weary of them, and their soul also loathed me'. The good shepherd was then sold for thirty pieces of silver; in that day the covenant that God had made with the two nations was broken, and the brotherhood between Judah and Israel was dissolved (Zech. 11:4-14). This indicates that when the good shepherd would be sold for thirty pieces of silver, the old order, the covenant of the fleshly brotherhood, would pass away. With its passing Jesus would gather into one flock both Jews and Gentiles (Homer Hailey, *That You May Believe*, 53,54,55).

The death of Jesus would be voluntary. He would do what He did in complete harmony with the Will of His Father.

Again the words of Jesus caused division and controversy among His hearers. Some viewed what He said as lunacy, and attributed it to His being possessed of a demon – hardly a new charge. Others said a man possessed by a demon could not work the miracles that Jesus had done.

The Mission of the Seventy (Luke 10:1-24)

This event seems to follow the activities of the Lord in Jerusalem connected with the Feast of the Tabernacles in John's account. John tells us that Jesus was in Jerusalem for the Feast of the Tabernacles and for the Feast of Dedication (John 10:22). Some hold that the healing of the man born blind took place at the time of the Feast of Dedication. However, it seems more reasonable that in the two months interval between the feasts, Jesus spent His time evangelizing Judea, along with this event.

Because of the great need and the limited amount of time for the work to be done, the Lord commissioned seventy of His disciples to go into the area of Judea and Perea, and prepare the way for His personal arrival by their teaching. They were sent two by two for mutual encouragement and for added power to their testimony, just as Jesus had done with the Twelve.

Why seventy? We understand the twelve apostles corresponding to the twelve tribes of Israel; but why seventy? Different reasons for this number have been suggested. For instance, some have suggested the seventy elders appointed by Moses (Number 11). Others mentioned the Sanhedrin with its seventy members and presiding officer in imitation of Moses and the seventy elders. Still others have suggested that it was seventy because this occurred at the close of the Feast of Tabernacles and seventy bullocks were offered during that feast. A large number was needed, and Jesus chose seventy of the most capable of His disciples.

They were to go as "lambs in the midst of wolves," an obvious reference to the growing hostility toward Jesus and His followers among the Jewish leaders. This was a dangerous mission indeed. They were to go quickly, not making the normal preparations for such a journey. They were to take no money, no extra shoes, and not waste their time in extended social pleasantries. They were to trust God and depend upon those to whom they were sent for their necessities.

When they came to a village, they were to seek lodging in whatsoever house they entered, first determining if the residents of that house were receptive. Finding them to be so, they were to remain there as long as they worked in that area. The disciples were not to waste their time engaging in the customary social activities of the East, nor seeking to find better accommodations. Whatsoever was set before them they were to eat and drink, not viewing it as charity, but as wages, "for the laborer is worthy of his hire." They were to eat just what they were given. They were to be neither greedy nor fastidious. It is easy to sense the urgency and the great need Jesus felt. Indeed, "The harvest truly is great, but the laborers are few."

They were given the power to heal the sick, and were entrusted with the message that "the kingdom of God is come nigh unto you." They were to preach about Jesus and His work. They were to use the power given to them to substantiate what they were saying. They were to prepare the area for the impending arrival of Jesus Himself. This was to be done in the cities that received them.

To the cities that did not receive them, they were to issue a stern warning. Shaking the dust of that city off of their feet as an indictment against it (Mark 6:11, Acts 13:51), they were to tell them that the kingdom of God was nigh. Again, Jesus issued a scathing denunciation of certain Galilean cities that had rejected the truth in spite of the abundant evidence they had seen in the form of miracles. Indeed, if such ancient cities of iniquity as Tyre and Sidon had witnessed the miracles that Chorazin, Bethsaida, and Capernaum had seen, they would have accepted the truth and repented. But these cities of the Jews that should have been prepared and receptive, rejected the truth in the face of abundant evidence.

These seventy disciples were acting as emissaries of Jesus. To hear them was to hear Him. To receive them was to receive Him. On the other hand, to despise His emissaries was to despise Jesus, and to despise Jesus was to despise the Father who had sent Him.

It is interesting that Chorazin is only mentioned in the New Testament here and in Matthew 11:21, a similar passage. Many miracles were worked there by Jesus but we do not have the details of them. This emphasizes the truthfulness of John's statement in John 20:30, "And many other signs truly did Jesus in the presence of His disciples, which are not written in this book," and in John 21:25, "And there are many other things which Jesus did, the which, if they should be written every one, I suppose that even the world itself could not contain the books that should be written."

As they returned the seventy were rejoicing in their work, even having had the ability to cast out demons by the authority of Jesus. When the Twelve had returned their reaction was more subdued due to the death of John the Baptist.

Verse 18 is interesting and two interpretations are plausible. One, the eternal Jesus saw Satan fall from heaven when he was cast out by God because of rebellion (Jude 6), and this was a portent of the casting out of demons by the disciples through the power of Jesus. Second, in the victory of His disciples over the demons, Jesus saw evidence of the final victory over Satan and his plans. Verse 18 is paraphrased in the following ways, "You are elated at your victory over the demons, and are proud of your spiritual powers. Beware of spiritual pride. There was a time when I saw Satan himself fall from heaven owing to this sin." Also, "You are overjoyed at finding that demons are subject to you; that is no great thing. I once saw their sovereign cast out of heaven itself, and their subjection was involved in his overthrow."

Certain that the disciples of Jesus were physically protected on this mission, verse 19 contextually refers to the forces of evil. Rather than rejoicing over this power they had received, they should rejoice over the fact that they were faithful servants of the Lord, and as such, had their names written in heaven.

While the leaders and the scholars of the Jewish nation had, for the most part, rejected Jesus and the truth He taught, this faithful band of followers had accepted and believed. The affection Jesus had for His followers is evident in His words. While the aristocratic scholars had failed to accept Him, Jesus had all things from His Father. The leaders did not know who the Son was, but the Father did; and they did not know the Father, but the Son did. And those to whom Jesus revealed both the Father and Himself could know if they would believe.

Such were His disciples. They had been blessed to hear and see things that many prophets and kings had desired to see through the eyes of faith.

The Good Samaritan (Luke 10:25-37)

Jesus was evangelizing in Judea and Perea in the period between the Feast of Tabernacle and the Feast of Dedication. As was often the case, the Lord was teaching a group of people in a location. It has been suggested that it was near Bethany because of Jesus' habit of using local customs to teach a lesson and Bethany was on the road from Jerusalem to Jericho. While Jesus was teaching, a certain lawyer stood to draw attention to himself and to indicate he had a question to ask or a comment to make.

Lawyers were a very learned group of scholars, usually Pharisees, who specialized in the exposition of the Law. Being different from the scribes who copied the Law, the lawyers expounded upon it orally. Some think Matthew and Mark use "scribes," and Luke uses "lawyers." They are one and the same.

This particular individual asked the question, "Master, what shall I do to inherit eternal life?" to tempt or make trial of Jesus. As an expounder of the Law, we cannot say there was maliciousness to his question. Talking about the Law and studying it was what this man did. His question dealt with eternal life and suggests he was a Pharisee – a group noted for their belief in the resurrection. Jesus' response placed the burden upon the lawyer himself. He was a specialist in the Law. What did the Law say?

His answer was from Deuteronomy 6:5 and Leviticus 19:18. The statement from Deuteronomy 6 was a natural answer for the lawyer to give. It was recited every morning and evening by the Jews and was written on their phylacteries.

> Phylactery – A prayer band consisting of short extracts from the law of Moses, and worn on the forehead or on the arm. (Matt. 23:5) The phylactery eventually assumed the form of a small case, made of parchment or black sealskin. The one for the forehead contained four compartments, in each of which was placed a strip of parchment inscribed with a passage of scripture. The four passages were Ex. 13:2-10, 11-17, Deut. 6:4-9, 11:13-21. It was fastened with straps on the forehead, just above and between the eyes. The other case, which was bound on the left arm, contained but one compartment, in which a strip of parchment was placed bearing the same four quotations from the law (*Davis Dictionary of the Bible*, 461).

The second, from Leviticus 19:18, was perhaps not so frequently quoted, but a beautiful passage, which, along with the other, comprised the basis of the Law.

Jesus commended the lawyer's answer but also made a fine distinction. His answer was correct, but a person had to do more than say it; he had to do it.

Why did the lawyer feel the need to "justify" himself in asking the question, "Who is my neighbor?" as pointed out in verse 29? Perhaps it was because the Lord had answered his question skillfully and he felt foolish in having asked it. Or perhaps it was because what he knew to be the truth and the way he was living did not match. Whatever might have been his reason, it set the stage for one of the greatest and most beloved of Jesus' parables. Some contend that Jesus is recounting history here, but it seems to have all of the earmarks of a parable. Either way the lesson is clear.

A certain man (obviously a Jew) was on his way from Jerusalem to Jericho. It may be asked why the trip from Jerusalem to Jericho, a trip northeast, is described as "down?" The reason is simple. Jerusalem sits on the backbone of a mountain range, approximately 2600 feet above sea level. Jericho, 18 miles away, sits in the depression of the Jordan River valley, approximately 1300 feet below sea level. So in 18 miles there is a drop of close to 3900 feet. It was not unusual for men to be attacked along this route.

> About two miles from Jerusalem it (the road) passes through the village of Bethany, and for the rest of the 18 miles it passes through desolate mountain ravines without any habitation save the inn, the ruins of which are still seen about half way to Jericho. This district from that time till the present has been noted for robberies, and Jerome tells us that the road was called the "bloody way" (McGarvey and Pendleton, *The Fourfold Gospel*, 476).

The man was robbed, stripped of his clothing, wounded, and left half dead on the road. Three individuals came upon the man. The first two, a priest and a Levite, both saw the man and passed by on the other side of the road and offered no assistance whatsoever. Maybe there were reasons for their lack of assistance because it was a dangerous place. Perhaps they viewed his situation as hopeless. Whatever their reasoning, it was not worthy to be mentioned.

Then another man came by, a Samaritan, the hereditary enemy of the Jew. He saw the injured man and had compassion on him. As far as human reasoning goes, this man would have had a better reason to pass by without helping than the other two. The injured man was a Jew, he was a Samaritan – hence, no obligation. That is how the lawyer would have interpreted the Law. He could also have encountered trouble at home for helping a Jew. As the Jews felt about the Samaritans, so too did the Samaritans feel about the Jews. But he did not do that. He saw a man in need and he helped him. He dressed his wounds, set him on his own animal, and took him to an inn where he took further care of him. The next day he departed but left money for additional care and promised more if it was needed.

We would obviously think that the answer about the neighbor would be anyone who needs help. But Jesus turned it from "Who is my neighbor?" (or "Who am I obligated to love?") to how love itself is embodied. Jesus answered the question by demonstrating the humility and compassion of love. Remember when Jesus told the lawyer, "Thou hast answered right: this do, and thou shalt live"? Jesus was showing again, by this parable, that the Law was not just for studying and arguing; it was for living.

Mary and Martha (Luke 10:38-42)

Here we receive insight into the character of the two sisters of Lazarus, Mary and Martha.

It is one of the most exquisite among the treasures which Luke alone had preserved; and the coincidence between it and John 11 with regard to the characters of the two sisters, the incidents being totally different, is strong evidence of the historical truth of both (Plummer, *Commentary on Luke*, 290).

But the characteristics of the two sisters are brought out in a very subtle way. In Luke the contrast is summed up, as it were, in one definite incident; in John it is developed gradually in the course of a continuous narrative. In Luke the contrast is direct and trenchant, a contrast (one might almost say) of light and darkness. But in John the characters are shaded off, as it were, into one another (Lightfoot, *Biblical Essays*, 38).

The certain village that Jesus entered was Bethany (John 11:1) and the home of Mary and Martha. We are told that Martha "received" Jesus into her house, treating Him as a guest. Mary sat at His feet, treating Him as the Teacher. Martha, going about serving food to our Lord, gave little time to listening to Him. She was distracted, going in different directions as she worried about serving Jesus. Mary sat at the Lord's feet and listened to what He had to say, even to the point of arousing Martha's anger. Martha said, "Lord, does thou not care that my sister hath left me to serve alone? Bid her therefore that she help me." She does not blame Jesus for Mary's failure to help, but implies Jesus' lack of caring to lend her help.

In response, Jesus rebuked Martha, gently, by repeating her name. Martha was hustling and bustling about physical things, and those are important. Only one thing is needful and that is food for the soul, spiritual sustenance. Mary had chosen the good part, seeking first the kingdom of God and that was the best choice to make.

Discourse on Prayer (Luke 11:1-13)

Jesus taught His disciples to pray by example (as in this particular case) and by precept (Matt. 6:7-15). At this time Jesus was praying in a "certain place." If this event is in the correct chronological order, then it follows closely with the visit in Bethany and would have taken place somewhere in the vicinity of Jerusalem. Seeing Jesus praying prompted at least one of the disciples to make a very important request, "Lord, teach us to pray." This disciple also remembered how John had taught his followers to pray.

The model prayer Jesus used here is very similar to the one found in the Sermon on the Mount in Matthew 6:9-13, but it is not exactly the same. The King James Version renders it practically identical but the manuscript evidence for it to be translated that way is very weak. Here are the general manuscript differences:

Matthew	Luke
• Our Father	• Father
• Who art in heaven	
• Hallowed be thy name	• Hallowed be thy name
• Thy kingdom come	• Thy kingdom come
• Thy will be done as in heaven	
• So on earth	
• Give us this day	• Give us this day
• Our daily bread	• Our daily bread
• And forgive us our debts	• And forgive us our sins
• As we also have forgiven	• For we ourselves also forgive
• Our debtors	• Everyone that is indebted to us
• And bring us not into temptation	• And bring us not into temptation
• But deliver us from the evil one	

The simplicity and brevity of this prayer makes it a wonderful model for us. Notice that God is addressed as Father and not addressed as "The Lord God of Israel." There is a universality of teaching here. Also, He is not addressed as Almighty, Creator, Ruler, or any other appropriate designations, but the comprehensive term "Father." At the same time, "Father" brings to the forefront love and relationship.

The same prayer shows God is to be given reverence, homage, and respect – "Hallowed be thy name." God's name must be up held with majesty, purity, and praise. In our prayers we must first recognize the relationship God has with all His children and glorify His name.

When this prayer was uttered, it was fitting to say, "Thy kingdom come," because it had not yet come. The idea was to identify their interests with the interests of the kingdom. It was God's Will that must be done.

"Give us this day our daily bread." This was a recognition of complete dependence upon God, and remembering this in all of our prayers serves to keep that dependence ever before us.

> The asking each day for the bread of the day carries with it efforts on our part to earn our daily bread. We are to work for it. When we pray for the kingdom to spread, we obligate ourselves to work for the spreading of the kingdom; so when we pray for our daily bread, we are pledging ourselves to cooperate with God through all the laws He has given for the production of bread (H. Leo Boles, *New Testament Commentaries, Luke*, 230).

"And bring us not into temptation." We will be tempted, and it is right to pray that the temptations will be few and that we will be able to bear them. 1 Corinthians 10:13 assures us that we will not be tempted above that which we are able to bear.

The Gospel of Luke has been called the Gospel of Prayer because of the emphasis upon the prayer life of Jesus and the instructions in regard to prayer. This parable is very similar to that of the unjust judge (Luke 18:1-8). Both are recorded by Luke. They offer good illustration of the proper method of interpretation of parables; i.e., to seek for the fundamental principle taught rather than attempt to make each detail fit. Persistence in prayer and the assurance of an answer to prayer are the fundamental principles. The conduct of the man who, at first, refused to accommodate his neighbor was churlish. The verb is not the one to lend on interest as a matter of business, but to lend as a friendly act. The man did not refuse because he did not want to lend the bread, but because he did not want to be troubled. All this is scenery and no part of the fundamental meaning of the parable. The key to the parable is found in v. 13, "If ye then, being evil, know how to give good gifts unto your children: how much more shall your heavenly Father give the Holy Spirit to them that ask him?" (R.C. Foster, *Gospel Studies, Vol.3*, 43).

Verses 9-10 give us assurance that God hears our persistent prayers. When Jesus used the verbs "ask," "seek," and "knock," they are in the present tense and denote continuous actions; keep on asking, keep on seeking, keep on knocking. Why the need for persistence? Persistence in prayer accomplishes a number of things. (a) It helps to develop faith if we pray properly. (b) It motivates us to action on our part. (c) It causes us to shape the prayer on the anvil of our knees until it is brought into harmony with God's Will. (d) It causes us to examine ourselves.

Denunciation of Pharisees (Luke 11:37-54)

There are differences of opinion concerning this Pharisee and the purpose of his invitation. Some feel that he was just a Pharisee who had a friendlier disposition toward Jesus than the others and merely wanted to have Him as a guest at a meal. Others, and I am more inclined to this view, hold that it was an attempt to remove Jesus from the crowd and entangle Him in a fresh discussion. There is no doubt they were after Jesus by this time and plans were being formulated to bring about His death. The Lord responded forcefully, which would seem to indicate again the ill will of the Pharisees, again.

The invitation was extended and Jesus accepted it. When He sat down to eat, the Pharisee marveled that Jesus did not wash first. He marveled because of the elaborate system of utterly meaningless washings and cleansings that had been instituted by the various rabbinical schools, all of which had come from the simple directions in the Law concerning cleanliness. According to the traditions of the elders, the Pharisees washed their hands before eating each meal, and if they had been in a public place where they might have been touched by some unclean person, they were known to wash their entire body. Jesus did not keep these man-made practices.

Even though Jesus was a guest in the house of this Pharisee, He spoke unsparingly in condemnation of the traditions preventing the Pharisees from accepting the truth. While Jesus would make many of these same comments in Matthew 23, there are subtle differences that show these comments were made on different occasions.

The Pharisees had many outward, ceremonial acts that they performed, presenting quite an impressive display of religiosity. Jesus charged them with making the outside clean but neglecting the inside. To be a godly, man both the inside and the outside had to be clean. It was foolishness to think they could please God by cleansing the material while leaving the spiritual polluted and full of corruption.

In verse 41, Jesus was saying to give of one's self, love, mercy, and compassion—and such inward purity would cleanse the outward.

> The translation here should run, but rather give the things that are in them as alms, etc. The thought of the contents of these cups and dishes here is evidently in the Lord's mind. 'Ah!' He seems to say, 'what you Pharisees and your schools of formalism indeed want is knowledge of that great law of love' (the law Jesus was ever teaching in such parables, for instance, as that of the good Samaritan). 'I will tell you how really to purify, in the eyes of God, these cups and dishes of yours. Share their contents with your poorer neighbors.' Let them do one single loving, unselfish act, not for the sake of the action itself, not for any merit inherent in it: but out of pure good will towards others, and their whole inward condition would be different (*The Pulpit Commentary, Vol. 16*, 307).

Jesus pronounced woes upon the Pharisees. In the matters of tithing they were scrupulous and exacting, even to giving a tenth of mint (a garden plant like spearmint), rue (a shrub of about two feet used for flavoring wine and medicinal purposes) and all manner of herbs (generally garden plants used primarily for flavoring). It was good they did this – it was not condemned. Jesus said, "These ought ye to have done." The "woe" was pronounced because they were careless and neglected the weightier matters of the law, such things as judgment and love. This is reminiscent of Matthew 9:11-13, "And when the Pharisees saw it, they said unto His disciples, Why eateth your Master with publicans and sinners? But when Jesus heard that, He said unto them, They that be whole need not a physician, but they that are sick. But go ye and learn what that meaneth, I will have mercy, and not sacrifice: for I am not come to call the righteous, but sinners to repentance."

In verse 43 the Greek for the word seats is singular, meaning "chief seat" and refers to the semi-circular bench elevated at one end of the synagogue and facing the congregation. They wanted the top spot in the public eye and all of the reverential salutations, titles, and praise of men. They wanted to stand out and be praised everywhere for their piety and scrupulous devotion to the Law. It was this attitude that Jesus pronounced "woe" upon them.

In Numbers 19:16, anyone who touched a grave was rendered unclean for seven days. Jesus said the Pharisees were like graves hidden from view. When men walked over them, not being aware that they were there, the individuals were defiled. In much the same way, people were defiled through association with the Pharisees, injured and corrupted by their influence without even being aware that it was happening. Let's notice some comments concerning "Lawyers:"

> It did not follow that all these professed jurists were of the Pharisee sect; some, doubtless, were Sadducees. It seems, however, probable that the greater proportion of these professional teachers and expounders of the Law did belong to the Pharisees. The oral and written Law, based upon the comparatively simple Mosaic code, had now become the absolute guide and director of the whole life of the people in all its smaller details. The various copyists, lecturers, teachers, and casuists, who debated the many doubtful points constantly arising in the perplexing and elaborate system, were all known under the general term "scribes". The lawyer was the scribe who had especially devoted his attention to the unravelment of the difficult and disputed questions which arose in the daily life of the people.
>
> This lawyer was certainly, considering the company he was associated with, of the strictest sect of Pharisees. This person could not believe that this able Rabbi from Galilee – for that they must all, after the morning's discussion, have allowed Jesus to be – could include him and his holy order in his terrible denunciations, the truth of which the learned scribe not improbably discerned (*The Pulpit Commentary, Vol. 16*, 308).

The "burdens grievous to be borne" placed upon the people were the religous leaders' interpretations added to the written law. They made it harder than God ever intended it to be, leaving nothing to the judgment of the individual, but regulated everything with a man-made rule. It appears, however, that by their interpretations they managed to exempt themselves from the burdens they imposed upon the people.

The sepulchers were hollowed out of the rock in the sides of cliffs and hills. These lawyers went to great lengths to decorate the entrance to the tombs of the prophets, showing the great honor they had for these men of God who had been slain by their forefathers. In actuality they were walking in the footsteps of their fathers. Their fathers had rejected the word of God through these prophets. They were rejecting the word of God through Jesus and seeking to kill Him. What utter hypocrisy!

In verse 49, "the wisdom of God" may refer to Jesus Himself; or may refer to the general trend or tenor of several Old Testament prophecies (such as 2 Chron. 24:19-22, 36:14-16). By adding the word "apostles", Jesus is coupling them with the Old Testament prophets to demonstrate the continuing revelation of God and the continuing rejection of it by the Jews. That generation who was now hearing the final phrase of God's revelation – the fulfillment of all that had gone before - and that had the fullest opportunities, was following in the footsteps of those who had preceded them. They did not learn from the disobedience of their forefathers. They were doing the same thing.

Abel was the first recorded martyr in God's Word (Gen. 4:1-8). Zachariah, the son of Jehoiada, was the last. He was the last because his murder is recorded in 2 Chronicles 24:20-22, the last book of the Old Testament according to the Jewish order of the scriptures. So, going from one to the other, the entire spectrum of Old Testament martyrs is contained. All had been looking forward to the coming of the Messiah. All had been pointing toward its fulfillment, which was happening before their eyes, and that generation continued to reject God's truth.

The "key" that opened the door of knowledge mentioned in verse 52 was Christ. The Pharisees had it within their power to turn the whole nation to Jesus because of their position of leadership and teachers. However, they not only rejected the truth themselves, they threatened and berated the common people who showed a willingness to believe.

In verses 53 and 54, Jesus had laid bare the hypocrisy of the Pharisees, and their attempt to depict Jesus as rejecting Moses had failed. Now they are protrayed like fighters who have lost their heads and come out swinging wildly. They are firing question after question at Jesus trying to get Him to say something that they might be able to use against Him. It was not a matter of seeking the truth; it was a matter of "laying in wait for Jesus, seeking to catch something out of His mouth, that they might accuse Him."

Warning against the Fear of Men (Luke 12:1-12)

While all of this was taking place in the home of the Pharisee, a great multitude was gathering. In their eagerness to see, hear, and be near Jesus, they were pressing in on each other. Jesus had much to say to these people by way of warning. Some of it was a repeat of things Jesus had said at other times, such as in the commission to the twelve and the Sermon on the Mount. First, He spoke to His disciples.

"Beware of the leaven of the Pharisees, which is hypocrisy." Hypocrisy is pretending to be what a person is not. It is deception of real character and feeling. The Pharisees were guilty of presenting themselves as pious, devout, spiritually-minded leaders of the people, when in reality many of them were more concerned with appearances than truth. They performed their religious rites and traditions to be seen of men, and not out of loyalty and love for God. Their motives were wrong.

Being a follower of Jesus would result in persecution, and there would be the temptation for some to hide their faith in Him. But true faith cannot be hidden; it does not allow the one who possesses it to remain quiet. It is of such a nature that it must be proclaimed from the housetops.

Yes, there would be fear among the disciples when persecution came; that was natural. However, the one to truly fear was not man. The worst thing a man can do is kill another man. The hand of man does not reach into the grave. God does. God is the One who is to be feared, for His hand reaches into the grave and eternity. Man cannot send a single person to heaven or hell.

Two farthings would be equivalent to less than two cents today. A person could purchase five sparrows for that amount in the days of Jesus. Yet these sparrows, of such little value in the eyes of man, were not forgotten by God. No matter what the disciples of Jesus might be called to undergo, they could take comfort that God was watching over them.

The fear of being cast out of the synagogue and the disgrace that would come with it was a temptation for the disiciples. If they denied Christ, it would mean they would be disgraced in the presence of the entire angelic band. When they stood and confessed the Lord before men, regardless of the consequences, Jesus would confess them in the presence of the angels.

There would be times when the Lord's disciples would be brought before the leaders of the Jews and others. They would be urged to deny Jesus and to attribute His miraculous works to a diabolical agency (blasphemy against the Holy Ghost), but they must remain strong. It was possible for a disciple in the first century to be tempted in this area. To prevent this from happening, Jesus admonished them to rely upon the Holy Ghost. Along this line, think of Stephen in Acts 7, Peter's defense before the Sanhedrin, and Paul before Felix and Agrippa.

The Parable of the Rich Fool (Luke 12:13-21)

One of those in the multitude who heard Jesus deliver such a powerful warning against the fear of men (as embodied in the Pharisees) took this opportunity to ask Jesus to arbitrate a dispute he was having with his brother. Under the Law of Moses, when an estate was being divided, the elder brother received 2/3, while the younger brother received a third (Deut. 21:17). It is not known if this was the younger brother complaining or the elder brother who had not received the 2/3 portion that was to be his according to the Law. Jesus' response concerning covetousness shows it was the root of the problem.

The request made of Jesus was indicative of an erroneous view concerning His mission and purpose. The people generally saw it as earthly, related to material things, but Jesus was seeking to turn them from the earthly, and the lust for those things, to the spiritual and heavenly. He was not here to act as an arbiter or judge in secular matters.

Covetousness made one of the brothers say "divide" and it made the other say "no." Covetousness is an unlawful desire for the property of another, a greedy and unlawful desire for anything. It is expressly called idolatry in Colossians 3:5. How silly it is to be so desirous of material goods when all the goods in the world cannot lengthen a man's life or preserve it in any way.

The parable itself shows that all the earthly possessions of the man did not save him. In fact, his earthly possessions led to his condemnation because of his attitude toward them. He wasn't dishonest. His wealth was apparently gained honestly from the fruitfulness of his lands. His abundance was so great that he did not have sufficient room to store his goods. So he tore down his old barns, built bigger ones, and decided to take it easy: "Thou hast much goods laid up for many years; take thine ease, eat, drink, and be merry." The man was demonstrating a perverted sense of what was important as well as selfishness. Six times the man used the pronoun "I," and said nothing about what could be done for others. His love of his possessions was shown by the use of the pronoun "my" five times.

God called this man a fool. He was a fool because (a) he devoted all of his attention to gaining earthly goods; (b) he hoarded instead of giving and sharing; (c) he did not think of his duty to God or his fellowman; (d) he thought he could feed his spirit with earthly things; (e) he forgot, or never considered, that death ends earthly pleasures (no matter how abundant they might have been) and brings judgment.

All of the goods that he had accumulated while on earth would be left behind for other people. Perhaps even to have someone say, "Master, speak to my brother, that he divide the inheritance with me."

Exhortation to Trust God (Luke 12:22-34)

The next portion of the Lord's discourse at this time followed the warning against covetousness. Why should there be covetousness when material things will not prolong life or provide security and happiness but trusting in God does? Much of what Jesus said at this time was already presented in the Sermon on the Mount, but a new crowd and a different set of circumstances warranted Jesus repeating them at this time. We are told that Jesus spoke these things directly to His disciples, but nothing is said if it was in private. Remember, there was a multitude gathered, and while Jesus was speaking to His disciples, He was teaching lessons that all needed to hear.

We must not allow the focus of our lives to be on the material and physical. We cannot feed our spirit with material goods; it just does not work. We have need of those things and just as God cares for the ravens, providing for their necessities, He cares for us. All the worrying about physical things and all the emphasis placed upon them cannot add one second to our lives.

Verse 26 argues from the least to the greatest. To add a little to life is a small thing with God, but to give life and sustain it, to give the fruits of the field and the animals for food -- that belongs to the greatest exercise of infinite power. The point is to trust God and keep our priorities straight.

Jesus used "the lilies of the field" to show the folly of anxiety over clothing and other things. The lilies, a wild flower cut down with the grass of the field, did not spin nor toil, yet they were more beautifully arrayed than even

Solomon in all his splendor. God did it. Are we not more worthy than they? Have a firm faith in God and do not be disturbed over the material things in life. They are important, yes, but not the most important. Worldly people are continually trying to get pleasure and satisfaction from their possessions. They will not find it there. God knows what we need and He has promised to take care of His children. Seek God first, make Him the focus of life, and He will care for us. A good reminder is Psalm 37:25, "I have been young, and now am old, yet have I not seen the righteous forsaken, nor his seed begging bread."

Verses 32-34 are uplifting. As the Good Shepherd, Jesus addressed the people with a term of endearment, "little flock." When God is put first in our lives there is nothing to fear. It is God's delight to "give us the kingdom." At that time the kingdom (the church) had not yet come; but it would, with all of its privileges and blessings. Priorities need to be right. Do not hoard material possessions as if satisfaction and security are to be found in them; do good with them, distribute to those who have need. In so doing we are laying up treasures that do not decay, treasures that fail not in heaven, and riches that cannot be stolen. The treasure and the heart go together. That which we treasure most, must be spiritual.

The Parables of the Waiting Servants and the Wise Steward (Luke 12:35-59)

The purpose of both of these parables, as well as the accompanying remarks, was to teach the need for preparedness, the need to always be watchful and ready. The parable of verses 35-38 is found only in Luke. While it would be most unusual for the master to serve the servants, it probably refers to the peculiar and special blessings to be enjoyed by disciples who persevere unto the Lord's return. The point of the second parable is simple. The person who is prepared avoids loss and must be ready.

In verse 41 Peter questions the parameters of the application. Was it only for the Apostles, or was it broader, "even unto all?" His question brought about the third of the Lord's parables at this time and He emphasized personal responsibility. Each follower has the responsibility to see to his own faithfulness as a steward. What was presented was the case of one who not only failed in his stewardship, but abused it. Jesus introduced punishment for unfaithfulnes in contrast to the blessings for faithful service that He had been discussing. Each one is held accountable for faithful stewardship according to their knowledge and opportunity.

In verses 49-56, Jesus was speaking of the "fire" of division and strife that came into the world with His coming. His coming excited men and stirred up their passions, causing division and discord. Look at the opposition of the Pharisees to Jesus. The fire having been kindled, what was there for Jesus to do: to suffer and die. Jesus said, "I have a baptism to be baptized with." As a man, He was distressed by the anticipation of the suffering that was awaiting Him.

Jesus spoke to them of the difficulty being His disciple. He came to overcome evil with good, but that is a conflict in which the good must suffer. His warfare was not a struggle against Rome, but a struggle against the evil within and around them. As long as such evil exists, so do the divisions.

If those who heard Jesus were capable of reading the signs of nature, why were they not capable of reading the signs of what was happening all around them spiritually? All the Old Testament had revealed in anticipation of Jesus' coming and the events up to John the Baptist were happening. Why could they not see? Verses 57-59 act as a summary.

Discourse on Repentance (Luke 13:1-9)

There were those present who gave voice to a popularly held view that calamity is the direct result of grave sin on the part of those involved. The case of some Galileans, whose blood Pilate had mingled with their sacrifices, were in Jerusalem at the time of this event. Nothing is known about what prompted Pilate to have them killed. Pilate had brought troops to Jerusalem at the times of the great feasts and Galilee was a hot-bed of the Zealots. Put it all together and it is probable that this was some uprising of Galilean rebels during a feast in Jerusalem. The fact that these Galileans were killed as they offered a sacrifice in the temple probably represented a particularly cruel and bloody suppression. But such occurrences were not unusual in the latter days of the Roman oppression.

In His response, Jesus did not give the popular view any credence and introduced the eighteen individuals who were killed when the tower of Siloam fell on them. Did this mean that they were greater sinners than all the others who dwelt in Jerusalem? No! Siloam was a village located across the brook Kidron southeast from Jerusalem on the lower slope of the Mount of Olives. The "tower of Siloam" means the "well-known tower" surrounded by the buildings of the town. Instead of speculating about the death of those individuals being the result of direct divine wrath, they needed to remember all men are sinners and all must repent or perish. Eternal separation from God is what matters.

What was the point of the parable Jesus spoke at this time? It was to demonstrate the patience of God with a sinful people.

> The severity of His warning of God's justice upon all who refuse to repent, is joined with the reminder of how long God has been pleading with the nations and with that generation. The fig tree represents the nation; it seems to mean the individual also. The three years is part of the background. A fig tree was supposed to bear fruit in three years. If it failed then, it was considered useless to wait. Some mystical interpreters suggest this means the three years of Christ's ministry, but the Jewish nation had been unfruitful many years before and the destruction was not till 40 years later (R.C. Foster, *Gospel Studies*, Vol. 3, 59).

Discussion Concerning the Sabbath and the Coming Kingdom (Luke 13:10-21)

This is the last time Jesus is pictured in the gospel accounts teaching in the synagogues, and the hostility of the Pharisees was probably responsible for that. This event appears to have taken place somewhere in Judea.

Jesus displayed courage by being in this synagogue preaching! From John 9:22, the hierarchy of the Jews in Jerusalem had already issued an edict that if any man should confess Jesus to be the Christ, he was to be put out of the synagogue. Obviously, that edict had to have been made by the rulers of the synagogues. Now Jesus Himself was in this synagogue.

A woman, obviously a Jewess for she had access to the synagogue, was present. For eighteen years she had suffered from an affliction that rendered her unable to straighten up and caused by a demon; she is said to have had a "spirit of infirmity."

While Jesus was teaching, He saw and spoke to this woman. He called her to come, laid His hands upon her and said, "Woman, thou art loosed from thine infirmity." She was able to stand straight, perfectly released from her torment. This miracle was unsolicited. It was wrought immediately, and she glorified God.

By calling this woman forward, Jesus had focused the attention of those gathered in the synagogue upon her. He put pressure upon the ruler of the synagogue, whose duty was for all things to be done decently and orderly. It is interesting that this ruler sought to attack Jesus by attacking those who came to be healed on the Sabbath day. There is no indication the woman had come for that purpose but that was the approach taken. If the people did wrong by coming to be healed on the Sabbath, then obviously Jesus did wrong by healing them on the Sabbath day.

Jesus responded sternly in His rebuke of the ruler and those who sympathized with him. "Hypocrites" is what Jesus called them. Most likely, each one of them had led his ox or ass from its stall to be watered that morning and did not consider themselves in violation of the Sabbath law. This whole exchange brings to mind the Lord's teaching in Matthew 12:11-12. How did it get to the point where the leaders missed the mercy that undergirded the letter of the law? The Pharisees were leading the people into spiritual destitution by their man-made rules and traditions. The people were like sheep that wander aimlessly about without a shepherd because their leaders were not properly leading them.

> The response of the multitude shows the inability of the system of religion which the Pharisees had developed to satisfy the hearts of the people; it shows the extent of the popular revolt against the hierarchy. This revolt hastened the desperate determination of the leaders to destroy Jesus; they saw their leadership slipping from their hands. But the rejoicing of the people was not merely negative in turning from a religion which was

barren; it was a positive response to the glory of the Son of God (R.C. Foster, *Gospel Studies, Vol. 3*, 61).

What follows are two brief parables, repeated from an earlier time in the Lord's ministry. The one is the mustard seed that grows to great size from such a small beginning. The other is leaven and the idea that just a little leaven accomplishes a great deal. From such a small beginning would grow the kingdom of God.

The Feast of Dedication (John 10:22-39)

Although no one is certain how Luke and John fit together at all points, there are some things that lead to this time. Both Luke and John give material that is not recorded in Matthew and Mark. This additional information emphasizes the closing period of the Lord's ministry – the time between the close of the Galilean ministry after the feeding of the 5,000 and the final week in Jerusalem. John mentions three different visits to Jerusalem in this time period. They are the Feast of the Tabernacles (7:2), the Feast of Dedication (10:22), and the last Passover (12:1). Luke also mentions three times that Jesus went to Jerusalem during this time frame; 9:51, 13:22, and 17:11. Luke was briefly noting the three visits to Jerusalem which John described in greater detail. John was focusing on the visits to Jerusalem and filling in some missing information. There is a change in time indicated in John 10:22-24 from the discussions recorded immediately before it. From the way Jerusalem is specified, as well as the time of the Feast and the season of the year, it implies at a return of Jesus to Jerusalem after being away from the city since the Feast of Tabernacles.

What is the Feast of Dedication? This is a feast held by the Jews for eight days, beginning on the 25th day of Kislev (December). It commemorates the cleansing of the temple and the dedication of the altar by Judas Maccabees after its desecration by Antiochus Epiphanes ("Illustrious" Antiochus IV), king of Syria.

> Antiochus now issued a decree that all nations in his empire should abandon their own customs and become one people. All the Gentiles and even many of the Israelites submitted to this decree. They adopted the official pagan religion, offered sacrifices to idols, and no longer observed the Sabbath. The king also sent messengers with a decree to Jerusalem and all the towns of Judea, ordering the people to follow customs that were foreign to the country. He ordered them not to offer burnt offerings, grain offerings, or wine offerings in the Temple, and commanded them to treat Sabbaths and festivals as ordinary work days. They were even ordered to defile the Temple and the holy things in it. They were commanded to build pagan altars, temples, and shrines, and to sacrifice pigs and other unclean animals there (1 Maccabees, 1:41-47).

> On the fifteenth day of the month Kislev in the year 145, King Antiochus set up 'The Awful Horror' on the altar of the Temple, and pagan altars were built in the towns throughout Judea. Pagan sacrifices were offered in front of houses and in the streets. Any books of the Law which were found were torn up and burned, and anyone who was caught with a copy of the sacred books or who obeyed the Law was put to death by order of the King. Month after month these wicked men used their power against the Israelites caught in the towns. On the twenty-fifth of the month, these same evil men offered sacrifices on the pagan altar erected on top of the altar in the Temple (1 Maccabees 1:54-59).

This feast was in the winter. So Jesus walked in Solomon's porch, located on the southeast side of the Temple, overlooking the Kedron Valley. It was covered and provided some protection from the weather. Most believe it was called Solomon's porch because the wall of the temple next to the porch was built by Solomon.

This was a national feast day. So, many people, filled with patriotism, were in the city of Jerusalem. The leaders of the Jews took advantage of the situation and tried to force Jesus to make a statement that would give them a reason to execute Him immediately. The statement, "Then came the Jews round Him" seems to imply that they encircled Him, separating Him from His followers, seeking to isolate Him. Then they demanded, "Don't keep us in suspense any longer. If you are the Christ, plainly tell us." They had decided to close their minds to the Lord's teaching, to His miracles, to the evidence of His life. They were seeking to ensnare Jesus in His words and kill Him.

Jesus' response was so powerful! "I have told you."

> He had told them that whatsoever His Father did, He did; that He would, in the place and by the authority of the Father judge all men; that He was the Light of the World; that if they believed not on Him they would die in their sins; that His Father was always with Him; that children of Abraham though they called themselves, they were not free till He made them free; that if a man keep His sayings He shall never see death; that before Abraham came into existence, He is; that He was the door into God's fold; that He was the Shepherd of the sheep; the Good Shepherd, who knew His sheep, and had power not only to lay down His life for them but to take it again (M.F. Sadler, *Sadler on John*, 271, 272).

Jesus had made His identify clear by His words and His works. It was not that these leaders of the Jews could not believe because they were not of

His sheep; it was because they would not believe. The Lord's sheep, unlike the unbelieving Jews, are those who hear His voice and are obedient to His word.

> There is an interesting and significant parallelism in the relationship subsisting between the Lord and His sheep. They (a) hear his voice and (b) follow Him; He (a) knows them; (b) gives them eternal life; (c) assures them that they shall never perish and (d) determines that no one shall ever snatch them out of His hand. The sheep, in hearing the Lord's voice, do much more than merely listen; they hear in the sense of heeding; of responding; in full obedience to His will. In consequence, they "follow" without questioning, His guidance in all matters; and they imitate, as far as it is possible, His disposition and manner of life (Guy N. Woods, *New Testament Commentaries, John*, 219).

No man can take a disciple away from Jesus as long as the disciple meets the qualifications: hears the Lord's voice and follows Him (obeys Him). A disciple can remove himself by no longer hearing and obeying the Lord.

Contextually, Jesus' statement in verse 30, "I and My Father are one," refers to what had just been stated in verses 28 and 29. They are one in purpose, protecting the followers. They are one in essence, possessing the divine nature equally. There are those who say Jesus never claimed to be God, but the Jews of that time knew exactly what Jesus was saying. They thought they had what they needed to put Him to death – blasphemy – because the Lord's statement was in fact an assertion of deity. It doesn't seem likely that there were stones lying around Solomon's porch, although perhaps repair work was being done on the temple and that made them available.

Jesus brought to the forefront, once again, His miracles (called His "good works") and demanded to know for which one of those they desired to kill Him. It set His good works above the wickedness of what they were doing.

Verses 34-36 need close examination.

> The Lord's answer to their charge of blasphemy because of their allegation that he was no more than a man is answered in two parts and continues through v. 36. His first answer is in v. 34. The "law" to which he alludes is set out in Psa. 82:6. Ordinarily, the term is used to refer to the law of Moses only; occasionally, however, it is made to embrace the whole of the Old Testament. He called it "your law" because it was from the law the Jews affected to draw their grounds for the charge of blasphemy. Jesus would show that the very law they professed to reverence did not support their view. In Psa. 82:6, civil authorities, because of their high position and official capacity, are referred to as "gods", in keeping with the concept that those who are God's representatives are gods, i.e., persons of great dignity. Other instances of this usage will be seen in Ex. 7:1, 4:16. The conclusion the Lord drew

from this, is that in keeping with this rare, but occasional usage in the law, he might properly call himself God's Son without being blasphemous; if this concept was permissible for magistrates and other civil authorities, he, being far greater than they, ought not so to be charged. If the scriptures use the word god in application to dignitaries and others of high office, it was not blasphemy for the term to be applied to him, since the scriptures cannot "be broken", set aside or annulled, at will; moreover, Jesus had been sanctified by the Father and sent into the world on a divine mission, which certainly elevated him far above the magistrates called gods in the Old Testament, and proved that his claim was not blasphemous as the Jews averred. Thus both in his official position and because of his mighty works he had far more right to be called the Son of God than did those of the Old Testament period who were regarded by these Jews as properly being called by the term, gods. The argument of Jesus was designed to stop the mouths of his opponents by the use of the very scriptures they sought unsuccessfully to turn against him. To this argument there was no valid answer and the Jews did not attempt one (Guy N. Woods, *New Testament Commentaries, John*, 223, 224).

Jesus could not have performed the works that He did if He were not the Son of God and He rested His case on their evidential power. "Though you believe not me, believe the works; that ye may know, and believe, that the Father is in me and I in Him."

Retirement from Jerusalem to Perea (John 10:40-42)

After the events during the Feast of the Dedication in Jerusalem, Jesus crossed the Jordan River and entered into the region of Perea. If we understand John 1:28 is referring to the initial site of John's baptizing, then Jesus travelled to northern Perea to the region around Bethabara. Some contend that Bethabara was referring to Bethany beyond Jordan, and would be directly across the Jordan from Jericho. In any case, Jesus remained active there, teaching the people.

John the Baptist had worked in this region, and it is apparent the people remembered John. John worked no miracles himself, but his work of "preparing the way of the Lord" was most effective, for the people recognized all John had spoken concerning Jesus, the "one who was to come after him." With Jesus in their midst, teaching and working, many believed on Him. This was quite a contrast to those in Jerusalem who had sought to take Him and kill Him.

Discussions in Perea (Luke 13:22-35)

If Jesus had travelled to northern Perea, to the region around Bethabara, as it appears He did, then the statement of verse 22 describes the leisurely character of this ministry in Perea. Jesus gradually worked His way through the region as He made His way back to Jerusalem and ultimately to the cross.

In one of the cities of Perea, Jesus was asked, "Lord, are there few that be saved?" The one asking the question could have been a disciple or someone there listening, friend or foe. Among the Jews of that time there were many different theories concerning salvation. Some schools of thought said every Israelite would be saved and others few would be saved (as when, of all the adults that came out of Egypt only two entered into Canaan). It seems that the man had the Jews in mind, so Jesus took it farther in His answer.

"Strive to enter in at the strait gate..." is how Jesus began His response. The word "strive" literally means to "agonize." It is the word used to describe the effort put forth by athletes in the Grecian games. They strove, or agonized, expending every ounce of energy they had to win. That is the idea here and the verb is present tense, expressing continued action: i.e., "keep on striving to enter; strain every nerve in trying to enter."

The word "strait" means "pent up, narrow, difficult to enter." Here it means that the way to heaven is pent up, narrow, and not easily entered. The way to death is open, broad, and thronged with people. Jesus was using the familiar cities of their time, cities surrounded by walls and entered through gates. Some of those gates were very large, and wide admitting a multitude of people at one time. Others were not so large, admitting only a few at a time. It is narrow with few on it. To walk the broad path is easy and requires no special effort, but to walk the strait path that leads to heaven requires effort. It is not entered without diligence.

When Jesus said, "Many, I say unto you, will seek to enter in, and shall not be able...," He was speaking of those who delay their efforts until it is too late. Hospitality was important to the Jewish people and He used this to illustrate the meaning. A man opens his house to his friends at the proper time and welcomes them, but there is a time when he shuts the doors, and to seek entrance is improper.

Jesus continued in His response and made the point that some of those who are denied entrance are going to be surprised and complain, "Weren't we acquainted with you, walked with you, ate with you, even heard you teach in our streets? Weren't we your friends?" Their acquaintance would not be enough; obedience was necessary, and their disobedience is what would keep them out.

There will be weeping and gnashing of teeth when the wicked see the righteous entering into the kingdom of God. Why mention Abraham, Isaac, and Jacob? Because, as the forefathers of the Jewish race, they are mentioned with "all the prophets" to show that the faithful Jews would be saved, along with faithful Gentiles, "They that shall come from the east, and from the west, and from the north, and from the south", would also be saved. However, some of the Jews, indeed the majority, who were first in terms of their opportunities to know God's Word and to hear and obey, would be last by virtue of their failure to make the most of those opportunities.

Verses 31-32 are interesting. The Pharisees may have come of their own accord or sent by Herod. Whether Herod actually made a threat or they perceived that he might, or if there was a real danger or the Pharisees used this as an excuse to get rid of Jesus, we do not know. But there does appear to be a certain probability about what they were saying. Herod killed John, a troublesome religious leader as far as he was concerned. It is probable that Herod wanted to rid himself of another spiritual troublemaker, one with a larger following than John, and avoid any problems similar to the ones he had with John. The Pharisees would certainly have been glad to pass along the threat and disturb the ministry of Jesus and frighten off some of His disciples.

It did not work, and the fact that Jesus called Herod a "fox," emblematic of cunning and treachery, indicates that the sending the Pharisees had been Herod's way of trying to trick Jesus into leaving his territory.

The remainder of the Lord's message to Herod was this: He had a definite program, a definite work to accomplish, and no threat of Herod's was going to stop Him or the work. His reference to "three days" and "the third day I shall be perfected" referred to that definite time. He would continue as He was for a time, then He would go to Jerusalem where He would die. All would be accomplished in God's time, not in Herod's time. The statement, "For it cannot be that a prophet perish out of Jerusalem" seems to refer to the stubborn, rebellious character of the nation demonstrated by its slaying of one prophet after another in Jerusalem.

The meaning of verses 34-35 is the same as it is in Matthew 23. With this simple statement Jesus gave the history of Jerusalem. They had killed the prophets, yet God still sent His Son to them, and they would kill Him. There would be no more opportunities after Jesus. No one else was coming.

Healing in a Pharisee's Home on the Sabbath (Luke 14:1-24)

The incidents in this passage are divided in the following way: (a) dinner in the home of a Pharisee on the Sabbath and the healing of the man with dropsy who was present (vs. 1-6), (b) the parable of the banquet which is about humility (vs. 7-11), (c) the discourse on hospitality (vs. 12-14), (d) the parable of the Great Supper (vs. 15-24).

The events of verses 1-6 were most likely still in Perea, where Jesus was invited into the home of one of the chief Pharisees for dinner on the Sabbath. Just exactly what the "chief Pharisee" means is uncertain. Perhaps he was a ruler of the local synagogue or a member of the Sanhedrin. He was, however, a man of influence and reputation. It is interesting that Luke says, "They watched Him." They had their eyes fixed upon Jesus, waiting to see if He would do anything on the Sabbath for which they could accuse Him of wrongdoing. With His usual courage and insight, Jesus went right to the crux of the matter.

There was a man in attendance sick with dropsy, a disease that is marked by an accumulation of watery liquid in any cavity of the body or tissues. We don't know if the man was there as a guest or if he had been invited to ensnare Jesus. The Pharisees certainly knew that Jesus had healed on the Sabbath before and it had generated a great deal of controversy.

Jesus knew the thoughts of the lawyers and Pharisees present and went immediately to what was on their minds. If He healed the man at once, they were ready to accuse Him of laboring on the Sabbath; if He did not heal him, they would have been ready to report a failure to extend mercy or a sign of fear. It is interesting to note how Jesus dealt with them. He asked, "Is it lawful to heal on the Sabbath day?" We are told "They held their peace." They could not say it was lawful, for that would defeat their purpose and leave them open for the same ridiculous charge they intended to level at Jesus. They could not say it was not lawful, for the law did not forbid it.

Jesus healed the man and sent him on his way. Then, He used the same illustration in Matthew 12:11 to show the lawyers and Pharisees their hypocrisy. If it was lawful to save one of their farm animals on the Sabbath, then it was certainly lawful to save the life of a man. They knew Jesus was right for they could not answer Him.

The whole point of the parable in verses 7-11 was not to teach social etiquette but to show certain truths about fundamental elements of character. The way we act shows a great deal about us. Are we egotistical, conceited, and haughty or humble?

The lesson taught in verses 12-14 is that the motive for hospitality determines its genuineness. True hospitality is that which is utterly unselfish. We are not to be hospitable for what we get from our guests in return. The reward for true hospitality will be enjoyed eternally.

In the next parable, the man who made supper is representative of God; the supper represents the provisions and blessings of God for the salvation of man; and the invitations represent the offer of salvation God makes to men through His Son, particularly the Jews. In rejecting the invitation, there are no valid excuses – none! Earthly things first and spiritual things last are deadly, resulting in a revocation of the invitation.

To summarize, it is obvious that not a single man of all those first invited would partake of the supper and they had all, without exception, made excuse. The master of the house determined that somebody would enjoy it, but not one of those who had spurned his invitation would do so. Jesus had offered the blessings of the gospel to the Jews; for the most part they had rejected His invitation. They offered various excuses (none of which held any weight), and they had rejected Him. The Gentiles (others more worthy) would receive the blessings first extended to the Jews.

Sermon about the Cost of Discipleship (Luke 14:25-35)

Jesus was still in Perea. The exact location at this time or the direction in which He was traveling is not indicated. There was a multitude with Him and from the Lord's words to them, it appears they were probably filled with Messianic excitement and expectations. This prompted Jesus' discourse concerning the high cost of following Him.

It is easy to be part of a multitude following the Lord. It is another thing to truly be His disciple and follows all His commands. Seeing this large multitude of people, Jesus pointed out that being His disciple does not come without cost, and He showed them the wide difference between mere lip service and adhering to Him.

The word "hate" in verse 26 means to "love less." To paraphrase, Jesus was saying, "He that comes to Me and does not love his father, mother, wife, children, brothers, sisters, and even his own life less than he loves Me, cannot be my disciple." To be a follower of Him, a person must be willing to place Jesus before all, even before those people and things he holds most dear. Anything less than total dedication and devotion is insufficient. It reminds me of Paul's statement in Philippians 3:8, "Yea, doubtless, and I count all things but loss for the excellency of the knowledge of Christ Jesus my Lord: for whom I have suffered the loss of all things, and do count them but dung, that I may win Christ."

There will be suffering involved in being a disciple of Jesus, and He wanted people to know this. The idea of "bearing the cross" is figurative and means that a disciple of the Lord is willing to endure whatever comes along as a result of that discipleship. If it be physical torment, so be it. If it be mental or verbal abuse, so be it. Whatever comes as a result of following the Lord must be accepted.

The two short parables are used by Jesus to emphasize the seriousness, as well as the possible difficulty, of following Him. He used these parables to show discipleship is not something to be entered without forethought and consideration.

> Common sense teaches men not to begin any costly work without first seeing that they have wherewithal to finish. And he who does otherwise exposes himself to general ridicule. Nor will any wise potentate enter on a war with any hostile power without first seeing to it that, despite formidable odds (two to one), he will be able to stand his ground; and if he has no hope of this, he will feel that nothing remains for him but to make the best terms he can. "Even so," says our Lord, in the warfare you will each have to wage as My disciples, despise not your enemy's strength, for the odds are all against you; and you had better see to it that, despite every disadvantage, you still have wherewithal to hold out and win the day, or else not begin at all.." (Jamieson, Fausset, & Brown's *Commentary on the Whole Bible*, 1010).

Jesus wasn't teaching that it is better to not try at all than to try and fail. He was teaching that it is pure foolishness to begin without first considering the cost. A person must be ready to place Jesus before everybody and everything in his life – family, friends, and material possessions, or he cannot be the Lord's disciple.

Verses 34-35 constitute another warning against half-hearted discipleship. That which appears to be salt, yet has lost its savor, is good for nothing. One who appears to be a disciple but has none of the preserving power of salt within him, is a disciple in appearance only and good for nothing.

If we do not deliberately resolve to leave all things, to suffer all things that may be laid on us, and to persevere to the end of our days in the service of Christ, we cannot be his disciples. No man can be a Christian who, when he makes a profession, is resolved after a while to turn back to the world. Nor can he be if he expects that he will turn back. If he comes not with a full purpose always to be a Christian; if he means not to persevere, by the grace of God, through all hazards, and trials, and temptation; if he is not willing to bear his cross, and meet contempt, and poverty, and pain, and death, without turning back, he cannot be a disciple of the Lord Jesus (Albert Barnes, *Barnes' Notes On The New Testament*, 227, 228).

Parables of the Lost Sheep, Coin, and Son (Luke 15:1-32)

The fact Jesus freely mingled with the multitude offended the Pharisees and the scribes. They believed they demonstrated their own righteousness by their exclusivity, their refusal to associate with those they considered spiritually unclean. They accused Jesus of two things: (1) of allowing sinful people to come into His presence; (2) of going into their midst and eating with them.

Consider verses 3-10, and be careful interpreting the two parables. There is no point in seeking to allegorize them, as so many commentators do. Recognize the setting in which our Lord spoke and the principle of God's love for each of His children as the primary lesson.

The lost sheep and the lost coin are representative of sinners, such as the publican and the others with whom the Pharisees took offense. Each sinner is important to the Lord, just as the lost sheep is to the shepherd and the lost piece of silver to the woman.

The concern for the lost sheep does not mean the shepherd lacks love for the 99 that were not lost. He does not neglect them, mistreat them, or expose them to danger. The nine precious pieces of silver that were not lost were well protected during the search for the one missing.

The point of both of these parables is God's yearning, care, and patient effort for the recovery of the sinner and the abounding joy in heaven in the restoration of that which was lost. The statement, "Joy shall be in heaven over one sinner that repenteth, more than over ninety and nine just persons, which need no repentance," does not mean that God finds more satisfaction in a repentant sinner than in a saint that need not repent. The Lord was referring to the penitent publicans and to the self-righteous Pharisees.

Verses 11-32 present one of the Lord's most beloved and well-known parables – the parable of the Prodigal Son:

Here we have perfectly described the experience of the repentant sinner and also the unsympathetic attitude of the disdainful Pharisee. The first is represented in the story by the prodigal and the second by the conduct of his elder brother.

In describing the waywardness of this younger son, Jesus gave a complete picture of the character and consequences of sin… Its results are sketched in appalling colors. We are shown all its disillusion, suffering, slavery, and despair. As a picture of the inevitable consequences of sin, no touch could be added to the scene of the prodigal in the far country when he had spent all, when the famine had arisen, when he had sold himself to feed swine and was unable to be satisfied even with the coarse food he was providing for the beasts.

Nor is there any more beautiful picture of repentance than was drawn when the Master described the prodigal as "he came to himself…" He remembered a former time of joy and plenty in his early home. He realized his present desperate need; he resolved to arise and go to his father. Most of all, he saw that his offense had been not only against a loving, earthly parent but against God, and that he was wholly undeserving of fellowship with his father. Repentance is not only sorrow for sin; it is an acknowledgment that the offense has been committed against a holy God; it is a change of heart toward him, and a resolution for a new life which manifests itself in definite action, "He arose and came to his father."

Strictly speaking, this is the end of the parable of the prodigal son. In another sense the most beautiful part immediately follows. It is a description of the matchless love shown by God to every repentant soul. The father had never ceased to love the prodigal or to hope and yearn for his return. He had been eagerly looking for his wayward son. The first sight of the prodigal filled his heart with compassion; he "ran, and fell on his neck, and kissed him." The prodigal was ready to confess his fault. The father commanded the servant to "bring forth quickly the best robe, and put it on him; and put a ring on his hand, and shoes on his feet: and bring the fatted calf, and kill it, and let us eat, and make merry." It is a picture not only of pardon but of complete restoration. It assures the sinner that as he turns to God he will be received into the closest fellowship of a son and heir and that his return will give joy to the heart of God who will regard him as one that "was dead, and is alive again," as one who "was lost, and is found." The picture of the elder son is unquestionably intended to describe the loveless Pharisees who envied the joy of the repentant publicans and sinners. When the eldest son learned that his brother had been welcomed to the home, he was filled with anger. He refused to enter the house and when his father came out to entreat him, he accused him of partiality and unkindness. His words described admirably the self-righteousness of the Pharisees, "I never transgressed a commandment of thine," they also show how little he appreciated his true privileges, "thou never gavest me a kid." The reply of the father intimates the possibilities which he never had appreciated and the privileges which he never had enjoyed. "Son, thou art ever with me, and all that is mine is thine". It had always been possible for the Pharisees to enjoy the grace and mercy and love of God; but to them religion had been a mere burdensome round of rites and duties.

We do not know whether the elder son yielded to the entreaty of his father or not. It was an appeal to the Pharisees; would they accept the grace of God and further His plans for the salvation of the lost, or would they continue to criticize and envy the repentant sinner? (Charles Erdman, *An Exposition, The Gospel of Luke*, 144,145).

The Parable of the Unjust Steward (Luke 16:1-18)

The parable of the Unjust Steward appears to be the most perplexing of all the parables spoken by Jesus. It protrays a man who robbed his master but received his master's praise and used by Jesus as an example for His followers. Also, it also seems to indicate that a place in heaven can be purchased with money. But a more careful reading shows that the praise was not for dishonesty, but for prudence and foresight; good qualities that the Lord would have His followers imitate.

The parable tells the story of a steward in charge of his master's property. Word got back to the master that his steward had wasted his goods. An accounting was demanded and he was certain to lose his position. So the steward seized the opportunity that was still his to use the wealth entrusted to him to make friends who would provide him a home when his stewardship was lost.

The story is intended to illustrate the importance of wise stewardship. Everything that one possesses has been entrusted to him by the Lord, to be used wisely in accordance with His will. There will be an accounting called for eventually. It is therefore wise and prudent to use that which is entrusted to us in preparation for eternity. The stewardship of material possessions is a training ground for the stewardship of that which is truly important, the spiritual, called by Jesus in verse 11, "true riches."

Finally, the motive which inspires fidelity in a steward is love. The one who truly loves his master is faithful in the use of that which is entrusted to him. The danger is in divided allegiance. A person cannot be devoted to the Lord and to the world. It cannot be done.

The Rich Man and Lazarus (Luke 16:19-31)

Jesus had just taught some extremely important lessons in the parables of the Prodigal Son and the Unjust Steward. He had instructed His disciples on the righteous use of money and warned them of the dangers of the love of riches. In response, the Pharisees scoffed at Jesus, or literally, "turned up their noses" at Him. Why? That's easily answered. They were lovers of money. The Pharisees were known for their meticulous observance of the letter of the Law, as well as their own traditions, and for their opulent living. They regarded their wealth as the reward due them for their strict observance of the Law and their traditions concerning it. They were living proof that righteousness and riches went together, according to their belief. When they heard Jesus teaching the necessity of benevolence and the unselfish use of money, as well as the possible dangers when one possessed a great deal of wealth, they laughed at Him.

It is difficult to see the connection of verses 16-18 with the previous ones. Luke has given a condensed version of the discussion. The Law and the prophets were the only guide until John came. With the coming of John, new revelation was proclaimed and was continued by Jesus. Men, such as the Pharisees, were trying to enter in a violent way the kingdom that was being proclaimed as "at hand." They were turning it to suit their own ideas and purposes. But they would not succeed in perverting the truth, or in overturning and destroying the smallest part of the Law.

Jesus illustrated this truth by a reference to the seventh commandment. The Pharisees were known for their interpretations concerning marriage and divorce. Jesus showed their interpretation didn't change the law. Adultery was adultery; it was sinful!

> Earlier in His ministry, while still in Galilee, Jesus had given a similar rebuke concerning the effort of the people to wrest the kingdom to their own purposes. The reading in Matthew, "men of violence take it by force" makes it clear the efforts to turn Jesus' movement into a political kingdom. The statement in Luke "every man entereth violently into it" or "every man presseth into it", is more difficult. Not everyone was attempting to follow Jesus, nor is violence necessary in entering the kingdom; it, therefore, does not mean that everyone was making a strenuous effort to follow Jesus, but rather that they were all full of excitement because of the revelations concerning the nearness of the kingdom and were making violent effort to enter into it and further their own ideas and interests. The kingdom was not established as yet, hence the present "entereth" means "is trying to enter". They could not enter it until it was established and they could never enter it by violence. (R.C. Foster, *Gospel Studies, Vol. 3*, 94).

Jesus had taught the need for the proper use and attitude toward riches. This parable showed the consequence of failure in either case. The Lord immediately made clear the contrast between the two individuals. There was the rich man, clothed in purple and fine linen, eating sumptuously every day. In contrast was the poor man, "a certain beggar," named Lazarus. He was laid at the rich man's gate. The gate, or entrance to the house or estate, was the obvious place to attract the most attention and to have the opportunity for someone to take pity on him. The poor man's body was full of sores, with the only medical attention being received when the dogs came and licked them. It isn't clear if their licking increased his misery or gave momentary relief; but the point was the extent of his suffering. The rich man was surrounded by servants and attendants; Lazarus' very existence was a scramble with dogs. Lazarus desired only to have the crumbs that fell from the rich man's table and Lazarus was laid daily at the gate of the rich man, not driven away, but was evidently ignored.

Lazarus was the only individual given a name in a parable of the Lord. Lazarus means "God a help," and was a common name among the Jews. There are many reasons that have been suggested for this, but the giving of a name supplies a distinctly historical flavor to this parable and makes it not so much a parable as actual history. It is important to understand, however, that whether this is a parable or actual history does not change the lessons taught and parables are comprised of elements that are real if not historical.

The contrast continues after Lazarus' death. Notice his burial was not mentioned. Since burial was a part of Jewish custom, it is assumed he was buried but in a "potter's field" type of burial. The angels received him into Abraham's bosom. Abraham's bosom (Paradise) is that part of the Hadean realm where the righteous wait in a state of happiness for their final reception after judgment into heaven.

The rich man also died, and it says he "was buried," perhaps indicating the pomp and pageantry of a fancy burial, a fitting end to a life of luxury. But he ended up in that part of Hades reserved for the lost, a place of torment. The rich man was now in misery; Lazarus was blessed and happy. The rich man was represented as being able to see Abraham "afar off, and Lazarus in his bosom." The "afar off" illustrates the great gulf between the two parts of Hades, a gulf that can never be crossed.

Now, the rich man wanted Lazarus, the man he had ignored in life, to help him. Isn't this an interesting parallel between the crumbs that Lazarus had desired and the drop of water this man wanted? He begged Abraham for relief, calling him, "Father, Abraham."

Abraham's reply did not mean the rich man received his earthly riches as a reward for doing good. Nor did it mean that Lazarus suffered earthly misery because of his sins and that he had suffered enough, therefore being received into Paradise. The character of each man and what had been demonstrated by their life was the focus of Abraham, not their riches or poverty. The point is the use and abuse of opportunities.

There is included in this story an obvious warning for the Pharisees and they should have seen themselves in the rich man. They were notorious for their scrupulous observance of the Law and their traditions, but they were also notorious for their lives of luxury and indulgence.

The rich man asked for Lazarus to be sent to his five brothers who were still living and warn them. He may have expressed concern for them, or was making a veiled excuse for himself, such as "If I had received more warning..." If that be the case, it makes the reply even more significant. "They have Moses and the prophets; let them hear them." And, "If they hear not Moses and the prophets, neither will they be persuaded though one rose from the dead."

Those whose hearts are not right with God won't be convinced by a miracle either. God's Word is sufficient. One who fails to observe God's Word in the use of wealth and all other opportunities is under condemnation and in danger of eternal hell fire.

Faithfulness and Duty (Luke 17:1-10)

Some contend there is a break between the end of chapter 16 and the beginning of chapter 17, presenting a different time altogether. Others say that it is a continuation of the same discussion and that the sayings at the beginning of chapter 17 are pertinent to what has already been said. Others say that is the same occasion, but these statements are now being directed to the disciples and not the Pharisees. This is the most plausible. If they are connected, the connection is difficult to ascertain.

Verses 1-2 warn about causing others to stumble, to sin. In the world in which we live, it is inevitable that offenses will come, that occasions of stumbling will present themselves. But Jesus pronounced a woe upon anyone who brings the occasion. He declared that it would be better for such a person to be drowned in the sea rather than to allow himself to be guilty of causing others to sin. Obviously Jesus wasn't teaching anyone to drown himself or anybody else, but He was emphasizing the seriousness of causing someone to sin.

There is an obvious connection between verses 3 and 4, and verses 1 and 2. It is not enough to avoid causing others to sin, but when we are sinned against, be willing to forgive. This is not advocating weakness or indifference to sin. Jesus taught that a brother who offends another should be rebuked. One should be made to feel and value the seriousness of what was done. If he sincerely repents, he is to be forgiven. Even if he struggles with the sin and repeats it frequently. The expression "seven times a day" implies an unlimited amount of times. Thankfully, God is willing to forgive repeatedly.

The apostles then asked, "Lord, increase our faith," and we see the connection with what preceded their request. The willingness to forgive often and freely is a hard saying, and difficult to do. Perhaps this is why the apostles asked for an increase of faith in order to put the Lord's teaching into practice in their lives.

There is an implied rebuke in Jesus' reply as well as a promise of the wonderful power of faith. If they had real faith, even in so minute a portion as to be compared to "a grain of mustard seed" (a tiny little object), they would be able to accomplish incredible results. Speaking figuratively, they would be able to cause a tree to be plucked up and planted in the sea, just at their word of faith. True faith opens the door to unbounded possibilities.

If an individual possesses great faith and is able to do great works in the service of the Lord, and if he has been blessed with wonderful talents and abilities and uses them appropriately, he or she will never be able to work their way into heaven. They will have done that which is their duty to do.

This does not mean that faithful service to the Lord will not be rewarded. It most definitely will. But it means that the reward is not of debt, but of grace. This removes all ground for boasting and at the same time emphasizes the necessity of works. In doing what the Lord commands, we have done that which is our duty to do.

The Raising of Lazarus (John 11:1-44)

Lazarus, (Eleazar in Heber, meaning "God a help" or "God has helped"), was a resident of Bethany, a town located about two miles east of Jerusalem. He was a brother of Mary and Martha, about whom we read in Luke 10:38-42. It is obvious from the narrative that he was a dear friend of Jesus. The anointing mentioned concerning Mary had not yet occurred. It would occur just before the final Passover of Jesus' life and is recorded in John 12 and Matthew 26. It is not to be confused with the sinful woman of Luke 7.

The two sisters sent word to Jesus that their brother was sick. They referred to him as "he whom thou lovest." In their message there was no request that Jesus come, but in the nature of friendship, they knew He would.

In verse 4, Jesus wasn't saying Lazarus was not going to die. Nor was He saying the sole purpose of the sickness and subsequent death was the opportunity for Him to work a miracle. He meant that the result of this sickness would not be continued death but the manifested glory of God with Lazarus being raised from the dead. Upon hearing the news, Jesus waited two days before going. His waiting was God's will that He do so and He came to do the Will of the Father. Any other comments concerning the delay would be pure conjecture.

Verse 5 presents us with another interesting picture of Jesus. As the Son of God, Jesus loved all men with divine love; but as the Son of Man, there were those close to the Lord and loved by Him in true human friendship. Yes, Jesus was fully God, but He was also fully man. What is more human than the close attraction of certain individuals who are our friends?

After the delay Jesus said, "Let us go into Judea again." He had been in Perea; now it was time to return. Note that Jesus did not say, "Let us go to Bethany." No, He was much more direct than that. "Let us go into Judea" - where they were waiting for Him. The apostles immediately understood that the leaders of the Jews were waiting for Jesus there. They had tried to kill Him previously and failed. Would Jesus go back there again?

The Lord's reply showed His acceptance of His mission and His confidence in God that He would be able to carry out the Father's Will. Nothing would stop that!

When Jesus referred to the death of Lazarus as "sleep" and His intent to go and "awake him out of sleep," the disciples thought He meant Lazarus was sleeping. Then Jesus told them that Lazarus was dead and they were going to witness something to increase their faith.

Thomas spoke, still not understanding. He understood that going to Judea was a prelude to the death of his Lord, and at this point in time, he was willing to die with Him.

The primary message of the raising of Lazarus is found in verses 25-26, "I am the resurrection, and the life: he that believeth in me, though he were dead, yet shall he live. And whosoever liveth and believeth in me shall never die."

These words were spoken in reply to the Martha's request. She heard Jesus was coming and was the first to act. She went out to meet the Lord, while Mary remained in the house. She greeted Jesus with the words, "Lord, if thou hadst been here, my brother had not died." There was no complaint or rebuke in her words, although some think so. They were words of regret that Jesus was not there at the time of his death, able to keep Lazarus alive. She continued. "But I know, that even now, whatsoever thou wilt ask of God, God will give it thee." That indicated a belief in the ability of Jesus to make bringing her brother alive again.

Jesus replied, "Thy brother shall rise again," which Martha thought referred to the resurrection in the last day. It was the Lord's design to awaken in Martha the realization that He could and would raise Lazarus from the dead. Jesus proclaimed Himself to be the "resurrection" and "the life." That certainly implied that the power of resurrection and life was in Him. Jesus said "I," using the personal pronoun, and said, "He that believeth in Me, though he were dead, yet shall he live; and whosoever liveth and believeth in Me shall never die." A follower of Jesus, though he will die physically, lives forever spiritually. And the one who is a believer will never die spiritually again. It is important to note that the verb "believeth" signifies continuous action. In other words, it is the one who "keeps on believing" who is blessed. Martha did not fully comprehend the meaning of all Jesus said, but she had complete faith in all He said because believed Jesus was the Christ, the Son of God.

In verses 28-37, the human sympathy of Jesus is seen. It was seen in His coming to Bethany, in His words to Martha, and now.

Jesus sent a message to Mary through Martha that He wanted to see her. She greeted Jesus with the same words her sister had used, "Lord, if thou hadst been here, my brother had not died," even as she wept. Seeing Mary, as well as those who accompanied her, weeping, we are told that Jesus "groaned in the spirit, and was troubled." It is difficult to determine the exact meaning of "groaned in the spirit." It obviously involves intense emotion. Some have suggested that "groaned in the spirit" refers to the sound of agony or anguish that often escapes from a man when overwhelmed by emotion. The idea of "was troubled" refers to a shudder, a shaking of His body. It is clear when we read, "Jesus wept."

What we are witnessing is human sympathy. Jesus knew He was going to raise Lazarus. He knew the tears and sorrow of Mary, Martha, and friends who had gathered, would be turned to joy. Yet the thought of the death of His friend, the anguish of Mary and Martha, and the tears of the Jews who had gathered, moved the Lord to tears of sympathy and empathy. But do the tears of Jesus only show us His humanity? No! They show His deity in that Jesus came to show God's love and mercy, and how God cares for us and feels our suffering. The crowd was moved by the tears of Jesus; some, being aware of the miraculous things that Jesus had done, speculated He could have prevented Lazarus' death if He had been present.

The miracle itself was (a) an actual resurrection which cannot be explained by natural law. He had been dead four days. (b) It was unquestioned, even by a large crowd that contained many hostile witnesses who ran to the Pharisees. (c) It was declared by Jesus, as no other of His miracles, to have been wrought specifically to produce faith. They were all faith producing, but it is particularly emphasized by the Lord in this one. "Lazarus, come forth!" And He did!

Plots to Kill Jesus (John 11:45-54)

There were two immediate results from the raising of Lazarus. First, many who witnessed it came to believe on Jesus. Secondly, some of those who saw, ran to the Pharisees and told them all that had happened. This resulted in a deeper hatred of Jesus in the hearts of the rulers and a stronger determination to put Him to death.

The Sanhedrin came together to discuss the situation.

> They proclaim a crisis in the life of the nation; the growing excitement over Jesus' miracles makes imminent an outbreak against Rome which would bring ultimate disaster on the nation. This was a real peril in the light of the numbers and power of the Zealot party. Jesus continually changed location or methods to prevent the Zealots from capturing His movement. The hypocrisy of the Sanhedrin is apparent, however, in their frank admission that Jesus is actually working miracles. The immediate conclusion is that He speaks the message of God and they are obligated to obey. Any sort of political crisis is insignificant compared with obedience to the voice from heaven. The real folly of their objection is seen when it was actually presented before Pilate (Jesus "King of the Jews"): he tore the cover from their hypocritical claim that Jesus was a rival of Caesar. Their wicked determination not to believe and repent, was the real ground of their objection (R.C. Foster, *Gospel Studies*, Vol. 3, 112, 113).

Caiaphas, the high priest, rebuked them for their hesitancy and urged immediate action, saying that the life of the nation was at stake. It was better that one man die for the sake of the nation, than for the nation to perish.

The high priest served in the position for life according to Jewish law, but the Romans interfered to appoint whomever they wanted. Sometimes they permitted a priest to serve as high priest for one year or longer. Annas ruled from A.D. 6-15. He was deposed by Gratus but kept his influence, and several of his sons held office. His son-in-law, Caiaphus, was appointed in A.D. 18 and held the office until A.D. 36 during the reign of Pontius Pilate. It has been suggested, with a high degree of probability, that the phrase, "The high priest that same year," means that "fateful year," the year of the Lord's death. It has also been argued that it means the year when the final atoning sacrifice was offered (the death of Jesus), and the office of high priest was no longer necessary.

We know certain leaders had been planning to kill Jesus for some time, but their planning had been spasmodic and disorganized, usually occurring when something Jesus did or said made them angry. Now it changed. From this time on, they were determined to bring their wickedness to pass.

> To escape the agitation caused by the raising of Lazarus from the dead, Jesus withdrew with His disciples to Ephraim, a town on a steep hill about five miles northeast of Bethel. Its modern name is et-Taiyibeh. Jesus' sojourn in Ephraim probably lasted about two weeks, after which He made the fifteen mile journey back to Jerusalem (*Baker's Bible Atlas*, 206).

The Passover was at hand, and it led many of the Jews to speculate about Jesus. Would He show Himself at the feast or not? Meanwhile, the chief priest and the Pharisees let it be known that those who knew the whereabouts of Jesus should tell them so they could take Him.

The Healing of the Ten Lepers (Luke 17:11-19)

As we have seen, Jesus was in Ephraim, a city in northern Judea about five miles northeast of Bethel. Verse 11 tells of a journey to Jerusalem but mentions Samaria before Galilee. Jesus was making a northward swing along the borders of Samaria and lower Galilee into Perea if Ephraim was correctly located. This is why this account of Luke is placed here in the chronology.

As Jesus was entering into "a certain village," He was met by ten lepers. The Old Testament law excluded lepers from general society and compelled them to warn all who ventured near that they were lepers. Naturally, those who suffered the same affliction would band together. We notice they stood "afar off." This was in compliance with the law.

> And the leper in whom the plague is, his clothes shall be rent, and his head bare, and he shall put a covering upon his upper lip, and shall cry, Unclean, unclean. All the days wherein the plague shall be in him he shall be defiled: he is unclean: he shall dwell alone; without the camp shall his habitation be (Lev. 13:45-46).

Instead of crying out, "Unclean, unclean," they lifted up their voices and said, "Jesus, Master, have mercy on us." Jesus' response to them was in exact accordance with the law, "Go show yourselves unto the priests."

> This shall be the law of the leper in the day of his cleansing: He shall be brought unto the priest: and the priest shall go forth out of the camp; and the priest shall look, and, behold, if the plague of leprosy be healed in the leper; then shall the priest command to take for him that is to be cleansed two birds alive and clean, and cedar wood, and scarlet, and hyssop (Lev. 14:2-4).

As they responded in obedience to what the Lord told them to do, their skin became clean. Of the ten, one of them, as soon as he saw that he was healed, turned back and cried out with a loud voice, glorifying God. He fell down prostrate at the feet of Jesus, giving Him thanks. There is no doubt that he would go to the priest, but his appreciation moved him to thank Jesus first. This particular individual was a Samaritan. Nine chose not to return with thanks in their hearts and on their lips.

> They had faith enough to be healed, but not love enough to return and thank Jesus. They were like nominal Christians who profess faith and repentance and are baptized, but do not appreciate what has been done for them enough to live nobly for Christ. Numerous are the excuses which have been suggested as probably in their hearts: (1) Anxiety to get back in haste to their families and business and society. (2) Thoughtlessness of their great debt to Christ. (3) Influence of example: some went on because others did; the majority refused to return - so the weaker ones went with the crowd. (4) Procrastination: some quieted their conscience by promising themselves they would return later and find Jesus and give him thanks (R.C. Foster, *Gospel Studies*, Vol. 3, 116).

After crying out against the ingratitude of the nine, Jesus spoke to the one who showed his gratitude, "Arise, go they way: thy faith hath made thee whole."

Sermon Concerning the Time of the Coming of the Kingdom (Luke 17:20-37)

Jesus taught that the kingdom of God was nigh, or at hand. He instructed His disciples to teach the same. The Pharisees wanted the particulars: "When will it come?" Bear in mind that what they were anticipating was a physical kingdom, ruled by an earthly king, one that would overthrow the shackles of Roman oppression. But our Lord's response indicated that it wasn't going to be what they expected. The approach of the kingdom could not be observed with the senses. It was a spiritual kingdom and could not be judged by outward signs, by political and military triumphs. It was not of such a nature that they could point to it and say, "Here it is" or "There it is."

"The kingdom of God is within you." The Greek can be translated correctly in two ways, "within you, in your hearts" or "among you, in your midst." The first would indicate the entirely spiritual nature of the kingdom, while the second would indicate that the King of the kingdom was in their very midst now in the person of Jesus. Its meaning is of an entirely spiritual nature of the kingdom "within you, in your hearts." At this point Jesus moved from a discussion of His kingdom to a discussion of His return.

The question of the coming of the kingdom is on the minds of the Lord's disciples as well. There are numerous indications of this in the gospels. So, turning from the Pharisees, Jesus began to address His disciples.

He told them that there would come a time when they would long to see "one of the days of the Son of Man, and they would not see it." He spoke of the days ahead, after the establishment of the church or kingdom, when they would be enduring severe trials and persecution. Their longing would be for His return.

Jesus told them that there would be many false messiahs after Him, do not go after them. His return would be like lightening: sudden, unexpected, and unpredictable, seen by all. At His return there will be no question of who it was or what was happening. But before any of this took place, Jesus had to suffer many things and be rejected of that generation. He had to be put to death! Jesus presented this to keep His disciples from getting caught up in the future glory and forget the present rejection and death awaiting Him.

Verses 25-32 are open to different interpretations. It is possible that these verses refer to the day of judgment on the nation of the Jews when the Son of Man comes in judgment through the destruction of Jerusalem. There is considerable similarity between these verses and several found in Matthew 24, in which the destruction of Jerusalem is under consideration. It is, however, very possible that the discussion here is limited only to the second coming.

In verse 33, Jesus gave further warning against any effort to save material things, or even one's life, when the destruction comes, whether it be Jerusalem or the destruction that will occur at the second coming. One should not give so much concern to earthly life or the material things that sustain it. The words of verse 33 constitute the only saying of Jesus that is recorded in all four gospels.

Verses 34-37 have reference to the second coming. The "one taken" and the "other left" means one taken home in glory to heaven, the other left for eternal destruction.

Jesus' disciples asked, "Where, Lord?" indicative of the fact they were viewing things from a purely physical standpoint. "Where is this going to happen?" That is what they wanted to know. Our Lord's reply was (taken from the NIV), "When there is a dead body, there the vultures will gather." Jesus took the opportunity to teach that judgment will not be confined to any one spot but will be inflicted where sin is found. Just as vultures gather around a lifeless body, so too will the Son of Man come to judge.

Parable of the Unjust Judge (Luke 18:1-8)

Jesus had been speaking of His return, and this parable is spoken with that particular reference. The uncertain time of the Lord's return, the importance of being prepared for it, and the powerful pull of the things of the world, make it imperative they be persistent in prayer for help from God. This is applicable to all Christians at all times.

The argument was this: if an unjust judge, who doesn't care for God or man, would yield to persistent appeals of a poor widow just because he feared she would annoy him even more by her repeated requests, how much more would a loving and righteous God answer the prayers of His children if they are persistent in prayer?

Jesus' question, "Nevertheless, when the Son of Man cometh, shall he find faith on the earth?" has a touch of the mournful to it, but reflects upon man's wisdom and loyalty. Jesus had repeatedly taught only a few (comparatively speaking) would walk the narrow way that leads unto life. The answer to His question is that faith will be found in the hearts of the loyal few, and is a warning of having faith to endure.

Parable of the Pharisee and the Publican (Luke 18:9-14)

This parable was designed to teach humility in prayer and in all areas of approach to God. The Pharisee had gone to the temple to pray. He stood in a place where all could see him, and although he addressed God, the prayer was not real. He began by saying, "I thank thee," but he was addressing everybody else, including himself, and not God. He was so self-righteous. "I thank thee that I am not as other men…" He told God how faithful he was and all the good works that he had done.

On the other hand the publican was a study in humility. He would not even look toward heaven, but beat upon his breast and cried out, "God, be merciful to me, a sinner."

The publican was justified and forgiven by God. That was not the case with the Pharisee. He did not ask for forgiveness because he did not think he needed to be forgiven. There was no recognition of unworthiness on his part because he thought he was worthy. His attitude makes one wonder why he bothered to pray in the first place except to be seen by people.

Jesus in Perea, Teaching Concerning Divorce (Matt. 19:1-12, Mark 10:1-12)

The focus is upon Matthew's account. Jesus was slowly making His way to Jerusalem and was now traveling through Perea as He did so. He had pushed into the southern part of Perea. This was the Lord's final departure from Galilee, He would not return. It was His final journey to Jerusalem and its environs. As was so often the case, there were great multitudes following the Lord. Some of them were sick and Jesus healed them.

There were also some Pharisees present who came to the Lord, and in an attempt to test Him, or try Him, they asked Jesus the following question, "Is it lawful for a man to put away his wife for every cause?" Mark states their question in a more general way: "Is it lawful for a man to put away his wife?"

Most approach this question as relating to the two most prominent rabbinical schools of the day and their interpretation of Deuteronomy 24:1. That verse reads as follows, "When a man hath taken a wife, and married her, and it come to pass that she find no favor in his eyes, because he hath found some uncleanness in her: then let him write her a bill of divorcement, and give it in her hand, and send her out of his house." The controversy comes from a short description in the Talmud of a first (or perhaps an early second century) rabbinical dispute.

> Beth Shammai says: a man should not divorce his wife unless he has found her guilty of some unseemly conduct, as it says, because he hath found some unseemly thing in her. Beth Hillel, however, says (that he may divorce her) even if she has merely spoilt his food, since it says, because he hath found some unseemly thing in her. R. Akiba says (He may divorce her) even if he finds another woman more beautiful than she is, as it says, it cometh to pass, if she find no favour in his eyes (Tractate Gittin, Mishnah 9,10).

The most logical view of the question of the Pharisees is that they were attempting to align Jesus in opposition to the Law of Moses and not some particular rabbinical school of thought. Earlier, in Matthew 5:31-32, Jesus had expressed the truth about the subject. Perhaps it was their knowledge of His previous statement, and additional times Jesus had spoken on this subject, that made them think they could ensnare Him by making it appear He was teaching something contrary to what Moses had taught.

It is very important to note that Jesus did not begin His response by appealing to the Law of Moses. Jesus went back to the beginning and referred to Genesis 1:27, "So God created man in His own image, in the image of God, created He him; male and female created He them." Then Jesus quoted Genesis 2:24, "Therefore shall a man leave his father and his mother, and shall cleave unto his wife: and they shall be one flesh." This union is by God's decree, and man does not have the right to interfere and separate that which God has joined together.

This either puzzled the Pharisees or caused them to think: "Now we can show that He is opposing Moses." So they asked, "Why did Moses then command to give a writing of divorcement, and to put her away?" What Moses permitted (or tolerated, suffered) was for the hardness (dried up, tough) of their hearts. It was not God's original intention, and God's law did not approve of divorce for just any reason. Malachi 2:16 makes it very clear how God feels about divorce: "For the Lord, the God of Israel, saith that He hateth putting away…"

Moses' law did not give God's approval of divorce. It states a contingency; in other words, "If a man divorces his wife, here is what he must do."

Understanding the Lord's teaching in verse 9 is not difficult, but understanding it has not been the problem. The problem lies in accepting what the Lord said. The basic law is this, "Whoever shall put away his wife, and shall marry another, commiteth adultery: and whoso marrieth her which is put away doth commit adultery." Mark showed this is applicable to both men and women when he adds in Mark 10:12, "And if a woman shall put away her husband, and be married to another, she committeth adultery." Making this applicable to women as well as men was unheard of in that day and time.

Divorce for any reason is not allowed. If one divorces his or her spouse for any reason and marries again, he or she commits adultery. Not only that, but the one who was put away commits adultery upon remarriage. To complete the picture from Matthew 5:32, the one who did the putting away is guilty of causing his or her spouse to commit adultery.

There is one, and only one, exception given by Jesus in Matthew 19:9. It is also found in Matthew 5:32. It is "except it be for fornication." If one divorces a spouse for the cause of sexual immorality, then the clear implication is that there is no adultery committed upon remarriage for the innocent one. The put-away party commits adultery upon remarriage. This is not difficult to understand, but it is hard to accept. This is seen in the response of the disciples and in what Jesus had to say about those who would remain celibate for the kingdom of heaven's sake.

The disciples who were listening to Jesus certainly understood what He was saying. They said, "If the case of the man be so with his wife, it is not good to marry." They saw that Jesus was teaching that marriage was a fixed and irrevocable bond. If the only reason for divorce was "fornication," then the union with a woman who was quarrelsome and ill-tempered would create an intolerable situation as far as they were concerned. If that was the case, then they thought that it would be better not to marry. Jesus gave the same right to women, something that had not even been considered previously. The disciples most assuredly understood.

The teaching to which Jesus referred in verse 11 was not what He had said concerning marriage and divorce in verse 9, but rather the statement the disciples had made, "It is not good to marry." Not all men were able to live a celibate life and forgo marrying.

Jesus and the Little Children
(Matt. 19:13-15, Mark 10:13-16, Luke 18:15-17)

This is a beautiful picture and shows the approachability of Jesus and the comfort parents felt in bringing their children to Him. It doesn't appear in the accounts that the children were being brought to Jesus to be healed of some disease, but for Him touch them, praying God's blessings to come upon them. As we look at the different words used to describe these people (Luke called them "infants", Matthew and Mark referred to them as "little children"), it is evident they were children of various ages.

The disciples issued their rebuke because the bringing of the children was viewed as an interruption in the teaching of Jesus. Jesus' response showed that He in no way saw it as an interruption. Mark stated, "He was much displeased." Jesus was always eager to receive and help all who desired to come to Him. He even had time for the little children. It was the act of the disciples in attempting to prevent the children from coming to Him that made the Lord angry.

Citizens of the Lord's kingdom are to be "such as" little children. Not childish, but child-like. It has nothing to do with age and everything to do with character. Children are characterized by humility, teachableness, innocence, unselfishness, loyalty, and so on. A disciple of Jesus must be childlike. One receives and enters the kingdom by hearing God's Word with absolute trust and belief and by total submission in humble obedience to that Word.

The Rich Young Ruler
(Matt. 19:16-22, Mark 10:17-22, Luke 18:18-23)

This individual was a "young man," because of the reference by Matthew. He was a ruler, for Luke called him a "certain ruler," and all three accounts make it clear that he was wealthy. As a young man he probably was not a ruler of the Sanhedrin, but perhaps of a local synagogue. He showed energy and enthusiasm, along with a concern for things of a spiritual nature. He had youth, riches, and authority, but continued to be dissatisfied. The dissatisfaction was not over what he possessed, but a concern that he may have been lacking something spiritually.

As Jesus finished His teaching concerning the little children, this young man came running to overtake Him. His reverence was shown when he knelt before Jesus. He asked the Lord, "Good Master, what good thing shall I do, that I may have eternal life?"

The response of Jesus was very interesting. Some have foolishly claimed that by the statement, "Why callest thou me good?" There is none good but one, that is, God…" Jesus was saying that He Himself was not good, and in so doing, denying His divinity. Others have suggested that Jesus was essentially saying, "Either I am not good, or I am God." That is true, but not the point.

Jesus was calling into question the young man's usage of the word "good." He was tossing it around very freely, "Good Master" and "good thing," without really understanding the meaning of the word. There is only one who is truly "good" in the absolute sense of the word. That one is God. The young man needed to be very careful about how he described people and things, himself included.

This ruler was a Jew and very well acquainted with the Law of Moses. By mentioning the commandments, Jesus was telling him that God had already told him how to be pleasing in His sight. Jesus added, "Thou shalt love thy neighbor as thyself." The young man replied, "All these things have I kept from my youth up: what lack I yet?" Some have said this young man was demonstrating an arrogant, haughty spirit with this reply. But Mark tells us that "Jesus loved him..."

It is apparent that the young man thought he had done his best and kept the commandments. He felt dissatisfied and thought there might be something more. He was more spiritually-minded than the Pharisees because he asked, "What lack I yet?" and most of the Pharisees did not believe that they lacked anything. He felt there was room for improvement. He had kept the letter of the law, which was necessary; but it was the spirit of the law that was concerning this young man.

"If thou wilt be perfect, go and sell that thou hast, and give to the poor, and thou shalt have treasure in heaven: and come and follow me."

> The command to sell all is not a general one, but a special precept needed in this case. 1. To dispel the ruler's self-deception. On the negative side his character was good, but on the positive it was deficient. He had done his neighbor no harm, but he had also done him very little good. 2. To show impartiality. The invitation of Jesus shows that the ruler desired to be in some manner a disciple, and hence he is subjected to the same test which the other disciples had accepted, and of which Peter soon speaks. Paul also was rich in self-righteousness like this man, but cheerfully sacrificed all, that he might follow Christ (Phil. 3:6-9). Moreover, the reference to treasure in heaven and the invitation to follow Christ tested the ruler's obedience to the first four commandments of the Decalogue as condensed in the great summary or first commandment (Matt. 22:37-38). Though the ruler perhaps did not fully realize it, those who heard the conversation must afterwards have been impressed with the great truth that the ruler was called upon to make his choice whether he would love Christ or the world, whether he would serve God or mammon. The whole scene form an illustration of the doctrine expressed by Paul, that by the law can no flesh be justified (Rom. 3:20), for perfection is required of those who approach God along that pathway; those therefore, who have done all, still need Christ to lead them (McGarvey and Pendleton, *The Fourfold Gospel*, 545, 546).

Whatever it is that rules our lives and keeps us from surrendering completely to the Lord must go.

The young man went away sorrowful. He wanted to follow Jesus, and be pleasing in God's eyes, but he was not willing to pay the price. The importance of his riches was evidenced by what he did. He was not angry, but sorrowful. Though the ruler was sorrowful as he turned away, and that Jesus loved him, we notice that Jesus did not modify His demands to gain an influential disciple.

Perils of Riches and Reward of Disciples
(Matt. 19:23-30, Mark 10:23-31, Luke 18:24-30)

The reaction of the rich young ruler prompted Jesus to make the statement concerning the difficulty of a rich man to enter heaven. Why is it so difficult? It is because of the "love" of riches. Consider 1 Timothy 6:10. Wealth tends to make one think he is self-sufficient and independent, wanting more. This takes the place of supreme importance in his life, and entices with entanglements of sin.

When the disciples responded with amazement, Jesus repeated His words and added the illustration of the camel through the eye of the needle. This was a proverbial expression meant to show absolutely no possibility. Some have tried to lessen the force of Jesus' words by saying He was referring to two gates of the city -- the large one for beasts of burden, and the small one for foot passengers. This smaller gate is now called "The Needle's Eye," but there is no evidence whatsoever that it was so called in the time of Jesus.

Once again the disciples were astonished. They were accustomed to viewing the possession of great wealth as evidence of divine favor. There is even good indication that they thought their positions in the kingdom could well be filled with riches and honor. Jesus spoke about how difficult it is for a rich man to enter into heaven. If this seemingly virtuous rich man could not enter into the kingdom, who then could be saved? With God, a man's heart can be changed and he can be saved.

Three questions need to be considered now.

> What suggested Peter's question? He has heard the conversation with the rich young ruler and that which followed. The young man had been challenged to leave all and follow Christ, and had refused. As Peter sees him disappearing in the distance, returning to his riches, worldly cares, and pursuits, and closing the gates of the kingdom against himself, the thought comes that the apostles have done what the young man refused to do. If earthly riches are so perilous, of what sort is to be the reward that awaits those who renounce all for Christ?
>
> What is the regeneration and the throne? The New Testament proclaims a new heaven and a new earth: God is to make all things new in the glorious time when His Son shall come to judge the world. This is the regeneration. The apostles who have sacrificed and lived for Christ shall have special places of honor in that day. The other interpretation refers the regeneration to the day of Pentecost and setting up of the church. The twelve apostles are upon twelve thrones judging the twelve tribes of Israel in the sense of proclaiming the means of pardon at Pentecost and following. The closing warning of this discourse confirms the former interpretation

How receive a hundred fold? This does not mean a hundred fold in kind or it would invite the very thing which Jesus has denounced. Men would seek the kingdom and surrender earthly riches in order to get more earthly riches as an investment proposition. It does not mean that if a person has to part company with his father and mother in order to do God's work, he will receive a hundred fathers and mothers, but that the fellowship in the kingdom will more than compensate for any worldly and godless people with whom he has had to part, no matter how close the blood relationship has been; the joys of the spiritual kingdom will outweigh by far the earthly riches and pleasures surrendered. (There will be a multitude of people who will be as father and mother, brother and sister to the Christian who has had to part with his family.) Note the significant "with persecutions" contained in Mark's account which makes perfectly clear the spiritual character of this promise (R.C. Foster, *Gospel Studies*, Vol. 3, 137, 138).

This discussion closes with a warning against pride.

The Parable of the Laborers in the Vineyard (Matt. 20:1-16)

The particulars of the parable are these: the owner of a vineyard went out to find workers early in the morning. He found some, talked with them, and struck an agreement that they would work for a denarius each. The King James Version says a penny. The denarius was a Roman coin worth about $.20 and was the regular rate of pay for a day laborer. In Palestine a man was hired at dawn and paid at sunset.

The early morning hours pass and the owner went again to the market place in search of additional workers. He found additional workers at the third, sixth, ninth, and eleventh hours. The Jews divided the daytime into twelve equal parts. The length of the hour depended upon the length of the day. The third hour would be approximately 9:00 a.m., the sixth about noon, the ninth would be mid-afternoon, and the eleventh hour would be about 5:00 p.m. As the owner contacted different workers throughout the day, no agreement was reached concerning pay. He said, "Whatsoever is right, I will give you." It might also be important to note that it appears he hired all he could find, and none of them refused to go into the vineyard. They evidently did not feel themselves to be in a position to bargain; they wanted a chance to work, and they committed themselves to the goodness of the owner.

The Law of Moses stated in Leviticus 19:13, "Thou shalt not defraud thy neighbor, neither rob him: the wages of him that is hired shall not abide with thee all night until the morning." Deuteronomy 24:15 states, "At his day thou shalt give him his hire, neither shall the sun go down upon it..." So in the evening the laborers were called in and given their wages, beginning with those who were the last hired. They were generously treated, paid in full according to what those in the early hours had agreed. And so it went with all the rest -- payment in full although they had worked only a partial day. Then it came time to pay the workers who had been hired first, those who had labored the entire day. These, having seen what the others were paid, expected to receive more. They were paid the same amount and responded with anger, saying, "These last wrought but one hour, and thou hast made them equal unto us, which have borne the burden and heat of the day."

The owner responded with, "I do thee no wrong: didst not thou agree with me for a penny? Take that thine is, and go thy way: I will give unto this last, even as unto thee. Is it not lawful for me to do what I will with mine own? Is thine eye evil, because I am good?"

There are those who connect this parable with the rich young ruler and believe it to be teaching that many who are first in the eyes of the world with wealth and fame will be least in heaven because of failure to use their gifts and opportunities. This would indicate degrees of reward and that is not substantiated. The parable implies that both the first and the last were saved alike, so it cannot be interpreted in that fashion.

Others connect it with the self-assurance of Peter (Matt. 19:27), taking it for granted that the Apostles, having left all to follow Jesus, would be saved. But what would be their reward? Peter was warned, "But many that are first shall be last: and the last shall be first." Others make the "first" and "last" refer to those who are first and last in time of following Jesus (by this is meant the apostles and early disciples versus Christians of later ages).

The fundamental principle of this parable is that salvation is the free gift of God, and we cannot dictate to God how He is to give it. God keeps His promises. Each who labors faithfully according to his opportunities will be graciously rewarded of God.

In the kingdom of heaven, equality is the rule. The work performed by the disciples of the Lord, any disciple, is transcended by a reward equal for all, even though the work and the time engaged in it varies from individual to individual. When a person becomes a Christian through obedience to the gospel, he does not receive a calculated portion of forgiveness, reconciliation, peace, joy, happiness, and the assurance of heaven based upon how much time he has to labor in the kingdom.

The eleventh hour cannot be used to represent people who have rejected the Lord all their lives and then give Him the last few minutes in what has come to be called "deathbed confession." When the owner went into the marketplace, he did not find men who had refused earlier invitations to work. He found "others" who had not yet had the opportunity. Those individuals hired in the eleventh hour represent those who respond when they have the opportunity and then do the best they can for the remainder of their lives.

Another Prediction of the Death of Jesus
(Matt. 20:17-19, Mark 10:32-34, Luke 18:31-34)

Now Jesus turned with determination to go to Jerusalem. Mark tells us that "Jesus went before them." The disciples were amazed and afraid, following behind. This is definitely different from previous times Jesus had gone to Jerusalem.

> Mark does not explain whether the feelings of the apostles result from the change implied in Jesus' looks, attitude, and conduct, or from their fearful anticipations as to the results of this journey. Perhaps both influenced them. They were filled with awe at Jesus and afraid to remain in His immediate company; hence they hung back, not at His command, but because of the atmosphere about Him. They also were afraid as they anticipated the desperate crisis which is about to ensue at Jerusalem. They believe Jesus to be the Son of God, but he has predicted His own death and intimated He will not defend Himself from His foes. What then? (R.C. Foster, *Gospel Studies*, Vol. 3, 140).

Jesus took the twelve disciples apart from the rest. This was for their ears only. When Jesus spoke of His death before He said such things as, "We must needs go to Jerusalem." Now Jesus said, "We are going."

The details of the prediction were specific. Jesus spoke of the betrayal by Judas, His condemnation, His being turned over to the Gentiles and mocked, His scourging and death by crucifixion, and His resurrection on the third day. In light of all the discussion concerning wealth and rewards, surely Jesus uttered this prediction to keep the materialistic desires of His apostles in check and to prepare them for what would happen very soon.

Luke tells us that they did not understand, that the saying was "hid from them," not knowing the things that were spoken. Their previously held views of what the Messiah would be and the nature of His reign were so strong that they could not or would not grasp the significance of what Jesus was saying. It was as if they somehow thought His word could not be literal concerning His death. How could this possibly be?

Rebuke of James and John for Asking for Chief Honors
(Matt. 20:20-28, Mark 10:35-45)

According to the Gospel of Mark, James and John made the request, while Matthew informs us that the mother of the two came with them and made the initial request. However, Matthew shows that when Jesus responded, He did not respond to the mother, but to James and John. By explanation, Mark does not tell of the mother's initial request, for it was the sons who were making it. And Matthew does not tell if the request was made in an attempt to get Jesus to fulfill it before it was asked. Like a child about to make a request of his parents and prefaces the request by saying, "Promise me you won't say no until I am done asking." The use of the mother to make the request and the way it was asked is evidence that James and John were ashamed of what they asked in the first place.

The request is further evidence of the physical view the apostles held of the work of Jesus. Earlier, in Matthew 19:28, Jesus had said, "Verily I say unto you, that ye which have followed me, in the regeneration when the Son of Man shall sit in the throne of his glory, ye also shall sit upon twelve thrones, judging the twelve tribes of Israel." James and John decided to ask for the chief seats on the right and left of the throne. In spite of the fact Jesus was telling them of His impending death, they could not rid themselves of the idea that He was about to ascend to the "earthly" throne of David and they were going to occupy positions of preeminence in this earthly kingdom. They did not understand the nature of the kingdom nor the difficulty of what they were asking. The word "cup," as Jesus used it in His response, meant whatever portion was to be experienced, either of pleasure or of sorrow. Most frequently, it was used in reference to sorrow, and that is how Jesus was using it. The "baptism," to which Jesus referred, was the baptism of suffering, which means to be overwhelmed by it.

James and John were not lacking in courage. Jesus was saying that suffering was to be involved, possibly death, and they asserted their ability to go through it. Jesus affirmed that they would share in His suffering and be baptized with the same baptism of suffering that He endured. James was killed by Herod Agrippa, and it is believed that John, after years of exile, died a natural death in Ephesus.

Some believe that Jesus acknowledged in His statement that there are to be chief seats in heaven, positions of honor. "But to sit on my right hand and on my left, is not mine to give, but it shall be given to them for whom it is prepared of my Father." The next verses indicate that Jesus was pointing out that the whole idea of one above another, the whole idea of elevating oneself, was contrary to the kingdom. What we might think elevates a man is not what God thinks. Indeed, Jesus Himself did not come to occupy a position of honor among men, but He came as a servant. That is to what we all should aspire.

Healing of the Blind Men at Jericho
(Matt. 20:29-34, Mark 10:46-52, Luke 18:35-43)

There are several differences in these narratives of the same event. Matthew tells us that it was two men; Mark and Luke only mention one. Can this be harmonized? Certainly it can. The one individual was quite the more forceful personality of the two and Mark gives his name, "Bartimaeus, the son of Timaeus."

Mark also says, "As he went out of Jericho," and to this Matthew agreed. But Luke says, "As he was come nigh unto Jericho." Can this be harmonized? Yes it can. Several different explanations have been offered.

First, as Jesus entered Jericho, Bartimaeus called for help but was too late to be heard as Jesus was in front of the large crowd, and the blind man did not realize who He was until He had passed. Determined to be healed, he circled the town, joined by another blind man, appealed to Jesus, and was healed. It seems as though John Calvin originated this explanation and it has been adopted by many, including J.W. McGarvey. It is possible, but it requires a great deal of speculation.

The second, the city of Jericho, captured by Joshua, had long been in ruins, but two others are identified and referred to in the Old Testament and the New Testament. Josephus also mentioned them. They laid a short distance apart, directly in Jesus' path, whether He came across the Pilgrim's Ford from Perea or crossed the Damieth Ford near the mouth of the Jabbok, traveling down the western bank of the Jordan River. If pursuing either course, Jesus would have passed through the older Jericho and across the plain into the newer Jericho; between the two, the miracle took place. Matthew and Mark refer to the older city, while Luke refers to the newer. This explanation probably originated with Macknight and adopted by many, including A.T. Robertson.

The third explanation is that it was a scribal error in the transmission of Luke's gospel and that could explain the difference. This is the simplest of the explanations.

All three gospel writers tell us of the large multitude present. Coming from the north, the northwest, the east and the northeast, several highways converged at Jericho into one main road leading to Jerusalem. Considering the time element, large crowds headed to Jerusalem for the coming Passover. Bartimaeus, hearing the passing of the great multitude, wanted to know what was causing the excitement. He was told that it was Jesus of Nazareth passing. So he cried out, "Jesus, thou Son of David, have mercy on me." This is a Messianic title, the same title the crowd at the triumphal entry into Jerusalem acclaimed the Lord (Matt. 21:9, 15). Even though the crowd tried to silence him by rebuke, Bartimaeus cried all the louder, "Thou Son of David, have mercy on me."

The reaction of the crowd is interesting, especially when considered from the normal reaction to the healings of Jesus. Several suggestions have been made to explain why the crowd wanted to silence Bartimaeus.

It has been suggested that the Pharisees and other enemies of Jesus tried to silence the blind man because they were angered by his publicly proclaiming Jesus the Son of David. Others believe that Jesus was teaching as He walked along and the crowd resented the interruption. Still others suggest that with their worldly views of the Messiah and the kingdom, the crowd had their hearts set on Jesus marching straight into Jerusalem, destroying His enemies, and establishing the kingdom. They did not want Him turned aside from that mission even to help this blind man. There are a few who believe the crowd to have been hard-hearted. So, they tried to silence Bartimaeus because they did not want to hear his repeated cries for mercy. All of these suggestions are speculative, but possible.

Jesus sent messengers to the blind man, telling him to come. Mark makes an interesting comment in connection with the man coming. He says, "And he, casting away his garment, rose, and came to Jesus." Why cast away his garment? Perhaps he did it so his movements would not impede his getting to Jesus.

Jesus asked him, "What wilt thou that I should do unto thee?" The response was, "Lord, that I might receive my sight."

All three accounts give us different details of the miracle. Matthew says Jesus touched the eyes of the two blind men; Luke tells us that He gave a command, "Receive thy sight." Both Mark and Luke include, "Thy faith has made thee whole." Mark adds the comforting, "Go thy way..." Each account gives different details and by putting them together we can see the entire picture. Bartimaeus, now able to see, followed Jesus, glorifying God. The multitude also gave praise to God for what they had witnessed.

Jesus and Zacchaeus (Luke 19:1-10)

Luke is the only writer to mention this event and he adds the geographical note, "And Jesus entered and passed through Jericho." Also, Luke is the one who wrote, in connection with the healing of the blind men, that it occurred as "he was come nigh unto Jericho." This lends validity to the second explanation of there being an old and new Jericho with the miracle taking place between the two. Now Jesus has entered into the new Jericho and as He passed through the city, or some suburb of the city, He came in contact with Zacchaeus.

Zacchaeus was a Jew, which is the same as Zaccai, and means "pure, just, or innocent." He was also "chief among the publicans," or the "chief publican." The Greek word rendered "chief publican" is found here and while the exact meaning isn't clear, it is clear that it was an official title indicating a high rank in the tax system. Since Jericho was a "port-of-entry," for caravan routes and highways leading to Jerusalem, it was a natural location for a high ranking official of the tax system to be stationed. Luke mentions his wealth, a natural consequence of his position and indicating the difficulty of his accepting Jesus.

Zacchaeus had heard of Jesus because he sought to see Him as He made His way through Jericho. However, because of the multitude and his small stature, Zacchaeus couldn't see. So he did what he could. He ran ahead and climbed a sycamore tree (fig-mulberry tree, having fruit like the fig and leaves like the mulberry, a very different tree from the sycamore tree known in the United States). Surely this showed him to have been a man of energy and determination, as well as a man of forethought. He knew Jesus would pass by this spot and now he would be able to see Him.

When Jesus came He looked up and saw Zacchaeus. He said to him, "Zacchaeus, make haste, and come down; for today I must abide at thy house." Maybe Zacchaeus was surprised when Jesus spoke to him. Jesus not only saw Zacchaeus, but He looked upon his heart. Jesus knew what brought Zacchaeus to that tree and climb it. Jesus knew his heart and what he needed. If Zacchaeus had been surprised when Jesus spoke to him, imagine how much greater his surprise when Jesus told him to come down and He would abide at his house that very day. Zacchaeus came down and joyously received Him.

The murmuring done was characteristic of the Pharisees and some must have been part of the multitude. They may have influenced others in the multitude to join their murmuring. The murmuring is easy to understand, however, given the generally held view by the Jews concerning publicans. As far as they were concerned, no faithful Jew would ever eat in the home of a publican. That made it more inappropriate for one that was a prophet or a teacher to go into such a home. Being the "chief of publicans" would certainly have made Zacchaeus a man of some notoriety, a "notable sinner."

Jesus taught those gathered at the dinner as this was His custom. At the close of the dinner, Zacchaeus "stood" and declared his faith in Jesus. "Behold" is how Zacchaeus began, calling attention to what he was about to say. "I give half of my goods to the poor." The verb is present tense meaning "now and in the future," a continuous action. When he said, "If I have taken anything from any man by false accusation," it was actually an admission of guilt. The "fourfold" restitution was called for under the Law of Moses in a case of robbery (Exodus 22:1).

While those things were good, and a blessing to the poor and to those whom Zacchaeus had wronged, they pale in comparison to the blessing Zacchaeus received. Jesus said, "This day is salvation come to this house, forsomuch as he also is a son of Abraham. For the Son of Man is come to seek and to save that which was lost."

The Parable of the Pounds (Luke 19:11-28)

There were two distinct reasons given for Jesus teaching this parable: (a) "Because He was nigh to Jerusalem," and (b) "because they thought the kingdom of God should immediately appear." They were approaching Jerusalem and the crowd was very excited, filled with anticipation of Jesus' arrival and confrontation with His enemies. They expected Jesus to exert His power and overthrow all opposition, establishing His kingdom as Messiah. So the parable was taught to prepare their hearts for His entrance into Jerusalem and to correct their false ideas about the kingdom. Two different groups were addressed by this parable—those who believed in Him and fully expected Jesus to declare Himself and set up His kingdom, and those who were His enemies and determined to thwart His movements and see Him destroyed.

Parables use everyday things, common things that the people were familiar with, to teach spiritual lessons. Josephus tells of several times when journeys to Rome were made by members of the Herodian family to be confirmed in rule over Palestine. There seems to be a direct reference in the parable to the journey of Archelaus to Rome in 4 B.C., upon the death of Herod to seek the throne in Jerusalem that had been granted him by his father's will. The Jews sent an embassy of fifty of their ablest leaders to oppose Archelaus, but Augustus sustained Herod's will. Archelaus was granted the kingdom, although not as king, but tetrarch.

In the parable, the nobleman represents Jesus, the servants represent His disciples, and the citizens represent His enemies. There is an emphasis here that spoke directly to the expectancy of the crowd about the kingdom being set up immediately. The parable warned that He must go away, be away for a long time before He returns, but that He will most certainly return and reward both His friends and foes.

One servant was given jurisdiction over ten cities because he had shown the ability by producing ten pounds from one; another was given the same with five. Yet another of the ten came with just the one pound he had been given originally. His reasoning was that his master was an exacting man, and out of fear he had returned to him exactly the amount he had been entrusted.

The main point of the parable is that wise use of talents and opportunities demands their use and increase. The refusal to use even a very small gift means the loss of that which we have. Verse 27 suggests the terrible destruction of Jerusalem at the hands of the Romans in A.D. 70, as well as the eternal destruction that awaits those who refuse to obey the gospel of the Lord Jesus Christ.

Arrival at Bethany (John 11:55-12:1, 12:9-11)

After the raising of Lazarus, Jesus had withdrawn to Ephraim, a town about five miles northeast of Bethel. From there He made a northward swing along the borders of Samaria and into lower Galilee, crossing the Jordan River into Perea. As He made His way south through Perea, a multitude journeyed with Him. They were probably making their way to Jerusalem for the Passover, going early to allow for ritual purification. Jesus would have crossed the Jordan near Jericho and made His way to that city, where there was the healing of the blind man and the dinner in the home of Zacchaeus.

The last Passover of the Lord's life was at hand, about a week away, and several people were already in the city to purify themselves for participating in the feast. The law did not specifically demand purification "before the Passover," but the principle of ceremonial cleansing had been applied to the feast of the Passover (2 Chron. 30:16-20).

Jerusalem itself was filled with excitement. Would Jesus come? The raising of Lazarus caused great excitement, generating more anger and hostility among the leaders. The construction of the sentence in verse 56 tends toward the negative; in other words, "He's not going to come to the feast, is He?"

The chief priests and the Pharisees had given an edict that if any man knew where Jesus was, he should make it known to them that they might take Him. Obviously they wanted to "take" Jesus to kill Him. But Jesus did not hide or do His works in secret. Multitudes followed Him. What they really wanted was a time when they could get Him away from the crowds and take Him.

Jesus arrived at Bethany.

> His arrival there undoubtedly preceded the onset of the Sabbath, which began at sundown, since He would not have traveled on the Sabbath day. The Passover was celebrated on the 14th of the Jewish month of Nisan (Leviticus 23:5), between the evenings

(that is, between sunset and the time darkness fell, Exodus 12:6); the paschal meal was eaten at the end of the 14th day, and at the beginning of the 15th; six days previously would be on the 8th of Nisan, Friday (G. N. Woods, *New Testament Commentaries, John*, 252).

Lazarus was mentioned because of the great excitement his raising had generated. When word got out that Jesus was in Bethany, many went there to see Jesus, and Lazarus. Many believed in Jesus because of the risen Lazarus that the chief priests actually entertained the idea of putting Lazarus to death as well.

Anointing By Mary (Matt. 26:6-13, Mark 14:3-9, John 12:2-8)

Only by looking at the three texts together are we able to see the entire picture of what took place at this time. Of the three, it appears that John places it in its chronological order. We see the arrival in Bethany six days before the Passover, and the anointing by Mary (probably on Saturday night after the Sabbath had ended; thus the beginning of Sunday according to the Jewish method of keeping time), and then the triumphal entry into Jerusalem in the daylight hours of Sunday. Matthew and Mark seem to speak of it out of order, but as a partial explanation of the actions that Judas took.

Jesus entered into the home of Simon the leper. Some have conjectured that he was the father of Mary, Martha, and Lazarus. Still others, that he was the husband of Martha. He was not a leper at this time, because if he had been, he would not have been inviting people into his home. He was a disciple of Jesus, who had been a leper and healed by Jesus, and now the two households, his and the household of Mary, Martha, and Lazarus, have joined together in this hospitality to Jesus (this is also conjecture).

Again, Martha was the one who did the serving. From Luke 10, she was concerned about the physical things necessary in hospitality and it was said of her, "Martha was cumbered about much serving." Mary, who "sat at the feet of Jesus, and heard His word" (Luke 10:39), took an alabaster box (or cruse) of precious ointment, pure nard, broke the cruse and poured the ointment over the head of Jesus. She anointed His feet as well and wiped them with her hair. John adds the beautiful detail, "and the house was filled with the odor of the ointment."

The "alabaster cruse" would have been the vessel in which the precious nard was shipped from the Far East. It would have been sealed to protect its contents, with the vessels themselves being delicate and beautiful. "Nard" was a liquid perfume distilled from an odorous plant and mingled with oil. A "pound" or "litra" was a Greek measure of weight amounting to almost twelve ounces.

The attitude and character of Judas showed itself here. While Matthew says "the disciples" had indignation," and Mark says, "some had indignation," John makes it clear that Judas was the one who brought it up, and his motive was not concern for the poor. Judas was successful in stirring the others to indignation over the perceived waste of this fine ointment. This ointment could have been sold and the money, over 300 shillings, given to the poor. But giving the money to the poor was not the motive behind Judas' objection. John says that Judas was the one who kept the bag containing the funds of the Lord and His apostles. Judas was the treasurer, so to speak, and he was a thief. Those 300 shillings could have been his for the taking.

Jesus described what Mary had done as "a good work," an act of kindness and love. He rebuked the disciples for their criticism of her actions. Perhaps Mary knew Jesus was about to die, and if so, the emphasis Jesus placed upon her actions was made known. "She hath anointed my body beforehand for the burying." Thus her actions were absolutely fitting. So significant and beautiful was this work of Mary that Jesus said it was to be spoken of wherever the gospel was preached as a memorial for her. There is considerable controversy in the religious world concerning "who" did this anointing:

> John clearly names Mary of Bethany as the woman. The most surprising efforts had been made to identify Mary of Magdala with the sinful woman of Luke 7:36-50 and identify them both with Mary of Bethany. Those who hold there was only one anointing usually attempt to identify all three. Bernard attempts the unusual in trying to identify three women as one and yet hold that she anointed Jesus twice, once in repentance as she left the life of a harlot to rejoin her family, and again in devotion to her Savior... This is the Roman Catholic position. Early Christian writers show great divergence of views about the identity of the anointing and the women, but from the time of Gregory the Great, the Roman Catholic Church has identified the three women as Mary of Bethany. The Feast of St. Mary Magdalene on July 22 attempts to teach this theory and presents Mary as a great sinner who became a great saint. But how can Magdala in the plain of Gennesaret of Galilee be identified with Bethany on the Mount of Olives? It is in vain to suppose that Magdala is some unidentifiable place on the Mount of Olives for Mary Magdalene is clearly represented as a woman of Galilee and Mary of Bethany a woman of Judea. They suggest that Mary, Martha, and Lazarus formerly lived in Galilee; this is without foundation for they are always associated with Bethany (Luke 10:38-42 does not name the village, but it evidently is Bethany). Moreover, there is not the slightest reason for casting reflections upon either Mary Magdalene or Mary of Bethany by trying to identify them with the repentant harlot of Luke 7:36-50. Bernard's effort to interpret, "Mary hath chosen the good part" (Luke 10:42) as meaning not the good part of hearing Jesus instead of serving with Martha, but the good part

of becoming a disciple as contrasted with a life of shame she had lived before, is monstrous. Such an effort is proof of the lack of any real evidence (R.C. Foster, *Gospel Studies*, Vol. 4; 3, 4).

The Entry into Jerusalem
(Matt. 21:1-11, Mark 11:1-11, Luke 19:29-44, John 12:12-19)

It was now the daylight hours of Sunday. Having left Bethany, Jesus began to make His way to Jerusalem. He approached Bethpage, "The House of Figs," which was a small suburb on the eastern side of the Mount of Olives, close to Bethany. To this village, or perhaps to another nearby, Jesus dispatched two of His disciples; which two we do not know.

The instructions were clear. Jesus told them that when they got to the village they would find an ass and a colt (Matthew is the only one who mentions the ass) tied. They were to untie and bring the animals to Him. If anyone questioned what they were doing, (the owner, who Luke wrote did ask), they were to say, "The Lord has need of them." Matthew writes, "All this was done, that it might be fulfilled which was spoken by the prophet, saying, tell ye the daughter of Zion, Behold, thy King cometh unto thee, meek, and sitting upon an ass, and a colt the foal of an ass." Thus, this was in fulfillment of Zechariah 9:9. Mark and Luke describe Jesus actually riding upon the colt. This would be indicative of His great meekness.

Mark mentions "and straightway he will send him back hither." There are a few possible meanings of this statement. It could be referring to the owner, and the idea that the owner would immediately send the animals back with the disciples. It could mean that Jesus was informing the owner He wanted the animals for only a short time and would send them back when finished.

This colt was to be one upon whom "no man ever yet sat." The fact it had not yet been used by man fitted it for such a sacred purpose. Consider Numbers 19:2, "This is the ordinance of the law which the Lord hath commanded, saying, Speak unto the children of Israel, that they bring thee a red heifer without spot, wherein is no blemish, *and upon which never came a yoke.*" This principle is repeated in Deuteronomy 21:3.

Having secured the animals in exactly the manner Jesus had said they would, the disciples brought them to Jesus. Evidently they did not know which animal Jesus would choose to ride, for they put their garments on both of them. This provided a place to sit and was also a sign of honor (2 Kings 9:13). These garments refer to the cloak worn over the tunics or shirts.

As Jesus came over the summit of the Mount of Olives, a great multitude began to rejoice and praise God. News spread that Jesus was coming, and many took palm branches to go meet Him, shouting, "Hosanna; Blessed is he that cometh in the name of the Lord: Blessed is the kingdom that cometh, the kingdom of our father, David: Hosanna in the highest." The people were proclaiming Jesus as the Messiah and King, and He accepted it. Even when the Pharisees complained to Jesus that He should rebuke His disciples for what they were saying, Jesus responded with, "I tell you that, if these shall hold their peace, the stones will cry out." A carpet of branches and garments were laid across the Lord's path. Many who had been with Jesus when He raised Lazarus were present, giving testimony and increasing the excitement of the crowd. "Hosanna" is rising up to the heavens, meaning "Save, we pray." Originally a prayer, it was at this time a phrase of praise and exhortation. What a thrilling time it must have been.

As the procession led by Jesus continued its descent of the Mount of Olives, the city of Jerusalem came into view. Jesus was moved to tears as He saw it. The verb indicates "wailing and sobbing." Jesus was weeping and making lamentation over the city. Why? Because He loved the people and knew what would happen to the city and its inhabitants because of their rejection of Him.

Over and over in their history the Jews had been guilty of rejecting God's messengers. On another sad occasion, recorded in Luke 13:34-35, Jesus had said, "O Jerusalem, Jerusalem, which killest the prophets and stonest them that are sent unto thee: how often would I have gathered thy children together, as a hen doth gather her brood under her wings, and ye would not! Behold, your house is left unto you desolate: and verily I say unto you, Ye shall not see Me, until the time come when ye shall say, Blessed is He that cometh in the name of the Lord." They were doing it again. Jesus was referring to the fact they proclaimed Him and shouted, "Hosanna in the highest," but they did not understand. If they had understood and accepted Him as the Christ, they could have saved themselves and the city from untold misery. But, they would not.

Luke 19:43-44 has reference to the destruction of Jerusalem. The account of that destruction, given by Josephus in Book VI of his *Wars of the Jews*, demonstrates how accurately the Lord told what would come to pass. When Jesus said in verse 44, "because thou knewest not the time of thy visitation", He was referring to the glorious opportunity they had. They were being visited by the Christ, the Son of the living God, and they did not know it.

Mark tells us that as Jesus entered into Jerusalem, He went right to the heart of things, into the temple, exactly where His enemies were. We are told that He "looked around about upon all things," and He saw a great many things taking place in the courts of the temple that were not right. This appears to be the meaning for it was now "eventide," and on the next day Jesus repeated an action He had taken about three years earlier, cleansed the temple.

John tells us how the enemies of Jesus viewed this whole event: "Behold how ye prevail nothing: lo, the world is gone after Him." All of their attempts to ensnare Jesus in His words, all of their threats against those who would believe in Him, all of their attempts to discredit Jesus or to heckle Him -- none of it had been successful. Those who were urging more severe measures, death, were saying to the more moderately minded, "Your ways have failed, look at how the people proclaim Him. Now it is time for death." In less than a week, that would come to pass.

Cursing the Fig Tree and Second Cleansing of the Temple (Matt. 21:12-17, 18-19, Mark 11:12-18, Luke 19:45-48)

After His triumphal entry into Jerusalem and His viewing of the temple, Jesus left the city and returned to Bethany where He spent the night. The following morning Jesus came back to Jerusalem and He made His way back to the city. He was hungry, one of only two times that is mentioned (the other was during the temptation). The gospels mention the work of Jesus being so great that He did not have time to eat (Mark 6:31). At another time, the disciples were upset with Jesus because He was engrossed in His labors and did not eat with them (John 4:31-34). The burdens on Jesus were heavy at this time because it was His final week before the crucifixion.

As Jesus and His apostles made their journey to Jerusalem, they saw a fig tree down the road. Mark says "afar off," while Matthew tells us it was "by the wayside." The tree was still off in the distance a bit when they first saw it, and it was right by the road. It was covered with leaves, suggesting that it also had fruit. When Jesus arrived at the tree, He found the tree only had leaves, no fruit. Jesus then cursed the fig tree, that it would bear no more fruit. The idea of cursing here is not one of anger or malice, but "devoted to destruction." Since it was not what it appeared and failed to produce the fruit, it would wither away and die.

Most of the commentators indicated a similarity between this fig tree and the Jewish nation at the time—all appearance, but no fruit. Most held the fig tree to symbolize the Jewish nation. The day before Jesus was praised, but in less than a week, they would crucify Him.

Mark also mentions "for the time of the figs was not yet." Several explanations have been offered. One, and the most probable, is that the tree was blooming a little out of season, and while it was not time for it to be producing fruit, it was not time for it to be producing leaves neither. Another explanation offered is Mark's statement referring to the "time of the gathering of the figs." Thus, it was time for fruit to be on the tree and before the time when the fruit would be normally gathered, making it a surprise when the tree was found to be without fruit. There will be more said about this tree later, but we need to note that the statement of Jesus was not meant for the tree, but as Mark informs us, "and His disciples heard it."

When they came to Jerusalem, Jesus entered into the temple. The first area of the temple into which He would have stepped was called the Court of the Gentiles. This was the largest of the courts of the temple. Gentiles could enter into it but proceed no further. It was considered the least sacred part of the temple by the Jews, and they had no problem with conducting business within its confines.

The business related to the worship, with animals being sold for sacrifice and money-changers needed. The money-changers were those who would exchange, for a fee, the Roman coin for the Jewish coinage necessary to pay the temple tax and freewill offerings. Such a place of business was needed, but it was to be conducted honestly (and there is clear indication that all was not being done honestly), and it was not to be done within the confines of the temple. You might note that Mark even mentions "and would not suffer that any man should carry a vessel through the temple." The idea is a vessel related to business. The temple was not a place of business. It was a place of prayer and worship.

This is not the first time that Jesus acted this way in the temple. The first time occurred almost three years earlier and is recorded in John 2. At that time Jesus made a scourge and drove the animals out, but no whip is mentioned at this incidence. Jesus' personality and the righteousness of what He was doing were irresistible. Those who were most upset by Jesus were not hirelings in the temple. It was the Sadducees and other Jewish leaders.

The effect on the scribes and chief priests was to seek a way to destroy Jesus and Mark tells us why: "For they feared Him." The Sadducees controlled the temple and Jesus had just accused them of dishonesty. He said that they had made the temple into a "den of robbers." It was a direct challenge to them, a challenge not only of their methods but of their motives.

The effect upon the crowd was amazing. They were astonished at His teaching, and all "hung upon Him, listening." The blind and the lame came to be healed and the children shouted out what had been said in the triumphal entry the day before, "Hosanna to the son of David." When the chief priests and the scribes heard it, they rebuked Jesus with, "Hearest thou what these are saying?" (the obvious idea being "stop them"). But Jesus answered, "Have you never read" and then quoted from Psalm 8:2. It is a psalm of praise to God, and His use of it implied the children were correct. To praise Jesus was to praise God.

Discussion about the Fig Tree
(Matt. 21:20-22, Mark 11:19-26, Luke 21:37-38)

Jesus left the city of Jerusalem that night and lodged in Mount Olivet. The next morning He and His disciples once again came to Jerusalem and came upon the withered fig tree. What a contrast there must have been from a tree covered with leaves the day before to a tree completely withered. Peter brought it to the Lord's attention and the disciples asked, "How did the fig tree immediately wither away?" Jesus gave them the following answer:

> Have faith in God. For verily I say unto you, That whosoever shall say unto this mountain, Be thou removed, and be thou cast into the sea: and shall not doubt in his heart; but shall believe that those things which he saith shall come to pass; he shall have whatsoever he saith. Therefore I say unto you, What things soever ye desire, when ye pray, believe that ye receive them, and ye shall have them.

To understand the Lord's teaching concerning prayer at this time, His teachings of prayer in other New Testament books is to be remembered. God answers prayers. He who asks in faith (not doubting), in accordance with the will of the Father, in harmony with the teaching of Jesus, with the understanding prayers to be uttered with a "not my will, but thine be done" attitude, will have his prayers answered and accomplish great things.

Jesus' emphasis on forgiveness at the end of this discussion was to make certain His disciples did not misunderstand the action He had taken concerning the tree. Nothing was done, nor is it to be done, out of vindictiveness.

Discussion of Authority (Matt. 21:23-27, Mark 11:27-33, Luke 20:1-8)

Once again Jesus arrived in the city of Jerusalem and went to the temple. Notice all who were involved in this challenge of the Lord's authority. There were the "chief priests," including the high priest and those eligible to the office; or the reigning priestly family. There were the "elders," the members of the Sanhedrin. And there were the "scribes," the scholars of the nation who were invariably Pharisees. Thus, the entire leadership of the nation was arraying itself against Jesus. The leadership had been strongly rebuked publicly and had been humiliated by the actions of Jesus in the temple the day before. It is apparent that they had to do something to regain the upper hand in the eyes of the people. Perhaps they could show that Jesus usurped their authority and had no right to do the things He did. If they could discredit Jesus in the eyes of the populace, their plan to arrest and destroy Him would be easier to carry out.

They asked two questions: (1) "By what authority doest thou these things?" (2) "Who gave thee this authority?" It is important to recognize in His response that one must have authority to act in religion and that authority must come from the right source. The Lord's response was, "I will tell you by what authority I do these things if you will answer one question. The baptism of John, where did it come from? From heaven or from men?"

The validity of the questions Jesus had been asked is seen. John acted by authority, but whose authority? There are only two possible sources of authority in religion. It is either from God or it is from man.

There was no attempt by the Jewish leaders to answer truthfully; they were concerned only with expediency. Their attempt to ensnare and discredit Jesus had already backfired. If they said that John's authority was of God, then Jesus would have accused them for not believing him. On the other hand, if they said that John's authority came from man, they were afraid of the reaction of the people because they held John to have been a prophet. So instead of honesty, they chose expediency and said, "We know not."

When Jesus told them "Neither tell I you by what authority I do these things," He was showing the people gathered in the temple the corrupt nature of their leaders. What courage Jesus showed! This was just the first of many conflicts that Jesus would have with the leaders on this most perilous day. It was Tuesday of His final week.

The Parables of Two Sons, Vineyard, Wedding Garment (Matt. 21:28-22:1-14, Mark 12:1-12, Luke 20:9-19)

Next, Jesus used two parables directed at the leaders of the Jews. The parables were designed to force them to pronounce sentence on themselves. He begins with two sons. Some have asked why just two sons? When you get right down to it, there are only two types of people—those who do God's will and those who don't. In this case, one refused to do God's Will, then repented and did it. One promised to do God's Will, then failed or refused to do it.

The inevitable question Jesus posed to His audience, "Who was the obedient son." The chief priests and the elders of the people could no longer hide behind feigned ignorance. They were forced to answer, even though they realized that the parable talked about the ecclesiastical hierarchy of Israel. They said that the son, who at first refused but later changed his mind, did the will of his father.

Jesus illustrated what the story of the father and his two sons really meant in the spiritual context of his day. The first son was the personification of the tax collectors, and the prostitutes who refused to do the will of God. But when John the Baptist came..."preaching a baptism of repentance for the forgiveness of sins" (Mark 1:4), the social and moral outcasts of society repented, believed, and entered the kingdom of God. Thus they did the will of the Father.

The second son portrayed the attitude of the religious leaders of Jesus' day. They were the ones who do everything for men to see. They were the people who did not practice what they preached. John the Baptist came to them showing them the way of righteousness. They listened to his words but did not believe. They saw, however, that the tax collectors accepted John's message and were baptized. Nevertheless, they rejected God's purpose for themselves, refusing to be baptized by John (Luke 7:30).

> The application of the parable is dynamic. Tax collectors and prostitutes had refused to obey the will of God. Yet when they heard the message of repentance, they turned to God in obedience. The religious leaders who presumably were experts in the law of God put on an outward show of compliance. Inwardly, however, they refused to accept the Word of God, whether it came via the written word of the prophets or the spoken word of John the Baptist and Jesus. They were like the son who said to his father, "I will, sir," but did not (Simon Kistemaker, *The Parables of Jesus*, 85,86).

Jesus continued with His discourse, turning His attention now to the people (Luke makes this clear), but the leaders were still listening. They were feeling the sting from the message of the previous parable.

In this one, the householder represented God, while the vineyard represented the Jewish nation. The description indicated how well blessed and protected the nation had been. The rulers of Jews were represented by the husbandmen given charge of the vineyard. God expected the Jews to bring forth goodly fruits; love, joy, peace, and so on. And, He looked to the leaders to bring forth such results; He sent the prophets to the rulers and people to encourage them. The rulers abused, mistreated, and killed the messengers of God.

So, He sent his Son, representative of Jesus. The householder was tender and forgiving, unwilling to resort to extreme measures. Surely the husbandmen would reverence his son. How did they treat him? They killed him. What were the leaders of the Jews plotting at that very moment to do to Jesus? They were plotting to kill Him.

What did the householder do to those husbandmen? That was the question Jesus asked, and they answered correctly. He destroyed those miserable men and let out the vineyard to other husbandmen who did right and brought forth fruits.

In application Jesus referred to Psalm 118:22-23. The Pharisees and other leaders were anxious to set up the kingdom of the Messiah. They were like unskilled workers who reject the corner stone of the building they sought to erect. That stone represented Jesus. The ones who fell "on the stone" refer to those who condemned the Lord. They would be judged. The ones upon whom the stone "fell" would be all the lost when Jesus comes in judgment. (It could also have reference to those Jews who still refused Him at the time of the destruction of Jerusalem in A.D. 70).

The final of the three parables delivered in the temple at that time depicted a judgment. Many guests were invited to the wedding of a king's son, but few honored the invitation. Most treated it with neglect, even scorn, making various excuses. Others took the servants of the king who delivered the invitation and abused and killed them. So after the destruction of those wicked people, the king extended his invitation to those out in the highways, both good and bad. They would be separated when the king came.

The ones initially invited represent the Jews. The servants, who were abused and killed, represented the prophets and the Lord. The city of murderers represented Jerusalem. The people called from the highways represented the Gentiles, and the coming of the king to the wedding feast represented the coming of the Lord in final judgment. The individual without the wedding garment was anyone found in the church at judgment who was not a true follower of the Lord. Many believe that the destruction Jesus spoke of in verse 7 referred to the destruction of Jerusalem.

Question of Tribute to Caesar
(Matt. 22:15-22, Mark 12:13-17, Luke 20:20-26)

Having failed in their attempt to discredit the Lord's position by questioning His authority, and having felt the brunt of His rebuke in the three parables, the Pharisees now took council to determine their next course of action. This happened on the same day. They decided to send some of their disciples to Jesus to ensnare Him in His talk. Perhaps these younger men, desired to learn, and would be able to trick Jesus into saying something that could be used against Him. Even more disturbing was their inclusion of the Herodians in their plot.

The Herodians and the Pharisees were natural enemies with the Jewish community. They were on opposite sides of practically all things religious and Jewish. The Herodians actually supported the Herod family, which ruled thru the favor of Rome. That made them favor the paying of tribute to Caesar.

The Pharisees, on the other hand, viewed the paying of tribute to a foreign power as a national tragedy. They did not advocate open rebellion against Rome because of it, but they definitely were not in favor of it. They were both willing to lay aside their differences because of their common hatred of Jesus.

If these disciples were in fact younger men, learning at the feet of the Pharisees, is not it sad they had learned their dishonest and devious ways? Notice how they tried to soften Jesus with their words of praise. What they said was true, but their motives for saying it screamed their blatant hypocrisy. They said that Jesus was: (1) A true man, and He was. (b) That He taught the way of God in truth, and He did. (c) That He had no fear of any person, and He did not. (d) That He was not going to be swayed by the person to whom He was speaking, and He wouldn't be. Their approach is a reminder of Proverbs 27:6, "Faithful are the wounds of a friend; but the kisses of an enemy are deceitful."

The question was, "Is it lawful to give tribute unto Caesar or not?" Consider the dilemma in which they had placed Jesus. The Jews were required by law to pay a large sum of money each year to the Roman government as acknowledgement of their being in subjection to them. It has been estimated to have been approximately 600 talents. A talent of that day was worth somewhere between $960 and $1180. This money was spent upon the maintenance of the province itself -- roads, harbors, government buildings, etc. -- with any leftover sent to Rome.

About twenty years before this, time Judas of Galilee had stirred the people in a revolt against Rome that included refusal to pay this tribute. The revolt was viciously crushed, but the masses of the Jews were bitterly opposed to this tribute. So, if Jesus said they were to pay this tribute, the Pharisees felt that He would alienate Himself from the common people who were listening, which would make putting Him to death much easier. On the other hand, if Jesus said that they should not pay the tribute, the Herodians were there to hear, which would have placed Jesus in open rebellion to the policy of Rome.

Knowing full well their trap, and rebuking them for their wickedness, Jesus asked to be shown the tribute money. Receiving a denarius, He asked, "Whose image and superscription is on this?" Told that it was Caesar's, Jesus said, "Render unto Caesar the things that are Caesar's, and unto God the things that are God's."

What an incredible answer! The question had involved "giving" tribute. Jesus' reply was "pay" it; two different words with two different meanings. Jesus used "apodidomi," meaning pay for value received. They did receive benefits from the Roman government and that part of His answer satisfied the Herodians. At the same time, Rome permitted them the freedom to exercise their religion, so they were free to give God the things that belonged to God.

Once again, the Lord's enemies had failed in their attempt to ensnare Him. Luke tells us, "And they could not take hold of his words before the people." They "marveled at his answer."

A Question of the Resurrection
(Matt. 22:23-33, Mark 12:18-27, Luke 20:27-40)

The Sadducees, the Pharisees, and the Herodians had all joined forces in their desire to kill Jesus. In this particular situation, the Sadducees had put forth this question concerning the resurrection to Jesus.

The Sadducees were a corrupt, skeptical, politico-religious party. One of their peculiar views was that there was to be no resurrection of the dead. Instead of a political question, they asked a religious, or doctrinal, question. They hoped to show that Jesus' teaching concerning the question of the resurrection was ridiculous; just imagine seven men fighting in heaven over the one woman.

As a basis for their question, they used the law of Levirate marriages. Deuteronomy 25:5-6 states, "If brethren dwell together, and one of them die, and have no child, the wife of the dead shall not marry without unto a stranger: her husband's brother shall go into unto her, and take her to him to wife, and perform the duty of an husband's brother unto her. And it shall be, that the firstborn which she beareth shall succeed in the name of his brother which is dead, that his name be not put out of Israel."

The purpose of this law was to prevent a family from becoming extinct, "that his name be not put out of Israel," and to secure the property of a family from passing into the hands of a stranger. Using this well-known law as a basis, the Sadducees believed that they had placed Jesus upon the horns of an unanswerable dilemma. They were wrong.

Notice how Jesus answered and pointed out three areas where the Sadducees were deficient, causing them to err. (1) They did not know the scriptures. (2) They did not know the power of God. (3) They assumed that things in the resurrection, if there was to be a resurrection, would have to be as they were on earth. By appealing to the scriptures, Jesus showed the doctrine of the resurrection was there and the Sadducees should have believed, without adding that men would have to live in the resurrection as they had on earth.

The passage Jesus quoted was Exodus 3:6, 15. When God made this statement, Abraham, Isaac, and Jacob had been long dead. Yet God spoke of them as still being their God. How could He be the God of someone who has ceased to exist altogether? That was ridiculous. Therefore they had to live on. Once again, there was astonishment at the Lord's teaching.

The Question of the Greatest Commandment
(Matt. 22:34-40, Mark 12:28-34)

As the Pharisees listened to the reply of Jesus to the Sadducees, they recognized He had answered them with no opportunity to ensnare Him. Next, they put forth a questioner who from Mark's account appeared sincere, but from Matthew's account was being used as part of the general attack on Jesus this day.

The question was, "What is the great commandment in the law?" "What commandment is first of all?" Evidently, this was a question argued among the rabbis. Which commandment was the greatest? Some believed it to be the laws concerning sacrifices, others the wearing of phylacteries, and still others about purification. Any way Jesus answered, He would be offending some who held to a particular view.

Jesus responded by quoting Deuteronomy 6:4-5. This is the first commandment; this is the greatest because it is the foundation of the entire law of God. It forbids all sins against God and demands love for and of Him. The second is from Leviticus 19:18, relating to our relationship with man. We will not mistreat those we love, and we are to love others as we love ourselves. These two laws encompass all aspects of the Law and the Prophets.

This man, perhaps a true seeker of truth being used by his fellow Pharisees, was fair-minded about what Jesus said, recognizing the depth of His reply. The way the man responded showed his deep thoughts about this subject. He understood how the outward signs of religion, while very important, were secondary to the actual, living devotion of the soul to God and one's duty toward his fellow man. Even in the midst of such rancorous questioning and dangerous circumstances as Jesus was facing on this day, less than a week from His death, His love and mercy were seen as He recognized this man's spiritual discernment and told him, "Thou art not far from the kingdom of God." For a short while the Lord's answers silenced His enemies on this fateful day.

A Question about the Son of David
(Matt. 22:41-46, Mark 12:35-37, Luke 20:41-44)

As the Pharisees gathered together, Jesus asked them a question. While their questions had been to entrap and ensnare, Jesus' question was meant to teach them, to save them, to help them understand what they were doing by their rejection of Him.

When Jesus asked, "What think ye of Christ? Whose Son is he?" the Pharisees were able to answer, "The Son of David." The Old Testament made that abundantly clear (2 Sam. 7:8-29, Isa. 9:5-7, 11:1-10, Micah 5:2). But when Jesus continued on and quoted from Psalm 110:1, they did not answer.

Jesus' question was to have them explain the use of the title "Lord," by David, when he spoke of his own descendent? How could the Christ be David's son and David's "Lord" at the same time? Jesus attempted to help them understand the divine character of the promised Messiah, and in so doing, help them to understand the divinity of the One they planning to destroy. His question and His logic dumbfounded the Pharisees.

Denunciation of the Scribes and Pharisees (Matt. 23:1-39, Mark 12:38-40, Luke 20:45-47)

By following the series of events that had taken place, it is apparent that it is still Tuesday before the crucifixion. Jesus arrived in Bethany on Friday (before the Sabbath). On Sunday, He made His triumphal entry into Jerusalem. On Monday, He cursed the fig tree and cleansed the temple. On Tuesday, He discussed the withered fig tree upon His return to Jerusalem. The account of what happened on this day in the life of Jesus is more complete than any other, with the possible exception of a day in Galilee when Jesus delivered the sermon of parables, calmed the sea, and healed the Gadarene demoniac.

On this final Tuesday, the question about our Lord's authority, the question of tribute to Caesar, the question concerning the resurrection, and our Lord's question about the Christ are seen. The parables of the Two Sons and the Wicked Husbandmen, as well as the Wedding Garment are told. The denunciation of the scribes and Pharisees, the incident of the Widow's mite, and the wonderful sermon about life and death are protrayed. There is also the private instruction give to His apostles and recorded in Matthew 24 and 25.

The Lord's scathing denunciation of the scribes and Pharisees was delivered to the multitude. The reason for this sermon is well stated by Foster.

> The work of construction and destruction go together. Before the new house can be built, the old one must be torn down. Before the nation can be won to the spiritual ideals of the kingdom of God, the false teachers and worldly motives of the hypocritical leaders of the nation must be uncovered. Facing the national leaders in this crisis and in the hearing of the vast multitude, Jesus challenged His disciples to disown the whole false system which the Pharisees had bound upon the nation. He clearly upheld the Old Testament law as of God, but denounced the Pharisees as false teachers. If these leaders, themselves, are ever to be turned to God, they must be brought to realize their own despicable conduct and condition. This He attempts to do (R.C. Foster, *Gospel Studies*, Vol. 4, 60).

Focusing on Matthew's account, Jesus recognized the authority of the Law of Moses and recognized the teachers of that Law were worthy of being heard because they upheld and taught that Law. However, the scribes and Pharisees were not to be viewed as examples in observing the law, for they would say and do not. They did not practice what they preached. In addition to being guilty of not observing the Law, they added to it innumerable traditional interpretations and minute rules, all of which went to form a wearisome burden that God did not require. And, to add to their hypocrisy, they did not keep all of their traditions themselves, inventing ways to get around them as in Matthew 15:4-6.

There was also the matter of ostentatiousness. Jesus expressed it so well with the words, "For all their works they do to be seen of men." The Lord gave two examples: (1) "They make broad their phylacteries." A phylactery was a small leather box with tiny manuscript verses from the law written thereon. It was worn hanging from the forehead, the arm, or the breast. There was nothing wrong or sinful about wearing a phylactery; but making it big to show off their piety was. (2) They "enlarged the borders of their garments." Numbers 15:37-39 commanded the Israelites to make fringes in the borders of their garments with a narrow strip of blue on the fringes. What the Pharisees did was to make it bigger, to make a show of how carefully they "observed" the Law.

They loved to be placed in the most prominent seats at feasts and in the synagogues. They loved to be recognized as "religious leaders." The Lord taught a basic message in this passage; the Christian is not to wear or assume a religious title that indicates superiority over others. While Jesus rebuked the desire for preeminence among the scribes and Pharisees, He also taught the disciples once again the principle of true greatness. True greatness comes in service and humility.

Jesus accused the scribes and Pharisees of "shutting up the kingdom of heaven against men." This they did by refusing to accept Jesus as the Messiah, by binding people to observance of their own man-made traditions, by opposing the work of Jesus, and by doing everything they could to keep others from becoming His followers. This did not mean that the kingdom was in existence at that time anymore than it means that the scribes and Pharisees were the gatekeepers of the kingdom. They had great influence over the people and they used it to keep them from accepting Jesus.

Concerning "widow's houses" and "long prayers," Barnes noted:

> The word houses is here used to denote property or possessions of any kind. You take away, or get possession of, by improper arts and pretenses. This was done in two ways: (a) They pretended to a very exact knowledge of the law, and to a perfect observance of it. They pretended to extraordinary justice to the poor, friendship for the distressed, and willingness to aid those who were in embarrassed circumstances. They thus induced widows and poor people to commit the management of their property to them as guardians and executors, and then took advantage of them and defrauded them. (b) By their long prayers they put on the appearance of great sanctity, and induced many weak women to give them much, under pretense of devoting it to religious purposes (Albert Barnes, *Barnes' Notes*, 109).

They sought to make converts to Pharisaism, not to the truth. Then, they made their converts fanatical to the precepts of the Pharisees causing them to be twice as bad as those who taught them. What a terrible indictment! They made them "twofold more the child of hell" than themselves.

There is another terrible indictment. These religious leaders engaged in some unholy reasoning. They taught that certain oaths were binding and others were not. For instance, an oath "by the temple" was not binding, but an oath "by the gold of the temple" was. The Lord's point was, if a man takes an oath, he is bound before God to perform it, no matter what the ungodly reasoning of the Pharisees might be.

They were scrupulous in their observance of the smaller matters of the law, even to the tithing of the smallest of garden herbs. However, they neglected the larger matters of judgment, mercy, and faith that gave meaning to the whole law in the first place. The little things needed to be done but never to the neglect of the larger. Mere observance of the ordinances of God's law without the proper motivation is meaningless.

The Pharisees and scribes were concerned with outward appearances, and not with the inside which is of the utmost importance. Jesus compared them to someone who washed the outside of the dishes and left the inside filthy. In their case, the filth was extortion and self-indulgence. He compared them to whited sepulchers, to beautiful, whitewashed tombs, but "within full of dead men's bones, and of all uncleanness." The scribes and Pharisees looked good on the outside, but inside they were full of hypocrisy and lawlessness.

Jesus indicted them for falsely professing to surpass their forefathers in righteousness. They built the tombs of the prophets who were dead, decorating them and denying that they would have done the same thing if they had been alive at the time of their forefathers. Professing themselves to be superior to their ancestors, they showed themselves to be of the same moral character. Their fathers had rejected and destroyed God's earlier messengers and now they planned to fill the cup of their unrighteousness by slaying God's Son.

In verses 34-36, Jesus did not say the Jewish people to whom He spoke would be held personally responsible for murders that they had not committed, but He said the climax of all such defiance of God was about to be seen in their murder of His Son. Theirs had been the divine gift of revelation; theirs the terrible sin of rejection. All the murders from Abel to Zachariah is akin to saying everything wicked from Genesis to Malachi was about to be culminated in the actions of that generation.

Jesus spoke of the judgment that would come upon that generation, upon the people, most likely the destruction of Jerusalem. Here is His lament over the city and the people He loved. God sought to secure the repentance of the people; now Jesus Himself pleaded with them to accept Him and receive salvation. They rejected Him; punishment would come.

The Widow's Gift (Mark 12:41-44, Luke 21:1-4)

After the long and arduous discussions Jesus had on this difficult day, He "sat down," as Mark tells us, close to the treasury. Jesus lifted up His eyes to view those who were making offerings, as Luke informs us.

It is not known for certain if there was a special building in the temple known as The Treasury, but in the Court of Women there were thirteen boxes, shaped like trumpets, into which the people cast their offerings. It was written upon each box what the money would be used to accomplish. Perhaps Jesus was watching the offerings being given in that manner.

Many wealthy came and cast into the treasury out of their abundance, while a poor widow cast in two mites, equal to about two fifths of a cent. It was actually unlawful to offer less than two mites. The test of what we give is not the amount offered, but how much is kept. The rich men gave large gifts, but their gifts were very small in comparison to what they had. The widow gave an insignificant amount, but not in God's eyes. God measures gifts, not in terms of how much monetarily, but in terms of devotion and dedication. In that way the widow gave more than all the others He saw that day. Isn't this picture of the widow giving all she had an interesting and refreshing contrast after our Lord's dealing with the hypocritical, self-righteous Pharisees and scribes?

Sermon Concerning the Significance of Life and Death (John 12:20-50)

This is the only event that John records of the last week between the triumphant entry and the Last Supper. It took place toward the end of that Tuesday of controversy, and was the last public discourse of Jesus before His arrest.

These Greeks were Greek converts to Judaism, proselytes, and were in the outer court of the temple. They may have approached Philip because he had a Greek name indicating a Hellenistic background. Philip did not immediately go to Jesus with their request, but first consulted with Andrew. These individuals may or may not have been escorted into the presence of Jesus, but His words constituted a reply to their request.

> "You would see me," He seems to say; "then you have arrived at exactly the right time, for the hour has come for the Son of man to be glorified." In his death and resurrection he is to be revealed in his true character, as the Savior of the world. The Greeks did not need to hear his words or to see his miracles; his death was what they needed to witness. His cross would be the attractive power which would draw to himself all those multitudes of the Gentile world represented by these inquirers.

> Jesus illustrates the absolute necessity of his death by reference to nature (v. 24); a grain of wheat must first be buried, its coverings must decay, it must perish as a grain before it can produce a multitude of grains like itself. He applies to Himself (v. 25) this great law of life through death, of service and influence through self-sacrifice, and that by so doing he would secure and bestow

blessings that are eternal. He applies this same principle to His disciples (v. 26) (Charles Erdman, *The Gospel of John*, 119).

Looking at verse 27, Jesus understood the necessity of His death, but He was not blind to the pain and anguish it would bring. In His troubled spirit He raised the question of what He should pray to the Father. Should He pray, "Save me from this hour?" Jesus came into the world to fulfill this "hour." But, His sacrifice was necessary. His prayer was "Father, glorify Thy name." God answered Jesus with a voice from heaven. He repeatedly glorified His name in the ministry of Jesus and now, as the final hour of death approached, He promised future glorification. It would be in the death, burial, resurrection, and ascension of Jesus and in the worldwide proclamation of the gospel.

People heard the voice but did not know where it came from or what was said. Jesus declared that it had been uttered for their sakes. It was designed to make them realize the importance of His death. His death would be "the judgment of the world." By it the moral character of the world would be revealed and its sin condemned. The prince of this world would be "cast out," defeated (v. 31). By His death, all men would be drawn to the Lord.

Jesus gave them a final warning. "Yet a little while is the light with you. Walk while ye have the light, lest darkness come upon you: for he that walketh in darkness knoweth not whither he goes. While ye have the light, believe in the light, that ye may be the children of light." After those words, Jesus departed and hid Himself from them. For all intents and purposes, the public ministry of Jesus was now over.

Verses 37-50 appear to be a summation. In them, the consequences and causes of unbelief are presented. It consists of two paragraphs, the first of which is from vs. 37-43. The miracles of Jesus should have been sufficient to produce faith in all who witnessed them, but most did not believe. As an explanation of why, Isaiah 53:1 and Isaiah 6:10 were quoted. They speak of spiritual blindness. Also, some did not openly accept Jesus because their hearts were not right. "They love the praise of men more than the praise of God."

The last paragraph, consisting of verses 44-50, summarizes the words of Jesus, giving the solemn and awful consequences of unbelief. To reject Jesus is to reject God. By their refusal to believe on Him, they judged themselves in the last day by the words that He had spoken.

Prediction of the Fall of Jerusalem and the Second Coming (Matt. 24:1-51, Mark 13:1-37, Luke 21:5-36)

As Jesus left the temple on that fateful Tuesday after His scathing rebuke of the Pharisees, His apostles called His attention to the magnificence of the structure. It must have been something to behold. It has been said that the building covered an area of approximately nineteen acres. There were those who viewed it as one of the wonders of the world. The Talmud says, "He that never saw the temple of Herod never saw a fine building." Jesus took the opportunity to make an incredible prediction. He said, "See ye not all these things? Verily I say unto you, There shall not be left here one stone upon another, that shall not be thrown down." Within forty years this prophecy was fulfilled.

In examination of this teaching of Jesus, which He did privately with His apostles, the focus is on Matthew's account.

Jesus had predicted the destruction of the marvelous temple, the center of Jewish worship. Surely to the apostles such an event could only mean the end of the world. To them, the two events were inseparable. So, they asked Jesus, "Tell us, when shall these things be? And what shall be the sign of thy coming, and of the end of the world?"

Mark writes, "Tell us, when shall these things be? And what shall be the sign when all these things shall be fulfilled?"

Luke 21:7 says, "Master, but when shall these things be? And what sign will there be when these things shall come to pass?"

Even though the apostles viewed their questions as related to the same event, Jesus did not. He divided His answer into two sections. First, Jesus addressed the destruction of Jerusalem and the temple. He told them when it would happen and the signs to indicate that it was about to happen. He told them that it would take place *before that generation passed away.* Next, Jesus addressed the Second Coming. Concerning that event, Jesus said there would be no signs to indicate that it was coming and that no one knew when it would be.

All sorts of signs indicate that the destruction of Jerusalem was nigh. There were deceivers who claimed to be the Christ. Josephus certainly verified that by saying there were many who made such a claim toward the time of Jerusalem's fall.

Not only were there false messiahs, there were "wars and rumors of wars." Revolts were constantly breaking out in different parts of the Roman Empire prior to A.D. 70. Josephus even mentioned wars among the Jews instigated by the Zealots. Famines and pestilence were a problem. In Acts 11:28 we read of a terrible famine that took place during the time of Claudius Caesar, which would place it sometime between A.D. 45-54. Even earthquakes occurred. Alford numbered five great earthquakes during this time.

The church suffered tremendous persecution before the destruction of Jerusalem. Read the book of Acts and see that this came to pass. Christians were driven from their homes, arrested, beaten, hauled into prison and before civil authorities, and even killed. Not only did the church have to deal with such outside persecution, it also had to deal with false teachers from within. Think of Hymenaeus and Alexander, Philetus and Phygellus, as well as Hermogenes to name a few. Yet the gospel went into all the world. Paul wrote of this being fulfilled in Romans 10:18 and Colossians 1:23. The book of Romans was written in late A.D. 57 or early 58, while Colossians was penned sometime in A.D. 58.

The "abomination of desolation" refers to the time when the standards and the idolatrous symbols of Rome would rise in the holy place of the temple. In Luke 21:20 we find, "And when ye shall see Jerusalem compassed with armies, then know that the desolation thereof is nigh."

When the disciples saw the armies, they should have know it was time to flee. To show the urgency of their flight, Jesus said that if they were on their housetops when they saw the armies coming, they were not to take the time to gather any of their household goods. If they were in the field when they saw them, they should not return to the city. It would be a difficult time for mothers with nursing children, and they should pray that it would not occur in winter for that would make their flight more difficult. They should pray that when the time came it would not be on the Sabbath day, for the gates of the city would be closed.

Many different things happened to show them that it was time. The Son of man was coming in judgment and the Roman armies were going to be the tool that He would use. The Romans were the "eagles" (or vultures) and Jerusalem was the "carcass." Jerusalem would be destroyed just like a carcass is consumed by hungry vultures.

Following immediately upon the heels of the destruction of Jerusalem, certain other signs occurred. The language of verse 29 is similar to language that was used in the Old Testament in reference to the fall of nations. Ezekiel wrote of the fall of Egypt in similar language in Ezekiel 32:7-8. The fall of Babylon was described by Isaiah in much the same way in Isaiah 13:10. It is reasonable to believe that the fall of Jerusalem could be depicted in the same way. When considered carefully, with the fall of Jerusalem and the destruction of the temple, the sun of Judaism was setting. It would shine no more.

This was all indicative of Christ coming in power. The events in Jerusalem showed that Jesus was executing judgment.

Verse 31 is very interesting. "Angel" means a "messenger." That is how it is used here. Once the hindrance of Judaism was removed, the gospel was easily spread to the four corners of the earth. Just as they know summer was coming when the fig tree blossomed, they could know that the fall of Jerusalem was close when they saw the signs.

Verse 34 is crucial to understanding this message from Jesus. It tells us *when* all of the events talked about in verses 2-33 were going to take place. Jesus said, *"This generation shall not pass,* till all these things be fulfilled." The word "generation" means the present generation, a contemporary race, a people living at the same time. In Matthew 11:16, 12:38-45, 23:36, the same word is used. Jesus said, *"This* generation." That is an adjective that described the generation. It was *"this* generation," the people living when Jesus spoke. This would surely come to pass. They could depend upon it.

Verse 36 is the "transitional verse." It marks the Lord's change to a different subject as He answered their second question. He talked about the destruction of Jerusalem, now His subject is "that day and hour," an expression used several times in the New Testament with reference of the Second Coming and final judgment (Matt. 7:22, 11:22; John 5:28-29; 1 Thess. 5:2; 2 Thess. 1:10; 2 Tim. 1:18, 4:8).

There would be no signs given to indicate that the Second Coming was at hand. Just like in the days of Noah when everybody continued in the normal affairs and did not know when the rain would come, that is how the return of Jesus would be. The statements about one being taken and the other left is the separation that will occur at that time. Jesus would expand upon that as He continued His teaching to His apostles. Obviously, since the time of the return is not known, all must be constantly ready. If a man knew when a thief intended to break into his home, he would prepare himself. Well, "In such an hour as ye think not the Son of man cometh." A faithful servant is always prepared for the return of his master."

Parable of the Ten Virgins (Matt. 25:1-13)

This parable stressed the need to be prepared, specifically to the Second Coming of Jesus. According to ancient custom, the bridegroom went to the home of the bride to bring her to his own home. The company of virgins gathered at the home of the bridegroom awaiting the return. All ten virgins went to sleep. They were not blamed for sleeping. Actually the fact of their sleeping has no significance in the parable except to explain how they passed the time of waiting. The wise had oil sufficient even for the delay in the coming of the bridegroom, while the foolish had oil only for the early evening hours. When the coming of the bridegroom was delayed, their oil ran out. The lesson is the virtue of forethought and preparedness versus the folly of being unprepared.

This parable taught that lost opportunities cannot be regained. When the bridegroom came, the foolish virgins were out buying oil. On returning, they found the marriage feast had begun. They missed their one chance, and did not seize their one great opportunity.

The Parable of the Talents (Matt. 25:14-30)

Once again the point of this parable is faithfulness. It follows easily the Parable of the Ten Virgins since both emphasize the departure and the return of the master and the need for constant watchfulness and fidelity. Perhaps we could say that the Parable of the Virgins emphasized more the inner life, what we are, and the Parable of the Talents emphasized the outward activity, what we do.

In the parable the three men were given varying talents according to their ability, but they were judged on the basis of faithfulness rather than success. It was possible for the man of average talents to increase his, as did the one with extraordinary talents. If the man with the one talent had made the effort to make some use of the money and add at least the interest, he would not have been condemned. His sin was not drunkenness or any wild excesses by which he squandered his one talent. His sin was neglect and the failure to realize his responsibility to work for the master.

Discussion of Final Judgment (Matt. 25:31-46)

Some consider these verses another parable. It is much more than a parable; it is a realistic prediction of the future judgment of all before the Son of man. Jesus Himself is the Son of man, and in keeping with His Father's wish, He proceeded to judge the nations. He made division among them like a shepherd who separates the sheep from the goats. In Palestine the task of distinguishing between them was not difficult. The sheep were white and the goats were black. He placed the sheep at his right hand, the position of honor. He turned the goats aside and placed them on His left hand. Then the awards were announced. To the righteous, the Son says, "Come, ye blessed of my Father, inherit the kingdom prepared for you from the foundation of the world." They lived in sympathy and self-sacrifice. Now they were rewarded. However, the very characteristics that won for them the Son's approval were the same characteristics, when absent, that caused the others to be rejected. Those on the left hand showed no pity and had practiced no self-denial. The kingdom prepared was not to be theirs; nothing was to be theirs except eternal punishment prepared for the devil and his angels. Judgment is coming. We must be prepared.

Fifth Prediction of Jesus' Death (Matt. 26:1-5, Mark 14:1-2, Luke 22:1-2)

It was Tuesday afternoon when Jesus left the temple and delivered the discourse to His apostles. If it was late in the afternoon, after 6:00, then it would have been the Jewish Wednesday. It was the early moments of Wednesday and the Lord's public ministry was over. The brief time remaining until the Passover and His death was now upon Him. Jesus spent it with the apostles and in solitude with His Father. Wednesday was spent in retirement; there was nothing recorded concerning the events of that day. There is nothing recorded concerning Thursday, except for the preparations for the Passover Feast. The "'two days" were from Tuesday evening to Thursday evening.

The reason for the fifth prediction of His death by Jesus was to establish the faith of the apostles. The time was upon them and they needed to know it was going to happen quickly. It is interesting that even as the chief priests and other members of the Sanhedrin were planning to postpone their efforts to destroy Jesus until after the feast, He was saying that they would actually crucify Him at the time of the Passover. The leaders of the Jews wanted to arrest Jesus secretly and condemn Him before the people could intervene. Remember, just days before, the general populace had acclaimed Jesus as the Messiah. Most would change their minds.

The Plot of Judas (Matt. 26:14-16, Mark 14:10-11, Luke 22:3-6)

Judas went to the High Priest offering to deliver Jesus to them. This appears to have been after their conference concerning Jesus. What prompted Judas and motivated him to do what he did? The Bible does not say a great deal.

Luke states that the devil entered into him. The emphasis on money, the thirty pieces of silver, certainly indicated greed. Remember Judas' anger when Mary anointed Jesus in John 12. It wasn't concern for the poor that prompted his anger, it was his greed. So, greed and avarice were certainly part of his character. John mentions in 13:2, the devil's part in this act. Judas was not a subject of demonic possession and could not resist. Judas opened the door and the devil came in. He deliberately yielded to temptation.

Judas was paid his thirty pieces of silver in advance to seal the bargain, and from that moment on he looked for an opportunity to do his deed -- to deliver Jesus to the chief priests at a time when He was away from the crowd.

Preparation for the Passover Meal
(Matt. 26:17-19, Mark 14:12-16, Luke 22:7-13)

The first day of unleavened bread was the day before the Passover. The Jews were required to remove all leaven from their homes one day before the Passover and keep it out for a week. Mark and Luke make it clear that "the first day of unleavened bread" was the day on which the lambs were killed for the Passover Meal. The Feast of Unleavened Bread began on the 15th of Nisan, but the removal of the leaven from the houses on the day before the Passover (14th of Nisan) caused it to be called the first day of unleavened bread. As soon as the evening of Nisan the 13th arrived (6:00 pm), the Jews searched their houses for leaven, proceeding in silence and with a light.

The day on which the Passover lambs were killed began at sunset of Nisan 13th and extended to sunset of Nisan 14th. The lambs were killed in the afternoon from approximately 2:30 to 5:00. The priest caught the blood of the animal in a bowl and poured it at the foot of the altar of burnt offering. The lamb was carefully prepared and roasted. The unleavened bread and the bitter herbs to be eaten with the lamb were roasted and prepared.

How the site of the meal was selected is an example of the foreknowledge of God. In order to go into the city, they entered through a gate. Jesus either instructed them concerning which gate to enter, or He already knew what gate they would use. He knew the moment they arrived at a certain point; this particular man, and no other, carried a jar of water. Jesus knew the journey of this man (unquestionably a servant) to his home and the fact that the master of that home gladly allowed the use of his large upper room by Jesus and the apostles. The way Jesus was identified to this man as "The Teacher," indicated that the master of the house was a disciple. The large upper room, the guest chamber, would be "furnished and ready." It would have all the usual furniture needed for such an occasion.

Matthew alone recorded the statement of Jesus, "My time is at hand." By this He meant the time of His betrayal and death.

The Passover Meal
(Matt. 26:20, Mark 14:17, Luke 22:14-16, 24-30)

After the preparations for the meal to be eaten after sunset had been made, Jesus sat down to eat the Passover with His apostles. The Lord said, "With desire I have desired," which is a Hebraism that means "I have desired exceedingly." This was the last occasion that Jesus and the apostles celebrated this feast together.

In Luke 22:16 the statement, "For I say unto you, I will not any more eat thereof, until it be fulfilled in the kingdom of God." Jesus did share the meal with them at that time, evidently so. The Passover was "fulfilled in the kingdom of God" when "Christ, our Passover, was sacrificed for us" (1 Cor. 5:7). Every time we partake of the Lord's Supper, we remember that sacrifice. In this sense, Jesus shares with us on each Lord's Day in the solemn commemoration of His sacrifice on our behalf.

Concerning the contention among the apostles, McGarvey and Pendleton suggested Jesus was about to set up an earthly kingdom, having misconstrued His statement made earlier, "My time is at hand." It was known that the apostles had contended about positions of authority and power for themselves (Luke 9:46). Once again, Jesus showed that true honor and greatness stems from service, not from being served. The word "temptation" is used for trials and tribulations. The words concerning eating and drinking at the Lord's table in His kingdom and sitting on thrones judging the twelve tribes of Israel referred to the ancient custom of bestowing honor and distinction. This indicated that the apostles would share in the Lord's exaltation and joy in the end.

The Washing of the Apostles' Feet (John 13:1-20)

Consider this in light of the apostles' contention among themselves. That contention probably occurred when they seated themselves for the feast; hence John said, "Before the feast of the Passover." Jesus had responded to their contention, teaching them that true greatness was seen in service. Now He took the opportunity to teach them a stunning object lesson.

In verse 1, Jesus knew that "his hour was come that he should depart out of this world unto the Father." The absolute knowledge by Jesus about His death being near made what He was about to do a revelation of true love and greatness. He was about to depart from this world. He was about to undergo tremendous pain and suffering, but He must leave His apostles in the world where they were going to have to continue on and proclaim His message to the world. They needed His love and help. Foreknowledge intensified His suffering, but their need took precedence in His heart.

He loved them all along, but now Jesus demonstrated His love for them in the sacrifice of His life on the cross.

The mention of Judas' treachery in verse 2 enhanced the glory of what Jesus was about to do as He stooped to wash the feet of the one He knew was in the process of betraying Him. Jesus rose from the supper, girded Himself with a towel, and took a pitcher of water and a basin. Stooping down, He poured the water from the pitcher over the feet of His apostles, the water running into the basin, and wiped them with the towel. This was a chore normally reserved for the lowliest of household servants.

> His act was interrupted by a notable dialogue between Himself and Peter, which reveals the spiritual significance of the scene. The disciple is hesitating to allow his Master to perform for him so menial a service; and even though assured that Jesus has a purpose which Peter will understand afterward, he objects: "Thou shalt never wash my feet." Jesus replies, "If I wash thee not, thou hast no part with me," indicating not only a part in the Passover supper, but in the friendship of Jesus, and in all that he was that night to impart to his disciples. Peter now turns impulsively to the other extreme: "Lord, not my feet only, but also my hands and my head." And Jesus answered: "He that is bathed needeth not save to wash his feet, but is clean every whit." It is at once evident that Jesus refers to a spiritual cleansing which he was seeking to effect. He did wash his disciples' feet to give them physical comfort. No servant had appeared, as the supper was served, to perform that usual, necessary task; no one of the disciples, disputing as they were as to relative greatness, dared to so humble himself as to perform this lowly service. Jesus therefore washed his disciples' feet; but he did more; he cleansed their hearts. As the disciples behold his matchless humility, and as he touched their feet, all their envy and bitterness and unkindness and wrath were gone. They were ready then to listen to the marvelous discourses which fell from his lips. He knew that the disciples loved Him..but He also recognized their need of having their present state of mind altered. He was aware that the heart of one was filled with deadly enmity: "Ye are clean, but not all. For he knew him that should betray him."
>
> The act was followed by a word of explanation, in which Jesus makes plain to his disciples that they should imitate him in loving, lowly service, and aim to secure not merely the physical comfort of others, but their moral and spiritual cleansing as well: "For I have given you an example, that ye also should do as I have done to you." He declares the blessedness of such service: but recalls a prophecy which shows that from such blessedness one of their number, the traitor, will be excluded (Psa. 41:9); the rest, however, will have the dignity of being thus the very representatives, not only of their Master, but of his Father" (Charles Erdman, *The Gospel of John, An Exposition*, 127, 128).

The question is often asked, "Did Jesus institute foot-washing as an ordinance of the church?" The apostles who were there, who heard His words and had their feet washed by the Master, never practiced foot-washing as an ordinance of the early church. The widows of 1 Timothy 5:10 performed foot-washing as a natural part of hospitality, not as a religious ordinance.

Judas Pointed Out as Traitor
(Matt. 26:21-25, Mark 14:18-21, Luke 22:21-23, John 13:21-30)

Even though He had full knowledge of what Judas was doing and was going to do, it did not make it any less painful for Jesus.

> By the use of the word "betray" Jesus revealed to Judas that he had perfect knowledge of the peculiar crime which he was about to commit. To induce repentance the enormity of the crimes is pointed out in two ways: A. It was the act of one, an act in which no other could be found willing to have a part. B. It was the act of one whose hand rested on the table, who was admitted to the closest intercourse and fellowship (McGarvey and Pendleton, *The Fourfold Gospel*, 652).

Obviously the disciples were amazed at this news and wanted to know who would do such a thing. When they asked, "Is it I, Lord?" the meaning is "Surely it is not I?" Jesus narrowed the possibilities by saying, "It is one of the twelve, he that dippeth with me in the dish." At such a gathering there would have been two or three bowls into which they would dip their bread. So, it would have been one of those sitting close to Jesus. John was sitting the closest to the Lord, "the disciple whom Jesus loved," and Peter encouraged John to find out who it was. When John asked, "Lord, who is it?" Jesus said, "It is he for whom I shall dip the sop, and give it to him." Jesus then dipped the sop, and gave it to Judas. So, it went from twelve, to three or four, to one – Judas. This seems only to have hardened Judas. His question, "Is it I?" wasn't to repent, but to continue the deception. By doing that, the language seems to indicate it was the giving of himself to Satan. Note now, Jesus did not command the deed, but since it had already been determined by Judas, Jesus dismissed him with the words, "What thou doest, do quickly." Judas had refused all appeals; it was time to do what he had decided to do.

Understand that Jesus was following a path that He had come to follow; it was why He came to earth. But Judas did not have to do what he did. Don't apologize for Judas. He had a choice and he made it.

There is a certain pathos in "and it was night." The light of day had faded for Judas. Because of what he was doing and would do, only night and doom remained.

Disciples Warned
(Matt. 26:31-35, Mark 14:27-31, Luke 22:31-38, John 13:31-38)

The order of these warnings would have probably been John 13:31-38 first, followed by Luke 22:31-38, of which Matthew and Mark are parallel accounts. This would make two distinct predictions of Peter's denial and two distinct protests from him.

These warnings were given to help prepare them for what was about to happen. The hour of the arrest was nigh. They would not be able to stand before it. They would flee. But these warnings would also help them recover from their failure. Jesus predicted not only their failure, but His return and their repentance and recovery. It seems probable that there were two warnings. One delivered in the upper room before the statements of John 14, and the other delivered as they were preparing to leave the room.

In Luke's account, the additional information that the devil was focusing his attack on Peter was given, attempting to "sift" him, to separate the good from the bad. But, even as His hour was drawing near, Jesus was not deserting Peter to battle Satan alone. Jesus said He was praying for Peter.

The Lord had also predicted persecution and death in their evangelistic labors for Him, but that had not come to pass. Now, He reminded them that the time of the fulfillment of those things was at hand. Luke 22:36 was not a case of the Lord advocating violence in the spread of the kingdom. He was telling them, in a dramatic way, that things were about to change. They understood His words literally. They declared they had two swords in the company and Peter would use one in Gethsemane. Jesus did not correct their misunderstanding at that time. He dismissed the subject for now by saying, "It is enough." Two swords would not have been enough to defend them against those sent by the High Priest if it was a question of physical force. Indeed, with Jesus no force would have been necessary and could have stopped it all at any time. He would correct their misunderstanding in Gethsemane.

The Lord's Supper Instituted
(Matt. 26:26-29, Mark 14:22-25, Luke 22:17-20,
1 Corinthians 11:23-26)

None of the gospel writers give us the exact time of the institution of the Lord's Supper except to place it during the Passover meal. Matthew uses the phrase, "And as they were eating..." Mark says, "And as they did eat..." Luke wrote, "Likewise also the cup after supper..." And Paul wrote, "After the same manner also he took the cup, when he had supped..." Putting all of this together, it is apparent that the institution of the Lord's Supper took place toward the close of the Passover meal. It is also evident that Judas had already left.

Jesus took unleavened bread, as this was the only kind of bread used in the Passover meal, blessed it and broke it. We are to follow the example of the Lord as He commanded, and only use unleavened bread which is blessed and distributed; blessed being in the sense of giving thanks (1 Cor. 11:24). This bread was representative of His body, and not His actual flesh. As He spoke to them, the Lord's body had not yet been given nor had His blood been shed. John 6:63 helps us to understand this truth.

After the supper, Jesus also took the cup. Luke distinguishes between the cup taken during the meal and the cup taken after. The first cup belonged to the Passover meal; the latter to the institution of the Lord's Supper. Jesus said of that first cup in Luke (which would probably have been the last of four cups passed during the Passover meal) that He would "not drink of the fruit of the vine, until the kingdom of God shall come." This does not mean He did not partake of the cup of communion with them when the Lord's Supper was instituted. It meant that after that night He would not partake of the Passover cup, but would share the institution of that which was the fulfillment of the Passover with them. He would not partake of it again until the coming of the kingdom on the day of Pentecost, when He would share communion with Christians each and every Lord's Day (1 Cor. 10:16).

This blood was called "my blood of the new covenant." It was the practice of the eastern people to use blood in making any pact or covenant. Jesus presented Himself as the victim from which the blood was to be taken to seal the new covenant, and He made the contents of the cup the symbol of that blood. Hebrews 9:15-22 shows how the shedding of blood was necessary in the sealing of the Old Covenant and how the death of the testator was necessary for a will to be in force, or for a testament to be in force.

This blood was "for the remission of sins," and to make forgiveness of sins possible, including those that took place under the first covenant (Heb. 9:15).

> It is to fulfill in a new and more complete fashion the purpose of remembrance (as in the Passover). The actual redemption of man from sin by the death of Christ is to be kept in remembrance by this simple feast. It is a memorial. (2) It is to bind them together in a new fellowship. Even in the last hours of parting, they have the assurance not merely that they shall partake of it together in the kingdom, but that Christ will share it with them. It is a communion together. (3) It is to recall to the mind of the Christian his sins and lead to self examination. "Which is poured out for many unto the remission of sins." What are these sins? Why was such terrible suffering of Christ necessary? Everything connected with the events of this night leads to "examine yourselves." Paul's account of the words of Jesus also shows: (4) It is to show forth the death of Jesus to the world. All who witness are led to inquire the meaning of the feast. It is thus a proclamation of the gospel to the world; as also is baptism. (5) It looks forward to His second coming as it looks backward to the cross. It is thus a prediction of His coming again and furnishes us an opportunity to confess each Lord's Day our Faith, Hope, and Love (R.C. Foster, *Gospel Studies*, Vol. 4, 127, 128).

Paul gave us these words of Jesus, "this do in remembrance of me" and "this do ye, as oft as ye drink it, in remembrance of me." The practice of the church in the first century under the guidance of the inspired Apostles was to partake of the Lord's Supper every first day of the week (Acts 20:7). This is our responsibility as well.

Jesus' Farewell Discourse (John 14:1-31)

It had been an extremely difficult week full of conflict and drama. Jesus revealed that one of His own apostles was going to betray Him. He had told them that His death was near. Their minds must have been reeling with much anxiety, emotion, and fear. Then Jesus gave them words of comfort and beauty that have supported and calmed the fear of believers from then to now.

He told them to have faith; believe in God and believe in Him. That is the remedy for hearts that are troubled. Jesus used the figure of a large house, a permanent residence, filled with rooms that are available for all guests. If His death was going to be the culmination, then Jesus would have told them, however, that was not the case. Jesus was going to prepare a place for them, a place of permanent residence, in the Father's house. He told them that He was leaving, that He would die; now the reason became clear. He was going to die so He might come again to take them back with Him. Obviously the reference is to the Second Coming.

The way to the Father's presence is through fellowship with Jesus in His suffering and death. Obviously, the Apostles did not understand Jesus' destination or the way there.

Then came the startling reply, "I am the way, the truth, and the life: no man cometh unto the Father, but by me." The only way to the Father is through Jesus; there is no other way. That implies belief in, obedience to, and imitation of the Lord.

Jesus also stated that He is the truth, the source of all truth, and through Him truth was communicated. Indeed, Jesus is truth personified.

And of course, Jesus is the life, the source of life and the way to spiritual life. If they had known and understood these things, then they would have known and understood His teaching. In His death, burial, resurrection, and ascension, they would come to know.

Philip expressed a universal desire of men—to see God. It was delivered with gentleness, yet full of pathos. For three years Jesus was in their midst. They saw Him raise the dead, cast out demons, heal the sick, and teach the most profound lessons ever heard; but they did not know Him. JESUS IS THE REVELATION OF GOD! As Paul wrote in 1 Timothy 3:16, "And without controversy great is the mystery of godliness: God was manifest in the flesh..." The apostles needed to believe and understand. The words Jesus spoke were the words of God. The works Jesus did were the works of God. Once again, the Lord emphasized the works He had performed and they proved who He was.

The greater works to which Jesus referred were not miracles. How could one miracle be classified as greater or more impressive, than another? No, the greater works referred to the conversion of the lost, the evangelization of the world. Truly the conversion of one soul is intrinsically more divinely wonderful than miracles. We know that there is joy in heaven over one sinner who repents (Luke 15).

At the right hand of the Father, Jesus would be mediating for His people. Jesus showed the union of the Father with Himself by promising His people that prayers offered by His authority would be answered.

Further evidence of the Lord's union with the Father would be the sending of the Holy Spirit. Since, however, the worldly-minded could neither receive nor understand the Spirit, the promise to send Him to the Apostles is prefaced by the exhortation to "keep my commandments." One who would not obey did not receive the Spirit.

On the next day Jesus would be crucified and leave this earth for good, only to return to take the church home. But He was not going to leave His children comfortless. Jesus' promise to "come to you" in verse 18 has reference to His coming through the Spirit. In John 16:13-14, "Howbeit when He, the Spirit of truth is come, He will guide you into all truth: for He shall not speak of Himself; but whatsoever He shall hear, that shall He speak; and He will show you things to come. He shall glorify Me, for He shall receive of Mine, and shall show it unto you."

On the day, referred to as "that day" in verse 20, when the Spirit came on the day of Pentecost of Acts 2, then they would know the absolute union of Jesus and the Father, and know the union of Jesus and those who are His through obedience to His commands. Verse 21 is interesting:

> Here, the Lord indicated the grounds upon which the divine indwelling exists; he is in those and those alone who keep the Lord's commandments. The words, "he it is that loveth me," are in a construction which emphasizes who it is that loves the Lord, literally, "That one it is who loves me," i.e., the one who had and keeps the commandments. It will be observed that two things are affirmed of this one. To have the commandments is to treasure them in one's heart; to keep them, is to obey them fully. Thus, the requirement is more than a slavish adherence to a set of rules or the outward mechanical conformity to a plan neither understood nor appreciated, but an intelligent, meaningful and precious conformity to the commandments because of him who imposed them. Through such faithful conformity to his will the obedient one will be privileged to have an awareness of the presence of Christ in his heart and his life. It is in this way, and in no other, that the Revealer of truth, the Holy Spirit, abides in the heart, as also the Father and the Son (Guy N. Woods, *New Testament Commentaries, John*, 314).

This time Thaddaeus interrupted Jesus with the question, "Lord, how is it that thou wilt manifest thyself unto us, and not unto the world?" Jesus' answer emphasized the spiritual nature of this coming manifestation and that it is conditioned upon obedience to the Lord. Those who abide in His word, keeping His commandments, have the Father, Son, and the Holy Spirit abiding in them; this is the only way this abiding takes place.

Jesus went on and gave further assurance that the Comforter, the Holy Spirit, would come and teach them all things, bringing to their remembrance all Jesus had taught them. There were to be many trials, tribulations, and sufferings coming, not only in their immediate future, but in their lives of service to Jesus. But, through obedience to His commandments and His abiding presence they would have peace. It is a peace from within, a peace that does not depend on what is happening around us.

> In spite of his promised spiritual return, the disciples were to endure the anguish of seeing him depart by way of death. They were going to lose his bodily presence. Jesus assures them therefore that his going away was a necessary condition of his spiritual return; that his very prediction of death would later strengthen their faith; that while they were now to separate, and Satan was to assault him, he was to gain no abiding victory, but only to aid in manifesting to the world the loving obedience of the Son to the will of his Father. In these last sentences Jesus uses the phrase, "The Father is greater than I," and it has been interpreted as intimating that he did not claim actual deity; but could any mere man, unless insane or blasphemous, use those words in comparing himself with God? It is true that the Son, in the mystery of his relation to the Father, was, in the days of his flesh, or in his eternal Sonship, subordinate to the Father; but these words, like many in this sublime chapter, are true witnesses to the conscious deity of the God-Man, Jesus Christ our Lord (Charles R. Erdman, *The Gospel of John, An Exposition*, 137).

The Parable of the Vine (John 15:1-27)

The word "parable" is not the best description to emphasize the union of the Father, Son, and the believers. Similitude is actually better. In it, Jesus is the vine, believers are the branches, and the Father is the husbandman.

The branches are a part of the vine, with the vine supplying the nourishment the branches need. Without the vine the branches would be lifeless and die. However, each branch is expected to bear fruit as a result of being part of the vine. If a branch does not bear fruit, it is pruned and cast away to be gathered and burned.

The apostles, Judas having departed, were said to be clean "through the word which I have spoken unto you." It is God in Christ who cleanses the soul, but this cleansing is effected through hearing, believing, and obeying the Word.

The continued purity of every disciple is dependent upon his abiding in Jesus, which is dependent upon obedience. Remember, "If a man love me, he will keep my words: and my Father will love him, and we will come unto him, and make our abode with him" (14:23). Part of this abiding is the bearing of fruit, further evidence of "keeping His commandments."

In verse 10 the union of the Son with the Father, and the Son with believers, is emphasized: "If ye keep my commandments, ye shall abide in my love; even as I have kept my Father's commandments, and abide in his love." All of these things were spoken to sustain them in joy – not only in the immediate future through the dark hours of seeming defeat, but continually in their lives.

The supreme commandment is love. They were to love each other as passionately and intensely as Jesus loved them. How great was this love? He was going to die for them and for all men.

The commandments of Jesus are to be obeyed in the spirit of love and friendship, not like that of a bondman. Again, the closeness of the union between Jesus and His followers is emphasized in verses 14-16: "Ye are my friends, if ye do whatsoever I command you. Henceforth I call you not servants; for the servant knoweth not what his lord doeth: but I have called you friends; for all things that I have heard of my Father I have made known unto you. Ye have not chosen me, but I have chosen you, and ordained you, that ye should go and bring forth fruit, and that your fruits should remain: that whatsoever ye shall ask of the Father in my name, he may give it you."

John 15 closes with a contrast between the love of believers for one another and the hatred of the world. The world for the most part hated the Lord, some out of ignorance, and others out of malice and neglect. Both are without excuse. They saw the Lord, heard the Lord, and witnessed His works. They were guilty of rejecting the Messiah. Since the world hated the Lord, His followers would not be surprised when they were hated. Jesus said in verse 20, "The servant is not greater than his lord. If they have persecuted me, they will also persecute you: if they have kept my saying, they will keep yours also."

Nonetheless, the Apostles, having been with Jesus from the beginning, would bear witness of the Lord, the Holy Spirit testifying through them, telling the world of Jesus.

Further Solemn Instruction (John 16:1-33)

The Lord continued to instruct His apostles on that fateful night before His death. He had many things to tell them as He prepared for the devastating events just hours away.

All that Jesus told them was to keep them from being offended when the opposition of the world came. They would be cast out of the synagogues, thus losing status and position in the Jewish community. They would even be killed by their own kinsmen. While Jesus had predicted many of these things earlier in His discussions with the Apostles, now He was repeating them and telling His Apostles what would happen, with the addition of the coming of the Spirit.

They had not needed the Comforter while Jesus was with them, but now they would since He was leaving.

The Lord was about to depart and then the Apostles would bear the brunt of the persecution. They were grief-stricken at what they heard. But again, Jesus told them that His death was necessary. He had come to die and the completion of His work demanded it. It was expedient for them that this should happen because the coming of the Spirit was dependent upon the Lord's departure. Their work was to be done through the Spirit.

In the world, the work of the Spirit is not a direct operation; it is through the Word. The Spirit's work involves "convicting" or "convincing." To convince or convict is to place the truth of a matter in a clear light before someone in such a way as to demand that it be acknowledged as the truth. The Spirit does this through the revelation. He would show the world they were lost in sin, salvation is available in the righteousness manifested in Jesus and practiced by those who follow Him, and the inevitability of judgment.

There was much for the disciples to know but they could not bear it yet. It was necessary for Jesus to die, be buried, be raised from the dead and ascend to heaven; then the Spirit would come. Jesus is the Way. The Spirit is the Guide; Jesus is the Truth. The Holy Spirit is the Guide into "all truth."

God glorified the Son and was to crown His earthly ministry with heavenly glory. After the ascension, the Holy Spirit was to unfold the full majesty of the person of Jesus and the supreme value of His ministry. The manifestation of the full truth as it is in Christ glorified Him.

The first "little while" referred to the period between the Lord's death and resurrection, a time when they "would not see Him." The second "little while" referred to the time after the resurrection but before the ascension, a time when they "would see Him." They did not understand, and they experienced a swirl emotions.

"Weep and lament" referred to the violent manifestations of grief they would feel when they saw Jesus condemned, tortured, and put to death. It was the kind of grief they would feel as they deserted Jesus and fled. "Ye shall be sorrowful" referred to the kind of dull, deadened suffering one feels after the initial flood of emotion has passed. The wicked world would rejoice over the cause of their sorrow, the death of Christ. However, the sorrow of the Apostles would be turned into joy, referring to the resurrection. Their joy would overshadow any sorrow they felt, and, unlike the sorrow, would remain.

After Jesus' ascension they would not ask Him any more questions for He would not be with them in the flesh any longer. They would turn to God in prayer. Previously they had not been taught to offer prayer in the name of the Lord, or by His authority. After His ascension and the coming of the Spirit, they would understand the relationship of Jesus to the Father and the efficacy of prayer in His name.

When Jesus said He would no longer speak in proverbs He referred to the time after His resurrection. He would be able to explain the purpose of His death and the reality of His resurrection in a way not possible before.

In verses 26-27, the following paraphrase was given by M.F. Sadler:

Do not think that when I speak of interceding for you with the Father, I am interceding with One who is unwilling to grant what I ask for you. It is not so. The Father is willing to grant all that I ask on your behalf or that you ask through Me, for He Himself, the Father, loveth you because ye have loved Me (M.F. Sadler, *Commentary on St. John*, 398).

Consider what verse 28 tells us about Jesus: "I came forth from the Father" - His preexistence, deity, and mission. "And am come into the world "- His virgin birth and His Incarnation. "I leave the world" - His death for the sins of the world and His resurrection. "And go to the Father" – the ascension and coronation.

Have you ever had a thought suddenly appear in your mind and clear up a problem or question? This is what happened to the Apostles. Understand that their grasp was not complete as of yet. Jesus understood their difficulties and addressed their questions before they asked them or understood enough to frame the questions, so this helped to assure their faith.

Jesus was not questioning their faith, but trying to prepare them for the shock they were about to receive. They would temporarily desert Him but He would not be alone. The Father would be with Him.

Having predicted His betrayal, denial, desertion by the Apostles, and His arrest, torture and death, Jesus said, "Be of good cheer; I have overcome the world." This was spoken as His death loomed in the shadows. What peace and calm assurance! What a triumph! As Satan appeared to conquer, Jesus triumphed.

The Prayer of Jesus (John 17:1-26)

This is the longest recorded prayer of Jesus and appears to have been spoken out loud. It seems to follow naturally on the heels of chapter 16 and was offered on the way to Gethsemane according to John 14:31. In this passage, Jesus solemnly dedicated Himself to be offered on the cross and His disciples gave themselves by spreading the message of salvation. The prayer is devoted to the disciples that they remained faithful and united in faith and love.

In verses 1-5, Jesus began by lifting up His eyes to heaven and acknowledging the "hour is come." The time for the fulfillment of His mission on earth, the time for Him to die and to be raised, then return to the Father, was upon Him. It was not a failure, but a triumph. It was not a humiliation, but a glorification.

Jesus, the Creator and Sustainer of men by God's authority and power, was their Savior as well. Eternal life is the reward for all who accept God's invitation and obey His commands. This is the meaning of "as many as thou hast given him." The knowledge that results in "life eternal" does not mean a mere acquaintance with the facts or an intellectual acceptance of them but a complete direction and devotion of life in harmony with the will of God and an intimate fellowship with Jesus.

The absolute certainty of Jesus is seen in His declaration, "I have finished the work which thou gavest me to do." This was a statement of a future event spoken as though already accomplished. Jesus was going home.

Verses 6-8 are transitional verses in the prayer as Jesus began to pray for His disciples. The word "name" is used to represent everything a name implies — authority, rank, character, majesty, power, and excellence. Jesus taught these individuals and revealed the Father to them. They arrived at their state of faith and needed help for what lay ahead.

At this particular time of crisis, Jesus prayed for His disciples. That is the meaning of "I pray not for the world…" The world entered the prayer before it was over, but at this point Jesus was concerned for His followers. The disciples glorified Jesus by their faith in Him and their declaration of that faith. They were living monuments and vehicles of His glory through their teaching, acts, and works.

Jesus was about to leave His earthly campaign in the hands of this small group of men. If they failed, if the evil succeeded in destroying their devotion to Jesus, all was lost. It was of supreme importance that they maintain love, harmony, and faith among themselves.

This group of men remained faithful while Jesus was in their midst, with the exception of Judas, called the Son of Perdition (meaning Son of Destruction or Loss). There are different meanings of the word "lost" found in verse 12, but here W.E. Vine comments its meaning being "the loss of eternal life." The scripture reference is probably to Psalm 41:9, a passage cited by John earlier in 13:18, speaking of the treachery of Judas. It may perhaps refer to Psalm 109:7-8.

Verses 13 and 14 provide an interesting contrast. This is a prayer that the joy of the Lord, the joy of self-sacrifice and victory, would abide with them. It connects well with 15:11 and 16:24. Having received the Father's word, the disciples were experiencing, and would to a greater degree, the hatred of the world. This was, and is, the inevitable result. The world demands conformity to its view and lifestyle

In verses 15-17, how far can Christians join with life in the world and not be contaminated by it? The Jewish element on one side and the heathen element on the other encompassed the early church. In truth, a Christian would have to leave the world altogether, physically remove himself, to avoid any association with wicked people. Since wicked people need to hear the gospel, that cannot be. Nevertheless, the follower of Jesus is to keep himself pure even in the midst of the world.

In faith, purpose, conduct, and in the whole manner of life, the disciples of Jesus were not of the world, just as Jesus was not of the world. Christians are set apart, sanctified, dedicated to the service of the Lord and not defiled by common or profane usage. This sanctification is accomplished through the Word, which is Truth. Jesus is, in a real sense, the embodiment of the Word of God (John 1:1, 14).

As Jesus was "set apart" for use by God, He was "setting apart" the Apostles for use as His special messengers to the world. Note three things which Jesus prayed for the Apostles: (a) That they would be united; (b) That they would be kept from the world and the devil; (c) That they might be set apart and equipped for the service.

Verses 20-26 constitute a prayer for the church. When Jesus mentioned the "word" in verse 20, He had reference to the preaching of the gospel from Pentecost on through all the years. Jesus prayed that all who believed in Him through the preaching of the gospel be united and that unity lead the world to believe. That unity of believers is illustrated by the unity of Jesus and the Father. Notice, the world has entered into the prayer of the Lord.

The "glory" to which Jesus referred in verse 22 is the glory Jesus manifested in the flesh, in dying for our sins, and being raised to give us the assurance of life. Indeed, the glorious gospel of our Lord Jesus Christ is the basis of the unity of believers.

And then finally, Jesus prayed for His own that they might be united together in His presence in eternity and there behold His "glory," the glory Jesus had before the foundation of the world which He left to come to this earth. They would see the ultimate and final vindication of their choice and all their labors. Once again, Jesus closed His prayer with reference to the Apostles. They had been through so much together, and it was probable that even now as they made their way to Gethsemane, another group was also on its way ready to arrest the Lord.

The Agony in the Garden
(Matt. 26:36-46, Mark 14:32-42, Luke 22:39-46, John 18:1)

Both Matthew and Mark use the Greek word for "garden" which means a spot or a place, and evidently denotes a small enclosure or field. "Gethsemane" is the Greek form of a Hebrew word that means "oil press." This shows the enclosure was an olive orchard with its oil press in the midst. It was a secluded spot that offered the privacy Jesus desired. John tells us that it was across the brook Kedron. The other three evangelists tell us that it was on the Mount of Olives.

The Apostles were divided into two groups. Eight were left at the gate. Maybe this was to prevent interruption. The other three, Peter, James, and John, came further into the garden with Jesus. To put into words what Jesus went through in the garden is difficult to express, but Frederick Farrar expresses it quite well:

> Jesus knew that the awful hour of His deepest humiliation had arrived – that from this moment till the utterance of that great cry with which He expired, nothing remained for Him on earth but the torture of physical pain and the poignancy of mental anguish. All that the human frame can tolerate of suffering was to be heaped upon His shrinking body; every misery that cruel

and crushing insult can inflict was to weigh heavy on His soul; and in this torment of body and agony of soul even the high and radiant serenity of His divine spirit was to suffer a short but terrible eclipse. Pain in its acutest sting, shame in its most overwhelming brutality, all the burden of the sin and mystery of man's existence in its apostasy and fall – this was what He must now face in all its most inexplicable accumulation. But one thing remained before the actual struggle, the veritable agony, began. He had to brace His body, to nerve His soul, to calm His spirit by prayer and solitude to meet that hour in which all that is evil in the Power of Evil should wreak its worst upon the Innocent and Holy. And He must face that hour alone: no human eye must witness, except through the twilight and shadow, the depth of His suffering. Yet He would have gladly shared their sympathy; it helped Him in this hour of darkness to feel that they were near, and that those were nearest who love Him best. "Stay here," He said to the majority, "while I go there and pray." Leaving them to sleep on the damp grass...He took with Him Peter and James and John, and went about a stone's throw farther. It was well that Peter should face all that was involved in allegiance to Christ; it was well that James and John should know what was that cup which they had desired preeminently to drink. But soon even the society of these chosen and trusted ones was more than He could bear. A grief beyond utterance, a struggle beyond endurance, a horror of great darkness, a giddiness and stupefaction of soul overmastered Him, as with the sinking swoon of an anticipated death. It was a tumult of emotion which none must see. "My soul," He said, "is full of anguish, even unto death. Stay here and keep watch" (Frederick Farrar, *The Life of Christ*, 575,576).

Much of mystery is found in all life, so it is small wonder if the dual nature of Jesus presents insoluble problems. It perplexes many to find that the divine in Jesus did not sustain Him better during His trial in the garden. But we must remember that it was appointed unto Jesus to die, and that the divine in Him was not to interfere with this appointment, or the approaches to it. For want, therefore, of a better expression, we may say that from the time Jesus entered the garden until He expired on the cross the human in Him was in the ascendant; and "being found in fashion as a man," He endured these trials as if wholly human. His prayer, therefore, is the cry of His humanity for deliverance. The words "if it be possible" with which it opens breathes the same spirit of submissive obedience which is found in the closing words. Reminding the Father of the limitless range of His power, He petitions Him to change His counsel as to the crucifixion of the Son, if His gracious purposes can be in any other way carried out. Jesus uses the words "cup" and "hour" interchangeably. They are both words of broad compass, intended to include all that He would undergo from that time until His resurrection…(McGarvey and Pendleton, *The Fourfold Gospel*, 686, 687).

Evidence of the Lord's tremendous mental anguish is found in the "bloody sweat," a phenomenon that occurs under the greatest stress and of which there are several documented cases. Three times Jesus came and found His apostles sleeping. Three times He returned to His Father in prayer. At the last, His betrayer arrived. As Jesus said, "The hour is come; behold, he that betrayeth me is at hand."

The Arrest
(Matt. 26:47-56, Mark 14:43-52, Luke 22:47-53, John 18:2-12)

Note the careful preparation of those who came to take Jesus. There were the temple guards ready to do whatever they were told. There was a band of Roman soldiers (the word is "cohort" in John 18:3) who came with swords and staves if it proved necessary to fight. They had lanterns and torches to light their way; maybe the moonlight would prove insufficient or they would have to search dark corners to find Jesus. They brought cords or chains to bind the prisoner (John 18:12). They were guided by a traitor, one of the twelve Apostles, and there was a prearranged signal to identify Jesus and to prompt them to act. There may have been some of the chief priests with the mob, and high priests, including Annas, who knew what was happening, and would have prepared themselves for the mockery of the trial to take place as quickly and quietly as possible.

> When the crowd approached, Jesus awakened the disciples; the eight who were at the gate of the garden were evidently called in or else Jesus went out of the garden and met the crowd outside. The crowd surged on rapidly, for Mark says, "And straightway while He yet spake, cometh Judas," (Also Matthew and Luke). Jesus stood forth and calmly identified Himself to the whole crowd: "Whom seek ye?" "…I am He." The multitude then fell to the ground in awe and fear (John 18:4-6). The request of Jesus that His disciples be permitted to leave showed to all that Jesus did not plan to resist arrest. Judas came to Christ to kiss Him and Christ uttered two words of gentle rebuke, "Friend, do that for which thou art come," (Matt. 26:50); then, just after Judas kissed Him: "Judas, betrayeth thou the Son of Man with a kiss?" (Luke 22:48). Judas was in front of the crowd. The pause in the rapid action gave the disciples time to bestir themselves and as the multitude advanced again, the disciples cried, "Lord, shall

we smite with the sword?" Peter did not wait for an answer, but rushed boldly to attack and wounded a servant of the high priest. Jesus rebuked him and healed the stricken man (Luke 22:49-51). The crowd had before started to seize Jesus (Matt. 26:47-50). But He had revealed His divine majesty to them and caused them to fall to the ground. Now they boldly take Him prisoner. The disciples fled. One disciple started to follow, but as they attempted to arrest him, he also fled (Mark 14:51). The accounts are independent and seem at points contradictory, but this is merely the result of the story being told four times from slightly different points of view and interest, and with various details added or omitted. It was one of those swift moving scenes when so many things were occurring almost simultaneously that it is not easy to tell it in chronological order. The only doubtful phases of the above arrangement are whether or not the actual arrest of Jesus preceded the attack of Peter (they may well have been simultaneous) and whether or not Jesus' revelation of Himself to the crowd preceded the kiss of Judas (R.C. Foster, *Gospel Studies*, Vol. 4, 174).

A lot of things have been written about Judas, many of them in an attempt to cast Judas in a more favorable light and somehow lessen the heinous crime. But, when the actual betrayal and the manner in which it was carried out is studied, all such efforts fail. Matthew 26:48-49 indicates that Judas laid out the betrayal and took the leadership in planning and executing. He said, "Hail Master," and the word used to describe the kiss means "to kiss effusively or in a demonstrative fashion." He had witnessed His power, and yet Judas knew that Jesus would not use His power to protect Himself.

Jesus called Judas "friend," meaning comrade or companion. If Judas was paying attention, that address would have shown Judas the absolute baseness displayed in betraying one who was his comrade.

Jesus' remarks to Judas can be interpreted in the following ways: "Friend, this is that for which thou art come?" In other words, "I know your treachery." Or it could be "Friend, is this for which thou art come?" And "Is a kiss fitting for what you are doing?"

In His rebuke to Peter (Matt. 26:52-54, John 18:11), Jesus set forth the fundamental principle that His cause was not to be advanced by violence and whoever resorts to bloodshed was to suffer the same. He also made it clear to Peter and the others that God's Will was being carried out in the events taking place. The statement in John 18:11, "The cup which the Father hath given Me, shall I not drink it?" certainly indicates that Jesus' earlier prayer in the garden was answered. There was acceptance and resolve in the words of Jesus.

The Trial before Annas (Luke 22:54, John 18:12-14, 19-23)

Jesus was first taken to the house of Annas, an older man who had been high priest but removed from that office by the Romans. The Romans had placed Caiaphas, the son-in-law of Annas, in his former position. The Jews regarded Annas as the legitimate high priest because, according to Numbers 20:28 and 35:25, the office of high priest was held for life. Annas exercised considerable influence, not only with the Jews in general, but with his son-in-law, the "official" high priest.

The reference to Caiaphas in verse 14 recalled an earlier event recorded by John in 11:49-50, when Caiaphas had given "counsel to the Jews, saying it was expedient that one man should die for the people." This shows the type of man Caiaphas was and what kind of "justice" Jesus expected.

In verse 19, Annas was the high priest mentioned here and Jesus was before him for a twofold purpose: (a) To gain the sanction of the legitimate high priest for the actions being taken against the Lord; (b) To question Jesus for the purpose of gaining some information that could be used against Him in framing a suitable accusation before the Romans.

In reply to Annas' questions concerning His disciples and His teaching, Jesus immediately showed their hypocrisy and the hatred with which He was being confronted. The secret arrest, the hasty night trials, the whole nasty atmosphere -- why question Him about His teaching and His disciples? They already knew what He taught and had determined that He was to be put to death.

While Jesus had often taught His disciples in "secret," everything He taught them was in harmony with everything He taught publicly. The disciples had been commanded to proclaim the teaching that He had given them privately from the housetop.

Lacking truth and credible testimony, wicked men have turned to violence to sustain their cause. One of the officers of the temple struck Jesus. The Greek word used for "struck" showed what Jesus received was a "slap on the cheek, given with the open hand by way of insulting rebuke rather than with the intention of inflicting bodily injury." In reply to this physical abuse Jesus denied that He had spoken in an improper way. He was protesting against the illegal and brutal proceedings but was doing so in a dignified way by letting testimony against Him be presented. Surely judgment and violence should not precede the hearing of the whole matter.

The Trial before Caiaphas
(Matt. 26:57, 59-68, Mark 14:53, 55-65, Luke 22:54, 63-65, John 18:24)

Jesus was led from Annas to the trial before Caiaphas. It would have been in a hall that was sufficiently large to accommodate the Sanhedrin which had come together. This was not a formal session as a court; it was more like a committee or a caucus.

Reference is made in John 2:19-22 to a statement that Jesus had uttered long before. At the time of that statement, His words were misunderstood as applying to Herod's temple. Now it appeared that the Jewish rulers, hearing the Lord's prediction that He would raise from the dead after three days (Matt. 27:62-63), came to understand what Jesus had been saying. In trying to build their case, the idea of tearing down the temple and rebuilding it in three days was a claim to deity, even though they knew that Jesus had reference to His body and not the temple.

While the testimony presented before the council might have been used to show that Jesus was a boastful man, it was certainly insufficient to justify a sentence of blasphemy. A threat to destroy the temple might be construed, but a promise to rebuild the temple, if destroyed, was altogether different. Caiaphas sought to force Jesus to give some additional evidence against Himself. With cunning and effrontery he assumed the testimony given was all that could possibly be desired and then demanded of Jesus an answer to it. But Jesus gave him no answer or explanation.

In desperation Caiaphas asked Jesus plainly and bluntly. His question was twofold: (a) Art thou the Christ? (b) Art thou the Son of God? The latter constituted blasphemy, the former, by showing a boastful spirit, tended to confirm the charge. It could also be that Caiaphas anticipated the future and saw how useful the claim to be the Messiah would prove when the hearing before Pilate took place.

Caiaphas had no legal right to ask either of those questions. No man could be compelled to testify against himself, but he knew the claims of Jesus, and realized that if Jesus repudiated them He would be shamed forever; if He asserted them He would be charged with blasphemy. Taking advantage of the situation, Caiaphas put the question to Jesus with the usual formula of an oath. This gave power to the question because a person was guilty if he refused to answer a question put to him in that manner.

Jesus freely confessed the truth. "Right hand of power" was commonly understood to mean the right hand of God. By the words, "nevertheless" and "henceforth" Jesus brought His present state of humiliation into contrast with His future state of glory. Hard as it might have been for them to believe, the day would come when He would sit in judgment and they would stand on trial before Him.

Even though Jesus' answer was exactly what Caiaphas wanted to hear, he pretended to be shocked and tore his clothes. "What need we any further witnesses? Ye have heard the blasphemy; what think ye? And they all condemned Him to be guilty of death" (Mark 14:63-64). This was not the final, formal sentence. It was the mere determination of the council.

When Jesus was turned over to the soldiers after this examination, He was subjected to taunts and humiliation. He was spat upon, struck, and humiliated.

The Denials of Peter
(Matt. 26:58, 69-75, Mark 14:54, 66-72, Luke 22:54-62, John 18:15-18, 25-27)

First, going back to Gethsemane and the arrest of Jesus, Peter and John (called "another disciple") followed Jesus from a distance to the court of the home of the high priest. John, acquainted with the high priest, probably from a business arrangement (Mark 1:19-20), entered into the court of the high priest and spoke to the female porter at the door to gain entrance for Peter.

It is early morning and the high elevation of Jerusalem caused it to be cool before dawn in the early spring. A fire was burned in the courtyard for heat and Peter was determined to see what would happen to his Master. He evidently felt that the boldest course of all was the safest, that the very best place to be inconspicuous was right in the middle of the crowd of soldiers around the fire. So, he went and sat down by the fire among the soldiers of the court.

We need to understand who first challenged Peter and why. Matthew, Mark, and Luke say it was a maid who first challenged Peter. John says it was the maid who admitted him at the door. Some suppose that the first challenge was given at the door at the time of entrance. But Matthew, Mark, and Luke put the first denial in the court by the fire and John appeared to do the same thing in 18:17-18. Each gospel writer gave three denials and Jesus said that Peter would "deny me thrice." It is not likely that the first denial in John is different from the first denial recorded in the Synoptics. Evidently, the maid who admitted Peter started to wonder about it and came into the court to search for him. Looking at his face as closely as possible in the light of the fire convinced her that Peter was one of the of Jesus' followers.

All four accounts agree to the first challenge. Mark said the same maid gave the second; Matthew said another woman; Luke said a man; and John said a group. The female gate keeper, bothered by the situation, left her post and looked for Peter in the courtyard. When she found him, she challenged him. Another maid joined her in the challenge along with a man servant. Peter retreated before this onslaught to the campfire where a whole group added their accusations. Thus, the second and third denials represented a succession of attacks or challenges. Peter, assailed on all sides, repeatedly denied. Mark indicated this by the graphic and exact imperfect tense, "He kept on denying." In the third denial, Matthew and Mark said a group; Luke said another man: and John said a kinsman of Malchus. This showed another succession of accusations and denials occurred, all in rapid succession that the event is viewed as one.

After the repeated denials of Peter, the cock crowed. In Luke 22:60-62, one of the most heart-rending is passages recorded in God's word, "And Peter said, Man, I know not what thou sayest. And immediately, while he yet spake, the cock crew. And the Lord turned, and looked upon Peter. And Peter remembered the word of the Lord, how He had said unto him, before the cock crow, thou shalt deny me thrice. And Peter went out, and wept bitterly."

Can you imagine the feeling when the "Lord turned, and looked upon Peter?" With anguish of heart Peter went out and wept bitterly, remembering what Jesus had said.

Final Condemnation by the Sanhedrin (Matt. 27:1, Mark 15:1, Luke 22:66-71)

It was now morning, the day was Friday, and the Sanhedrin came together to formally charge Jesus and condemn Him. By law the Sanhedrin only met as a council in the day. All the preliminary work had been done. In truth, they had already condemned the Lord. Their coming together at this time was to make it final and give it the appearance of legality.

Even though the questions of Luke 22:67 and 70 had already been asked of Jesus the night before, they were asked again now that the whole council assembled together. The questions addressed the most serious charge to the council. Jesus' response to their first question or demand, "Art thou the Christ, tell us," was a protest against the violence and injustice of this mockery of a trial. They asked Him these questions with their minds already determined. It did not matter what Jesus said; they had no intention of seeking to ascertain the truth of His claims. They were trying to condemn Him by assuming that He was not the Christ.

In the KJV, Luke 22:68, Jesus said, "And if I also ask you, ye will not answer me, *nor let me go.*" The phrase, *"nor let me go"* is not found in the best manuscripts. In fact, the manuscript evidence for it is extremely weak.

Seizing upon the Lord's statement that they would see Him "seated at the right hand of the power of God," they asked, "Art thou the Son of God?" With Jesus' affirmative answer, they believed they had their official charge - blasphemy. John 19:7 showed this when the Jewish leaders said to Pilate, "We have a law, and by our law he ought to die, because he made himself the Son of God."

The statement of the council, "What further need have we of witness? For we ourselves have heard from his own mouth?" constituted an unconscious admission on their part that they had no evidence against Jesus. Having tried and condemned the Lord, but not having the legal power to put Him to death, the Sanhedrin now had to get a concurring sentence from the Roman governor. They took Jesus to Pilate.

Remorse and Death of Judas (Matt. 27:3-10, Acts 1:18-19)

In the gospel according to Matthew, Judas' remorse and suicide followed the condemnation by the Sanhedrin but preceded the condemnation by Pilate. It is probable that Judas' remorse and suicide followed the final condemnation by Pilate. McGarvey wrote, "The incident is introduced in advance of its chronological order so as not to interrupt the subsequent narration."

Seeing Jesus condemned to death, Judas felt the awful weight of what he had done. He had betrayed "innocent blood." There is an important point that must be made concerning the statement in Matthew 27:3 that Judas "repented himself."

> There are two Greek words which are translated "repented," the one properly so translated, *metanoeo*, which means literally "to know after" and which therefore means a change of mind or purpose; and the other, *metamellomai*, which is used here and which means literally "to care after," indicates a sorrow for the past. The first should be translated "repent," the second, "regret." Trench draws the distinction thus: "He who had *changed his mind* about the past is in the way to change everything; he who has an *after care* many have little or nothing more than a selfish dread of the consequences of what he has done." Considering the prophecy which had been uttered with regard to Judas' act (Matt. 26:24), he had good reason to fear the consequences. While he testifies as to the innocence of Jesus, he expresses affection for him (McGarvey and Pendleton, *The Fourfold Gospel*, 720).

Judas found the priests in the sanctuary of the temple, indicating that he was standing outside of the Holy Place. Judas might have cast the money because he feared the consequences of what he had done, not out of any true remorse for his sin against Jesus.

The reasoning of the priests concerning the use of the money was hypocritical. They were willing to take money out of the treasury to purchase an unholy and terrible deed, but they were not willing to return it to the treasury because of its terrible use. The money was used to purchase "potter's field," a field devoid of use since it was stripped of its good soil for clay to be used in pottery. This was a place for strangers to be buried because Gentiles were not permitted in Jewish graveyards. Hence, this field was called the "field of blood."

There are those who understand Acts 1:18-19 to indicate that this field was the same field in which Judas hung himself. Judas "fell headlong" and "burst asunder in the midst, and all his bowels gushed out." That is the reason given in Acts for the field being known as the "field of blood."

The quotation in Matthew 27:9-10 is said to be from Jeremiah, but appears in Zechariah 11:12-13. There are two possible explanations for this: (a) It could be a scribal error. (b) It could have been found in one volume with Jeremiah's writings and went by the latter name since Jeremiah is the longer book.

First Trial before Pilate
(Matt. 27:2, 11-14, Mark 15:2-5, Luke 23:1-5, John 18:28-38)

The trial before Pilate was held in the "praetorium," which was the official residence of the Roman governor. Traditionally it is believed that Pilate had his headquarters in the Tower of Antonia that overlooked the temple area from the northwest. Archaeologists have uncovered a beautiful pavement under the present building that many think may have been the original Roman Court Room.

The original intention of the Jewish leaders was to get Pilate to accept their verdict and condemn Jesus solely on that basis without a trial. Pilate humored the Jewish leaders by going outside to hear the charges and then questioning Jesus inside the praetorium. The cruel and unjust sentence they were seeking to have carried out was the "defiling thing," not the location. They sought the death of the Son of God.

When Pilate heard the initial charges, he told them to pronounce their own sentence, but that did not serve their purpose. It was illegal for them to pronounce a death sentence, and their verdict called for death. Legally, Jesus could be put to death by the Romans and crucifixion would be the mode for that sentence. Unwittingly, the Sanhedrin, through its insistence upon the death penalty, was bringing about the fulfillment of prophecy (Isa. 53, Psa. 22, John 12:33-34).

With the reaction of Pilate, the Jewish leaders changed their tactics. Now it was, "We found this man perverting our nation, and forbidding to give tribute to Caesar, and saying that he himself is Christ a king." An examination of the charges revealed what they were attempting to do. The first charge was extremely vague and purposely so. The second charge was a deliberate falsehood. Remember Jesus saying, "Render unto Caesar the things that are Caesar's, and unto God the things that are God's"? The third charge, that Jesus claimed to be a king, was true; but not in the way they were using it. Their intent by these charges was to give the impression that Jesus was claiming to be a political king and thus have Him stand in rebellion to Caesar.

Pilate went into his residence to question Jesus privately. All four gospels record his first question, "Art thou the king of the Jews?" When Jesus responded with "Thou sayest," that was a Hebrew form of affirmation. He was saying, "Yes."

Jesus asked Pilate, "Sayest thou this thing of thyself, or did others tell it thee of me?" McGarvey and Pendleton's comments about this exchange:

> Jesus admits that he is a king, but asks a question which forms the strongest negation that he is a king in the sense contained in the Jewish accusation. Had he been a king in that sense, Pilate would have been the one most likely to know it. The question also, by an indirect query as to the accuser, reveals to Pilate's mind that no Roman had accused him. He was accused of the Jews, and when had that restless, rebellious people ever found

fault with a man who sought to free them from the galling Roman yoke? The strong practical mind of the Roman at once caught the drift of Christ's meaning, so that it might be construed in some unpolitical sense. What this sense was he could not tell, for he was not a Jew. The mysteries of that nation were of no interest to him save where his office compelled him to understand them. Pilate concedes that the accusation against Jesus comes from an unexpected and suspicious source, and he asks Jesus to tell him plainly by what means he had incurred the enmity of the leaders of his people (McGarvey and Pendleton, *The Fourfold Gospel*, 706).

It was apparent that Jesus had done something to incur the wrath of the leaders of His nation, but He showed Pilate that He was not seeking to usurp the throne of Caesar. His kingdom was not of an earthly nature, and indeed, it never would be. Jesus' statement in John 18:36, "but now is my kingdom not from hence," has been misconstrued by some to mean that at a later time His kingdom would be earthly. The phrase, "but now" is logical, not temporal. It can be properly rendered, "seeing that it is so." *Vine's Expository Dictionary of New Testament Words* says of it, "Of logical sequence, often partaking also of the character of, now therefore, now however, as it is."

Yes, Jesus was a king. Again He affirmed it to Pilate, but it was the nature of His kingdom that Pilate needed to understand. Jesus came into the world to bear witness to and to reveal truth. The Jewish leaders had refused to "hear His voice," in the sense of accepting His words and obeying them. They refused to recognize the spiritual nature of His kingdom and that was the problem.

Pilate's question, "What is truth?" has been viewed as an earnest, true question, as a despairing appeal, and as a sneer. Instead of waiting for Jesus to answer, Pilate went back and informed the Jews that he found no fault in Jesus as a result of his questioning.

When additional charges were leveled against Jesus by the Jews, Pilate sought to get the Lord to defend Himself. Yet Jesus would not respond to the false charges. His refusal to speak in His own defense caused Pilate to marvel, but the charges kept coming, ending with, "He stirreth up the people, teaching throughout all Judea, and beginning from Galilee even unto this place."

Jesus before Herod (Luke 23:6-12)

When Pilate heard Jesus had begun in Galilee, he saw it as an opportunity to shift the case to another court. Herod was in Jerusalem for the Passover celebration. Luke says he was "at Jerusalem at that time" ("that time" referring to the Passover season). While Herod was not a religious person, showing respect for the Jewish festivals was important to his position and Pilate used this opportunity.

At an earlier period of the Lord's ministry, Herod was so troubled by a guilty conscience due to his murder of John the Baptist, that reports of the work of Jesus frightened him. Herod thought Jesus might have been John risen from the dead. This passage indicates the fear had passed and now he was curious about Jesus. He had heard about the miracles Jesus performed and now he thought he could see one. There was no indication of what Herod asked Jesus, but the Lord remained quiet before him.

The chief priests and the scribes vehemently accused Jesus before Herod, but the Lord answered nothing. Evidently, the silence of Jesus angered Herod, for he and his soldiers certainly treated Jesus with abusive contempt by mocking Him and dressing Him in a gorgeous robe. Finally, Herod sent Jesus back to Pilate having found nothing worthy of condemnation.

Perhaps it was the courtesy of Pilate in recognizing Herod's jurisdiction and giving him the opportunity to question Jesus that led to the reconciliation between these two infamous Bible characters who had been at enmity with one another.

Second Trial before Pilate
(Matt. 27:15-26, Mark 15:6-15, Luke 23:13-25, John 18:39-19:16)

When Jesus was sent back to Pilate, Pilate called together the chief priests and the rulers of the people. He told them once again that he had found no fault in Jesus. Even Herod had found nothing worthy of death. So, Pilate gave them the opportunity to have Jesus severely beaten and then released as per the custom of releasing a prisoner at the time of the feast. The Roman government attempted to calm the turbulent elements in the provinces under their control. The release of a political prisoner at the great feast of the Jews was one example of condescension to the conquered nation that they hoped would calm the seeds of rebellion. The people were gathering to demand the release; here was a good opportunity. They would get Jesus punished and Pilate would not have Him killed.

The choice was limited to Barabbas or Jesus. It seems as though Pilate chose Barabbas because he was such a notorious person who could not possibly stir the sympathy of the people, and they would demand the release of Jesus. The leaders of the Jews intervened and persuaded the people to demand the release of Barabbas and the crucifixion of the innocent Jesus.

Sometime in this process of judgment, Pilate was informed of a dream by his wife. He was encouraged to have nothing to do with Jesus. The specific dream was not told, except that it caused her to suffer many things, and based upon the innocence of Jesus.

When Pilate presented the people with the choice, they cried out, "Barabbas." When asked about Jesus, they said, "Crucify, crucify Him!" Pilate said to the crowd, "Why, what evil hath He done? I find no cause of death in Him. I will therefore chastise Him and release Him."

Pilate then gave orders for Jesus to be scourged. Pilate intended for the scourging to be the complete punishment. Often a prisoner died while the scourging was taking place. The scourge was a whip consisting of many thongs with pieces of bone or metal attached to the end of each thong. This instrument would be brought down time after time upon the stretched back, buttocks, and legs of the one being beaten. The prisoner would have been stripped of his clothing and fastened to a low post, thus bending the back and stretching the skin, exposing it to the cruelty of the whip. The Jews had a custom of forty stripes, save one. This was for fear of killing the one being beaten. Those executing the beating of Jesus were not Jews. They were Romans. The number of stripes Jesus received was not recorded.

After the beating, the Lord was crowned with a crown of thorns by the soldiers. A purple garment, the color of royalty, was thrown about Him. He was tormented by the soldiers and struck by their hands.

Once more Pilate went before the people, prepared to bring Jesus out before them, and told them once again he found no crime in Him. Jesus came forth, beaten, crowned with thorns, and wearing the purple garment! Pilate cried out, "Behold the man!" Surely this would stimulate some sympathy from the people as they viewed the pathetic sight before them. Yet the chief priests and the officers, upon seeing Jesus, cried out, "Crucify Him, crucify Him!" Pilate responded, "Take Him yourselves, and crucify Him: for I find no crime in Him!" In response the Jewish leaders now gave the real charge they were using, "He made Himself the Son of God."

After Pilate returned to his residence to question Jesus further, John tells us that he was "more afraid." Perhaps the interjection of God into the picture, coupled with the warning of his wife's dream, started to weigh on Pilate. He asked Jesus, "Who are you? Where do you come from?" Jesus gave him no answer. Again Pilate spoke, "Speakest thou not unto me? Knowest thou not that I have power to crucify thee, and have the power to release thee?" Our Lord's reply to this shows that the matter wasn't really in Pilate's hands, except by the deliberate choice of God. Pilate had no real acquaintance with Jesus other than what was happening right then. But the leaders of the Jews had opportunity to know better. They had personal knowledge of Jesus. They knew what He had done and what He had taught. They knew the prophecies of the prophets. Yet they rejected Jesus outright and delivered Him for death. Of whom much is given, much is expected. After this exchange Pilate sought even more to release Jesus, only to be threatened with an appeal to Caesar on the issue of his having set a man free who had been arrested on the charge of claiming to be a king and a rival of Caesar.

With this new threat Pilate determined that it was now time for this trial to come to an end. It had gone back and forth, in the residence, then back outside with the Jews. Now, the final verdict was to be rendered. In the place called "the Pavement," a spot for such an act located in the front of the palace. He told the Jews, "Behold your king!" They cried out, "Away with Him, crucify Him!" Pilate said, "Shall I crucify your king?" And the chief priests answered, "We have no king but Caesar!"

Pilate asked for a basin of water and figuratively washed his hand of the blood of Jesus, saying that he was "innocent of the blood of this righteous man," to which the Jewish people replied, "His blood be on us, and on our children."

It was about 6:00 a.m., Friday morning (John 19:14, using the Roman method of keeping time). Finally, from fear and lack of courage, Pilate released Barabbas and delivered Jesus to be crucified.

Torture by the Roman Soldiers
(Matt. 27:27-30, Mark 15:16-19)

It seems apparent that after the death sentence had been meted out by Pilate, the Roman soldiers continued the cruel sport of mocking the prisoner. Once again, Jesus was clothed in a scarlet robe as a king, with a crown of thorns taking the place of the royal crown. A reed was placed in His hands to sarcastically represent the scepter and to further ridicule His claim to be a king. They knelt before Jesus in mock humility, spat upon Him, and took the reed from His hands, beating Him about the head with it.

The Way to Golgotha
(Matt. 27:31-34, Mark 15:20-23, Luke 23:26-32, John 19:16-17)

Having finished with their cruel taunting, the soldiers took the robe from Jesus, put His own garments upon Him, and led the Lord away to be crucified. John tells us "and they took Jesus, and led him away. And he bearing his cross…" It was customary for the condemned man to bear his own cross (actually the crossbeam of the cross).

Jesus began the journey carrying that weight but must have been unable to bear up under it. When the tremendous emotional and physical abuse to which He had been subjected over the last 24-hour period is considered, it is no wonder that Jesus could not continue to carry that weight. Matthew tells us, "As they came out, they found a man of Cyrene, Simon by name; him they compelled to go with them, to bear his cross." Perhaps they had reached the city gate and Jesus could go no further. Mark's account says, "And they compel one Simon a Cyrenian, who passed by, coming out of the country." As the crucifixion party was going out, Simon was coming in. He was chosen by the Roman soldiers to bear the cross for Jesus. Luke makes it clear that two other individuals, criminals, were also part of the procession. These had been condemned to death and awaiting a suitable opportunity for their execution.

As the procession continued on its deadly journey, a great multitude of people were following. The women in the crowd lamented and wailed over the Lord. But instead of joining them in weeping and wailing for Himself, Jesus told them to weep for themselves and for their children. It is important to note that Jesus was not being overwhelmed and destroyed by a superior force; He was giving Himself voluntarily in fulfillment of the will of God. But the Jews by their actions were condemning themselves. Jesus warned them that because of their rejection of Him, destruction of a devastating nature would be their fate. This was a reference to the destruction of Jerusalem that would take place in A.D. 70.

Luke 23:31 says, "For if they do these things in the green tree, what shall be done in the dry?"

> The language here is obscurely proverbial. Jesus refers to the sorrows which the Romans were to bring upon the Jews, and the meaning may be, if the fiery persecution of Rome is so consuming that my innocence, though again and again pronounced by the governor himself, is no protection against it, what will that fire do when it envelopes the dry, guilty, rebellious city of Jerusalem? Or we may make the present and future grief of the women the point of comparison, and interpret thus: if they cause such sorrow to the women while the city is like a green tree, how much more when, like a dry, dead tree, it is about to fall (McGarvey and Pendleton, *The Fourfold Gospel*, 724).

The crucifixion site was outside the city walls but near to the city. Hebrews 13:12 and John 19:20 are specific about that and Matthew 27:32 and John 19:17 certainly imply it. The exact location of this site is not known, although it has been the site of much conjecture and tradition. Why it was called "the place of the skull" has also been a matter of considerable conjecture. Two plausible explanations have been offered: (a) The most unlikely is that skulls had been found at this particular location. (b) More likely it was so called because it was a hill that had a physical makeup giving it the appearance of a skull. No one knows for certain.

When they arrived at the crucifixion site, Jesus was offered a drink of wine mingled with gall and myrrh. It was intended to dull the senses of those being crucified and lessen the agony. After tasting it, Jesus refused to drink. Having come to this point, Jesus did nothing to lessen the suffering or dull His awareness.

The Death of Jesus
(Matt. 27:35-50, Mark 15:24-37, Luke 23:33-46, John 19:18-30)

The clothes of Jesus were taken from Him. Roman law awarded the clothes of the crucified individual to the soldiers of the crucifixion party. There was a quaternion (group of four) of Roman soldiers who were involved (John 19:23).

Stripped of His clothing and the crossbeam placed on the ground, Jesus was thrown down upon it. His arms were stretched out (but slightly bent to allow flexibility and to prolong the agony) and nails were driven through the small indentation at the front of the wrists. Heavy, wrought-iron nails were used. Then the crossbeam was raised into place and Jesus' feet were placed one on top of the other with another wrought iron nail driven through His arches into the wood of the upright. Jesus was crucified. About this time Jesus uttered the incredible words, "Father, forgive them; for they know not what they do."

Bear in mind that ignorance mitigates but does not excuse. Above His head was nailed the superscription, "Jesus of Nazareth, King of the Jews." It was written in three languages, and not told if this was customary. Likely, Pilate had this done to allow all who passed by the opportunity to read it and also to taunt the leaders of the Jews. They had forced him to have an innocent man executed. The superscription had the desired effect upon the Jewish leaders. They were furious and asked Pilate to change it to "He said, I am King of the Jews." Pilate refused. The two criminals who were part of the procession to Calvary were also crucified at the same time.

Having finished the crucifixion, the soldiers divided the part of the Lord's garments that could be divided into four parts, a part for each of the soldiers. For His coat or robe, the outer garment, they cast lots, for it was without seam and to divide it would have ruined it. This was fulfillment of Psalm 22:18.

Luke's account tells us that "the people stood beholding..." At scenes of tragedy and death, people stood and stared. Some that passed by railed on the Lord with insults, "Save yourself, come down from the cross." The rulers and the chief priests joined in what they obviously considered their hour of triumph.

> Their utterly base character is shown by their conduct. When a person dies, usually people refrain from criticism and leave judgment in God's hands, even when the person was infamous. Unable to bring any real charges against Jesus, they substituted venom and vehemence. The title draws their fire. The claim that He was the Son of God becomes the butt of their ridicule. (Little do they understand that they are about to set the stage for the culminating proof of His deity.) Their language reminds us of the words of the devil in the wilderness: "If thou art the Son of God." Their garbled version of His prediction of the destruction of the temple furnished them further sneers. Notice how their taunts become tributes in spite of themselves. "He saved others" (So they admit it!) "Himself He cannot save" (to prove the reason is to uncover the deity of Jesus and His infinite love for lost men). Their offer to believe if Jesus will come down from the cross reminds one again of the devil's suggestion in the wilderness for a joint rule of the world, if Jesus would abandon His plans to save lost men by dying on a cross and merely bow the knee to Satan (R.C. Foster, *Gospel Studies*, Vol. 4, 216, 217).

At the beginning it appeared that both of the robbers crucified with the Lord taunted Him; but one of them repented and thus gave the memorable account of the thief on the cross. The dignified conduct of Jesus on the cross must have made a tremendous impression on the one thief. This thief repented. As a matter of fact, his was the only voice to be raised in protest against the death of Jesus. His statement in Luke 23:42, "Lord, remember me when thou comest into thy kingdom" certainly indicated belief in Jesus and a belief, however primitive, that Jesus lives eternally. He didn't ask to be removed from the cross, but to be "remembered" when Jesus came into His kingdom. Someone once wrote, "Some saw Jesus raise the dead, and did not believe; the robber sees Jesus put to death, and yet believes."

The Lord's response was "Verily I say unto thee, today shalt thou be with me in paradise." It is such a shame that the thief has become the favorite of those who attempt to circumvent the command to be baptized for the remission of sins. Baptism for the remission of sins is into the death of Jesus (Rom. 6:3-5). While on the earth, Jesus forgave sins as He saw fit (Matt. 9:5-6). Having not yet died, Jesus personally forgave this man his sins. After His death and resurrection, and His ascension into heaven, all sins are forgiven according to the terms of His will, the New Testament. Both the thief and Jesus lived and died under the Old Law, the Law of Moses.

Who were the women specifically mentioned as "standing by the cross" (John 19:25)? McGarvey and Pendleton give an excellent explanation.

> Matt: Mary Magdalene, Mary the mother of James and Joses, and the mother of the sons of Zebedee
> Mark: Mary Magdalene and Mary the mother of James the Less and Joses, and Salome
> John: His mother, Mary Magdalene, Mary the wife of Clopas, the sister of Jesus' mother
>
> Matthew and Mark each name three women, whence it is thought that Salome was the name of the mother of James and John. But the solution of the problem depends on our rendering of John 19:25, which is translated thus: "but there were standing by the cross of Jesus his mother, and his mother's sister, Mary the wife of Clopas, and Mary Magdalene." Now, was Mary, the wife of Clopas named and also additionally described as sister to our Lord's mother, or was it the unnamed Salome who was her sister? Does John mention three or four women? The best modern scholarship says that there were four women, and that therefore James and John, the sons of Zebedee, were cousins of our Lord. In support of this it is urged: 1. That it is unlikely that two sisters would bear the same name, a fact, which, as Meyer says, is "established by no instance." 2. John gives two pairs of women, each pair coupled by an "and." The first pair is kindred to Jesus, and is unnamed, and is paralleled by the other pair, which is not kindred to Jesus, and of which the names are given. Hebrew writers often used such parallelism. 3. It accords with John's custom to withhold the names of himself and all his kindred, so that in his Gospel he nowhere gives his own, his mother's or his brother's name, nor does he even give the name of our Lord's mother, who was his aunt. 4. The relationship explains in part why Jesus, when dying, left the care of his mother to John. It was not an unusual

thing to impose such a burden upon a kinsman (McGarvey and Pendleton, *The Fourfold Gospel*, 225).

As Jesus looked down He saw His mother and John His disciple standing there. To Mary He said, "Woman, behold thy son!" To John He said, "Behold thy mother!" If it is true, and Salome was Mary's sister, then Mary would have been John's aunt. So, this was a matter of entrusting a kinsman with her care. The implication being Joseph was already dead. We last read of him at the time of the visit to the temple when Jesus was twelve years old. The last we read of Jesus' brothers and sisters was of their unbelief. As far as James, His brother, that would change. But at the time of Jesus' death there was no indication of belief on the part of His family members. Perhaps this contributed to Jesus charging John with the care of Mary.

At about noon, darkness covered the whole land. This could have been the land of Palestine or the entire earth. The language would permit both. It descended by miracle and all attempts to explain it in a purely natural way fail. Why the darkness descended is a matter of speculation. One reasonable view is that God was veiling the dying moments of His Son from the cruel, taunting multitude. That is certainly possible.

Matthew and Mark tell us that at about 3:00 in the afternoon, Jesus cried out, "My God, my God, why hast thou forsaken me?" This was a quote from Psalm 22:1, but it was a great deal more than that. God turns from sin (Isa. 59:1-2) and there is no fellowship between God and the unfruitful works of darkness (2 Cor. 6:14-16). It is possible that Jesus was bearing the weight of all the sins of the world combined in one incomprehensibly horrific mass and the Father turned from Him at that moment. His anguish was real and beyond our limited understanding or appreciation. He was there in my stead!

Some who heard the Lord thought He was calling for Elijah, having misunderstood His words. They believed Elijah had to come, based upon Malachi 4:5-6 and that he had not yet come. So, if Jesus was the Christ, Elijah had better get there, and it was now or never.

The Father heard Jesus' prayer and answered it. In just a short time Jesus would die with calmness and serenity, committing His soul to His Father. "My strength is dried up like a potsherd; and my tongue cleaveth to my jaws; and thou hast brought me into the dust of death," (Psalms 22:15). With death but moments away, Jesus cried, "I thirst." Someone placed a sponge upon a reed and held it to the lips of Jesus. After having received the drink, Jesus cried with a loud voice, "It is finished," and "Father, into thy hands I commend my spirit." Having said this, Jesus died, voluntarily yielding up His spirit.

Miracles Accompanying the Death (Matt. 27:51-56, Mark 15:38-41, Luke 23:45, 47-49)

At the time of Jesus' death, the veil in the temple that shut out the Most Holy Place was torn in two. It is obvious that there is great significance to this miracle. The way into the Most Holy Place in heaven was now made open to all by the death of Jesus (Heb. 9:24ff; 10:19ff). Also, it signified that the Law was nailed to the cross and the Old Dispensation was coming to an end.

There was an earthquake; rocks were rent and tombs were opened. The earthquake took place when Jesus died. The bodies of some who had been faithful but died, came forth and appeared to some in Jerusalem. This did not happen until "after his resurrection" (Matt. 27:53).

The centurion, who was in charge of the crucifixion, seeing the conduct of Jesus on the cross, knowing the claims that He had made, and witnessing the miraculous disturbances of nature taking place, weighed the evidence and reached his conclusion, "Truly this was the Son of God." Luke says that "all the people that came together to that sight, beholding the things which were done, smote their breasts, and returned." His disciples watched "from afar."

The Burial
(Matt. 27:57-60, Mark 15:42-46, Luke 23:50-54, John 19:31-42)

This was the day before the Sabbath of the Passover Week, and because of the festivities and significance of the events taking place, this Sabbath was a "high" or "great" day. The day before the Sabbath was called the "preparation." In the works of Josephus, the preparation for the Sabbath began on the ninth hour of the sixth day at 3:00 p.m. according to the Jewish method of keeping time.

Not wanting the bodies to be hanging on the cross on the Sabbath, the Jewish leaders requested of Pilate that the legs of the crucified men be broken so that they would die quickly and could be taken down from the crosses. The soldiers used large clubs to shatter the legs of the men, meaning that they could no longer push themselves up to breathe and would die quickly.

When the soldiers came to carry out their task, they broke the legs of the two criminals before they came to Jesus. The soldiers took care of their gruesome task with the other two, even though Jesus was crucified between them. Coming to Jesus, the soldiers found that He was already dead. To ensure that they had not made a mistake, a soldier pierced the side of Jesus with a spear, and blood and water flowed out. John stated he was there, saw it happen, and that his testimony concerning the matter was true. He wrote so that those who read his words could believe.

Even after His death, fulfillment of prophecy continued. John mentions, "A bone of him shall not be broken," from Psalm 34:20 and related to the Passover lamb. In the ultimate this referred to Jesus (1 Cor. 5:7). John also mentions, "They shall look on him whom they pierced."

A man, Joseph of Arimathaea, stepped forward to request the body of Jesus. He was evidently a member of the Sanhedrin, for Luke tells us that he had not consented to their counsel and deed, which would only be significant if Joseph had been in a position to consent. He was a good and righteous man as well as wealthy. He was all of these things, but John tells us that he was a "secret" disciple of Jesus for fear of his fellow Jewish leaders. He went to Pilate and requested the body of the Lord. When he did, Pilate was surprised that Jesus was already dead. There are accounts of individuals living an entire week on the cross. Death on the first day was rare.

When Pilate received assurance that Jesus was dead from the centurion in charge, he released the body to Joseph. Although Joseph made his request for the body of Jesus alone, he was assisted in the burial by Nicodemus, the same leader of the Jews who had first come to Jesus under the cover of night in John 3. He came with a mixture of myrrh and aloes, about 100 pounds, that they used in the burial. Again, it is apparent that the two of them removed the body from the cross.

The linen cloth with which Jesus was wrapped for burial would actually have been torn into strips for winding around the body. John mentions "linen clothes," indicating the many strips used in the burial. The spices that Nicodemus brought would be placed between the folds of the linen in order to partially embalm the body. In the same area where the crucifixion had taken place there was a garden. In the garden there was a tomb that had never been used, a cave-like structure, hewn out of the rock, belonging to Joseph. Jesus was laid in this tomb and a large stone was rolled to the door of the tomb. Joseph and Nicodemus left. The Sabbath day was drawing near.

The Watch at the Tomb
(Matt. 27:61-66, Mark 15:47, Luke 23:55-56)

While the burial was taking place Mary Magdalene and Mary the mother of Joses remained behind. They observed what was being done and where the body of Jesus was laid. Because of the time, Joseph and Nicodemus had hurried in their preparation of Jesus; and the women had returned home to prepare additional spices and ointments. They returned after the Sabbath.

Matthew 27:62 says, "Now the next day, that followed the day of the preparation, the chief priests and Pharisees came together unto Pilate." The Jewish day began at sunset, and the Jewish leaders would not have wanted the tomb of Jesus to go unguarded for an entire night. So, these leaders went to Pilate on what would be a Friday evening.

The hostile Jewish leaders requested a guard be placed at the tomb because they understood Jesus' statements concerning the temple and its raising again. Jesus said He would rise from the dead and they wanted to be sure the disciples of Jesus did not steal His body, claiming He had risen. They had to contend with the ministry of Jesus, which they felt had been defeated. But, if it spread throughout Jerusalem that Jesus had risen from the dead and the people began to believe it, then their difficulties would be multiplied.

Pilate granted their request and gave them their guard. For this task, a squad consisting of sixteen soldiers was used. It is probable that they kept four on watch in a rotating manner throughout the night.

The Jewish leaders secured the watch from Pilate, took them to the tomb, examined the tomb to be certain that the body was there, rolled the stone back in front of the tomb, and sealed it. The seal would have been a cord of some sort placed across the face of the stone, held in place by wax seals on either side of the rock. This did not prohibit someone from breaking in, but indicated if they had tampered with the tomb.

The Resurrection and Related Events
(Matt. 28:1-15, Mark 16:1-11, Luke 24:1-12, John 20:1-18)

The actual resurrection of Jesus is not described in scripture. We do not know exactly what took place when Jesus came forth from the grave. The account begins with the women coming to the tomb to anoint the body of Jesus. Their journey began very early on the morning of the first day of the week. Evidently when they began their journey the sun had not risen, but it had by the time they arrived. They brought the spices they had prepared for the task. Four women were named when we take all of the gospel accounts together. They were Mary Magdalene, Mary the mother of James, Salome, and Joanna. Joanna was the wife of Herod's steward.

On the way to the tomb the women wondered who would roll the stone away from the entrance for them, enabling them to enter. They did not need to worry about this, for there was a shaking of the earth caused by an angel of the Lord coming from heaven and rolling the stone away. The appearance of this angel affected the Roman guard. They "became as dead men," perhaps meaning that they fainted for fright. And the angel sat upon the stone. It is probable that Mary Magdalene left at the sight of the open tomb, confident the body of Jesus had been taken, but before the discussion with the angels. Matthew and Mark mention one angel, Luke mentions two. There is no contradiction because neither Matthew nor Mark states that there was only one.

The women first encountered the angel sitting upon the stone as they saw the door of the tomb was opened. They were told not to be afraid, nor seek the living among the dead. They were told that Jesus the Nazarene, the One who was crucified and whom they sought, was not there. He had risen! They were invited to come closer to see where the Lord had been laid and were reminded that it was necessary for Him to be delivered into the hands of sinful men, crucified, and on the third day rise again. They were told to go and tell His disciples that He would see them in Galilee.

In the meantime Mary Magdalene found Peter and John, told them the body of Jesus had been taken, and that she did not know where it was. The other women, having recovered from their surprise and fright, also returned and told the apostles, along with others, what they had seen and heard. Mary reported to Peter and John; the other women brought their news to the others, along with Peter and John.

The initial reaction of the apostles and the others was one of disbelief, but Peter and John raced to the tomb to see for themselves. It is believed that John was the younger man and outran Peter. Arriving at the tomb, he stooped and looked inside, saw the linen grave clothes lying there, but he did not enter.

When Peter arrived, he entered the empty tomb and beheld the grave clothes. He saw the napkin, that had bound the head of Jesus, rolled up in a place by itself. John now entered, saw the evidence, and believed. Peter left the tomb uncertain and confused.

As Peter and John ran to the tomb, Mary Magdalene was making her way back to it, too. The other three women were not with her as she returned. By the time she arrived back at the tomb, Peter and John had already left. As Mary stood outside the tomb weeping, she stooped and looked in the tomb. Jesus was not there, but the two angels in white were. One was sitting where Jesus' head had been and the other at the feet. When the four women had seen the angels earlier, we saw that they were frightened. There is no mention of such a reaction with Mary at this time. When the angels asked Mary, "Woman, why weepest thou?" her response was filled with emotion, "Because they have taken away my Lord, and I know not where they have laid him."

As Mary finished speaking she turned around and saw someone standing there. She did not immediately recognize that it was Jesus. Why did Mary fail to recognize the Lord? There have been many explanations offered.

> This is one of those remarkably vivid and autopic touches that carry conviction of truth, whatever may be the explanation or the conclusion to be drawn from it. How far was this lack of recognition due to her, and how far to this the first manifestation of "spiritual body" to human kind? Some have frigidly taken a commonplace explanation. Her eyes were blinded with continuous weeping; or the darkness of the morning; or Jesus may have stood in the shadows of the city wall, as the glare of the first beam of sunrise broke out of the purple mists on the Moab hills; or Christ's appearance was so changed by the agony through which he had passed, and by the recovery and reconstitution of his humanity, that the signs of his identity were obscured. He could not have clothed himself with the glittering garments of the Transfiguration, or with the dazzling robes of angels; for she mistook him for the keeper of the garden, either for Joseph of Arimathaea himself or his steward (*The Pulpit Commentary*, Vol. 17, 467).

Perhaps facial recognition was being withheld in a miraculous fashion, as was the case with the two disciples on the road to Emmaus. Also, some have thought a contributing factor to Mary's failure to recognize Jesus was not expecting to see Him.

Jesus said to Mary, "Woman, why weepest thou? Who seekest thou?" Mary's aim was to find the body of Jesus and perhaps this "gardener" could help her. "Sir, if thou hast borne him hence, tell me where thou hast laid him, and I will take him away." Mary must have turned away from Jesus, not knowing yet who He was. Initially, Jesus referred to her as "woman," but now He said, "Mary." There is no doubt that with the calling of her name, Mary knew this man was Jesus. "Rabboni," Mary cried, which means "Teacher."

It is implied that Mary, in her joy and wonder, must have sought to hug or embrace Jesus, hence His statement, "Touch me not; for I am not yet ascended unto my Father; but go to my brethren, and say unto them, I ascend unto my Father, and your Father, and to my God, and your God." Many questions have been raised about the meaning of Jesus' statement to Mary. The best explanation seems to be that Mary had work to do and there would be ample time in the next forty days to be with Jesus. She went and told the disciples.

As the other women were making their way back to the tomb, having delivered the message received from the angels to the disciples, Jesus met them. Their recognition of the Lord appears to have been immediate. They fell at His feet, took hold of them, and worshipped the Lord. Jesus had not permitted Mary to touch Him, but now allowed these women to do so. The best explanation for this seems to be that Mary was to serve as the messenger to the disciples to inform that Jesus had risen, and had seen Him. This was to be made known to them quickly, so she was sent on her way. There was time later for her to worship the Lord. These women were given the responsibility of telling the disciples to return to Galilee where Jesus would meet with them.

The women were in the process of performing the task Jesus had given them when some of the Roman guard that Pilate had granted to the Jews for the security of the tomb made their way into the city to the chief priests, Caiaphas and Annas. They gave them an account of what had happened. The chief priests obviously felt the news was of great import and assembled the whole counsel together to decide what to do.

> Notwithstanding all their caution, it was plain that the body of Jesus was gone. It was further plain that the disciples would affirm that he was raised. It was not improbable that Jesus would himself appear, and convince multitudes that he was the Messiah; and that the guilt of putting him to death would, after all their caution and cunning, be charged on them. They had been at great pains to procure his death. They had convinced Pilate that he was dead. They had placed a guard for the express purpose of preventing his being taken. It would be in vain, after this, to pretend that he was not dead; that he was in a swoon; that he died in appearance only. They had shut themselves out from this, which would have been the most plausible plea; and whatever course they might now adopt, they were obliged to proceed on the admission that he had been really dead, and that all proper measures had been taken to prevent his being stolen. They concluded, after consultation, that but one way was left – to bribe the soldiers, to induce them to tell a falsehood, and to attempt to convince the world that Jesus, in spite of themselves, and in the face of all probability, had been stolen (Albert Barnes, *Barne's Notes on the New Testament*, 144).

In addition to the large sums of money given to the soldiers by the Jewish leaders, there was the promise that if word of their failure reached Pilate, they would "persuade" him. In other words, they would take care of it. This was vital to the bribe because it was a capital offense for a Roman soldier to fall asleep while on guard.

Further Appearances
(Matt. 28:16-20, Mark 16:12-20, Luke 24:13-53, John 20:19-21:23, 1 Corinthians 15:6-8)

The appearance to the two disciples and their report to the others.

No one knows who these two disciples were other than the name of one was Cleopas. Some scholars have suggested that it was Luke himself. Early tradition from the twelfth century placed Emmaus at Nicopolis and if this is the case, then it was twenty miles from Jerusalem. Later tradition places it at El Kubeibeh, just seven miles northwest of Jerusalem. That makes more sense, but it is a traditional placement.

As these two were walking along, they were discussing the wondrous events that had taken place that morning. After a time, Jesus joined Himself to them as they journeyed, and through some divine measure, restrained their vision so that they did not recognize Him. Jesus interrupted their discussion wanting to know the topic of their talk. It appears that they were surprised by the question and the interruption.

Cleopas was the one who answered, indicating surprise that one would not know of the events that had taken place. His answer could be paraphrased in this way, "Are you the only person visiting Jerusalem who doesn't know about these things?" When Jesus said, "What things?" they continued with their answer, telling of His deliverance by the chief priests and the rulers of the Jews in order that He might be put to death by crucifixion.

Notice what they thought of Jesus. They said He was "a prophet mighty in deed and word before God and all the people..." That is true, but it doesn't go far enough. They looked for an earthly ruler, who would overthrow the Roman government. They hoped Jesus was that person. They said, "But we trusted that it had been he which should have redeemed Israel."

These two continued their answer, indicating once again that this was the very day of the resurrection – not meaning a strict 72 hours, but counting time just as we do, freely; this was Sunday. They mentioned the report of the women who had gone early to the tomb, saw the angels, and found the tomb empty. They also mentioned the reaction to the report, amazement. They told of Peter's and John's visit to the tomb and the fact they found it just as the women had said, but they had not seen Jesus.

Finally, Jesus spoke and the first thing He did was to charge these two disciples with being slow to understand and believe the things the prophets had spoken concerning these events. The prophets made it clear the Messiah would enter into His glory through His suffering, but they had not understood.

Jesus began with Moses and went through the prophets, showing them how all of the things spoken concerning the One who was to come were being fulfilled in Him (of course, at this time they still did not know who He was – their eyes being "holden"). They heard Jesus explain the types and symbols contained in the Old Testament that referred to Him. Jesus explained the statements and predictions of the prophets concerning Him.

Finally, they arrived at the village of Emmaus, and Jesus acted as though He intended to continue on. When the two urged Him to stay with them, Jesus did so. Together they went into their place of lodging, and as they sat down to eat, Jesus took bread, blessed it and gave it to them. Now, their eyes were opened and they knew that it was Jesus. Once He had revealed Himself to them, He vanished. Whatever the situation with the resurrected Jesus, He obviously was not bound by the physical limitations of time and space.

> Thus they admit to each other that the joy of beholding the risen Lord was but the consummation of a joy already begun through a right understanding of the truth contained in Scripture. The sight of the Lord was sweeter because it was preceded by faith that he ought thus to rise (McGarvey and Pendleton, *The Fourfold Gospel*, 750, 751).

Their news was too important for them to wait until the next day. They left immediately for Jerusalem to share the news with the eleven. When they got there, the eleven were discussing the resurrection and the Lord's appearance to Peter. This appearance is mentioned by Luke and by Paul in 1 Corinthians 15:5, but details concerning that appearance, have not been revealed. However, it appears the Lord took special care to help Peter after his denial and repentance. The women had been told, "Go your way, tell his disciples and Peter that he goeth before you into Galilee." Now, Jesus made an appearance to Peter alone.

The two disciples told the apostles all that had happened to them, and how they came to recognize Jesus when they sat down to eat. The scriptures make known that the apostles did not believe their report. Now, it is evident the apostles believed Jesus had risen from the dead. Perhaps they had difficulty believing the particulars of the report given by these two disciples.

Jesus appears to the ten disciples.

While this discussion was taking place, Jesus appeared in the midst of them. It is still the same day as the resurrection, the first day of the week. The scriptures describe them as being terrified and seeing a spirit of some sort. Bear in mind that Jesus appeared in their midst despite the fact that the door was closed for fear of the Jews. At His appearance, the Lord rebuked His disciples for their failure to understand and believe. Perhaps the two disciples had told them how Jesus demonstrated, through Moses and the prophets, all of these things were to come to pass. It is obvious that the apostles were confused and vacillated between belief and disbelief.

Then, Jesus asked them to see His hands and feet, touch Him, handle Him, and know He was not a disembodied spirit. Jesus showed them His hands and feet with the scars of the nails, and His side where the spear had been thrust. Now, they would know and believe with a belief that would not falter, that this was Jesus with whom they had spent the last three years. This was their Lord, and He had risen from the dead.

They were amazed at what they were seeing. Luke tells us, "And while they still disbelieved for joy, and wondered…" What does this mean? Have you ever said, "This is just too good to be true?" This is the same idea. Jesus asked if they had anything to eat and was given a piece of broiled fish, which He ate. This satisfied the apostles that they were not seeing a ghost.

With the apostles fully convinced this was the Master, Jesus repeated His salutation and commissioned them to go forth. There is some controversy about the statement, "He breathed on them, and saith unto them, Receive ye the Holy Spirit…" Obviously the phrase, "He breathed on them" calls to mind Genesis 2:7, "And the Lord God formed man of the dust of the ground, and breathed into his nostrils the breath of life; and man became a living soul." The two main views that have been presented are these: (a) "This significant gesture of Jesus suggests the power of a new spiritual life in the apostles, arising from their faith and fellowship with Him and empowered by the presence of the Holy Spirit… There is nothing contradictory between a further giving of the Spirit at this time and the baptism of the Holy Spirit on the day of Pentecost" (*Gospel Studies*, Vol. 4, 256). (b) "Symbolic of the baptism which they were to receive at Pentecost, He breathes upon them…"(*The Fourfold Gospel*, 753).

The apostles were to preach the gospel with its glorious message of the forgiveness of sins. The power to forgive sins did not rest with the apostles; that power belongs to God. However, they were commissioned to preach the message that salvation and forgiveness of sins would belong to all who believed their message and obeyed its commands.

Thomas, one of the twelve, had not been at this appearance of Jesus, and the reason for his absence was not given. The other apostles were completely convinced about Jesus and told Thomas they had seen the Lord. Thomas was not going to be fooled by emotion, so he said that he would have to see the wounds of Jesus personally before he would believe.

Appearance to the disciples on the next Lord's Day.

The apostles were still in Jerusalem one week later. Albert Barnes, Jamieson, Faussett and Brown, and R.C. Foster as well, state the usual free method of counting time is used here and so "after eight days" is the same as saying "on the eighth day," thus one week. That makes this the first day of the week.

Once again Jesus appeared in their midst, the doors shut, and greeted them with the same salutation as before. Jesus turned His attention to Thomas, now with them, and urged him to examine the evidence of the wounds He suffered, and "become not faithless." Of the phrase, "and be not faithless," A.T. Robertson wrote, "Present middle imperative of ginomai in prohibition, "stop becoming disbelieving" (*Word Pictures in the New Testament*, Vol. 5, 316). Thomas was becoming an unbeliever and the appearance of Jesus reaffirmed his faith. He believed on the basis of evidence personally seen. How wonderful it is to believe on the basis of testimony by accredited witnesses. Truly, all four of the gospels were written, not one of them claiming to be an exhaustive, complete recounting of all that Jesus said and did, to offer testimony about Jesus and produce faith in those who read them.

Jesus appears to the seven by the Sea of Galilee.

The apostles were in Galilee and fished through the night, but came up empty-handed. As the day was breaking, Jesus stood on the beach. The disciples did not recognize Him. This could have been because of the distance, or it could have been because Jesus did not want them to recognize Him.

The Lord asked them, "Children, have ye any meat?" In other words, "Have you caught anything?" The answer was no. At that, Jesus told them to "cast the net on the right side of the boat, and ye shall find."

> They did not recognize Jesus or pay any heed to Him so long as He stood on the shore simply watching. But the moment He addressed them, the title He gave them must have thrilled their hearts: the form of the question suggested actual knowledge of their plight: the command given implied miraculous insight into the depths of the water and the future. Their former experience would be instantly recalled (Lk. 5:1-11). Their situation was something like that when Jesus came walking on the water. They did not recognize Him. He addressed them and assured them of His identity. Peter challenged, "Lord, if it be thou, bid me come unto thee upon the waters." Jesus accepted the challenge: "Come." The miraculous test proved the identity of Christ both as their beloved leader and "the Son of God." He gives a command which implies miraculous power and which stirs them to recognize Him. They obey and the miracle makes their identification positive and complete (R.C. Foster, *Gospel Studies*, Vol. 4, 265, 266).

John was the first of them to recognize that this man was Jesus, and he told Peter, "It is the Lord." The impetuous nature and devotion of Peter is seen in his putting his coat upon him and diving into the water to swim to Jesus. The "nakedness" of Peter means that his outer garment, his coat or robe, was removed, and he was in his undergarment. The distance to the shore was about 200 cubits, in the neighborhood of 100 yards. The others followed in the boat dragging the net full of fish. When land was reached Jesus already had a fire burning with fish upon it. When the Lord told them to "bring of the fish which ye have now caught," Peter helped, possibly going back into the water and bringing the net to shore. John gives the specific amount of the catch, 153 large fish, a tremendous catch, yet their nets did not break. There may be special significance to the nets not breaking. It certainly was different from the previous experience (Luke 5:6).

By now they knew it was Jesus. He told them to come and eat, but it appears they held back, maybe due to reverence and awe, for we find that "Jesus cometh, and taketh the bread, and giveth them, and fish likewise."

While this was the Lord's seventh appearance: 1) to Mary; 2) to the other women; 3) to Peter; 4) to the two going to Emmaus; 5) to the ten apostles without Thomas; 6) to the eleven with Thomas; 7) by the seaside in Galilee, this is the third appearance to a number of the apostles and the third appearance witnessed by John.

After they ate, Jesus turned His attention to Peter. There are primarily two different views about the questions Jesus asked him. The first is that when Jesus asked if Peter loved Him more than "these," the pronoun was neuter and referred to the fishing nets, the boats, and so on. The second is that the pronoun was masculine (in the Greek it is dative plural and can be either), therefore referring to the other apostles. Recall in the upper room on the very night of His betrayal, Peter claimed to love the Lord more than any other; at least he implied such. In Matthew 26:33 Peter said, "Though all men shall be offended because of thee, yet will I never be offended." Most likely the question had reference to the apostles and was a threefold question because Peter denied the Lord three times.

Many commentators believe that a significant point is being made by Jesus' use of the word "agapan" and Peter answering with the verb "philein." In the third question, Jesus dropped the "agapan" and used the same word Peter used, "philein." They say that "agapao" is a higher type of love and "phileo" is a lower type of love. They have the Lord, in His third question, essentially asking Peter, "Do you love me even as you would love a friend?" thus descending in His questions. It appears that Jesus used the term that Peter used, and John writing, "He saith unto him the third time..." seems to indicate that the meaning of the three questions was the same.

Many commentators also see significance in the Lord's use of lambs and sheep, particularly those of the Roman Catholic Church. If the Lord meant a distinction in meaning by the two terms, it seems best to view it as "lambs" being the young Christians, and the "sheep" being the older, more mature saints.

Jesus spoke of the manner of Peter's death, which would take place when he was older. His freedom would be taken from him, others would bind him, and he would die. Some suggest that the phrase, "Thou shalt stretch forth thy hands" is a reference to crucifixion, and that "follow me" meant that Peter was to follow the Lord in that manner of death. This is possible, and tradition holds that Peter was crucified upside down.

John was with them, and Peter asked what the future held for John. Jesus' answer was essentially that John's earthly lot was none of Peter's business. Peter's concern was to be faithful himself. Jesus did not mean that John would not die. He was not addressing John's future. The Lord was making a point with Peter.

Jesus appears to the 500: The Great Commission.

The statement is made that this was an appearance that took place according to an appointment Jesus had made. From the very first announcement of the resurrection of Jesus, the women were told to tell the disciples that they should go into Galilee where Jesus would meet them. Jesus Himself repeated this in Matthew 28:10. It appears reasonable that this meeting would include not only the apostles, but the women and other disciples as well. Hence, it is probably the appearance that Paul wrote about in 1 Corinthians 15:6.

With this large crowd, some worshipped Him, but others doubted. The language of the passage seems to indicate that Jesus walked to them from a distance. Some, as they saw Him, immediately recognized that it was Jesus and began to worship. Others waited for Him to come closer, not being sure that it was the Lord from such a distance. However, Jesus came to them and spoke, removing all doubt. What He said is known as The Great Commission, consisting of a declaration of His absolute authority, a charge to go and make disciples of all nations, it is to be done by instructing the people, bringing them to belief, baptizing them by the authority of Deity, and then instructing them to continue in all that the Lord had taught. Never will the Christians be alone, for Jesus promised to be with them always.

In Mark 16:13-14, Mark wrote about the appearance of Jesus to the Apostles as they sat at meat in Jerusalem on the very evening of the Lord's resurrection. Jesus rebuked the disciples for their failure to believe the words of those who had seen Him. Mark then brought his gospel to a close by giving the Great Commission. This may have been a summary of the Great Commission given in Galilee, or another one given in Jerusalem. Mark does not speak of the time or place when it was given. 1 Corinthians 15:7 mentions an appearance of Jesus to James, but there is no information given about that appearance.

There were many things Jesus said during the time of His appearances, a time that lasted forty days, that are not recorded for us. While they were gathered in Jerusalem, Jesus promised them the baptism of the Holy Spirit (which would occur with the apostles ten days hence). He explained once again how all the events that had happened were in fulfillment of the law and the prophets, and the wisdom literature. He expounded to them the truth so they might come to understand. They did not yet completely understand (that was still to come), but it is clear their understanding was improving. Yet, despite all they had seen and heard, there was still the longing for a physical kingdom. The spiritual nature of the kingdom would be made clear to them when the Holy Spirit came.

Jesus gave another version of the Great Commission, telling His apostles to remain in Jerusalem until they were endued with power from on high. Then He arose, bodily, into heaven. The angels added their testimony to the promise that He would come again.

Epilogue
(John 21:24-25)

John witnessed these things himself and therefore was competent to attest to their truthfulness. The gospels were not intended to be exhaustive accounts of everything that Jesus did. If they had been, using an example of hyperbole, John said, "The world itself could not contain the books that should be written."

Index Of Scripture

MATTHEW

1:1-17	p.4	7:24-27	p.73	13:44-53	p.88
1:18-25	p.9	7:28-8:1	p.73	13:54-58	p.96
2:1	p.11	8:2-4	p.49	14:1-12	p.100
2:1-12	p. 16	8:5-13	p.73	14:13-21	p.103
2:13-18	p.17	8:14-17	p.47	14:22-36	p.105
2:19-23	p.18	8:18-22	p.89	15:1-20	p.111
3:1-6	p.21	8:23-27	p.89	15:21-28	p.114
3:7-12	p.22	8:28-34	p.92	15:29-38	p.116
3:13-17	p.25	9:1-8	p.51	15:39-16:4	p.117
4:1-11	p.27	9:9-13	p.53	16:5-12	p. 118
4:12-17	p.41	9:14-17	p.54	16:13-20	p.119
4:18-22	p.45	9:18-26	p.94	16:21-28	p.122
4:23-25	p.48	9:35-11:1	p.97	17:1-8	p.123
5:1-8	p.62	11:2-19	p.76	17:9-13	p.125
5:3-12	p.62	11:20-30	p.78	17:14-21	p.126
5:13-16	p.65	12:1-8	p.57	17:22-23	p.127
5:17-48	p.66	12:9-14	p.59	17:24-27	p.128
6:1-18	p.68	12:15-21	p.60	18:1-5	p.129
6:19-24	p.70	12:22-45	p.81	18:6-14	p.130
6:25-34	p.70	*12:31-32*	p.82	18:15-35	p.131
7:1-6	p.71	*12:38-45*	p.83	19:1-12	p.186
7:7-11	p.71	12:46-50	p.85	19:13-15	p.188
7:12	p.72	13:1-23	p.85	19:16-22	p.189
7:13-14	p.72	13:24-30, 36-43	p.86	19:23-30	p.191
7:15-23	p.73	13:31-35	p.87	20:1-16	p.192
				20:17-19	p.194

20:20-28	p.194	27:1	p.241	3:13-19	p.61
20:29-34	p.195	27:3-10	p.241	3:19-30	p.81
21:1-11	p.202	27:2, 11-14	p.243	3:31-35	p.85
21:12-17,18-19	p.204	27:15-26	p.245	4:1-20	p.85
21:20-22	p.205	27:27-30	p.247	4:21-25	p.86
21:23-27	p.206	27:31-34	p.247	4:26-29	p.86
21:28-22:1-14	p.207	27:35-50	p.248	4:30-34	p.87
22:15-22	p.208	27:51-56	p.251	4:35-41	p.89
22:23-33	p.210	27:57-60	p.252	5:1-20	p.92
22:34-40	p.211	27:61-66	p.253	5:21-43	p.94
22:41-46	p.211	28:1-15	p.254	6:1-6	p.97
23:1-39	p.212	28:16-20	p.257	6:7-13	p.97
24:1-51	p.216			6:14-29	p.100
25:1-13	p.219	**MARK**		6:30-44	p.103
25:14-30	p.219	1:1-6	p.21	6:45-56	p.105
25:31-46	p.219	1:7-8	p.22	7:1-23	p.111
26:1-5	p.220	1:9-11	p.25	7:24-30	p.114
26:6-13	p.200	1:12-13	p.27	7:31-8:9	p.116
26:14-16	p.220	1:14-15	p.41	8:10-12	p.117
26:17-19	p.221	1:16-21	p.45	8:13-26	p.118
26:20	p.222	1:21-34	p.47	8:27-30	p.119
26:21-25	p.224	1:35-39	p.48	8:31-9:1	p.122
26:26-29	p.225	1:40-45	p.49	9:2-8	p.123
26:31-35	p.225	2:1-12	p.51	9:9-13	p.125
26:36-46	p.234	2:13-17	p.53	9:14-29	p.126
26:47-56	p.236	2:18-22	p.54	9:30-32	p.127
26:57	p.238	2:23-28	p.57	9:33-37	p.129
26:58, 69-75	p.240	3:1-6	p.59	9:38-41	p.130

9:42-50	p.130	14:32-42	p.234	3:19-20	p.41
10:1-12	p.186	14:43-52	p.236	3:21-22	p.25
10:13-16	p.188	14:53, 55-65	p.238	3:23-38	p.4
10:17-22	p.189	14:54, 66-72	p.240	4:1-13	p.27
10:23-31	p.191	15:1	p.241	4:14-15	p.41
10:32-34	p.194	15:2-5	p.243	4:16-30	p.44
10:35-45	p.194	15:6-15	p.245	4:31-41	p.47
10:46-52	p.195	15:16-19	p.247	4:42-44	p.48
11:1-11	p.202	15:20-23	p.247	5:1-11	p.45
11:12-18	p.204	15:24-37	p.248	5:12-16	p.49
11:19-26	p.205	15:38-41	p.251	5:17-26	p.51
11:27-33	p.206	15:42-46	p.252	5:27-32	p.53
12:1-12	p.207	15:47	p.253	5:33-39	p.54
12:13-17	p.208	16:1-11	p.254	6:1-5	p.57
12:18-27	p.210	16:12-20	p.257	6:6-11	p.59
12:28-34	p.211			6:12-16	p.61
12:35-37	p.211	**LUKE**		6:17-49	p.62
12:38-40	p.212	1:1-4	p.1	*6:20-26*	P.62
12:41-44	p.214	1:5-56	p.5	7:1-10	p.73
13:1-37	p.216	1:57-80	p.8	7:11-17	p.75
14:1-2	p.220	2:1-7	p.11	7:18-35	p.76
14:3-9	p.200	2:8-20	p.12	7:36-50	p.79
14:10-11	p.220	2:21	p.13	8:1-3	p.80
14:12-16	p.221	2:22-38	p.13	8:4-15	p.85
14:17	p.222	2:39	p.18	8:16-18	p.86
14:18-21	p.224	2:40-52	p.19	8:19-21	p.85
14:22-25	p.225	3:1-6	p.21	8:22-25	p.89
14:27-31	p.225	3:7-18	p.22	8:26-39	p.92

8:40-56	p.94	14:1-24	p.171	22:1-2	p.220
9:1-6	p.97	14:25-35	p.172	22:3-6	p.220
9:7-9	p.100	15:1-32	p.174	22:7-13	p.221
9:10-17	p.103	16:1-18	p.176	22:14-16,24-30	p.222
9:18-21	p.119	16:19-31	p.177	22:17-20	p.225
9:22-27	p.122	17:1-10	p.179	22:21-23	p.224
9:28-36	p.123	17:11-19	p.183	22:31-38	p.225
9:36	p.125	17:20-37	p.184	22:39-46	p.234
9:37-42	p.126	18:1-8	p.186	22:47-53	p.236
9:43-45	p.127	18:9-14	p.186	22:54	p. 238
9:46-48	p.129	18:15-17	p.188	22:54,63-65	p.238
9:49-50	p.130	18:18-23	p.189	22:54-62	p.240
9:51-56	p.135	18:24-30	p.191	22:66-71	p.241
9:57-62	p.89	18:31-34	p.194	23:1-5	p.243
10:1-24	p.150	18:35-43	p.195	23:6-12	p.244
10:25-37	p.152	19:1-10	p.197	23:13-25	p.245
10:38-42	p.154	19:11-28	p.198	23:26-32	p.247
11:1-13	p.155	19:29-44	p.202	23:33-46	p.248
11:14-36	p.81	19:45-48	p.204	23:45,47-49	p.251
11:24-36	p.83	20:1-8	p.206	23:50-54	p.252
11:37-54	p.157	20:9-19	p.207	23:55-56	p.253
12:1-12	p.160	20:20-26	p.208	24:1-12	p.254
12:13-21	p.161	20:27-40	p.210	24:13-53	p.257
12:22-34	p.162	20:41-44	p.211		
12:35-59	p.163	20:45-47	p.212	**JOHN**	
13:1-9	p.164	21:1-4	p.214	1:1-18	p.2
13:10-21	p.165	21:5-36	p.216	1:19-34	p.28
13:22-35	p.169	21:37-38	p.205	1:35-51	p.30

2:1-11	p.31	13:21-30	p.224
2:12	p.33	13:31-38	p.225
2:13-22	p.33	14:1-31	p.227
2:23-3:36	p.35	15:1-27	p.229
4:1-42	p.38	16:1-33	p.230
4:43-54	p.41	17:1-26	p.232
5:1-47	p.54	18:1	p.234
6:1-14	p.103	18:2-12	p.236
6:15-21	p.105	18:12-14,19-23	p.238
6:22-71	p.108	18:24	p.238
7:1	p.111	18:15-18,25-27	p.240
7:2-9	p.133	18:28-38	p.243
7:10	p.135	18:39-19:16	p.245
7:11-52	p.136	19:16-17	p.247
8:1-11	p.138	19:18-30	p.248
8:12-59	p.140	19:31-42	p.252
9:1-41	p.144	20:1-18	p.254
10:1-21	p.147	20:19-21:23	p.257
10:22-39	p.166	21:24-25	p.263
10:40-42	p.169		
11:1-44	p.180	**ACTS**	
11:45-54	p.182	1:18-19	p.241
11:55-12:1	p.199		
12:9-11	p.199	**1 CORINTHIANS**	
12:2-8	p.200	11:23-26	p.225
12:12-19	p.202	15:6-8	P.257
12:20-50	p.215		
13:1-20	p.222		

www.ingramcontent.com/pod-product-compliance
Lightning Source LLC
Chambersburg PA
CBHW080602170426
43196CB00017B/2880